World Yearbook
of Education 1990

World Yearbook of Education 1990

ASSESSMENT AND EVALUATION

Edited by Chris Bell
and Duncan Harris (Series Editor)

Kogan Page, London/Nichols Publishing, New York

World Yearbook of Education 1982/83
Computers and Education
Edited by Jacquetta Megarry, David R. F. Walker,
Stanley Nisbet and Eric Hoyle

World Yearbook of Education 1984
Women and Education
Edited by Sandra Acker, Jacquetta Megarry,
Stanley Nisbet and Eric Hoyle

World Yearbook of Education 1985
Research, Policy and Practice
Edited by John Nisbet, Jacquetta Megarry and Stanley Nisbet

World Yearbook of Education 1986
The Management of Schools
Edited by Eric Hoyle and Agnes McMahon

World Yearbook of Education 1987
Vocational Education
Edited by John Twining, Stanley Nisbet and Jacquetta Megarry

World Yearbook of Education 1988
Education for the New Technologies
Edited by Duncan Harris (Series Editor)

World Yearbook of Education 1989
Health Education
Edited by Chris James, John Balding and Duncan Harris (Series Editor)

First published in Great Britain in 1990 by Kogan Page Limited
120 Pentonville Road, London N1 9JN

British Library Cataloguing in Publication Data

A CIP catalogue record for this book is available from the British Library

ISSN 0084-2508
ISBN 0-7494-0051-X

First published in the USA in 1990
by Nichols Publishing,
an imprint of GP Publishing Inc,
PO Box 96, New York, NY 10024

Library of Congress Cataloguing in Publication Data
Main entry under title:
World Yearbook of Education: 1990
1. Education – Periodicals
   ISBN 0-89397-364-5
   LC Catalog No. 32-18413

Typeset by DP Photosetting, Aylesbury, Bucks
Printed and bound in Great Britain
by Biddles Ltd, Guildford

Contents

List of contributors

Nunt Adler, Hadassah Vocational Guidance Institute, Israel — *Chapter 17*
John Bailey, Department of Education, Bhutan — *Chapter 22*
Antonio Calvani, Department of Educational Sciences, Italy — *Chapter 16*
Lynne Cameron, College of Ripon and St John, England — *Chapter 5*
Tshewang Choeden, Department of Education, Bhutan — *Chapter 22*
David Clemson, Liverpool Polytechnic, England — *Chapter 9*
Betty Collis, University of Twente, Netherlands — *Chapter 10*
A di Carlo, Liceo Scientifico E Majorane, Turin, Italy — *Chapter 14*
Avram Eskenasi, Institute of Mathematics, Sofia — *Chapter 4*
Maria Ferraris, Istituto Tecnologie Didattiche, Italy — *Chapter 12*
Maria Ferretti, Scuola Don Milani, Genoa, Italy — *Chapter 13*
G J Fishburne, University of Alberta, Canada — *Chapter 22*
Kim Foss Hansen, Research Institute for Pedagogy and Education, Denmark — *Chapter 2*
Claude N Kennedy, Ngee Ann Polytechnic, Singapore — *Chapter 18*
Robert Kowalski, Wolverhampton Polytechnic, England — *Chapter 6*
Lorento Laviosa, Scuola Don Milani, Genoa, Italy — *Chapter 13*
Michela Mayer, European Centre of Education, Italy — *Chapter 15*
Elchanan I Meir, Hadassah Vocational Guidance Institute, Israel — *Chapter 17*
Nigel N Nixon, CNAA, England — *Chapter 7*
Donatella Persico, Istituto Tecnologie Didattiche, Italy — *Chapter 7*
Chitra Pradhan, Department of Education, Bhutan — *Chapter 22*
Jaap Scheerens, University of Twente, Netherlands — *Chapter 11*
Tom Schuller, University of Warwick, England — *Chapter 8*
Blagovest Sendov, Bulgarian Academy of Sciences, Bulgaria — *Chapter 4*
Roger Singer, DRS Data & Research Services plc, England — *Chapters 19 and 20*
David Smith, Education and training consultant, Slough, England — *Chapter 3*
John Smyth, Deakin University, Australia — *Chapter 21*
G Trentin, Istituto Tecnologie Didattiche, Genoa, Italy — *Chapter 14*
J K Turner, University of Alberta, Canada — *Chapter 22*
Minchha Wangdi, Department of Education, Bhutan — *Chapter 22*
David Warren Piper, University of California, USA — *Chapter 1*

Introduction
Chris Bell

Assessment and evaluation are essential to education and training. Whether informal or formal, at their best they assist the learning process by providing feedback to 'learners' and 'teachers', facilitate quality assurance and control, and provide a mechanism whereby education and training can be attuned to the needs of the individual and society.

This edition of the *World Yearbook* focuses upon a wide range of assessment and evaluation issues from all over the globe. A number of themes emerge and, to present an overview of these themes, I have borrowed from each of the articles and produced a (more or less) coherent whole. There are differences in arguments presented, there are contradictions. Dip into the papers, there is much of value.

Quality (ie 'fitness for purpose') of education and training

It is no mere chance that the desire for high-quality education should arise just now. Today we emphasize the importance of knowledge; the technology of information is seeking to activate the passive written language. New work tasks presuppose and create the need for different training and education.

However, we have scarcely begun the work of constructing the educational path along which individuals of the future will need to tread. Time may be running out. We currently have a process of 'education' for an economic role rather than for active democratic citizenship; the implicit model underlying it is essentially a version of optimized batch production moderated by a notoriously imprecise and unreliable system of assessment. Instead of reconstructing education to support and nurture the intellectual development of all individuals, we are offering ever narrower training for tightly defined and fragmented tasks. If we are to cope with the threats and promises of the coming era, then it is clear that there is a need to devise pedagogies and educational environments which permit intellectual growth rather than narrow utilitarian training. The two main questions in connection with the discussion on quality are therefore: 'What should we teach?' and 'How should we teach it?'

What is required is a fundamental shift in the way that teachers perceive themselves. It is not that identification with the subject matter should get any less, but that teachers' identity as educators should be much stronger.

Focus upon the learner

It is those other than learners who are mostly concerned with the results of traditional assessments. In the context of self-directed learning, the information is at least as important to the learner as it is to the tutor. Student self-assessment and self-diagnosis is a natural outgrowth of student, as opposed to subject-centred approaches to course design and delivery. One of the main objectives of the teaching/learning process should be a deepening of knowledge by focusing attention on what is learnt and how it is learnt. Unfortunately, teachers often accept a behaviourist paradigm of the teaching/learning process and consider learners as *tabulae rasae*, empty blackboards where knowledge has to be chalked up.

This old assumption has to be revised in the light of the constructivist theory of learning. In one example, by acting as authors and testing their knowledge through critical review, learners become more responsible for what they learn and how they learn it.

Learners' and teachers' evaluation of curriculum innovations help ensure success, guiding the innovation, disseminating information and identifying and disseminating good practices. Structured review instruments (questionnaires and interviews) for use by learners and teachers are invaluable in this process. However, there is a tension between approaches. In the early days of formal evaluation, there was an almost universal adoption and acceptance of scientific method. Over the last 30 years there has been a growing appreciation that there is also a need for well-designed and thorough qualitative evaluation.

Focus upon the teacher

Portraying teachers as a much-maligned group within the community would not be hard, given the draconian nature of recent 'educational reforms'. But to engage in the assessment of performance is an issue of increasing significance within the public services generally. The core of the argument is that while the question of performance measurement and the use made of public resources cannot be ignored – nor left solely to internal dialogue among professionals – exclusively quantitative and externally imposed approaches not only suffer technical limitations, they are inherently dangerous to proper accountability.

Educational institutions have become vehicles of certification as much as places of learning. The assessment process is intimately connected with the achievement and continued maintenance of standards of academic excellence, and as such its importance to the educational process cannot be overstated.

I hope that you find the *World Yearbook 1990* of interest and value: I would like to thank all those who gave their time and expertise to make this edition a reality.

1. Quality control in British higher education

David Warren Piper

In the United Kingdom, all first degrees are, in principle at least, of comparable standard. Perusal of official and often ancient documents, which regulate universities, leaves little doubt that this notion of parity is deeply ingrained in British higher education. For instance, a passage from the 1843 University of Durham Calendar asserts: 'The standing of the degree of B.A., as for all other degrees, is the same as that which is required at Oxford'. The charter of the Victoria University (Manchester), 1888, requires that examiners be appointed from other universities for all degrees, for the evident purpose of ensuring that standards (in words taken from the regulations of London University, but typical of others) 'are consistent with that of the national university system'.

The reference to a national system is revealing because constitutionally no such system exists: each university is a discrete and autonomous entity, awarding its own degrees under a charter from the Crown. The polytechnics and colleges, on the other hand, can be said fairly to be part of a single system, at least for the award of degrees. These institutions do not possess their own charters, rather their degrees are given under a charter held by The Council for National Academic Awards (CNAA). Thus, whereas the universities are free to adopt whatever standards they wish, the rest of the higher education 'system' is not. In fact the universities have always maintained an accord on standards and the CNAA chose to join them: until 1988 the Council's regulations required that its degrees be 'comparable to the standard of an award conferred by universities in the United Kingdom'. Thereafter, the reference was dropped, on the grounds that the Council's standards were well established.

What is implied by this ideal of a universal standard? Clearly, more than one form of parity. There must be consistency within a degree programme, especially parity between course options. Standards must remain reasonably constant from year to year. Courses in similar subjects must be taught by all institutions to a similar level and the examinations marked to similar standards. It is also clear from the regulations quoted above, that standards are to be consistent between subjects. This view was recently reaffirmed by the Lindop Committee.[1] Implicit in this view is the notion of a quality of academic work which is independent of subject matter yet is manifest in all disciplines. (Or, at the least, sets of equivalent qualities which allow examiners in different subjects to discriminate between degree classes in ways which agree.) A further implication is that all examiners have a grasp of this common notion and can apply it consistently in drawing distinctions between several levels of student performance.

Implicit in the ideal of parity between all degrees, then, are a number of assumptions first, about the kinds of comparisons which might be made to establish the marking standards, and secondly, about the ability of examiners to make certain kinds of discrimination. They are assumptions which invite scrutiny. A recent investigation[2] undertaken by the author throws light on some pertinent questions and summaries of selected findings are presented below.

Four kinds of parity were identified above. First, a degree programme must be internally consistent, the same standards must be applied when marking all assessed work which counts towards a degree.[3] Achieving such consistency within a programme raises some problems. One such problem concerns the application of consistent standards to the marking of work done under different conditions – say, that done during a three-hour invigilated examination and that produced as a project completed under supervision over a period of months. The question is whether or not the marking should take into account the conditions under which the work was done. If the answer is 'no', then we might expect to get very different ranges of marks for work done under different conditions. As a consequence the distribution of degree results would be partly a function of the assessment methods chosen. If the answer is 'yes', we invoke the need for some kind of conversion table, understood and consistently applied by all markers.

Another problem concerns the marking standards to apply when some of the examined work is done before the final year. Should early work be marked to the same standard as the final examinations or should it be marked as, say, second-year work? Again, the second option implies some consistent and shared notion of standards not only for final-year work but for every year of a course. The task is further complicated if an elective course may be taken by students in different years.

To understand the potential significance of these problems we must first enquire into the combinations of work which typically contribute to assessment for a degree. The first problem concerned work done under different conditions. How many degree courses involve projects and other kinds of course work? Course leaders were asked the question and the results are presented in Table 1:

Is work other than that done under examination conditions, taken into account when determining students' final grade or marks?

	Univ*	P&C**
Yes, all students	77%	94%
Yes, for some students or course options	18%	4%
No	4%	1%

* Universities.   ** Polytechnics and Colleges

Table 1

The relative weighting given to examination marks in the overall determination of a candidate's degree class.

Weighting	Proportion of courses giving the weighting	
	Univ	P&C
0%–59%	18%	25%
60%–79%	45%	61%
80%–100%	37%	13%

Table 2

there are very few degrees indeed which are awarded solely on the basis of 'traditional' invigilated examinations.

How much weight is given to the marks awarded for examination performance compared with assessed course work of various kinds? Table 2 gives a summary.

From these data we can conclude that the resolution of the problem of how to reconcile the marking standards applied to different kind of work is potentially a major determinant of overall degree standards. It follows that if the issue is resolved inconsistently or differently from one course to another the ideal of parity becomes difficult to achieve.

What of standards? We might postulate that if the same standards are applied to project work as to examination scripts, the marks will be affected in two ways: the project marks will be higher and the variation between them will be less because students will continue to work on their project until they are likely to earn the required mark.

External examiners were asked both about the quality of candidates' work and about the standards by which it was marked. The results as they relate to course work and to projects or dissertations are summarized in Table 3. They suggest considerable variation between examiners' views on quality and inconsistent approaches to the adjustment of standards to take account of context.[4]

Assuming that the external examiners' views are correct we may conclude that the quality of course work and projects is higher than examination answers in a substantial number of cases but that the cases in which compensatory marking standards are applied is considerably less. More examiners report the same marking standards being applied to all kinds of work than the number who report the quality of work being the same, which implies that there are courses in which the distribution of marks is partly determined by the method of assessment.

The survey revealed no direct evidence that the range of marks on course work or projects was restricted although that was the view of some examiners among those who were interviewed. Should it be so, the possibility arises that on some courses items which carry the majority of examination marks are also the items which discriminate between the candidates the least, implying that items with low weightings are the critical determinants of overall degree class.

The quality of work and standards of marking as reported by external examiners.

	The proportion of external examiners who agree	
	Univ	P&C
In relation to examination scripts:		
Course work was of better quality	24%	37%
Projects/dissertations were of better quality	43%	49%
The same quality prevailed throughout (course work)	32%	20%
The same quality prevailed throughout (proj./diss.)	28%	19%
Higher standards were applied to course work	8%	8%
Higher standards were applied to projects/dissertations	11%	16%
Same standards applied throughout	54%	42%

Table 3

Such an outcome, should it occur, is presumably, the exact opposite of the intention behind the weighting scheme.

Overall it seems probable that there are a substantial number of courses in which marking standards are held constant regardless of the kind of work being marked, with the result that each kind of work yields a different distribution of marks with a consequent effect on overall degree standards. There are other courses where an attempt is made to take into account the conditions under which work has been done. The difficulty in those instances is putting some consistent numerical value on a qualitative difference which is likely to affect candidates in different ways (for example, one student might excel in formal examinations where another's temperament is better suited to project work). The survey yielded no quantitative data on the point but some written answers to open-ended questions referred to the matter. One respondent, for example, wrote:

An insolvable problem. There are so many uncertainties involved in the appraisal of course work that this is one of the main causes of imprecision in the examination process (eg the candidate who fails in the paper but passes overall on the basis of course work which may be suspect).

The second dilemma mentioned above referred to marking 'early' work: should it be marked at the same standard as final-year work if it counts towards the degree? The problem affects a large number of courses as returns to the survey suggest that on 78 per cent of courses candidates' degree results depend partly on work or examinations undertaken prior to the final year. The survey produced no statistical data on the weighting given to 'early' work in the computation of degree results. The general rule is that final-year work has the greatest weighting, yet work from previous years commonly counts for one-third of the total marks.

Course leaders and external examiners give compatible replies when asked about the relative standards applied to marking early work. Table 4 summarizes

Is any of the work from previous years marked to a different standard than that from the final year?

	Univ	P&C
Yes	15%	30%
No	82%	63%

Table 4

the answers given by course leaders and Table 5 the answers given to a similar enquiry of external examiners.

A similar pattern emerges to that from the questions about course work: on the majority of courses the same standards are maintained but there is a substantial minority of courses where some form of compensation is attempted. Examiners were asked if they were aware of any problems or ambiguities over the standards by which 'early' work was assessed. Eleven per cent reported that they were.

It seems clear that practice varies, and, *prima facie*, we might infer that the standards of degrees vary as a consequence. Of course, it is theoretically possible for the variations in marking standards to be compensated by weighting marks or by examiners taking into account the difficulty of the material.

The second form of parity identified above concerned standards from year to year. Course leaders were asked whether the examined work was judged against standards of work of candidates completing the same course in previous years. Twelve per cent of the respondents reported that such comparisons were not made, but only 7 per cent said that the comparisons were made directly between the work from different years. The remaining 80 per cent said that comparisons were made 'from memory and experience'. Only 4 per cent of course leaders reported that external examiners would have a selection of scripts from previous years, but 55 per cent said that they would have the distribution of marks from previous years. However, only 18 per cent of the sample of external examiners said that they had received a summary of the previous year's marks; most of whom (16 per cent) found it useful. Among the 82 per cent who did not receive a summary were 23 per cent who believed they would have found it useful.

Were the standards applied when marking work produced before the final year the same as those applied when marking work during the final year?

	Univ	P&C
Yes	67%	58%
No	12%	25%

Table 5

We may conclude that the ideal of consistent standards from year to year is widely accepted but that a good deal of reliance is placed on examiners' ability to carry the standard in their memory from one year to the next. The ability of humans to carry within themselves valid and implementable notions of marking standards has been challenged by a number of authorities, notably by Dale, who, writing in the Universities Quarterly in 1959, asserted that:

> One of the biggest obstacles to improvement . . . is the unreliability and uncertainty of university examinations and the greatest obstacle to reform is the ignorance of the staffs of universities about the pitfalls which surround the examiner, the calm assurance with which lecturers and professors alike believe that they can carry around in their heads an unfailing correct conception of an absolute standard of 40 per cent as the pass line is incomprehensible to anyone who has studied the research into the reliability of examinations.[5]

The theme has been taken up recently by Johnson (1988)[6] who, having reviewed some evidence drawn from studies of GCE examining boards (which employ elaborate procedures to enhance reliability) considers examining practice in higher education:

> No single person can possibly have complete insight into the sometimes subtle effects of mark aggregation, nor a 'feel' for absolute grading standards. The likelihood of any individual being able to 'absorb' a feel for the grading standards being applied by some other institution by reviewing examination papers and scripts must be even lower. And the possibility that such an individual, however experienced and long serving, could 'carry' applicable notions about universally appropriate grading standards must be remote.

Certainly the higher-education examination system is premised upon the assumption that examiners can make consistent judgements over time and one of the more intriguing questions is why there is such a contrast between the experimental evidence produced by psychologists and the experience reported from the field by practitioners. In the current survey it was common for interviewees to express surprise at the high level of agreement they found with other examiners, even when marking in ignorance of the other's mark. Whether such experience rests on distorted perception and selective memory, or whether laboratory experiments have failed to replicate crucial field conditions may not have been conclusively demonstrated, but the wealth of experimental data about the unreliability of human judgement is formidable evidence to set aside in the name of custom and practice.

The third kind of parity was that between similar courses taught in different institutions. It is, perhaps, to this form of parity that the external-examiner system is primarily addressed. Every board of examiners has at least one, and usually more, members drawn from other institutions; invariably they are well-established members of the academic community in the relevant discipline. This exchange of examiners is regulated by the CNAA for polytechnics and colleges and by a code of practice adopted by the universities. These regulations prohibit a direct exchange between two institutions and limit the number of concurrent external examinerships an individual may hold.

Probably the most efficacious pattern of interchange, for the purposes of maintaining parity of standards, is no pattern at all, but rather a thoroughly haphazard exchange, a kind of Brownian Movement of examiners across the system. Perhaps a systematic distribution could, in theory, achieve an even and thorough association between departments but in practice it would be prohibitively difficult to organize. Any pattern which isolates pairs of conglomerates of departments from the rest of the system invites divergence in the standards of marking.

As part of the study, the investigators selected four representative discipline areas (Electrical/Electronic Engineering, Chemistry, Sociology and English) and attempted to map the movement of external examiners between departments during the summer examination period of 1986. The results showed an evenly spread network of examiners across the system. There are very few pairs of departments which exchange examiners and nearly all individuals restrict themselves to one or two concurrent examinerships. Perhaps the most compelling evidence of the potential of the system for maintaining comparable standards is the small number of links along the chain of examiners which connect any one department with any other; the smallest was six for the English departments and the largest was ten for the sociology departments. There is one respect, however, in which the system is very lopsided. In the four subject areas studied there were virtually no polytechnic or college staff appointed as external examiners by universities, whereas around three-quarters of the external examiners appointed by polytechnics and colleges were from universities. So, although the network of examiners is pretty evenly spread, the flow of examiners through it is biased in direction.

Given the regulations mentioned at the beginning, we would expect all course leaders to report that marking standards are judged against similar courses in other institutions. Over 80 per cent do so, most agreeing that the comparisons are made 'from memory and experience', although a surprising 15 per cent (widely spread across subjects) reported that such comparisons were not made. The reasons for this last finding are not apparent.

The key question is whether or not the external-examiner system actually achieves the objective of comparable standards between institutions. There have been no direct comparisons of examination scripts in the United Kingdom[7] but two kinds of indirect evidence throw some light on the point.

The first comes from the current survey. Both course leaders and external examiners were asked how much variation they thought there was in the standards of degree class awarded in their own subject throughout the United Kingdom. The results are summarized in Table 6.

The following facts must be borne in mind when interpreting the figures in Table 6. A very high proportion of the external examiners would have been course leaders at some time in their careers; the reverse would not be true. All the external examiners in universities and the bulk of those in the polytechnics and colleges would be university staff. The variation in wording between questionnaires may account for some of the differences between course leaders and external examiners on the item: 'Standards vary (a little)'. On the whole the figures suggest that among those in the best position to judge (external examiners) few believe that standards vary a great deal. (It could be argued that as a group they have the largest vested interest in perceiving the external-

How much variation do you think there is between the standards of degree classes awarded?

	Course leaders.		Ex. Examiners.	
	Univ	P&C	Univ	P&C
More or less the same throughout the UK	25%	18%	48%	41%
Standards vary (a little)*	45%	48%	33%	41%
Standards vary a great deal	12%	20%	4%	4%
Don't know	16%	13%	9%	11%

* The words "a little" were omitted from the questionnaire to external examiners.

Table 6

examiner system as an effective moderating instrument.) The group containing the largest proportion of people who perceive a great deal of variation, that is, course leaders in polytechnics and colleges, is also the group which would contain the smallest number of people (less than half) who have experience as external examiners; virtually none of them would have experience as an external examiner in a university.

Those course leaders who reported that they thought standards varied either a little or a great deal (of whom there were 458) were asked whether they thought the variation was related to the 'binary divide' between the universities and the polytechnics and colleges sector. Of the university staff, a little over half believed that the variations were associated with the binary divide and all but one individual thought the universities had the higher standards. On the other hand, less than a quarter of the polytechnic and college staff believed that standards varied between sectors and of those few, three quarters believed that the higher standards were found in the polytechnics and colleges. This seems to suggest a higher incidence of confidence in the superiority of their own sector among university staff than polytechnic and college staff, who are more likely to see variations arising from departmental differences which have nothing to do with the binary divide.

The second kind of indirect evidence which throws light on the degree of parity between similar courses in different institutions is the distribution of degree classes awarded. If the marking standard for degrees is the same between departments then a higher proportion of first- and second-class degrees would reflect a higher quality of student work. This might be explained either by more successful teaching, higher student motivation or a more highly qualified student intake. If these do not provide an adequate explanation, variation in marking standards provides an alternative explanation. Most of the studies which have compared the distribution of degree results have been comparisons between subject, but a few have compared similar courses in different institutions. Two such recent studies[8] show the proportion of 'good degrees'[9]

The percentage of honours candidates awarded first class degrees (in both universities and polytechnics and colleges) 1971–1986

Computing & mathematics; physics	17%
Chemistry; engineering (general)	16%
Aeronautical engineering; chemical engineering	13%
Electrical engineering; mechanical engineering	12%
Metallurgy; mining engineering; technology (general)	11%
Art & design; civil engineering; industrial engineering	10%
Biology	8%
Combined science; English; health studies; pharmacy; philosophy; theology	7%
Architecture and planning; environmental sciences; history; modern languages	6%
Drama; education; music	5%
Economics; geography; hotel management/food sciences law; psychology; surveying	4%
Business studies; combined arts; social studies; other professional studies	3%
Accountancy; government & public administration	2%
(Medicine does not award classes of degree)	

Source: CNAA Transbinary Database.

Table 7

awarded in the same subject by different institutions varying, in one case by as much as 20 per cent and 70 per cent. It is a wide range to be accounted for and difficult to attribute to teaching practice, student motivation or student selection alone. Even more suggestive of the power of local norms in determining the distribution of grades is the remarkable stability of the grade profiles over time (eight years in one of the studies) when other possible determinants almost certainly fluctuate. A third study[10] has demonstrated how institutional norms governing the proportion of degrees assigned to the upper grades can mask the predictive value of General Certificate of Education scores.

Other studies have focused on the different ratio of good to poor degree grades associated with various subjects.[11] Tables 7 and 8 show the percentage of candidates awarded 'good degrees' in selected subjects. It is hard to explain these differences in any other way than that there are variations in the standards applied in different subjects: if an explanation were sought in the quality of student intake, for instance, we should still have to account for the reason why subjects appear in a different rank order in the two tables. The fact that the rank order differs not only supports the hypothesis that standards are determined by

Percentage of honours graduates awarded a "good" degree 1971–1986

History; philosophy	50%
Biology	48%
Art & design; drama; engineering (general); industrial engineering	47%
Chemical engineering; English; health studies; mining engineering; pharmacy	46%
Chemistry; physics	45%
Metallurgy; modern languages; psychology; technology (general)	44%
Computing & mathematics; theology	43%
Hotel management/food sciences; mechanical engineering	42%
Electrical engineering; environmental sciences; geography; music; surveying	41%
Aeronautical engineering; other professional subjects	40%
Civil engineering	39%
Education; government and public administration	38%
Combined science; social studies	37%
Business studies; combined arts	36%
Economics	35%
Architecture & planning; law	34%
Accountancy	30%

Source: CNAA Transbinary Database.

Table 8

subject-area norms, but strongly suggests that the relationship between the cut-off points between degree classes varies from subject to subject; it is not a simple matter of some subjects being generally harder or being marked more stiffly than others because the proportion of candidates assigned to each class varies.

The grade profiles not only vary between subjects but vary in different ways from one institution to the next. The variations between subjects are considerable, which brings us to the last form of parity: the notion of a universal, or rather a British, degree standard.

Despite the implication of a general standard found in official documents it is not uncommon to find scepticism expressed about the suggestion that all first degree courses pose the same intellectual challenge or require the same work load as each other. One can imagine the raised eyebrows in ancient university common rooms at the suggestion that theoretical physics as taught by the eyebrows' owners is on a par with International Hostmanship as taught at, say, Little Wallop Technical Institute. Not surprisingly, opinion is divided on the matter. When asked if standards on their own courses were 'judged against those which apply in other subjects, that is, against a general notion of a bachelor's degree course leaders split about equally between 'yes' and 'no'. However, there were differences according to institution and subject. Sixty-one per cent of respondents from polytechnics and colleges reported such cross-subject comparisons being made in contrast to only 44 per cent of those from the universities. Sixty per cent of respondents from social-science courses reported such comparisons, compared with 56 per cent in the arts and 42 per cent in the sciences.

It is difficult to see how examiners could make cross-subject comparisons. Quite aside from the conceptual problems of comparing performance in different disciplines or the technical problems of analysing candidates' performance according to psychological constructs supposedly applicable regardless of subject matter, there are few opportunities for examiners from different disciplines to work together. There was some evidence in the survey to suggest that cross-subject comparisons are reported more frequently on multi-subject courses than on single-subject courses by a factor of about 10 per cent.

Overall, the evidence throws some doubt on the tenability of assumptions implicit in the notion of a common degree standard. There seems to be a good deal of inconsistency in the way examiners adjust marking standards to circumstance; they vary in their views about the comparability of degrees; there is strong experimental evidence that making consistent judgements, especially over extended periods of time, is not *Homo sapiens'* strong suit and, finally, there is no mechanism for comparing standards between disciplines.

Are we, then, to conclude that parity of standards is an unattainable ideal? Is its pursuit a misguided policy? Should the external-examiner system be dropped as an expensive piece of window dressing which gives the impression of fairness while achieving very little? My own answer to all three questions is an unequivocal 'no', although, undoubtedly, many improvements could and should be made.

Is parity an unattainable ideal? The key issue is the *degree* of parity sought. Clearly standards do vary and are bound to do so. The question is whether the variation can be limied to acceptable proportions. Rather than seeking absolute parity as though calibrating so many scientific measuring instruments, an impossible task, a more realistic goal is a loose yet controlled bunching of standards, like a shoal of fish. Individual fish might be to the left or the right, high or low, forward or laggard, each following its own path, each with its own motive power; yet the shoal as a whole can veer in one direction or another. There are apparently mechanisms at work within each individual which keep it close to its neighbours. It seems, for instance, that there is a kind of reflex activated if the images captured by each eye of an individual differ: if more of its cousins appear in the image of the left eye than the right, the swimming muscles on the right beat more strongly, thus constantly propelling the individual to a central position in the shoal. Thus deviant individuals are returned to the mainstream. The relationship between individuals adjusts constantly but the shoal retains a constant steady progression. The external-examiner system is higher education's way of tapping deviant individuals back toward the centre: it may not position them exactly but it turns them in the right direction. This regression to the mean is assured, first by the number of individual examiners involved in determining each candidate's degree class,[12] and second, should a group of examiners build up increasingly deviant marking norms, by the external examiners, who are usually several in number and who, in any case, are replaced periodically. Overall, variations between examiners will be compensatory and in the long run deviant external examiners, who by definition are in the minority, will be replaced. Evidence concerning the unreliability of individual examiners' markings is not, of itself, sufficient grounds for concluding that an acceptable level of parity is unattainable. Research needs to focus on the overall effectiveness of the examining system in the field and on the policy issues which govern the degree of variation which is acceptable. Some work, such as that on the distribution of degree results, is of that kind and suggests that improvements are desirable. It would be premature and defeatist to assume that improvement is not possible.

Is the attempt to maintain parity between all degree courses misguided? It is a policy which has its critics. Martin Trow,[13] writing from an American perspective, has recently argued that it is the policy above all others which ensures that British higher education remains a shamefully exclusive privilege. Deregulation, he maintains, would allow institutions to adjust standards to suit the market and thus allow a move to mass higher education vitally necessary to a modern society. The counter-arguments are that all students have the right to expect that they will fare the same regardless of when and where they are assessed,[14] that a consistent standard of qualification is helpful to employers[15] and that under British law (perhaps changed by the time this article is published) all student fees are paid from public monies. As public authorities are keen to avoid charges of inequitable treatment of members of the public and the profligate use of funds, a system in which all courses cost the same and are of equal worth is attractive to them. If a loans system is introduced to replace the current student grants system, the argument for parity in degree standards will become that much weaker. However, there seems to be no appetite in the United Kingdom at present for allowing market forces to dictate tuition fees and degree standards. Mass higher education, if it comes at all, may come by other means.[16]

Should the external examining system be dropped? It was a common view among the external examiners interviewed that they could be effective at the margins. If course standards were grossly astray (an extremely rare occurrence by all accounts) it would be difficult radically to adjust marking standards on the spot; for one thing it would be unjust to the students who had been misled over what was required of them. They could, however, turn the examiners in the right direction so that, over time, anomalies could be redressed. The metaphor of the fish suggests that adjustment at the margins is sufficient.

Beyond its immediate efficacy, the external examining system has a great deal to recommend it. It is a manifestation of the great care which goes into assessing degree candidates. It is proof of a commitment to disinterested grading: an outside expert in the subject with no personal knowledge of the candidates (often not even knowing their names) can moderate the judgements of those who, knowing the students, can interpret the quality of their work more subtly yet may, by that very knowledge, be more susceptible to bias. Above all, the presence of external examiners on every examining board ensures that fundamental questions will be posed about issues apt to slip from the view of those at the chalk face, such as the original educational intent behind a course.

The periodic re-arguing of the bases upon which candidates have been evaluated and categorized is, perhaps, the greatest safeguard in the system. It is a safeguard against mark aggregation schemes which outlive their original intent, against the loss of fresh thinking in empty routines and against the gradual loss of rigour in applying standards. At the same time, those who serve as external examiners are messengers who take, from one institution to the next, news of innovations, of curriculum developments and of examination policy changes. For many academics, we were told, it is their only opportunity of discussing educational issues relating to their discipline; few academics attend education conferences or take courses on educational issues. Like Damon Runyon's crap game, the external-examiner system is the only permanent floating conference in town. Such periodic return to discussion of the basics is, I would argue, a far greater safeguard of the interests of both candidates and scholarship than could ever be afforded by the most sophisticated schemes for calibrating degree standards, however well founded they were on the latest psychometric principles.

None of that is to say that we may be complacent. The system has not realized its potential. Many improvements might and should be made. Our shoal of fish is rather more scattered than it need be; it could move with more definition and commitment; individuals could develop the use of sensitive antennae to be in closer touch with both their fellows and the environment in which they swim, relying, perhaps, just a little less, on their internal gyroscopes to plot their path.

Dale's attack on the ignorance of academics of some of the basics of educational practice might, in other professions or other circumstances, have been devastating. In fact, it went largely unnoticed in the groves of academe. Twenty years later Dale's thesis was taken up by Stones. In one paper having again reviewed the oft demonstrated shortcomings of traditional examinations and repeated follies of marking practices, he wrote:

> I wish I could have spared you this depressing recital but I fear that it is vitally necessary. The biggest block to examining in ways which genuinely test learning at high levels of rigour is the attitudes toward current methods that persist in the face of years of well documented evidence of their inutility. Only when we come to realise the illegitimacy of present practices are we likely to make progress toward methods that are more efficacious ... However, I recognise the fact that resistance to change resides in administrative structures as well as the minds of people.[17]

A related point arose from the current survey, concerning the professionalism of teachers in higher education. One of the defining characteristics of a profession is that its members share a body of knowledge and a set of theoretical constructs, as well as common ethical standards, often enforced by a professional body. Most teachers in higher education easily meet these criteria in respect of their academic discipline, but seldom in respect of teaching and examining. Many academics are highly experienced examiners and they draw mightily on that experience when assigning candidates to degree classes; moreover, external examiners give a very strong impression of people who take their responsibilities most seriously and are dedicated to the highest standards of integrity and concern for candidates; yet, equally, in the survey, most examiners gave the impression of very scant familiarity with the considerable body of knowledge about examinations and the measurement of human performance. This body of knowledge is not the esoteric province of educational research workers; it should inform practitioners' daily work. If they are to be regarded as professional educators (and that, after all, is what they are largely engaged to be, for the larger part of the higher-education budget is related to student numbers, not research programmes) it is the specialist knowledge which should define the profession.

What then, might be done to improve matters? In the final analysis what is required is a fundamental shift in the way that teachers in higher education perceive themselves. It is not that their identification with their subject matter should get any less but that their identity as educators should be much stronger, or, more precisely, the implications of perceiving themselves as educators could be more widely appreciated and accepted among academics. Such sea changes take time and possibly follow on from a hundred-and-one improvements in procedure which might more immediately be accepted.

Stones made some proposals for improving the way in which examinations are composed in his own subject (educational psychology).

I hold that the best we can do at present to ensure that our examinations are valid is to accept content validity as the most important form of validity and that its legitimation is dependent on the consensus of experts in the field. This is where the external examiner comes in. With this approach he does not merely moderate questions and examination scripts, he becomes a consultant in touch with the teaching institution throughout the year moderating students' work as it is produced and advising on questions of validity and levels of competence as and when necessary. His job is not to help the teaching institution to sort out the students more effectively but to advise on the degree to which he thinks the tests test the skills they purport to test.[18]

This last task is highly specialized and unlikely to be within the competence of academic staff other than psychologists. The rest of Stones's recommendations adumbrate those of the Lindrop Committee fifteen years later when it proposed that the role of external examiners in polytechnics and colleges should be extended:

The external examiner should contribute to the review and development of the curriculum by getting to know a course and its teachers in depth by such means as visits and discussions with the staff outside the examination period.[19]

This recommendation posed a problem for the Council for National Academic Awards because it seemed to confuse two functions for which the Council has distinct procedures: external examining and course validation. A working party of the Council responded by agreeing that external examiners had the freedom to comment on any aspect of a course but sought to confine their attention to examination material:

The external examiner should concentrate on a few essential concerns: quality of outcome, standards of award and the impartial treatment of students. All external examiners' judgements should be confined to what is reflected in the candidates' examined work.

Given a choice between two statements, to which are you personally inclined?

	Total	Univs		P&C	
Strongly inclined to A (Lindop)	21%	18%		25%	
			41%		55%
Marginally inclined to A	26%	23%		30%	
Indifferent	4%	3%		6%	
Marginally inclined to B	26%	30%		20%	
			55%		35%
Strongly inclined to B (CNAA)	21%	25%		15%	

Table 9

As part of the current survey external examiners were asked which of these two positions they were inclined towards. As can be seen from Table 9 the overall result was perfectly palindromic but the examiners in polytechnics and colleges were more inclined to the Lindop wording while those in universities leant more to the CNAA wording.

The figures suggest some considerable division of opinion as to whether the extended role would constitute an improvement. Part, but only part, of the problem is the extra time the additional duties would take. In answer to further questions it seems as though two-thirds of current external examiners would be willing to take on the extended role (about one-fifth already work in a similar way), but about half of them would want a higher fee for doing so. Of the third not willing to take up the role about three-quarters include matters of ethical principle in the reasons they give: either the advisory role constitutes an unwarranted incursion into the autonomy of fellow professions or it would conflict with the examiner's responsibility for impartial judgement (or both). If the objection is on ethical grounds rather than on grounds of time or payment, it suggests that the proposed extended role is seen as a retrograde step rather than a potential but expensive improvement. Whether or not the extended role will be introduced as standard practice is a policy matter yet to be resolved between the Department of Education and Science, the Council for National Academic Awards and the Committee of Vice-Chancellors and Principals.

Meanwhile, there is much that can be done at departmental and institutional level to improve quality control of degree examinations. What follows are some of the key points which emerged from the survey.

The total examination (that is, assessed work counting towards the degree as well as examination papers) should be carefully and systematically monitored against a previously adopted set of criteria. A checklist of basics for evaluating an examination might run:

☐ The syllabus should be adequately covered, yet candidates should not be assessed more than once on the same material (for example, an examination answer should not cover the same ground as a project report).

☐ The balance of *kinds* of performance required of candidates (for example, accurate memory, the application of fundamental concepts or principles to novel data, computational skills, problem solving, creativeness) should be deliberate and controlled, rather than the incidental product of the assembly of questions and examined tasks or of mark aggregation schemes.

☐ The examinations should accommodate equally well candidates at all levels of performance, that is both first-class candidates and borderline-fail candidates (and all those between) should have an equal chance of demonstrating the quality of their work.

☐ All candidates should have an equal choice among questions *de facto* as well as *de jure* (for instance their choice should not be limited by the combination of optional courses they have elected to take).

☐ A candidate's choice of question or project should not affect the grades that it is possible for them to achieve.

All examined work should be double blind marked. That is each marker should have no clues as to the other's assessment, such as are given by marginalia or an open grade. It is also good practice for a candidate's name and sex to be concealed, if possible, as both these can affect examiners judgements.

There should be thorough marking conventions, reflecting the educational purpose of the course and well understood by all markers. Where possible markings should be 'criterion referenced' rather than 'norm referenced'.[20] Where numbers allow, marks should be subject to statistical analysis to check for deviant markers and aberrant examination tasks. Similarly, the efficacy of examination papers should be monitored: which questions attract most answers, which are avoided and which cause problems; do the answers in total cover the syllabus as well as the examination questions do? The board of examiners should be aware of which examination tasks principally contribute to the discrimination of degree classes so as to be in a position to assess how well any mark aggregation scheme accords with the educational purpose of the course.

The means by which an array of marks is converted to a single degree class seem frequently to draw criticism from external examiners and can clearly be the source of difficulty. The variety of aggregation schemes is profuse and some are excessively complicated, but many share a common feature: the early stages involve the calculation of some form of average mark which later may be refined by reference to rules relating to the pattern of marks. (For example, no more than 20 per cent of a candidate's marks must fall in a degree class two below the overall class to be awarded.) Useful rules of thumb for the composition of aggregation schemes seem to be: prefer the simple to the complex; be sure all examiners have the same understanding of the scheme; ensure that the scheme neither subverts the original intent of the examinations nor disadvantages some candidates. Once adopted no scheme should be lightly set aside nor yet applied slavishly if justice is thereby jeopardized; a board of examiners should have the power to set aside an aggregation scheme in the interest of justice or the maintenance of appropriate standards.

All examiners, including external examiners, should be adequately briefed about the course, the examinations and the candidates.[21]

There should be a defensible rationale for the way in which an external examiner samples scripts. This concerns both the kind of sample (all work of selected candidates; all work from selected examinations) and the size of the sample (sufficient to draw relilable inferences).[22] The common pattern is for either all scripts or a selection of them to be sent to the external examiners. An alternative arrangement, however, has much to recommend it: that is for all examined material to be made available concurrently to all external examiners, at the examining institution, for one or two days before the meeting of the board of examiners. This arrangement greatly lessens security risks. It allows external examiners to confer with each other, with internal examiners and with candidates as required. It gives maximum freedom for examiners to adopt progressive sampling procedures which allow cross-checking and the follow-up of significant findings. It also limits the time an external examiner is required to work to a predetermined period.

An external examiner should not be required to undertake tasks which are better done within the home department. Examples from the survey are: referring to external examiners an excessive number of borderline candidates because the internal examiners are reluctant to assign degree classes; and referring disagreements between internal markers which should properly be resolved within the department. An example of the latter is a disagreement arising from different interpretations of course policy; disagreements which genuinely arise from differing judgements about the quality of a candidate's work, on the other hand, might legitimately be referred to an external examiner (but only after internal procedures have failed to break the dead-lock).

Certain principles governing the composition and conduct of a board of examiners can also contribute to the orderly maintenance of degree standards. A board of examiners may be regarded as an assembly of representatives of a collegium come together to exercise collective judgement on the quality of candidates' academic work. The main responsibility of the board is the exercise of judgement where regulations, marking procedures, guidelines or precedent are found to be inadequate or inappropriate. The business of the board should be conducted accordingly, so allowing this primary duty to be fulfilled with dispatch and lack of undue restraint.[23]

The detail of how these various principles are translated into procedures must be suited to local circumstance. Good practice inevitably depends upon context, and varies according to educational purpose, subject matter and type of department. Nonetheless, the items detailed above have broad applicability and can serve as a guide to departments and institutions reviewing their examination procedures. That is perhaps the first step towards the British higher-education system getting a firmer grip on the control of degree standards. Once that is done, institutions will be in a firmer position to apply some of the lessons implicit in psychological investigations of how people make judgements. Uncertain though that capacity may be, it is one of the last responsibilities we should assign to mechanical procedures whether bureaucratic or electronic.

Notes

1. 'Despite the notorious problems involved in trying to achieve comparability of standards between institutions even within a single subject, let alone between subjects, we believe that broad comparability is possible and desirable both between and within sectors.' Paragraph 6.4

Academic Validation in Public Sector Higher Education (Lindop Report) 1985, Cmnd 9501, HMSO, London.

2. The study was carried out between 1985 and 1987 under the aegis of the Economic and Social Research Council. The major components of the study were: a questionnaire sent to course leaders in 50 representative universities, polytechnics and colleges producing 757 returns; two questionnaires sent to the external examiners of the same courses producing returns of 1,000 and 645; and extended interviews with 81 external examiners. The results of the survey are presented in detail in a report submitted to the ESRC and entitled *The Role of External Examiners for Undergraduate Courses in the United Kingdom*.

3. It might be argued that internal consistency is not necessary, provided that the average standard is correct, but such an argument will not hold if there are optional courses allowing candidates to take different combinations of electives. Unless the alternative examinations are marked to the same standard, there will be variation in the standard of the overall degree.

4. The figures presented in Table 3 are taken from a more extensive array of data and so give only partial information. For precise interpretation they need to be considered in their context and readers are referred to the full report.

5. Dale, R R (1959) University Standards, *Universities Quarterly*: 13(2).

6. Johnson, S (1988) Implications for Degree Level Examinations of Two Decades of School-Level Examinations Research, *S.R.H.E. Annual Conference*, London. (Subsequently published in *Studies in Higher Education*.)

7. There has been one study in New Zealand in which departments exchanged scripts to mark: Crooke, T J (1979) Consistency of Standards between Departments and Courses, *Assessment in Higher Education*: 4(3).

8. Bee, M and Dolton, P (1985) Degree Class and Pass Rates: an Inter-university Comparison, *Higher Education Review*: 7(2). Connolly, K J and Smith, P K (1986). What Makes a 'good' Degree: Variations Between Departments.

9. First-class and upper-second-class degrees.

10. Sear, K (1983) The Correlation Between 'A' Level Grades and the Degree Results in England and Wales, *Higher Education* 12(5).

11. See for instance: Becher, T and Kogan, M (1980) *Process and Structure in Higher Education*. Heinemann; London p. 157; Bourner, J with Hamed, M (1987) Entry Qualifications and Degree Performance, *CNAA Development Services Publication:10*; Bligh, D et al (1980) 'A' Level Scores and Degree Classifications as a Function of University Type and Function. In Billing, D. (ed) *Indicators of Performance*, SRHE Guildford. Hindmarch, A and Bourner, J (1979) Examination Results: Universities and the CNAA. In Billings op cit. Turner, D J (1985) An Analysis of Differences in Marks Obtained by Students in Different Modules, *Teaching*: 12, Oxford Polytechnic.

12. Most undergraduate programmes involve a number of courses which are taught and examined by different members of faculty. On 71 per cent of university degree courses and 84 per cent of CNAA degree courses there are more than ten examiners involved; on 34 per cent and 46 per cent respectively there are more than 20 examiners. Thus the number of people whose judgements are being sampled goes some way toward ensuring that overall marks regress to a mean. Further stability may be added to the overall marks by markers tending to conform to a norm especially among colleagues who, through the convention of double marking (see below), become familiar with the marking standards of colleagues.

Most often some kind of guidance is provided for faculty marking examined work (on 59 per cent of university courses and 75 per cent of polytechnic and college courses); this most often takes the form of marking guides or checklists of criteria or educational objectives. Marking guides, it might reasonably be assumed, increase the reliability of examination marking, although there have been very few field studies to demonstrate that the effects noted in the laboratory are carried over to working practice. Another way of increasing the reliability of marks is to adjust them after they have been awarded so that they confirm to a common distribution. On only 10 per cent of courses are marks subjected to such statistical treatment yet marking is predominantly normative.

13. Trow, M (1987) Academic Standards and Mass Higher Education, *Higher Education Quarterly*, 41, pp 268–292.

14. An argument put in Williams, G and Blackstone, T (1983) *Response to Adversity*, (Leverhulme Programme Monograph: 10) SRHE: Guildford, in which they echo the 1963 Robbins' argument 'that in any properly co-ordinated system of higher education the academic grading of individuals should depend upon their academic accomplishments rather than upon the status of

the institution in which they have studied': *Higher Education* (Robbins Report) 1963, Cmnd 2154-11. HMSO, London.
15. But see Roizen for evidence that employers typically make distinctions between degree giving institutions.
16. After all, a country like the USA can quite correctly point to the very much greater proportion of its population earning first degrees, but that is not the same as claiming that a higher proportion of the population gets a better education. It is a matter of semantics: what kind of courses are to be included in the category of 'higher education'? However that is not to say that England is not weak in that kind of post-school education which in Britain would be offered outside the degree system but which in America is included within it.
17. Stones, E (1978) *The New Examiner*, paper delivered at a conference on external examining, 16 October, organized by CNAA.
18. Stones, E and Anderson, D (1972) *Educational Objectives and the Teaching of Educational Psychology*, Methuen.
19. Lindop Report, op cit.
20. With 'criterion referencing' marks are awarded according to previously specified criteria. The more precisely the criteria are worded the greater the potential for consistent marking. In simple schemes the criteria specify only information which candidates must include in their submissions in order to gain certain marks. More sophisticated schemes precisely specify levels of intellectual performance or analytic procedures or other academic virtues to discriminate between classes of degree. Such schemes may draw upon analytic models of types of learning and intellectual activity rather than referring to subject-based syllabuses. 'Norm referenced' marking essentially relies upon comparing the performance of candidates.
21. The following is a categorized list of items which external examiners report they do or would appreciate receiving:

☐ Information about the course:
- prospectus;
- course regulations and/or requirements;
- a description of duties or a code of practice for all examiners;
- syllabus (or preferably a fuller account of what is taught than is normally found in syllabuses);
- course objectives;
- information on teaching methods;
- rationale for the choice of examination methods in relation to educational objectives.
☐ Information about the derivation of examination marks:
- rules for combining and adding marks;
- marking guides and schemes.
☐ Information about the marks awarded:
- the mean and range of marks awarded for each question;
- the number of candidates provisionally awarded each class or grade of degree;
- the range of marks awarded by each internal examiner;
- the mean and range (or deviation) of marks awarded for each paper;
- summary of previous year's marks;
- summary of difficulties which have cropped up in assessment.
☐ Information about candidates:
- information about particular candidates (eg health);
- information about incidents during the examinations which may have affected performance or relate to the interpretation of candidates' marks (from disturbed examination rooms to suspected plagiarism.

These last two items might more appropriately be provided at the board of examiners' meeting than as part of an initial briefing.
22. In the British higher-education system the number of candidates sitting any given examination is small. Forty-two per cent of university courses have fewer than 20 finalists a year and the modal number is less than ten. Courses in polytechnics and colleges tend to be bigger: 71 per cent have beetween 20 and 74 finalists per year and the modal number is between 20 and 39. (Data from current survey.)
23. Respondents to the survey suggested a number of specifics designed to contribute to those ends. What follows is a compilation.

The examining board's regulations should include a rule that all other rules might be set aside in the interest of justice to candidates and the maintenance of standards but only with the explicit agreement of the external examiner(s).

The external examiners should be notified well before the meeting of any difficult or borderline cases, of any matters of principle raised by the examinations or the marks, and of any uncertainties or disagreements among the internal examiners. All relevant documentation and scripts must be made available to the external examiners in sufficient time for them to prepare for the meeting.

All candidates should have their interests equally well represented by the membership and procedures of the board. If, by way of illustration, the membership of the board includes the tutors of some candidates but not others, then all requests for special consideration of a candidate's results must be tabled before the meeting along with all pertinent documentation and a board member nominated to present the case, thus minimizing the opportunity for special pleading.

Normal rules and standards should be applied to the marking of all work in the first instance. Thereafter may consideration be given by the board to adjustments and exceptions. This implies that evidence in support of marks being adjusted (such as of a candidate being unusually stressed) should be disclosed only after preliminary marks of all candidates have been agreed but before candidates have been assigned to degree classes. Such avoidance should have been submitted to the examinations office beforehand and its contents revealed to the chairman to allow him to confirm the agenda and to the external examiners in time for them to consider their judgements. The external examiners should be satisfied that only those marks which may have been affected by adverse circumstances are adjusted (for instance only those marks earned during a period of bereavement).

The chairman should not admit unethical or irrational lines of argument to be advanced in determining a candidate's degree class: for instance, a proposal to discriminate between candidates with identical marks on the grounds that one chose easier questions than another.

The board's meeting should be conducted with a certain degree of formality and chaired so as to get through the agenda expeditiously while allowing discussions of principle to develop and run their course. Membership of the board should be unambiguous and attendance consistent, members staying either for the whole meeting or for the portion thereof for which their attendance is specifically required.

No unresolved decisions regarding marks from intermediate (or second-year) examinations should be carried over to the final year.

There should be no ambiguities about the respective responsibilities of the board and the institution over cases of suspected plagiarism. (The usual arrangement is for the board to determine whether or not plagiarism has taken place but to make no adjustment to the candidate's mark or grade. The institution is responsible for applying its regulations regarding any penalty, normally the withholding of its award or discounting the relevant part of the examination, in which case the affected work is regarded as non-existent and the pertinent examination regulations concerning non-completion are evoked. It is possible at this point that the case may again come under the purview of the examining board.

External examiners who are involved only in sub-boards should be informed of the eventual outcome of the deliberations of the main board.

A number of principles were espoused by various respondents to the survey relating to the assignment of degree classes. Among them were the following:

☐ Attempts should not be made to compensate for poor teaching by generous marking or differentially assigning candidates to degree classes; there is no way of doing it consistently and it invites punitive marking of candidates who have been well taught.
☐ Candidates should not be penalized for shortcomings in teaching and course administration.

These first two principles appear to conflict. Only in exceptional and well-established cases should an examination board take steps to compensate for inadequate teaching or administration possibly by placing less weight on the affected parts of the examination.

☐ The quality of a candidate's work at the end of a course should be the principle determinant of the degree class awarded.
☐ There should be an explicit and defensible policy as to whether degree class is to reflect the best work of a candidate (ie that of which he or she is capable) or some average of the quality exhibited in all examined work; mark aggregation schemes should make manifest the policy.
☐ On joint degrees a candidate's degree class should reflect the overall quality of work rather

than require equally outstanding performance in both (all) subjects for the award of a Class I or II:1 degree. (The argument is that otherwise joint degree candidates are disadvantaged in relation to single honours candidates who can compensate for weaker performance in one part of their examinations by a stronger performance elsewhere.)

2. Raising educational standards – improving the quality of education

Kim Foss Hansen

Summary: The question of how to improve the quality of education attracts much attention in Denmark these days. This article deals with some of the reasons why the debate arises just now, with a view of how education can be changed and improved, and finally with a description of a method which makes it possible to start a dialogue about desirable changes in education.

A brief description of the education system

The first nine school years: the 'folkeskole'

The *folkeskole* is a unified school covering the first nine or ten years of a child's education. Characteristics of the *folkeskole* are:

- ☐ that it is obliged to accept all children except those seriously physically/ mentally disabled;
- ☐ that the children are grouped in classes, based on age, which remain the same throughout all the school years. This means that pupils do not repeat classes because of slow educational attainment, that there are no classes for particularly bright pupils, that no marks are given until the 8th school year, and that all pupils take the same examinations at the end of the 9th, perhaps 10th, school year,
- ☐ that normally a pupil has the same teacher for a particular subject for several years;
- ☐ that the ministerial orders governing the contents of the curriculum provide a broad framework, which means that to a very large extent it is up to the teacher to decide at which stage it is easiest for the pupils to acquire certain knowledge;
- ☐ that the teachers have free choice of teaching method, ie they are free to choose the method considered most suitable taking into account the nature of the subject and the stage of development reached by the pupils;
- ☐ that within the financial limits imposed on the school the teachers are free to choose their own teaching material.

A consequence of the above is that in Denmark there is no tradition that a central body (such as the Ministry of Education) should instruct the schools and the individual teachers:

- [ ] which teaching method to apply;
- [ ] when to teach what;
- [ ] which teaching materials to use.

But they are expected to provide high-quality education – an education so differentiated that all pupils can obtain satisfactory results in relation to their abilities and potential.

The 10th to the 12th school years

In Denmark, the 10th to the 12th years of education can be taken at different types of school. There are five possible paths leading to higher education, the most common ones being via the 'gymnasium' or 'Højere Forberedelse'.

The curriculum for the 10th to 12th School years has been laid down by the Ministry of Education and is far more specified (through prescribed syllabuses) than is the curriculum for the first nine school years. At the end of the 12th school year an examination is held that gives access to higher education, which is provided by universities, technical universities and business schools. The contents of the examination depend on the combination of subjects chosen by the pupil during the school years. Also, in this case, the teachers may, to a large extent, choose their own teaching methods and teaching material, subject to the financial limits imposed on the school in question.

Changes throughout the past 20 years

The past 20 years have seen a number of changes in the school system, these changes being one of the main reasons why the Ministry of Education now stresses its wish to improve the quality of education. The changes are as follows:

- [ ] class hours in the *folkeskole* have been reduced by approximately 25 per cent;
- [ ] a unified school has been introduced, which means an increase from approximately 50 per cent of a generation completing a 10-year education in 1968 to more than 95 per cent today;
- [ ] from providing an education with the primary aim of giving 10 to 15 per cent of a generation the qualifications necessary to continue in the education system, the *folkeskole* has gradually changed towards providing an education catering for *everybody*;
- [ ] tenth to 12th year education is now offered by different types of school, appealing to different types of young people;
- [ ] in principle, an examination taken at any of the types of school gives access to higher education;
- [ ] the number of young people completing 12 years of education has increased from approximately 15 per cent of a generation in 1968 to approximately 50 per cent today;
- [ ] these days pupils have more options when choosing the combination of their subjects, which has reduced the percentage going for the 'old' combinations;
- [ ] higher education has chosen to introduce restricted admission instead of ability tests after eg the first year of study (admission examinations). It is

an average of a person's examination marks after the 12th school year which is decisive of whether or not he or she can start higher education.

Whereas there have been considerable structural changes, there have been few changes in syllabus or teaching methods, not taking into account the cuts in syllabus resulting from cuts in class hours.

However, the syllabuses have not been reduced as much as the reduction of class hours would indicate. This means that the teaching has already become more efficient.

Changes in society

In a society which is only changing slowly, changes in the education system can be effected through changes in the training of teachers. Changing university teacher training, for example, will produce teachers with a new and different background. The new teachers will subsequently introduce changes in the education system.

There is also time to let the development come from below and grow concurrently with the needs expressed by teachers and pupils.

The development may originate at the bottom of the education system, starting within small groups of teachers at the individual school while the majority of teachers at the school continue teaching the way they have previously, without really noticing the development project, which in that kind of society merely consists of a slow change of practice, replacing old and obsolete syllabus topics by new ones.

In a slowly changing society demands 'from the top' for quick changes in the education system are rare; Denmark has long ago passed this stage.

Danish society is characterized by change and adaptation to shifting conditions of life and production. Any change, in for instance the education system, is a consequence of a desire for change expressed both 'from the top' and 'from the bottom'. The present development of our society is described by some people as the third automation wave. Whereas the first two automation waves mechanized manual operations, the third one affects intellectual operations, exemplified by the robot replacing the spray-painter, the CAD system rationalizing the work of the architect or the draughtsman, or word-processing systems taking over the work of the typist.

The third automation wave not only affects the crafts and industries, but also the academic world. It is propagated into fields of activity that are considered not only intellectual but representing maximum intellectual performance. One example is expert systems; the mere thought that in a generation or two we may be able to replace maximum intelligence wholly or partly by machines is provoking and challenging in itself.

The development is not new, of course – this is the latest stage of an advance which started thousands of years ago. At an early stage the development produced a culture in which the central elements were the people of the culture and the spoken language. People could talk to each other, they could remember, they could pass on the experience of that culture orally, but they could not store experience and knowledge separately from the spoken language. The next step in development was a culture in which knowledge and experience were placed outside the person. People were not capable of storing experience in the form of tools (storing human skills) and in the form of a written language (storing human knowledge).

Today we emphasize the importance of knowledge – once we invented machines that could copy what we had created, now we try to develop machines that can copy the thoughts we have been thinking. The technology of information is seeking to activate the passive written language.

The development of society has meant more and more leisure for the individual as the amount of work a person has to do in order to fulfil their basic needs – satisfy their hunger or quench their thirst – is decreasing.

But the development also means that the tasks that society is facing nowadays are changing faster than before. Someone who became a smith 150 years ago could expect to work as a smith and to be able to use the skills he learned during his apprenticeship for the rest of his life. Someone who became a smith 70 years ago has experienced that the skills acquired during his apprenticeship did not suffice for much more than 10 years after he finished his apprenticeship. The machines and the work make new and further training necessary. Today the greater part of the working population has experienced changing jobs and has received further training several times after they finished what their parents thought was a training that would last them the rest of their lives.

New work tasks presuppose and create the need for different training and education, but that does not mean that 'old' training and education must be discarded; the fan structure of the development of society must also be presumed to apply to the development of the education system. Furthermore changes in training and education presuppose and create the need for teacher qualifications. We are talking about a dialectical process in which the prerequisites and the needs created can only be distinguished from each other in theory.

A logical consequence of the above is that the development of our education system must involve changes in the qualifications of teachers as well as changes in the education system. We are no longer a society in which it is possible to first change teacher qualifications and subsequently change education – and we are definitely not a society in which it is possible to change only the education system. Even when ignoring the human costs, it is a fact that Denmark does not have a manpower reserve within the education sector which would allow discarding the present labour force.

The desire for high-quality education

It is no mere chance that the desire for high-quality education should arise just now. In addition to the demands for new labour force qualifications caused specifically by technological development, other decisive factors behind the desire to improve the quality of education are:

☐ that the number of young people who want to study mathematics, physics, and chemistry is too small;
☐ that girls especially do not choose more technical subjects;
☐ doubt whether the educational establishments which give access to higher

education provide their pupils with equal qualifications;

☐ that it has been claimed again and again that educational establishments giving access to higher education do not provide their pupils with the qualifications that they are required to have when starting.

Add to this that change and development of the education system is considered a necessary condition for our country to remain an equal partner in a Europe seeking to open its borders; that our society can maintain its national character and culture in a world in which, through international information channels, we are daily exposed to the influence of foreign cultures; and that we can develop our democratic society in a world in which democracies are clearly in a minority compared with dictatorships.

Finally, the debate about quality in education is not new; however, it was reintroduced by the American government some years ago, because it was feared that bright pupils did not benefit sufficiently from their education and it was held that the basic skills of the pupils were too poor: many Americans cannot read, cannot participate in the most fundamental processes of society. They are referred to as functional illiterates.

The government initiatives in the USA have led to a back-to-basics movement, which is directed in particular towards the groups of society who traditionally have only had a very few years of schooling, as well as to more stringent demands for 'optional' in-service training of teachers – at their own expense – as a condition of continued employment.

In Japan the demand for quality has led to an increasing number of Japanese children and young people being taught in public as well as in private schools, the latter after normal school hours. The school day has thus been considerably prolonged. It does not burden the budgets of central or local authorities – only the budget of the parents!

In Western Europe the debate about quality has not yet left such drastic and visible traces, but because of the intensified competition and the fear of being left behind by the USA and Japan, the issue has been taken up at both OECD and EC conferences. In Denmark, these conferences were the forum for serious consideration of the matter, as a result of which a report was drawn up on the differences between Danish and foreign teaching conditions and traditions. On that basis Jesper Florander, the late manager of the Danish Institute for Educational Research, pointed out that for Denmark the two main questions in connection with the discussion of quality are:

☐ what should be taught?
☐ how should it be taught?

If these two questions are not posed – and answered – the question of quality is reduced to a question of:

☐ the benefits obtained daily by the pupils from their education (ie short-term goals);
☐ easily measurable skills.

If the term 'high quality' is used in reference to the fact that it is easy to check the acquisition of basic skills only because it is difficult to measure other aspects of education (such as learning how to deal with and solve a problem, learning how to work, learning how to acquire knowledge, learning how to get on and co-operate with other people) it indicates a debate without quality. We have to realize that we are living in a highly technological and industrialized society which will focus more and more on electronic aids. As employers and trade unions realized long ago, this type of society needs people who are familiar with cultural, social, political and historical relations. And learning how things are related to each other is not possible if only basic – easily measurable – skills are concentrated on.

It is first and foremost the basic skills that can be replaced by electronic aids, whereas, for instance, the ability to bring a certain event into other contexts than the one it was derived from is a human skill which will be very difficult to automate.

A society in which choices have to be made

When neither human nor financial resources are unlimited, priorities have to be made, ie even though the society is apparently a society in which all possibilities are open, it is also a society in which choices have to be made, choices which are binding once they have been made. When a choice has been made, it has consequences, one of them being the exclusion of all other choices. Spending the resources on one thing means not being able to spend them on other things.

In practice, this implies that it is not expedient just to issue new orders laying down the contents of education – ie changing and specifying the syllabuses – and to change the examination requirements, since society cannot wait the 10 or 12 years it takes from when a pupil starts their school education till they finish it to see if the changes are successful. Changes must be directed towards the actual educational process with the purpose of furthering an education containing the desired qualities.

Defining high-quality education

The term 'high-quality education' has not yet been defined. In Denmark it has been decided that choices concerning large fields – in this case the educational field – have to be political. They are carried out through legislation and directions given by the popularly elected politicians to the local authorities. But many choices are left to the local authorities and the institutions that are to carry out the decisions. This is crucial. One reason is the desire:

- ☐ that as many people as possible have an influence on their own life;
- ☐ to involve more and more people in a democratic decision-making process;
- ☐ to give those who know where there is a need for change the chance of making the correct decisions.

Another reason is that when society is changing as rapidly as in our case, it is very difficult to make a choice today which is still correct in five years. For example, it is difficult to predict which qualifications children and young people will need when they leave the education system and have to take their places in society as grown-up citizens.

Not many employers dare specify today which qualifications they will require of the people they are going to employ within the next 5 to 10 years, even though everybody knows that precisely those people are in the education system today.

As was realized long ago, it is difficult to make choices and decisions that have to be valid for more than five years. In many cases the politicians have consequently chosen only to create the legal frameworks and leave it to the local authorities and the people who carry out the activity in question to fill them in. Thus, it is to a large extent up to the techers to specify the syllabuses and choose their own teaching methods (decisions which were previously embodied in government reports and circulars).

Teachers have a very free rein, but also a great responsibility. They cannot protect themselves by saying that they 'just' acted in accordance with detailed directions – they have to defend their choices if they are later exposed to criticism based on the argument that they could just have made a different decision. But the free rein means that it is possible for the teachers to decide and influence development through the initiatives they take, most of which do not necessitate any change of the existing legal framework.

This type of development is usually considered a necessary condition that the education system can live up to the demands and needs of any time.

The main tendency in democratic development is thus that a number of choices have been left to people that are directly affected by them.

Also, so is the responsibility that the right choices are made. That means that new demands are made on the group that has become the new decision-makers. They are for instance required to be able to make competent decisions on the basis of an analysis of different possibilities. In consequence, the new decision-makers must require that the development projects that are launched are of a sufficient quality that future decisions on standards can be based on their results.

Using teachers as the basis for improvement of the quality of education

Teachers are the necessary condition of, and the basis for, development in the educational sector as it is they who, owing to previous experience, are in a position to change education so that it meets the requirements of society. It is essential to realize this; a development cannot be forced through.

Development depends on a detailed knowledge of current practice, and on this practice being compared with the desired changes. The individual teacher and the teaching staff of the individual educational institution are the people who have this knowledge and who must consequently head the development. It is their responsibility to compare new experience with earlier experience and on that basis establish new practice. But usually it is not possible for the individual teacher to head a development on their own as the various possibilities are brought to light in discussions with people who are capable of asking questions that give rise to careful consideration. The teachers need a catalyst to be able to concentrate on their main task, ie the pedagogical conveyance of knowledge of facts and processes.

Initiating development requires support, guidance, advice, debate and experiments.

High-quality education provides more than skills

In our efforts to improve the quality of education – which the majority of our teachers are constantly seeking to do – we must see the education provided in the light of the objectives of education and not only in the light of some of these objectives.

A characteristic of high-quality education is that it enables the pupils to achieve as much of their potential as possible. It takes the pupiles' abilities as its starting point and provides them with the qualifications they need to continue in higher education. Our education system has, and has always had, that quality concerning some of its pupils, but obviously not concerning others.

An assessment of the present quality of education is necessary, as the only human qualifications of any value on the labour market today are those which can be more cheaply acquired than the price of a production system that can do the same. For instance, computer systems will take over some of the functions today reserved for graduate engineers, architects, economists, geologists, and doctors. In some fields, technology will eliminate human work and consequently render human qualifications superfluous. But the continuous development of technology creates the need for new and different human qualifications, qualifications that are directly connected with the applications of technology and with the consequences of that application. We are beginning to realize that we cannot continue developing and applying technology without trying to analyse, assess, and consider its consequences.

As society is automating more and more of the skills which were previously reserved for the human labour market, and as it becomes increasingly necessary that more and more people are able to recognize complicated connections, participate in complicated decision-making processes, think our new plans and solutions, and co-operate with people from another background – educational, cultural, or linguistic – it will become essential that the education system provides a high-quality service for more and more pupils and students. We cannot afford to have an educational system which does not make allowances for the different ability levels of the pupils when they start their school education, or which is not capable of providing the pupils with the qualifications necessary to continue in the education system and take the education to which their abilities entitle them. This indicates that a debate about which qualifications the education system should provide the pupils with would not only be a debate about which basic skills a pupil is lacking when they enter (eg a gymnasium or a business school), or about which is the best way that they could acquire the missing basic skills. It would have to be based on the following assumptions:

☐ that the paid work which is going to predominate in future will mainly be the abstract activities, activities which cannot be automated, such as political decision-making and the development of new ideas, cultural and social life, and which are based on values, norms, and attitudes;

☐ that the participation in the processes of society will require similar qualifications of an increasing part of the population to ensure that the decisions made are competent.

High-quality education recognizes that human activities have produced changes, and that what were previously human activities are now performed by the results of those activities.

How to improve the quality of education

Which is the best way to obtain high-quality education? Where does development come from and who initiates it? – these are much debated questions.

Some people say that the way to improve the quality of education is through pedagogical development initiatives coming from the top (ie from the people who legislate and issue directions).

Other people say that high-quality education is obtained through a pedagogical development coming from the bottom (ie the development starts where education takes place). According to this view, development is initiated at the individual educational institution through the initiatives of teachers and pupils.

Neither of these views represents the whole truth. But the fact that the ministerial orders have changed (because of the rapid development of society) from prescribing detailed syllabuses and teaching methods to just providing a general framework, has meant a change in the developmental process. Development used to be initiated at the top; today it is often initiated at the bottom through development projects carried out by a small number of teachers and pupils at the individual educational institution.

At times the belief that pedagogical innovation comes from either the top or the bottom has resulted in a pointless debate in which they were presented as contrasts, sometimes even giving the impression that one excludes the other. Of course that is not the case, and it is more likely that the debate is caused by the differing opinions than the desired pedagogical development

☐ has not happened as fast as the legislature had hoped; or
☐ has not been possible because of legislative cuts in, for example, class hours.

In periods when the first opinion has been prevailing, there have been attempts to further the desired development through initiatives from the top whereas the second opinion has, when prevailing, unfortunately led to passiveness and discouragement.

In Denmark there is a tradition of central government with a high degree of local participation – that distinguishes us from the countries which, especially recently, seem to exert a strong influence on the pedagogical debate.

Throughout the past 25 years, grants to finance mainly the drawing up of reports and additional hours of work for teachers have given the folkeskole in particular the opportunity of testing new teaching methods and different structures of education. Until two years ago grants totalled about Dkr 4M a year; to this figure must be added considerable resources from the local education authorities, which are responsible for the operation of the schools. But two years ago Dkr 400M were set aside for development projects during the following four years. The results of these projects are to form the basis of a future reform of the Education Act.

Experience from 25 years of development projects shows that not all intiatives lead to permanent changes in the quality of education. The reasons are numerous, of course.

In some cases in the past it turned out that the project did not come up to expectations, or that it involved unforeseen measures and changes, or changes that were undesirable for reasons that had escaped the attention of the initiators at the time when they started the project.

In other cases the project was affected by additional resources so that success was caused by the resource increase and not by the other characteristics of the initiative. But the explanation may also be the very simple one that the development project was described and evaluated in such a way that it was of no benefit to anybody except the people who had undertaken it.

Therefore, any development project should be prepared in such a way that the people carrying out the project get immediate feedback and so that the results of the project are of use not only to the people behind the project but also to others who can relate them to their own practice and experience. A development project must thus be brought into the context of the people carrying it out as well as of future users.

Many development projects have failed because a sufficiently detailed description of the background of the initiative was not part of the preparations, that is:

☐ the instruction in the light of which the development project must be seen when it is evaluated must be described;
☐ before the project is started, the aims and objectives of the development project must be described and compared with previous aims and objectives.

Other projects have failed because evaluation did not commence early enough or was not carried out in such a way that the results obtained could be identified and applied by the people who were to determine future practice; an evaluation method must be used which provides results that can be identified by decision-makers as well as by teachers.

Types of developmental project

In order not to lose the dynamic feature of our education system, we must realize the possibility of carrying out development projects of different types and making them feasible through financial support. At least three different types of development projects are necessary in the efforts to improve the quality of education. The projects are classified not according to contents and methods, but according to fundamentally different aims and objectives.

The future-ensuring project

This type of project usually originates in the desire of a teacher or a group of teachers to try something which is different from what has so far been their own practice and from what is current practice. The aim of the project is usually to test new topics and/or teaching methods, but it could also be to test familiar topics in a new structural framework.

The development project is 'future-ensuring' in that it has the characteristics of an experiment: it is not possible to predict whether it will succeed or whether (even if the results are positive) it will lead to changes which it is desirable to make permanent under the present circumstances. It is in this category that there is room for making mistakes and learning from them.

It is essential to the education system that it can carry out projects of this type, as these projects represent the choices of the education system if the conditions under which education is provided are changed through for example the issue of government regulations and directives.

Without this type of project the education system would only be able to meet the outside demands with big delays and great difficulties, necessitating resource-intensive efforts.

The here-and-now oriented project

Characteristic of this type of development project is the existence of a description of detailed objectives and a project design. The purpose of the project is to determine whether the changes that the project is seeking to illuminate are to be made permanent after the conclusion of the project.

Projects of this category must be based on research, by which is meant that people with pedagogical/psychological and didactic knowledge have been involved in the planning of the project so that the objectives of the project are in accordance with the actual contents of the project. That is the condition that the results of the development project can be used by more people than the parties directly involved.

Furthermore the research basis of the projects means that owing to the method applied to collect experience the teachers who carried out the project can change current practice in accordance with the experienced gained from the project, and the teachers who did not participate can, thanks to the method of description applied, relate the new practice to the one they know.

In-service upgrading projects

This third category contains development projects with the aim of making a standard improvement. The project is based on experience from development projects of the here-and-now oriented type, which means that the contents of the development project are not actually new, but it is new to the group of teachers who carry out the project. That makes this type of project more educational than creative. In-service upgrading projects are the condition of a uniform development of the education system. Without them there would be an undesirable difference between the individual educational institutions.

The benefits of a development project

If development projects are to be of any pedagogical value, they must be of such a quality that the value of the project does not only consist in the fact that a teacher has participated in a development project. It will always be of benefit to a teacher to have participated in a development project, but that alone will not be sufficient in future.

A development project must be able to offer results and explanations that are of use not only to the teachers involved. It requires the participation of other parties in planning, carrying out, and evaluating the project apart from the teachers directly responsible for the instruction and for carrying out the project.

However, this does not mean that the influence of the teacher on the development project is diminished. The teacher still has the ultimate say, but the project must be carried out in co-operation with people outside the narrow circles of the education system. In future, development projects are to be based on research and carried out in co-operation with researchers to a higher degree than now.

It is important to realize that a development project which has been carefully planned will always yield results (often other results than the ones expected originally but generally useful ones). A development project which has been carefully planned cannot fail. The only unsuccessful projects are projects that for some reason fall apart, peter out, and come to nothing. That is characteristic of either insufficient planning and unspecified expectations or of insufficient needs analysis and the resulting lack of opportunity to establish any need for changes. On that basis the people behind the project will have to realize that there is no result to describe. Unsuccessful projects do occur, but they are rarely described.

A society desirous of development in its education system must have room for unsuccessful projects, but it must be characterized by a majority of projects that:

☐ have well-defined aims and objectives;
☐ have been carefully planned;
☐ are carried out in an instructive way;
☐ can be evaluated;
☐ result in a report after conclusion;
☐ are evaluated on the basis of a standard situation.

Before a development project is initiated, it must be decided how the collection of experience is to be conducted.

Describing the experience

The description of the experience gained from a development project must be of a quality so that it enables the people who carried out the project to compare the experience with the situation as it was before the development project was launched. Without having made this comparison it is very difficult to decide whether the experience gained should result in a change of current practice or whether it is better to preserve the status quo, or whether a new development project should be initiated before a decision on future practice has been reached.

Furthermore, the description must be of assistance to all parties in their work. It must meet the requirements made of it:

☐ it must enable politicians to take the main decisions;
☐ it must enable administrators to administer the changes; and
☐ it must be concrete so that other teachers can benefit from the experience.

In order to perpetuate any change in the teaching of a subject it is necessary that the method applied to collect experience differs in several respects from the methods that used to be applied in connection with reports on development projects (questionnaires, class room observation, and interviews).

A description of the instruction

The collection of experience can only be conducted and result in instructive reports if the basis of the changes or innovations to be tested in the development project is known before the project is launched.

One way of obtaining this knowledge is to interview the teacher about their instruction, while another is to conduct classroom observation. But as neither of these procedures makes the teacher very conscious of their own way of teaching, and as they are furthermore extremely resource-intensive, it is more expedient to let the teacher describe their own instruction by correcting and changing a standard description of how to teach the subject in question.

The teacher is given a concrete description of, for example, the teaching of mathematics; this description is called a prototype description and has nothing to do with the instruction provided by the teacher as such, except that it describes how others have taught the subject.

The teacher deletes, inserts, and makes corrections in the text so that in the end they feel that the prototype description covers their own instruction.

When the teacher has made corrections, they are incorporated in the prototype description and questions will be asked if they have expressed themselves unclearly. The new version is revised and sent to the teacher, who reads it through. Usually it will be found necessary to make further changes and corrections.

The procedure is then repeated, and when at last the teacher returns the description, declaring that now it covers their instructional techniques, they will receive a final version. Not only does the teacher in this way become conscious of what they are doing every day, but the person doing the collection of experience acquires a very profound knowledge of the instruction provided by that teacher; a knowledge which is a condition that the results of the actual collection of experience will be optimal.

For instance, it is far easier for the person doing the collection of experience to interview a teacher if they are known in this way than it would be if they were just total strangers.

Not all teachers can recognize their own instruction in the prototype description they are given as a basis of their description. It is simply too far from what they and their pupils are doing in practice. If they feel that it is not possible to change the prototype description into a description they can accept, there must be resources enough to allow them to start a description of their instruction from scratch. That is a big task and is usually experienced as being very difficult. By giving the teachers the opportunity to describe from scratch, the number of prototype descriptions available is gradually increased.

Detailed planning

The teacher's description of their instruction forms the basis of a detailed planning of the development project. Aims, objectives, intentions, desired contents, and choice of method are seen in the light of the instructional process into which the project is to be integrated. This makes it possible to specify which changes and developments need most attention.

This specification forms the basis for drawing up the diary leaves that the teacher uses during the development project. Thus, when the development project is launched, the following is available:

- ☐ a description of the teacher's instruction;
- ☐ a description of aims, intentions, and objectives;
- ☐ a number of observations made when working out the descriptions and planning the project.

Making the description of aims, intentions, and objectives requires a dialogue with the teacher about the definition of high-quality education. The teacher usually has a subjective opinion of what high-qualify eduction is. This opinion is based on experience, on interpretation of current educational objectives and of the requirements for the examinations that the pupils have to take (but which the teacher usually regards as covering only the measurable parts of the educational process).

The teacher's conception of high-quality education usually involves a number of notions that are difficult to make concrete. It may be that the pupils should like going to school, that they should retain the desire to acquire new knowledge, that they should learn how to learn, that they should retain the courage to meet new challenges, that they should become happy. How such intentions can be furthered is more of a psychological than a methodological/pedagogical question – and it has much to do with the personality of the teacher. But in a dialogue about such themes the teacher will often realize aspects that have not been noticed before.

The dialogue partner's conception of high-quality education also belongs in the dialogue. To that person it may mean to avoid pupils losing interest in a subject, that the pupils acquire a certain number of skills and an understanding of complex relations, or that they learn how to apply the methods of the subject, etc.

During the dialogue the teacher is asked how they believe that the features agreed on in the dialogue as characteristic of high-quality education can be furthered. Which teaching materials can further high-quality education? Which teaching methods, which pupils' activities, which role and attitude of the teacher?

This discussion of how to define and achieve high-quality education results in a number of aims and ideas which the teacher will try to carry out in their instruction during the following period of time. The definition and methods agreed upon are related to the instruction described by the teacher; that makes the strategies that the teacher is going to use more concrete.

Following the development project

The development project is followed through, on which the teacher notes down characteristic features of the project.

The teacher does not report in full every time a class has been taught. They note down key words referring to special events and observations which surprise them, or which they find worth remembering. It is important to note down these events as experience shows that it is very easy to forget precisely such events when describing afterwards the main impressions left by the project.

The amount of entry in the diary will thus vary from teacher to teacher. Depending on the length of the development project diaries are sent in when the development project is finished or halfway, with a view to making adjustments or midway summings-up.

The final questionnaire or interview

On the basis of the description of the objectives etc of the development project, the knowledge acquired, the description of the instruction, and the diaries, a questionnaire is worked out which the teacher is asked to fill in. The questions are based on the teacher's own description of their instruction as it was before the development project was launched.

A brief report

A brief report on the development project is drawn up on the basis of the diary leaves, the questionnaire, and perhaps an interview.

The report is sent to the teacher, who corrects, changes, and inserts in the same way as when the description of the instruction was made.

The actual evaluation

The actual evaluation is made on the basis of brief reports and a traditional questionnaire, which is sent to the teacher six to twelve months after the brief report has been finished. The final evaluation report is made available for all the parties involved, and is presented in a way so as to enable them to take the necessary decisions.

High-quality education according to the model

The above method is being developed in connection with the delivery of 250 development projects. The purpose of these projects is to make a well-founded and differentiated assessment of the pedagogical applications of computers in education, on which future decisions on the production and application of computer programs for educational purposes can be based.

The 250 development projects are spread over the whole country and cover all age groups and the greater part of the subjects taught in the folkeskole.

In conclusion of this article, a development project from the municipality of Holstebro is briefly described as an example of how the local authorities of one municipality have approached the desire to improve the quality of education by introducing the computer into education.

The municipality of Holstebro

The municipalityof Holstebro has 15 schools with a total of 5338 pupils and 407 teachers. Seven of the schools provide the first ten school years whereas the remaining eight only provide the first seven years of schooling.

PROGRAM-DESCRIPTION GROUPS

Five program-description groups were set up, each consisting of three teachers who got a reduction of 2.5 hours of work a week for the task of describing the programs which exist in the five academic fields covered by the groups, and which can be run on the available computers. The five groups covered history/geography/biology, Danish, arithmetic/mathematics, the foreign languages, and remedial instruction respectively.

The criterion of the choice of teachers was that they had to have a broad basis of teaching experience in that specific academic field; it is not important whether they had any experience in the use of computers.

The 15 teachers attended a 15-hour course before they started their task. During those 15 hours the project was discussed, the work was organized, and a word processing program was studied.

Working with the word processing program had the purpose of giving the groups a practical tool that they could use in their work as well as giving them an introduction to the computer and its operation.

Each group met once a week during the school year 1987 to 1988, and the work fell into the following phases:

☐ Looking through and describing the programs.
☐ Describing the instructional context.
☐ Making a a brief report.

In the course of the year, three meetings of four hours were held during which the work was discussed. These meetings had the purpose of providing an opportunity for the groups to discuss their work and the problems they met. Furthermore, problems arising in connection with describing and reporting were discussed.

The program-description groups attempted to find out how the programs in question could form part of the existing instruction as they agreed that they would not recommend an instruction which was based on a specific programe. In other words, they did not want to make changes in the syllabuses, only the methods of delivery.

The work of the program-description groups fell into two phases; first selecting from the group of programs chosen by the project leaders those that might be applicable in the instruction, going through them and describing them; then describing the instructional context required by the programs in question. The purpose of the program-description groups was thus to create the best possible conditions for the teachers who are testing the selected programs in their instruction this school year.

Many aspects were considered by the groups in their discussion of the relation between the instruction and the selected programs. As an example can be mentioned that the importance attributed to training programs for arithmetic/mathematics depends on whether it is believed that the underlying principles of the instruction in mathematics of recent years are:

☐ that the individual is not only a passive recipient of knowledge;
☐ that learning is considered the active gathering of experience, as a consequence of which the pupil's knowledge is presumed to result from an exchange process between realizing problems and gathering experience;

☐ that if the academic interests of the pupil are taken as a starting point, the pupil will participate more actively and eventually get a good grasp of the whole subject;

☐ that the main objective of the subject is that the pupils acquire skills within, for example, the four basic arithmetical operations; and

☐ that the acquisition of these skills should be strengthened in the daily instruction so that the cuts in mathematics lessons of recent years will not affect the skills of the pupils more than absolutely necessary.

It is also important to an assessment of, for example, the various tools for the subject, whether it is believed that the essentials of the instruction are:

☐ that the pupils are interested in solving problems, which makes it the teacher's duty to create working conditions that enable the pupils to solve the problems; and

☐ that it is the teacher's duty to help the pupil systematize and define the experience that they have gathered; and

☐ that the pupil gets an opportunity to verbalize their new knowledge, and, through verbalizing, gets the opportunity to structuralize it and fit it into existing knowledge;

or whether it is believed:

☐ that the organization of topics in the textbook systems is a sufficient guarantee of the necessary acquisition of knowledge.

Furthermore, it will be taken into consideration when a program is assessed whether it must be applicable in an instruction based on one of the mathematics textbook systems that are characterized by a spiral organization of the contents, aiming at the following learning process.

First, the pupils gather experience, which forms the basis of understanding and using concepts and terminology; then, when that has happened to a sufficient extent, systematizing and defining can take place, which is a condition that the pupils can start reasoning and drawing conclusions, eventually leading to deduction.

Alternatively it must be applicable in an instruction which only applies a textbook system to a very little extent and which is based on the view that the pupils must make a guess, founded on experiments and observations. The guess is proved, and if it is confirmed, the next step is reasoning. If the guess is not confirmed, new experiments and observations are made, one of the reasons for this being the fact that not all pupils are capable of, for example, systematizing and defining in the same time. Thus, the instruction is aiming at an acquisition of knowledge based on experience to a much larger extent than on skills.

BRIEF REPORTS FROM THE GROUPS

The program-description groups finished their work by drawing up brief reports, which were sent to the schools in the municipality. The reports (one from each group) contained a description of the typical instruction provided, a description of the programs that the group had examined, and the recommendation that test projects were launched.

As described, the program-description groups dealt with a number of pedagogical themes; they did not only concentrate on the individual computer program, but included the entire context in which the computer program is to be applied and tested. It is that context which will form the basis of an assessment of the applicability of the program. The descriptions by the groups form the basis of an assessment of the applicability of the computer program in question in that the experience gained and reported by the teacher during the test phase is related to the teacher's description of their instruction and to their description of the instructional process into which the program will be integrated.

Principally, the program description served to give the test teachers an introduction to the programs – and to support the teachers in planning and instructional process. Furthermore, the descriptions serve to save other teachers the very time-consuming task of going through and assessing computer programs.

On the basis of the reports the local authorities decided to support the testing of computer programs in 42 classes, distributed across the seven schools providing ten school years.

Prior to each test project a description was made, stating among other things the variables and constants applying to the individual test project. This is to make sure that test projects within the same subject, employing the same computer programs, can focus on different aspects of the use of computer programs. In the project plan it was recommended that other teachers than those who carried out the test projects do the reporting on the projects, and also that members from the program-description groups are included in the team that organizes, follows, and reports on the test projects.

The purpose of this recommendation was to give the project are additional function – hopefully with the result that a whole group of teachers will eventually be able to describe and assess computer programs, place them in an educational context, and give qualified help and advice to colleagues who wish to employ computers in their instruction.

The local authorities followed the recommendation, and consequently 42 teachers were approached, who did not necessarily have any experience in the use of computers. Thus, a total of about 55 teachers were involved in the projects as three teachers were both in the program-description groups and test teachers.

THE PROGRAM-DESCRIPTION GROUPS EDUCATED THE 42 TEST TEACHERS

With support from an EDP-consultant from the local authorities, who has put in an enormous deal of work making programs ready, guiding the program-description groups, ensuring that the computers work, and answering numerous questions, the program-description groups carried out the introduction of the test projects and the education of the 42 test teachers. It is considered of great importance that the test teachers were not educated by outsiders, but by people they knew and could talk to, people that were easy to get in touch with in case they needed assistance.

Other functions of the program-description groups

The program-description groups:

☐ provide the contact to the teachers carrying out the test projects,
☐ conduct the collection of experience in co-operation with the project
leaders and try to ensure that the purposes of the test projects are
achieved.

Furthermore, the reporting on each of the 42 test projects is conducted by the
program-description groups in co-operation with the project leaders and the test
teachers.

By the end of this school year all test projects will be finished, and a brief
report will be made on each of them. In the school year 1989–90 final reports will
be drawn up, which will result in a detailed proposal for the future application of
computers in ordinary education.

Present situation

Right now we are in the middle of the test phase, and it has turned out that the
desire among the other teachers at the seven schools to watch and try for
themselves is so great that the computer rooms are over-booked. It is difficult to
understand why the test teachers and datalogy lessons have first priority. This
situation is undoubtedly due to the fact that the 42 teachers are ordinary
teachers, known to the others as their colleagues with whom they are used to
discussing various pedagogical themes, whom they usually consult when an
educational question has to be settled, with whom they usually exchange
information when there is a new development. In other words, a new
educational element has been introduced into the circle of people who usually
exchange experience. They do so now as well, of course. And when the test
teacher communicates their impressions and experience, the other teachers also
feel like trying, getting support, giving their class permission, etc.

There is no doubt that the 42 test teachers perform the function of educating
the interested teachers; they are approached for advice and common problems
are discussed with them. Often they are met with questions such as: What did
you use that for?. . . What did you do then?. . . How is it possible to do this or
that?. . .

3. Assessment, technology and the quality revolution

David Smith

Introduction

The particular subject of this contribution is the relationship between some approaches to educational assessment and certain models, or ideologies, of industrial management. This relationship is both simple, direct and literal and at the same time complex and metaphoric: a duality which is sometimes a source of much confusion. It also involves discussion in the context of a minefield of 'essentially contested' concepts. It is therefore impossible to discuss what has been called 'performance technology' (Olsen & Bass, 1982) without running into matters which are political, in the sense that it concerns the welfare of the polis, rather than the usual party sense of 'isms' and 'ologies'.

I want particularly to explore the relationship between the tradition of management thinking which is rooted in FW Taylor's 'scientific management' ('Taylorism') and the growing trend towards the assessment of minutely described 'competences', as embodied, for example, in the national curriculum currently being introduced in England and Wales. I shall argue that this approach to assessment is based on an ideology which is already obsolescent as a basis for management practice. I shall point out that the 'Taylorist' tradition is rapidly being supplanted in many countries by a quite new approach (the so-called 'quality revolution'), and I shall question whether the tacit ideology of the 'neo-Taylorist' model of assessment might not in the end undermine progress towards the much-vaunted 'information society'.

FW Taylor and the 'control revolution'

The twentieth century to date has arguably been the era of FW Taylor's 'scientific management', often referred to simply as 'Taylorism' or even, more politically, 'Fordism'. This has been much refined, elaborated and developed since its original formulation by FW Taylor in the last decade of the nineteenth century, but it retains a strong subliminal hold on management thinking.

Taylor's original system analysed and subdivided work into its smallest mechanical components and activities, and rearranged these into the most effective combinations. Each component operation was timed and a standard time specified for each task. Taylor extended the division of labour into the division of time and ultimately to the division of thought. It was a harsh discipline. Taylor once said (Taylor, 1906) that:

> . . . in my system, the workman is told precisely what he is to do and how he is to do it, and any improvement he makes upon the instructions given to him is fatal to success. . .

Another way of looking at the period of ascendancy of Taylorist management is to think of it as the 'control era'. From this perspective, we can see scientific management and its various modern derivatives and counterparts operating through three levels of control:

- □ *Direct control:* giving orders, enforcing rules and regulations and imposing technological constraints on human actions;
- □ *Bureaucratic control:* specialization and standardization of work activities and the establishment of structured hierarchies;
- □ *Premise control:* effectively 'thought control', through the management of the ideas underlying work actions.

None of this is quite as sinister as it may sound, although it is certainly not necessary to look very far for examples where these basic principles have been carried to extremes (Lenin was an early convert to Taylorism!). But it is interesting to relate these three forms of managerial control to systems of education, and in particular, to systems of educational assessment. Examination systems and other forms of centralized assessment (however humanely intended, and however learner-centred) tend to display all three modes of control.

The quality revolution

It is arguable that only Taylorism could have made possible the massive industrial expansion of the early to mid 20th century which has transformed the world economy. However, one trouble with Taylorist management is that it works best with mature and well established manufacturing technologies. It has proven virtually impossible to control and organize genuine creativity within the bounds of scientific management principles (*see*, for example, Peters & Waterman, 1982). Really important inventions still have the habit of arising from unplanned actions by creative mavericks. For example Mike Cooley (Cooley, 1987) recalls that EMI's computer-controlled body scanner was developed using unallocated funds as a by-product of work on optical character recognition. Cooley argues that if its inventor had been forced to follow set objectives within a conventional management system, he might just have produced another optical character recognition machine.

Whether or not this latter assumption can be justified, Cooley's general argument is borne out at the Massachusetts Institute of Technology where much the same thing has been observed with their best work in the artificial intelligence (AI) field. Terry Winograd's famous program 'SHRDLU', which pointed to some major breakthroughs in natural language processing wasn't part of any formal project. As AI guru Marvin Minsky put it:

... Terry just did it. The successes of the Artificial Intelligence Laboratory were basically good ideas that students got. . .
(Reported by Brand, 1987)

Another trouble is that Taylorism is not necessarily conducive to high quality products and services. The scientifically managed factory or office is basically fault-tolerant within defined limits. The operative is there to carry out their specific task and it's somebody else's job to worry about quality control, other than in the crudest sense. Statistical quality control is used to ensure that quality is up to the required minimum level. But that's a rather high-risk strategy for modern high technology industry, where mistakes may be very costly indeed.

Ninety-eight per cent accuracy may be good enough for a plastic widget manufacturer, but it's disastrous when you are building communications satellites or nuclear power stations. To get such quality levels, however, you need people to be involved as people, rather than as pairs of hands. This implies a reversal of the trend towards Taylorism, towards what European workers are describing as the quality revolution.

Swedish researchers have seen the principal features of this quality revolution as being:

☐ emphasis on quality in production and innovation in work. (Workers are actively encouraged to design their own circuitry: see below!);
☐ giving humans the primary role in the production process and designing systems to encourage human commitment, rather than attempting to totally control workers' behaviour:
☐ rejection of the ideas of the 'technological fix' and the 'one best way' approach;
☐ no attempt to substitute technology for organizational solutions;
☐ development of integration, rather than fragmentation in work systems;
☐ broad multiskilling, as opposed to narrow deskilling;
☐ emphasis on labour/management cooperation.

This is not a mere pipedream. Factories in Scandinavia, Germany and elsewhere are increasingly being built around these principles, and a whole new generation of 'human-centred' tools and manufacturing systems is being developed for them, capitalizing on the fullest integration of human skills and knowledge and machine capabilities.

But the effective development and application of these new human-centred systems will depend on education. New styles of education will be needed to help people to make the most of the opportunities available to them through the new technology. Sadly, in countries such as the UK, education is one area of social policy which is currently strongly driven by ideas from the Taylorist past.

Back to the future?

We all have to come to terms with a sort of 'uncertainty principle' in social futurology. Everybody is blessed with 20/20 hindsight, but the fact is that we can know little or nothing about the future. The best we can do is to make broad-brush generalizations about society based on data of varying quality, and these predictions are often proved very wrong indeed – as witness recent events in Eastern Europe. The end of the second millenium of the Common Era is only a decade away. The coming century promises to be traumatic, perhaps even crucial for the survival of humanity. But we have scarcely begun the work of constructing the educational path along which the citizens of the future will need to have trodden. Time may be running out.

In the UK it is even, apparently, running backwards. Instead of taking courageous steps towards the future, politicians are busily building a kind of 'heritage schooling' – an idealized version of a glorious past of capes and bays – and educators are enthusiastically conniving at this degradation.

Education is beset by an enduring vision of a past golden age, when men were men, women were women, boys wore short trousers and girls were decorative creatures somewhere in between Kate Greenaway's books and the Laura Ashley catalogue. And they ALL knew their place. The heritage schooling approach incorporates the view that we have fallen from a state of grace to which we can be restored by the idealized reconstruction of a system of education based on recapture of a sanitized past. The key to economic salvation is, it often seems, an academic Yorvik in every neighbourhood.

Taylor-made education?

As Geoffrey Hubbard has pointed out (Hubbard, 1984), the system of public education in the UK owes as much to the factory system as to any great educational thinkers or reformers. We have a process of 'education' for an economic role rather than for active democratic citizenship and the implicit model underlying it is essentially a version of optimized batch production, moderated by a fault-tolerant system of statistical quality control (in the form of a notoriously imprecise and unreliable system of assessment). Much current development in the field of assessment technology can be seen as valid and worthwhile attempts to improve the basis of the quality control process without challenging the underlying organizational principle. Some, however, take a rather harder line (Noble, 1989) and argue that most recent developments in this field echo the manpower development requirements of the US military establishment, which is the largest research investor in educational technology.

The idea of education and training as 'infrastructural investment in human capital formation' seems to be a reasonable conception of one of the strategic functions of education. But it is not the only one. Education is not simply a means of regulating the quality of labour or even a route of access to economic competence for particular individuals. People are human beings, not industrial raw materials: a point which tends to be somewhat overlooked amid the instrumentalism and economic utilitarianism of much current educational argument. Nevertheless, it would be a brave person who claimed that current educational systems and structures were anything but inadequate. We have little idea what the mass of people are capable of achieving because in the past we have not required (or permitted) them to achieve anything at all. Our educational systems are shot through with a minimalist outlook which demands and expects very little of the vast majority of people and is neither surprised nor disappointed when little is attained.

Education, at whatever level, seems to be utterly non-developmental for the vast majority of those who experience it, and the phenomenon which I have labelled 'heritage schooling' represents what is, in the main, an honest but misguided attempt to remedy its more obvious defects. Other approaches, far more firmly rooted in educational theory and practice, are possibly equally mistaken, and it is towards these that the criticism in this article is particularly directed. I am referring here to developments in education (and training) for 'competency', in which the component subskills of a desired domain of performance are clearly identified and explicitly developed.

The problem as I see it is certainly not related to any low opinion of the good faith or the technical skill of curriculum designers. It is, rather, that many of the solutions which are being proposed are founded on mirages of the past rather than visions of the future. Analysis of the educational needs of the predicted 'information age' is underpinned by short-term political considerations, a general gut-reaction that something is wrong and a whole tangle of special interests, all pushing to ensure that society's blueprint for the future incorporates their particular chunk of the present. Educational technologists are as deeply involved in this struggle as any other group of people: after all, it's rather difficult to spend many years advocating a particular approach to learning, only to find that unfolding events have rendered one's insights irrelevant to a new version of the future.

The electronic sabre-tooth

I hope that I can be forgiven for drawing a lightning sketch of Harold Benjamin's minor masterpiece. . .

> Once upon a time, in the paleolithic era, there was a tribe of cavemen. Their life was simple, but hard. Then as now, there were few lengths to which men would not go to avoid the pain and labour of thought. But a thinker arose. His name was New-fist-hammer-maker (New-Fist, for short). He thought out ways in which life might be made better for himself, his family and his tribe.
>
> 'If I could only get children to do the things that will give more and better food, shelter and security', thought New-Fist, 'I would be helping the tribe to have a better life. . .' Having set up an educational goal, New-Fist proceeded to construct a curriculum. 'What things must we tribesmen know in order to live with full bellies, warm backs and minds free from fear?', he asked.
>
> New-Fist identified three factors which were central to the life of the tribe:
>
> clubbing woolly horses for food;
> catching fish with bare hands;
> scaring sabre-tooth tigers with fire.
>
> He constructed a curriculum accordingly.
>
> He educated his own children according to his new curriculum, and they thrived. Some of the other more intelligent members of the tribe followed

New-Fist's example, and eventually the teaching of horse-clubbing, fish-grabbing and tiger-scaring came to be accepted as the core of all real education.

Gradually, being a statesman as well as an educational administrator and theorist, New-Fist overcame all opposition (practical, theoretical and theological) to his curriculum. Long after his death the tribe continued to prosper.

But times changed. A new ice-age came. Fish grew difficult to catch with bare hands. The woolly horses migrated away and were replaced by fast, agile antelopes. The sabre-tooths died out and their place was taken by enormous cave bears which were totally unimpresed by fire. The tribe was soon in danger of following the sabre-tooths into extinction.

Fortunately for the tribe, there were still men in it of the New-Fist breed, men who had the ability to do and the daring to think. Between them they solved the survival problem by inventing fishnet making, antelope snare construction and the theory, practice and operation of catching cave bears in pits. Once again the tribe prospered.

There were a thoughtful few who asked questions as they worked. Some of them even criticized the schools. They asked why these new subjects should not be taught. But the majority of the tribe had long ago learned that schools had nothing to do with real life, and anyway, the wise old men who controlled education had an answer: 'That wouldn't be education; it would be mere training, and anyway, the curriculum is already too crowded. What our people need is a more thorough grounding in the basics'. The old subjects, it seemed, were taught not for themselves, but for the sake of generalized skills.

But the radicals persisted: 'Times have changed. Perhaps these up-to-date activities have some educational value after all?' The wise old men were appalled: 'The essence of true education is timelessness. You must know that there are some eternal verities, and the sabre-tooth curriculum is one of them!'

(Benjamin, 1938, republished 1975)

If the elements of this debate seem as familiar today as in the thirties when Benjamin was writing, perhaps it is a mark of our continuing failure to develop an educational system which, as Leon Bagrit said in his 1964 Reith Lectures (Bagrit, 1965), produced men and women who:

> . . . are able to understand the significance of the past, who are in the stream of current ideas, and who can make use of them, and who have the quality of imagination that is capable of foreseeing and welcoming the future. . .

We have all too often failed to appreciate, as New-Fist's successors had yet to learn, that once you have an educational system, then that system acquires objectives and priorities related to its own defence as a system, rather than to the service of the ends for which it was originally set in motion. We need to be fairly cautious in assuming that apparently fundamental innovations are not merely the defence mechanisms of a system under attack.

It is easy to mistake today's solutions for responses to today's problems. But because the advent of the microprocessor caught education largely unawares, the enormous lead-time required for the effective institutionalization of educational innovations means that many developments which appear to be responses to the 'challenge of the chip' actually predate it. The roots of educational developments such as the British National Curriculum, and the resurgence of the feigned precision of educational 'measurement' whereby, after a brief period of sanity, we are once again apparently prepared to allocate people's life chances on the basis of their scores on amorphous pseudomeasures of depressing banality.

The UK has a system of education attuned to the knowledge requirements of Taylorist industry and a highly stratified society still rooted in the feudal middle ages. And the whole system is being rendered even more overtly Taylorist by the introduction of a national curriculum which fragments knowledge into ages and stages (this at a time when the inherent weaknesses and contradictions in Taylorism are coming to be better understood). Consequently, much recent debate on educational assessment, particularly in relation to information technology, seems to be little more than debates about the arrangement of the deckchairs on the Titanic.

The dilemma we face is a choice between attempting to restore the putative harmony of the past, or recognition that new times require new means. We are not faced with the relatively simple task of fine-tuning an essentially satisfactory system, but with the need to convince ourselves that the whole thing is beyond economic repair. It is not enough for today's generation of New-Fists to look for new utilitarian objectives for education to replace the old. New educational delivery systems, new media and new methods are all irrelevant if the basic framework is left unchallenged.

Too many recent developments are deeply rooted in Taylorist principles, notably the implicit proposition that human skill and knowledge are ultimately reducible into elementary units. This is an idea which is today constantly reinforced by the subliminal message of our computer-dependent technological culture, since much current thinking in computer science appears to underwrite and to legitimate the reductionist approach to knowledge and skill which is at the heart of Taylor's ideas.

The fragmentation of knowledge

Taylor's system originally led to an increase in the quality of work carried out by clerical and managerial staffs. Taylor himself explained that the system was:

> . . . aimed at establishing a clear cut and novel division of mental and manual work . . . It is based upon the precise time and motion study of each worker's job in isolation, and relegates the entire mental parts of the task in hand to the managerial staff . . .

This enhancement of what now might be seen as the 'information processing' aspects of work in industry and commerce has prompted the assumption that the advent of the so-called 'information society' and the decline of manufacturing industry will inevitably lead to better jobs for all. But this is to completely fail to understand the inherent drive within Taylorism to de-skill all work wherever possible. Even computer programming has been largely reduced to routine clerical activity, as the short-lived 'cottage craft industry' approach to program production has given way to more scientific 'software engineering' methods.

Instead of the comforting prospect of everybody's work being progressively upgraded, we have the more probable scenario of the rapid transfer of information handling tasks from human brains to machines. Most people will be relegated to intellectually undemanding work, with increasing insecurity for those remaining 'brainworkers' whose work is still incapable of cost-effective implementation on state-of-the-art computer systems.

Despite all this, computer-based metaphors have held an enormous fascination for educators in recent years, to the extent that it is occasionally difficult to discern whether discussions about topics such as 'information handling capabilities' concern humans or machines.

But part of the human price of Taylorism's success as a management principle has been the way in which failure to distinguish between metaphor, analogy and homology has distorted much academic and managerial thinking. One frequently cited classic (Boguslaw, 1965) can perhaps serve as an illustration:

... Our immediate concern, let us remember, is the exploitation of the operating unit approach to systems design no matter what materials are used. We must take care to prevent this discussion from degenerating into the single-sided analysis of the complex characteristics of one type of systems material, namely human beings. What we need is an inventory of the manner in which human behaviour can be controlled, and a description of some of the instruments which will help us achieve that control. If this provides us with sufficient handles on human materials so that we can think of them as metal parts, electrical power or chemical reactions, then we have succeeded in placing human material on the same footing as any other material and can begin to proceed with our problems of systems design. There are, however, many advantages in the use of these human operating units. They are somewhat fragile, they are subject to fatigue, obsolescence, disease and even death. They are frequently stupid, unreliable and limited in memory capacity. But beyond all this, they sometimes seek to design their own circuitry. This in a material is unforgivable, and any system utilising them must devise appropriate safeguards.

The tone of this piece is clearly slightly flippant, and its argument ironic and metaphorical. It would normally be difficult to take at face value the proposition that one of the most precious attributes of humankind, the capacity to think for themselves (the 'ability to design their own circuitry') is now an undesirable inconvenience, to be deliberately suppressed, were it not for the fact that such attitudes seem to be deeply embedded in our culture as serious principles. And nowhere is this more apparent than in the culture of advanced computing technologies such as AI.

These technologies, influential, highly regarded and thoroughly permeating our life and language are tremendously powerful in setting the cultural climate in which other technologies, including educational and training technologies, are embedded. Many developments in assessment methodology can be understood in relation to such 'subliminal' cultural aspects of Taylorism, rather than its 'first-hand' impact as a practical system for managing organizations.

For example, part of the subliminal message which we get every day from the 'technoculture' in which we function is the ultimate inferiority of humans to machines: a prospect which even a hundred years ago prompted the novelist Samuel Butler to ask

> . . . may not man himself become a kind of parasite upon the machines? An affectionate machine-tickling aphid. . .
>
> (Butler S, 1874)

It is true that these days few serious computer scientists are as ready to belittle human intellect as the US 'guru' who once suggested that:

> . . . human beings will have to begin to accept their true place in the evolutionary hierarchy: animals, human beings and intelligent machines. . .

Or even the British academic who predicted in the seventies that computers would attain an IQ of 120 'within the next two decades', arguing that we would then have to decide whether computers were people or not (Cooley, 1987). (Where the vast majority of human beings with IQs less than 120 fit into his scheme of things is difficult to see, but we could guess that perhaps they don't rate very highly.)

But there is a rather curious paradox here. Humans were still needed to do the real thinking and creating. You can sell or buy computer-based systems because they don't get tired, need feeding, go on strikes or need holidays, but in the end, the productive operation of the systems needs people, who do all of these things. As one writer foresaw nearly twenty years ago (King-Taylor, 1972):

> . . . the innovative firm of the future will have a people-intensive firm, depending on the human resources of imagination, initiative and creativity. Fewer people may be necessary to produce a given result, but they will quickly become the necessary few, without whom managers will be left sitting idle in mahogany corridors . . .

The political implications of this interdependency are both significant and rather chilling. The idea that people will need to be made receptive to their symbiotic role by the systematic reduction of their inclination to dissent can easily become part of the 'control' agenda of education and training.

One counter to such 'progress' would be to put control of learning more firmly into the hands of learners, and by the evolution of existing formal institutions to accommodate and facilitate this new climate. We would need to abandon once and for all the passive concept of 'being educated' in favour of a move towards active learning and knowledge creation.

Educating citizens or programming proles?

It is worth referring at this point to a very thoughtful paper from the German teachers' union GEW (GEW, 1987). This union believes that all pupils, of both sexes, of school age should be put in a position both to comprehend the problems involved in using new technologies and to shape their applications in industry and leisure time in accordance with their own interests:

> . . . Schools must therefore not be allocated the task of promoting the

uncritical acceptance of new technologies but must rather above all provide qualifications that improve capabilities vis-a-vis co-determination and joint structuring of the use of these technologies. . .

It is significant that the concept of 'co-determination' is becoming very strong in Germany, to the extent that it is no longer a party political issue. GEW saw this in the context of a conception of vocational education such that it should contribute to enabling every person to realize their claim to a job that:

– has widely varied contents . . . and is of a demanding nature;
– affords the opportunity to co-determine the shaping of work conditions;
– provides an opportunity for social communication with other employees.

GEW thought that school should impart an understanding of the ways in which the new technologies function that is independent of products. Education should centre on providing a knowledge of the basics and interconnections, not simply practising user skills or superficially learning computer languages.

Far too much of the current debate on education and training, especially in the UK, focuses on narrowly instrumental and utilitarian conceptions based on totally outmoded models of process and purpose. H A L Fisher introduced his Education Bill to Parliament in 1917 with the argument that:

. . . The industrial workers of this country are entitled to be considered primarily as citizens and as fit subjects for any form of education from which they are profiting. . . They do not want education only to become better workmen and earn higher wages or in order that they may rise out of their own class, but to find an aid to good citizenship, a source of pure enjoyment and a refuge from the necessary hardships of a life spent in the midst of clanging machinery in our hideous cities. . .

A rather patrician view, but not a bad one! It is certainly a perspective which some of today's educators might do well to think about. It contrasts with a current trend towards what might be called the 'era of the human EPROM'. An EPROM is an Erasable Programmable Read Only Memory: a silicon chip which can be programmed for a specific function and then erased and reprogrammed whenever necessary. Instead of reconstructing education to support and nurture the intellectual development of all citizens, we are offering ever narrower training for tightly defined and fragmented tasks.

Instead of perhaps being given the opportunity of learning from and alongside older people with experience of the world outside schools, young people are subjected to increasing vocationalism. And as the supply of young people dries up, pressures grow to provide work experience and vocational orientation which may be little removed from the good old days of the juvenile chimney sweep.

Open learning or closed minds?

But if we are to cope adequately with the threats and promises of the coming era, then it is clear that careful attention must be given to the need and right of all citizens to be able to develop towards self-realization at their own pace and in their own ways. That is to say, we must reassert what we have always claimed education was about in any case!

The front-end model of education, with a few short years of childhood and youth providing a lifetime toolkit of practical and intellectual skills was no part of either the pre-industrial craft system or of academia before the move towards 'relevance' took hold. In both cases, a craftsman or a scholar continued to mature and develop throughout their working life. It was, rather, part of the process of labour quality management of the factory era. Now, ironically, this system is revealing itself as totally inappropriate to life in a rapidly evolving technological society.

As Morley Sage and I envisaged some years ago now (Sage and Smith, 1983):

> . . . specialised skills and knowledge will be increasingly short-lived, so that periodic updating and/or retraining will become normal and necessary features of working life for the majority of people, rather than for a small minority as at present. Knowledge based systems will relieve many workers of the need to memorise masses of facts, case knowledge, technical detail and so on. Consequently, many people . . . could be freed for imaginative thinking and creative problem-solving in the course of their everyday work. The pace of economical, social and political evolution will be accelerated as a result of the result of all this creative energy, and goods, services, processes and even whole industries will arise, flourish and decline at hitherto undreamt-of rates. . .

The problem is to devise pedagogies and educational environments which permit this to happen, rather than narrowly utilitarian training systems which often seem specifically designed to illustrate Hazlitt's dictum that:

> . . . Men do not become by nature what they are meant to be, but what society makes them. The generous feelings and high propensities of the soul are, as it were, shrunken, seared, violently wrenched and amputated to fit us for our intercourse with the world, something in the manner in which beggars maim and mutilate their children to make them fit for their future situation in life. . .
>
> (The great English essayist William Hazlitt)

One solution which has been mooted, and which is increasingly popular, is open learning. Indeed, the European Community's DELTA programme demonstrates substantial commitment to a Community-wide system of open learning, to be accessible to any citizen of any member state of the European Community. It seems highly likely that open learning in some form or other will be firmly established for many years to come.

The ideal of open learning offers us a chance to reconsider what it means to be educated or, for that matter, to be an educator. It is already obvious that the role and function of the teacher will have to change dramatically, towards a less direct and more complex relationship with learners. But it is also evident that other kinds of professionals may acquire new sorts of broadly educational roles and functions. For example, community-based information professionals (librarians) are particularly well-placed to adopt the function of mediators and advisors in knowledge transfer processes. All of this has profound implications for the development of assessment.

For example, if open learning is seriously concerned with increased personal autonomy, then we have to allow for situations where students actually have greater understanding of the tacit elements of a knowledge domain than their tutors/teachers or whatever. Indeed, this is already an issue to some extent.

Today's young (and not so young) people have grown up in a high technology televisual world, where 'language' implies more than the use of the written or spoken word. There is a 'visual language' which can have deep tacit influences on the identification, definition and representation of problems. Analogous questions may arise when students and teachers come from different cultural or ethnic backgrounds. It is conceivable that progress with a 'learning task' may be assessed by a student in terms which, though valid *per se*, are not grasped by a teacher. Assessment becomes much more complex than endorsement or rejection in relation to a dominant value system, rather it becomes a process of communication and learning on the parts of both 'teacher' and 'learner', to the extent that such role-defined labels become meaningless.

This is a relatively new relationship within education. The idea of mutuality in the construction of new knowledge, rather than the 'measurement' of the efficiency of data transfer has great significance for the whole idea of assessment. It does not, however, imply a sort of 'committee view', analogous to a moderation meeting. Open learning begins to imply open minds, rather than open doors. And instead of inhibiting consensus, the likelihood of multiplicity of viewpoint becomes a positive advantage. We perceive three dimensions precisely because our two eyes receive different images. Although both would need to have contact with related bodies of tacit knowledge, there is no need for 'teacher' and 'learner' to share exactly the same viewpoints, so long as they are able to tolerate diversity and uncertainty, and to resolve them within themselves.

A systems view of assessment

This is where what Checkland calls 'systems thinking' (Checkland, 1981) comes into its own as an analytical technique. Checkland's 'soft systems analysis': 'a technique for tackling ill-structured real world problems' may be particularly useful here.

The soft systems method attempts to define systems in terms of six dimensions (the CATWOE inventory):

CUSTOMER (client, beneficiary . . . or victim)
ACTORS (the agents who carry out the main process)
TRANSFORMATIONS (changes brought about)
WORLDPICTURE (the often unquestioned outlook or taken-for-granted framework which makes the system meaningful)
OWNERSHIP (who controls, overlooks or sponsors the system)

Applying this inventory (in a fairly non-rigorous way) to assessment, raises some interesting and significant questions:

CUSTOMER: who is intended to be informed by the process of assessment? Those who answer 'the student', are likely to have a very different view of the whole system from those who relate assessment to informing potential employers about a person's capabilities or to supplying academics with feedback about their own effectiveness.

ACTORS: who are involved? Is the system 'open' or 'closed'?

TRANSFORMATIONS: what changes is the system aiming to bring about? Is it about helping individuals to self-realization or perhaps enlisting them in their own exploitation?

WORLD PICTURE: what is the general political and/or philosophical context? This is the whole crux of the analysis, and the point at which the clash of essentially contested concepts becomes critical to understanding of the system.

OWNERSHIP: whose system is it? What interests are brought to bear on its operation? What interests are believed (whether correctly or otherwise) to be involved?

ENVIRONMENT: what limits are placed on the system? For example, the need for formal qualifications, the demands of potential employers, political constraints or even academic fashions in assessment theory.

If such an exercise is carried out with an arbitrarily selected group of educators, the sheer variety of system descriptions which emerges usually serves to point out that there is no naturally delimited system to which the process of assessment uniquely relates. However, for the purpose of this article, I shall consider the following systems contexts for assessment:

- ☐ truth in packaging system: concerned with quality control of the human resource input from the point of view of the employer;
- ☐ intelligent cannon fodder system: concerned with strategic aspects of 'human capital formation';
- ☐ ticketing system: regulating access to other systems and subsystems, such as universities etc;
- ☐ constructive custody system: pseudo training, removing otherwise unemployed people from politically damaging records;
- ☐ parallel currency system: a metaphor based on those countries which have two currency systems, one for the elite and another (devalued) currency for the rest;
- ☐ social location system: showing people their 'proper' place in society by leading them to discover their own limitations;
- ☐ education: what we all hope we are doing!

Discussion of assessment only begins to make sense in the light of some such analysis. The technicalities of assessment procedures are important, but they are secondary to basic philosophical considerations. And yet one of the more worrying features of the system of assessment instituted in the UK by the Education Act of 1987 is that it establishes an assessment framework ahead of the development of the curriculum to which it supposedly relates. This is an instance where soft system analysis could be particularly instructive!

Down with school!

It is clear that the humans at the centre of future human-centred systems would be 'educated' people, proud of their roots, aware of their rights, conscious of their needs and strengths and able to take on and solve real problems by applying the fullest range of tools available to them. Serious attention needs to be given to identifying the features of educational systems (seen in the broadest sense) which will most effectively support this progress.

There can't be many of us who haven't been tempted into a little crystal ball-gazing when it comes to the future of education. Indeed, education probably ranks with the direction of the economy and the management of the national rugby team as par excellence fields for saloon bar wisdom. And we are all inclined to lose sight of the fine dividing line which separates myth, reality and wishful thinking in all these cases. There are really two traps to avoid here. The first is over-estimating the pace and extent of short-term change. The second, however, is to under-estimate the extent of long-term change. The next two decades will see dramatic changes in education, but the principal factors underlying these changes are unlikely to be fully apparent until the early years of the next century. By then it seems probable that we shall have seen the end of schools and colleges as we now know them. Twenty years ago the educator Ivan Illich was regarded as a crank for advocating the 'deschooling' of society. Today we must take another long hard look at his ideas.

But we will almost certainly need to forget some of our 'school of the future' pipedreams and nightmares. The disturbing image of rows and rows of individualized learners silently beavering away at their VDUs is fortunately a long way from realization and probably receding. The sci-fi stereotype of the computer as a super-intelligent automated teacher substitute is more a product of the ways in which computers have been designed, managed and marketed in the past (a combined legacy of Von Neumann's architecture, 1960s industrial automation and Barnum and Bailey hokum) than serious future-oriented educational thinking! Nevertheless, digital computer technology will continue to exert its subliminal influence as what David Bolter (Bolter, 1984) has called the 'defining technology' of our age, and it remains important that we should at least be sensitive to this influence.

Modern information and communications technologies open up an enormous range of possibilities for de-institutionalizing education. And this could be done by private as well as public agencies. We could see the growth of alternative educational systems more popular, more effective and more powerful than anything the state can offer. In the wrong hands, coupled with workforce dispersal and fragmentation, such a system could become an extremely powerful medium for social and political control.

In principle there is no reason why we should not witness the development of a new form of samizdat open education, based on new technologies. This is already happening in corporate training in the USA, where the proliferation of communications satellites with spare capacity means that the potential cost of broadcasting or 'narrowcasting' to a restricted audience is getting lower all the time. However, the cost of producing high-quality television, perhaps combined with computer software educational materials is constantly rising in real terms. The entry costs are already almost prohibitive and seem likely to remain very high, while the numbers of specialist educators with significant competence in the new media are still low, despite development programmes such as OLYMPUS. All the indications are that we shall see the increasing commodity marketing of education and training as personal services, rather than their availability as a social good by right of citizenship.

Don't let's pretend that this is all impossible, or that it will not happen: it is already happening, and there are enormous commercial pressures involved. In the USA, businessman Jack Taub, inventor of the public database 'The Source' has proposed the 'Educational Utility', a sort of MacBurger approach to education, where educational materials are kept in a sort of electronic warehouse, and distributed by satellite to locations such as schools, who then sell them on, possibly through some franchising agreement. As a development in *publishing*, it doesn't, perhaps, raise too many problems, but it has also been hailed as a breakthrough in *education* (Middleton, 1986).

Such a market-based approach is likely to continue to promote a Taylorist model of assessment. Assessment directed towards tacit knowledge and the nurture of the personal qualities needed for independent participation in society is unlikely to provide simple answers to simplistic questions. The prospect of an educational system owned by media barons and contracting to deliver a standard quality labour force lurks nastily just around the corner!

References

Bagrit, L (1965) *The Age of Automation (1964 Reith Lectures)* London, Weidenfeld & Nicolson

Benjamin, H (republished 1975) The Sabre Tooth Curriculum. In Golby M, Greenwald J & West R (eds) *Curriculum Design* Milton Keynes, OU Press. 7–14

Boguslaw, R (1965). *The New Utopians: A study of systems design and social change.* New Jersey, Prentice-Hall

Bolter, J D (1984) *Turing's man: Western culture in the computer age* London, Duckworth

Brand, S (1987). *The Media Lab* London, Viking Penguin, p 163

Butler, S (1987) *Erewhon.* Revised ed., 1913, London AC Fifield, Ch XXIV, p 245

Checkland, P (1981) *Systems thinking, systems practice* Chichester, John Wiley

Cooley, M (1987) *Architect or Bee?.* London, Hogarth Press 40

GEW (1987) Unpublished report to IFFTU Conference, Washington DC

Hubbard, G (1984) Social and educational effects of technological change. *B J Educ Stud XXXII (2)* 108–117

King-Taylor, L (1972). *Not for Bread Alone: An appreciation of job enrichment.* London, Business Books

Middleton, T (1986) The Education Utility. *American Educator 10* 14–25

Noble, D D (1989) Cockpit cognition: education, the military and engineering. *AI & Society 3 (4)*

Olsen, J R & Bass, V B (1982) The application of performance technology in the military: 1960–1980. *NSPI Journal 21 (6)* pp 32–36

Peters, T J & Waterman, R H (1982) *In search of excellence: Lessons from America's best-run companies* Cambridge, Harper-Row

Sage, M W & Smith, D J (1983) *Microcomputers in education: A framework for research* London, SSRC

Taylor, F W (1906). *On the Art of Cutting Metals.* New York, ASME

4. Educational change and assessment in the age of information technology

B Sendov and A Eskenasi

Summary: The development of the educational system in Bulgaria is closely linked to, and determined by, the dynamic socio-economic and cultural development in the country as well as by the on-going revolution in science and technology. Correspondingly two basic trends emerge:
- close interdependence between the high school education system and the demands for highly qualified specialists in the sphere of economy, science and culture; need for a most up-to-date professional training on a broad polytechnic basis;
- correspondence between content and methods of education and the modern achievements in science and technology.

The educational system in Bulgaria is founded upon, and functions according to, the following principles:
- democratism: equal opportunities for general, polytechnic and professional education for all young people; accordingly education in Bulgaria is free and available to all;
- polytechnic character of education which determines both the general outlook of educational training and the professional orientation and training;
- attainment of high professional skills according to the demands of modern economy, science, culture, art and the interests of the individual.

According to the decisions of the Central Committee of the Bulgarian Communist Party (1979) reforms in education are being carried out in two directions:
- perfection of the existing system, a so-called 'transition period';
- building up a new system of high school education.

The main characteristics during the transition period are:
- a single type of education exists for the first seven grades (I–VII), except for the 29 schools of the Research Group of Education;
- partial admission of six-year-old pupils to the first grade has been started;
- the instructional contents of the general education subjects is unique for all kinds of high schools (5 years polytechnic high schools and technical high schools, and 4 years professional vocational schools);
- differentiation in instruction is introduced by optional disciplines and extra-curricular activities.

In parallel with the transition-period, work has been started on the realization of the new unitary polytechnic schools, with three levels of instruction within a 10 to 12 year course of education. This system also includes new two years post-high-school technical schools, special schools for care and training of handicapped children, three years only professional vocational schools (VIII–X grades) etc.

Introduction

In 1979 the Bulgarian Academy of Sciences and the former Ministry of

Education established the Research Group of Education (RGE). The main goal of this experiment has been to prepare the ground in schools for the wider use of information technology (Sendov 1987). Twenty-nine schools were attached to the RGE. The main intention is not so much the use of computers as instruments of school training, or information about and instruction for work with computers; rather, the goal is the thorough reorganization of educational curricula and methods through the constant and general use of computers in everyday life: in other words a man-computer symbiosis.

The basic hypothesis on which we are building our educational strategy in the information age is that the object of education has changed. What do we mean by this? We view the computer as an extension of the human mind. This concept is widely accepted and is realistic. It upholds the unique status of the human personality and removes any contradiction between man and computer.

From the concept of the computer being an extension of the human mind it follows that the aim of education in an information age is the training of children and young people who are equipped to use computers. Since education is basically dealing with the mind of the person being trained, it cannot itself remain unchanged as this mind is extended by the computer. In this sense the object of education has changed.

An analysis of the character of computers used in education shows that three main tendencies may be distinguished:

- ☐ the computer as an object of study;
- ☐ the computer as a training device;
- ☐ the computer as an extension of the human mind.

All three trends have their place and future development in education, but the third will lead to the most profound and essential changes.

What are the major effects of such changes in an information age? It is natural to expect a basic change in the methods, as well as in the content of education. Analysis shows that the change in school curricula is particularly significant. But this change cannot be carried out easily, let alone immediately. The reasons lie mainly in the traditional conservatism of the educational system (which also has its positive side), as well as in the constant and still fairly rapid improvement in computers. We do not mean that the object of education has already changed; it is still doing so. This means that adequate school training in an information age will develop as the result of a long and difficult process.

A great influence on the modern principles of curriculum development is exerted by the so-called Bloom's taxonomy concerning the hierarchic aims of education (Gronlund, 1976). The latter can be grouped together in three main domains:

- ☐ the cognitive domain, concerned with knowledge and its application;
- ☐ the affective domain, concerned with the emotional responses and values that are taught;
- ☐ the psychomotor domain, concerned with physical and manipulative skills.

As far as changes in education appropriate to an information age are concerned, the process will affect most substantially the first domain of Bloom's taxonomy. The second and third domains will undergo less significant changes. However, manipulative skills will probably change considerably.

From the history of pedagogy, we learn of the long and varied development of educational systems as they adjust to serve a particular society. The educational systems in all countries are strongly influenced by the historical and political development of the country. There are, nevertheless, universal trends and developments that may serve as a basis for international cooperation. The basic principle of the RGE is the integrity of knowledge. The principle of integrity, or wholeness, of education is not a new one. The idea of studying objects and phenomena from different points of view, involving knowledge of different school subjects, is a well-known approach, particularly in primary education. The very integrity of knowledge itself can have different characteristics. We may take account of the special features of the various subjects, while at the same time investigating and emphasizing their interconnections. Another approach is integration on the basis of fundamental ideas from different fields. Methods using projects are well-known, and achieved great popularity in the twenties and thirties in the USA, as did the method of complex training in the twenties in the USSR. These could both be considered as variants of an integrated approach in education.

The integrated approach of the RGE is of a particular nature and differs in principle from other methods of education quoted as integral methods. The basic difference lies in the emphasis placed on the need for the integration of knowledge as a consequence of a qualitatively new situation: the emergence of new information technologies. This new situation can be characterized by the following developments.

The school is no longer the sole nor most attractive source of knowledge. The availability and rapid development of the information technologies (radio, TV, computer networks, satellite communications etc) provide for the quick and unhindered acquisition of knowledge in a pleasant atmosphere. These sources therefore prove to be strong competition for the school. However there is one aspect of school education that cannot be challenged by other sources of information. This is the unique commitment and capacity of the school to provide systematized and well-structured knowledge. Hence in the age of highly advanced technologies the main preoccupation of the school should be the systematization and structuring of knowledge whereby emphasis is laid on fundamental and universally valid principles. In this sense, the integration of knowledge acquires a special significance. The purpose of the integral approach to education is not to continue the learning in different spheres of a certain body of facts needed to carry out a definite practical job, or to develop a project. What we have in mind is just the opposite. It is to have the attention of the student concentrated upon basic and valid principles from the viewpoint of a large number of scientific subjects, making possible further independent study and the utilization of specific information through the information technologies.

It is easy enough to formulate this requirement in principle, but it is rather more difficult to implement it as a particular learning process incorporating curricula, textbooks and study aids. The school is not in a position to provide sufficient knowledge for the entire range of man's working life. The amount of change that man will experience during his lifetime in the world about him is likely to increase enormously in the future, and this means that it will be no longer possible for a school to equip the future citizen with enough skills to serve a lifetime. There is no doubt that such a citizen will be compelled to study all their life.

So the main task facing the school of today is, above all, to teach the students how to learn. In this respect the integrated approach has indisputable advantages; it enables the student to observe natural and social phenomena from a different angle and cultivates the need for a constant search for new relationships and facts. According to the system adopted by the RGE, the entire period of schooling should be divided into four cycles:

☐ primary (4 years; age 6–9);
☐ junior secondary (3 years; age 10–12);
☐ senior secondary (4 years; age 13–16);
☐ terminal (one year; age 17–18).

It is the primary and junior secondary cycles for which the RGE has developed a more or less final version of its teaching materials and has amassed the greatest experience in implementation and evaluation.

The system of textbooks starts with a primer for use during the first semester of the first year. There is no other textbook during this time (use of a single textbook at any one time is characteristic of the entire primary cycle), and the primer is used in school rather than taken home. The main objectives of this first book are elementary reading, writing with block letters and digits, and adding and subtracting numbers up to 20.

Although there is only one textbook, we differentiate among eight activities: reading, writing, calculating; singing and instrument playing, concert visiting; drawing and modelling; design and construction; sports; reading books; studying one's homeland; and excursions. The first item represents the 'hard' studies (10 lessons per week) and all other items – the 'soft' (altogether 25 lessons per week). In grades 2–4 the schedule remains essentially the same.

The primary cycle has, as its objective, providing initial, non-systematic knowledge about the child's environment, and achieving a basic literacy in Bulgarian and Russian (the latter starting in the third grade). An attempt is made to reach this goal through an integrated approach and a relaxed atmosphere to stimulate the child's activity. Neither grading marks, nor homework are given. All the teaching materials (books, slides, tapes, etc) remain in school and are not taken home. Time at home, after a whole 'working day', belongs to the family. Every class is assigned to teachers: one senior teacher, who typically takes over the 'hard' lessons, and a junior teacher, who is responsible for the rest. There is usually a professional sports teacher available at most of the schools. In the junior secondary cycle emerges the first differentiation of disciplines, although the system still remains integrated horizontally among disciplines and vertically among grades. The next important feature is the advent of a second foreign language, English. The main disciplines (the 'hard' ones) are 'language and mathematics', 'Nature' and 'Society'. 'Language and mathematics' is a most unusual discipline and is intended as an amalgam of general and comparative linguistics, and mathematics. Linguistics (not just the native language) through phonetics, morphology and syntax, logically comes first, and an attempt is made to use simple mathematical tools to describe linguistic phenomena. This was the most difficult book to conceive, and it has not yet reached its final form.

(Incidentally, the same applies to a lesser degree to all our teaching materials, which were planned to be continually revised.)

A great difficulty to overcome was that the language and literature teachers on the one hand and maths teachers on the other usually form somewhat distinct groups and it is not at all easy to find and convince the same person to teach according to such a hybrid textbook. In practice, two teachers enter the class and team-teach, hopefully in a concerted way. Linguistics should be comparative, in view of the synchronized study of Bulgarian, Russian, English and some programming languages. The next discipline, 'Nature', deals with the sciences. It includes topics from physics, chemistry, biology, ecology, medicine, and related areas, in a more or less unified, systematic way, according to the increasing complexity of natural phenomena.

Broadly speaking, the third discipline, 'Society', represents the humanities, but it is in fact a history of civilization. The backbone of this discipline is history, the main emphasis is on the development of human society, its productive forces, the history of social formations and relations, the history of ideas, and especially the history of arts. 'Society' has as its objective the development of an open-minded citizen, respectful of other civilizations and cultures, and ready to live in a peaceful pluralistic world. Some other features are also characteristic of the junior secondary cycle. First of all, a computer-oriented approach is being attempted in all disciplines, but initially in 'Language and mathematics' and in 'Nature'. While in the primary cycle the only information technology equipment used is calculators, in the secondary cycle personal microcomputers are playing a more and more substantial role. Although we are at the beginning of such an approach, three textbooks on LOGO are already in use in the junior secondary cycle.

In addition to the three 'hard' disciplines we have discussed, several related optional activities are available. There are also two other important disciplines with their own textbooks: 'Daily life' and 'Manufacturing'. The first deals with home economics, especially cooking; the second covers simple crafts and agriculture.

To sum up, the junior secondary cycle is a closed one from a logical point of view, as well as from a chronological one. It is assumed that a subsequent cycle, on a higher level, will follow in the senior secondary cycle. The first clustering of concepts and phenomena arises in the junior cycle, elements of proofs emerge, and a first broad overview of human history adapted to this age is presented. Individual inclinations are given a first opportunity of appearing and developing.

A recent evaluation by an independent government educational laboratory has shown that the students of the RGE perform no worse than the average student, and yet have broader interests, are not afraid of school, are not intimidated and are more self-confident.

Independently of these results we are trying at the RGE to build up our own evaluation system. Objectivity should be an important characteristic of this system. Moreover, computers have been introduced in the RGE schools as a training device. Therefore it is quite natural to try using computers as an assessment tool. A stepwise approach has been devised to this end. Objective tests of multiple choice (MC) type have been chosen as an appropriate way of evaluation. Then a computer assisted testing system has been selected. This system, TEST, has been designed at the Institute of Mathematics (Bulgarian

Academy of Sciences). A very concise description of TEST follows.

From the viewpoint of the examined student, TEST may be described as follows: the student sits in front of the microcomputer, receives brief instructions (several sentences on the screen) and is offered a test, consisting of multiple-choice test items. The test item consists of a text whose answers are 3, 4 or 5, one of which is correct while the others are distractors. The answers consist of text and (optionally) colour pictures. The student is supposed to select the correct answer (answering with a digit). When no more test items are available, the results are stored in a file, which is further accessible to the examiner.

Database maintenance techniques are available to the examiner. Text and graphics are stored separately and supported in different ways. The textbase maintenance tools (text editor) represents an elementary menu and no preliminary knowledge is necessary to correct, update or delete text. The graphics base maintenance tools (graphics editor) enable the easy creation of various colour figures, which occupy minimal memory space, and are executed quickly. It is not hard to learn how to use the graphics editor. The examiner is able to require the generation of a test (using the data base) with particular characteristics – number of test items per test, subject area, global difficulty, time for test solution etc. Each test item is characterized by 'difficulty weight' and belongs to a certain subject area. Since the test items are selected within each subject area by a random generator, practically an unlimited number of distinct tests are produced if the data base is large enough. As mentioned before, the results of each examination are registered and generalized and can be printed as various reports on request.

TEST consist internally of 4 subsystems:

☐ text base maintenance (text editor);
☐ graphics base maintenance (graphics editor);
☐ test generation and examination;
☐ results processing.

A minimal hardware support is required – an Apple II (or compatible) with one diskette drive for each student to be examined.

After a 12 hour course with several RGE teachers, comprising general concepts of educational measurement, creation of MC test items and use of the TEST system (without the graphics editors), two of them volunteered to participate in our first experiment. They passed an additional 6 hours' instruction on the TEST graphics editor and were ready to start the experiment in their respective RCE schools in Sofia and Plovdiv. The main objectives were:

☐ to establish to what extent teachers are able to create an appropriate set of test items, using the TEST system;
☐ to investigate the students' reaction to a new and unusual way of examination;
☐ to compare examination results obtained by computer testing with results obtained by usual examination;
☐ to try finding out a general assessment scheme, based on computer assisted testing and appropriate results interpretation.

It should be taken into account that objective testing in Bulgaria is still applied in very rare and special cases, particularly in schools; that although the TEST system had been financed by the Sofia district administration of education it has not been implemented in schools up until now. That's why the experiment has also stressed some initial procedures, as mentioned above.

The experiment was carried out with the material comprising LOGO and taught in the third year of the junior secondary cycle. The teachers created 106 MC test items with graphics to 44 of them.

A first test was administered to 27 students in the Plovdiv school and 19 students in the Sofia school. Each test consisted of 10 MC test items, selected out of 20 available, the particular lesson 'word processing'. Each of the students received a different test.

A second test was administered to the same groups, this time comprising the whole second semester's material. 66 MC test items were available in the TEST data base and again 10 out of them were used to be randomly selected for each student immediately before examination. A last examination was carried out with a senior secondary cycle class.

The first conclusion is that the total instruction of 18 hours proved to be sufficient for both teachers. They created by themselves the hierarchic subject area classification scheme, needed by TEST in the stage of test item selection according to subjects. Only minor corrections were necessary in order to obtain final versions of the test items created by the teachers. Surprisingly fast the two teachers got familiar with the graphics editor and programmed, without further help, the graphics images for 44 of the test items. However, it should be taken into account they are teaching mathematics and informatics.

Information concerning the students' reaction was collected by direct observation and by interviews. The computer assisted test examination was met both with great interest and frustration. It should not be forgotten that there were two new aspects – test examination (almost new) and computer examination (entirely new). The majority of the students claimed to get a concrete mark immediately after the end of the examination and calculated by the computer itself. Some of them disapproved of the impossibility of correcting an answer after having once keyed it. (TEST allows temporarily skipping a test item, but does not allow corrections.)

Two evaluation procedures were completed. By the first one the teachers were allowed to intuitively establish an evaluation scale. The second was a standard criterion referenced scheme. The first one displayed an almost full match with the previous students' marks. The second positioned the test examination results (as an average) a little bit under the previous results.

What is not yet completed is the last point of our plan as mentioned above. But there is no doubt that RGE teachers are able to produce test items, to effectively use the TEST computer assisted system, to analyse the examination results obtained. It is also clear that students are ready to accept this examination approach.

References

Gronlund, N E (1976) *Measurement and evaluation in teaching* New York, Collier-Macmillan
Sendov, B (1987) Education for an information age *Impact of science on society*, no. 146, pp 193–201

5. Adjusting the balance of power: initial self-assessment in study skills for higher education – a case study

Lynne Cameron

Summary: Working from the belief that learner control of learning requires both self-knowledge and knowledge of the learning possibilities available, the procedure described here was developed to provide an entry point into a Study Skills for Higher Education programme. It was to yield useful diagnostic information about the learners' skills and, a the same time, assist in the creation of a relaxed and productive relationship between tutor and learners.

A questionnaire with built-in tasks was designed and trialled, taking into account the specific context in which it was to be used. The questions and tasks aimed to produce information on study habits and skills through an interactive process of action and introspection, at the same time giving the learner an overview of study skills that could be used in drawing up a learning programme. Trials of the questionnaire with potential learners revealed the advantages of this kind of approach, and some of the pitfalls.

Introduction

This case study describes one way in which learners can be enabled to increase the degree of control they have over the content of their learning and over the interactions between learner and tutor.

The learners in question were mature students in two very different types of programme, both aimed at improving study skills for higher education. One situation was of self-directed learning, where the learner, having decided support was required, attended an open learning workshop and worked on an individualized programme with the help of a tutor. The second was a class-based 'pre-sessional' course in language and study skills, organized for students arriving from overseas to study at British universities.

In the first context, a relatively equal distribution of power between learner and tutor is, to some extent, brought about by the one-to-one working situation, and a questionnaire-type instrument was required that would aid the selection of learning goals and the planning of the learning programme. Such learner control over content and methodology can only be real if the learner is assisted in becoming aware of the range of possibilities available. Awareness is also needed, by both learner and tutor, of the knowledge and skills already possessed by the learner, and this must be formulated in comprehensible terms.

Having initially been designed for the early stages of self-directed learning. The task-linked questionnaire, as it was called, was later used with the pre-sessional class, and proved to be transferable, with no need for major changes.

More importantly, the individual nature of desired outcomes showed through equally clearly in the class situation, making it difficult to avoid questioning the efficiency of class teaching in study skills.

In a class situation, the roles of learner and teacher are usually much more clearly defined in terms of power. Expectations that learners may have about their less powerful position in interactions are frequently confirmed by what takes place in the first sessions of a course. As in other interactions between people meeting for the first time, when learners first encounter their tutors, each sizes up the other before deciding how to act. Tutors usually adopt the role of prime mover in this situation – testing learners, dividing them into groups, and selecting teaching materials and methods for them. Learners complete tests, answer questions and, on the whole, do what they are told. Problems can then arise if learners feel the tutors' decisions about their learning are not appropriate for them. They can either try to add to the choices on offer, which is not easy, given the less powerful role they have been assigned, or accept the situation, with a likely loss of motivation for learning.

It also seems likely that this initial imbalance of power affects the way in which tutors and learners interact in future learning situations. An investigation into tutor/learner relations under the surface is described in another paper (Cameron, 1990), and shows worrying discrepancies between the informality being aimed at by tutors and the realities of learners' feelings.

In terms of assessing knowledge and skills, an initial procedure was required to serve some of the diagnostic purposes of traditional tests. However, the types of tests frequently given to students on pre-sessional courses were not seen as appropriate for us in the one-to-one situation for two reasons. First, the information flow is usually in only one direction – from learner to tutor – and one of the prerequisites of this procedure was that the learner should also be receiving information. Second, there is a problem with how the information is processed. Haertel (1985) defines tests as 'settings for structured observations designed to provide an efficient source of information about the examinees'. This information is generally converted into numerical scores which can then be extrapolated, correlated and otherwise manipulated. It is people other than learners who are mostly concerned with the results of a test. In the self-directed learning context, the information is at least as important to the learner as it is to the tutor and, because of this, it would, in some cases, be a hindrance to convert it into a numerical score.

An acceptable alternative to testing, for extracting information from learners in a situation where the purposes are course design and placement, is self-assessment and self-diagnosis. Use of questionnaire format as a tool for self-assessment and diagnosis has been described in literature (eg Rea (1981) Oskarsson (1978, 1982) and generally appears to produce assessments that correlate well with tutors' estimates and objective tests. However, Blue (1987), reporting on the use of self-assessment of language skills on a pre-sessional course in the UK, noted that students had some problems interpreting terms used in the questionnaire and, having completed the self-assessment found the next stage of prioritizing needs and deciding on learning goals difficult.

To try to resolve this and to enable the procedure to function as a learning process, modifications were made to the usual questionnaire format. The questionnaire that emerged covered most of the aspects of study skills and the linked language skills by relating them to the writing of a particular assignment. It was decided that questions to the learner were necessary but not sufficient for effective self-diagnosis. To facilitate this, a set of tasks was integrated into the set of questions. It was hypothesized that the process of completing the tasks and then responding to questions about the process would guide the learners towards constructive reflection on the strategies and skills possessed.

The initial context of use will now be described in greater detail, together with the purposes of, and constraints on, the task-linked questionnaire.

The initial context

This project was initially designed to meet the needs of a number of students at Bradford and Ilkley Community College, who enrolled in an open learning communication workshop to improve the form, rather than the content, of essays and assignments for their mainstream higher education courses.

The target group

The questionnaire was aimed at students in higher education studying at British universities or colleges, some of whom were bilingual speakers of English and East European/Asian languages, or speakers of English as a Foreign Language.

Having started an undergraduate or postgraduate course and having been faced with assignments and reading lists, some students are forced into the realization that they need to work on reading skills (such as skimming and scanning), use of indexes, etc, and writing skills (such as essay planning, paragraph construction, etc). The area in which students most frequently ask for help is note-taking.

The communication workshop

Students at Bradford and Ilkley Community College finding themselves in the situation described above are referred by tutors, or refer themselves, to the communication workshop. The workshop is open to college students, university students and others, and operates on an open access, one-to-one tutor/student basis. It provides self-access materials for external examinations in English (eg GCSE, AEB Basic English) and for particular areas of language study (eg spelling, essay-writing, study skills). When students come for the first time, they spend some time with a tutor discussing what they want to work on, and completing diagnostic tests. From this discussion, a programme of work is drawn up and the student is assigned a particular tutor to work with.

The purpose of the questionnaire

The questionnaire was designed to form part of the initial counselling session between tutor and student, providing a framework for discussion. The first stage in this type of self-directed learning takes the form of a needs analysis. It aims to increase the students' awareness of their current level of study skills and of the particular skills relevant to their course that they need to acquire. Since a student's analysis of his or her needs is often quite unsophisticated, the quesionnaire would only be the first stage in that process. This must continue alongside the work the student does, gradually becoming more detailed, more realistic and thus more useful.

The questionnaire was to be used to:

☐ Give learners a clearer idea of the nature and range of study skills. The questionnaire introduces the various aspects of study skills, breaking them down in some cases into subskills, and so presents the student with a range of possibilities from which learning goals can be selected.
☐ Enable learners and tutor to assess which skills have already been acquired, which need to be acquired and which may need to be modified for a new language or level of course.
☐ Enable learner and tutor to plan a programme of work to be followed in the workshop. Various purpose-written and published materials were already available. Constructing the questionnaire also enabled the identification of gaps in the materials available.

Constraints

While setting out to achieve these ends, the realities of the constraints imposed by the situation could not be ignored:

☐ The learner had to be able to work through the questionnaire mostly on their own, after an introduction by the tutor. This meant that the level of English used had not to be too difficult and tasks had to be easily understood, even if involving ideas new to the learner.
☐ 'Marking', to be done by tutor and learner together, was itself a learning process. A learner usually has a very urgent need for help and no time should be wasted if motivation to use the workshop is to be maintained.
☐ Since the questionnaire should aid the process of designing a programme of work, sections would ideally lead into particular books or materials in the workshop.
☐ The subject matter of the tasks would relate to the learner's course or background.
☐ Some diagnosis of a learner's problems in written English at and beyond sentence level was required.
☐ It would be useful if the questionnaire was also suitable for re-use for checks mid-way and at the end of the programme of work.

The design of the study skills questionnaire

The questionnaire consists of a series of 'items' interspersed with nine tasks. Both tasks and items follow a line of development (Low, 1986) which parallels the writing of an assignment, examining in turn the subskills involved in the various activities.

Line of Development	Tasks
Student attends lectures	
Handouts received	
	Understanding
Discussion with tutor	spoken English
Assignment given	Identifying key words in
	assignment titles
Finding books, journals	Use of catalogue
Selecting books	Use of contents/index
Reading for assignment	Scanning
	Close reading
Note-taking	Note-taking
Planning an assignment	Ordering a plan
Writing the first draft	Writing a paragraph,
Preparing the final draft	proofreading

The items are used to help develop the 'line of development' and move from one stage to the next. Items ask the respondents for facts concerning their course (3 items), for information about their study habits (21 items) and for assessment of their current state of understanding or level of skills (11 items). Twenty-seven out of the 35 items ask for a response on a four-point frequency scale, six ask for a Yes/No response, one has a four-point scale of degree and one asks for an open-ended response. It was considered important for ease of use to restrict the types of responses as far as possible. By formatting items in the form 'Do you have problems with – ?', the frequency scale can be used to ask about the learners' level of understanding or skill.

In order to help increase the confidence and independence of the respondent, items 1–7 include examples of all the types of items. It was intended that these would be worked through together with the tutor, with answers given orally first and then put on to the questionnaire, so that the learner would see the process involved. The tutor should then be able to leave the learner to work on their own, returning to help as and when necessary.

Tasks can be seen as fitting into the questionnaire format in the manner illustrated in Figure 2.

Tasks have the following purposes:

☐ providing concrete examples of the skill being discussed;
☐ enabling a deeper and more accurate level of assessment or diagnosis to be made by the learner and/or tutor;
☐ enabling the learner to assess specific subskills involved in the task;
☐ providing a check on responses to items;
☐ giving the tutor more detailed information for diagnosis.

The tasks involved two levels of response. All of them required the learner to carry out a skill-related task and respond by underlining, selecting, ordering or writing. Four of the nine also required the learner to reflect on what happened as the task was carried out. This took the form of:

NAME: _____   DATE: _____

1. How many lectures a week do you go to?   ☐

2. When you listen to a lecture, how much of it do you understand?
   very little   some of it   most of it   all of it
   ☐   ☐   ☐   ☐

3. Do you take notes from lectures?
   never   sometimes   usually   always
   ☐   ☐   ☐   ☐

4. If so, are the notes useful for

	never	sometimes	usually	always
re-reading to understand the lecture better?	☐	☐	☐	☐
writing assignments?	☐	☐	☐	☐
revision?	☐	☐	☐	☐

5. If the lecturer gives you handouts, do you keep them?
   never   sometimes   usually   always
   ☐   ☐   ☐   ☐

6. If you don't understand parts of a lecture, do you ever
        ask other students to explain?   Yes/No
        find out from books?   Yes/No
        ask the lecturer?   Yes/No
        ask your tutor?   Yes/No

7. Do you meet your tutor every week?   Yes/No

8. Is he/she helpful?

9. Do you have any problems in getting your tutor to understand you?
   never   sometimes   usually   always
   ☐   ☐   ☐   ☐

10. Do you have problems understanding what your tutor tells you?
    never   sometimes   usually   always
    ☐   ☐   ☐   ☐

Figure 1 *The first page of the questionnaire on study skills*

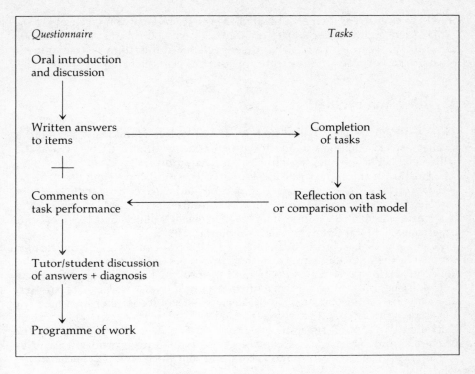

Figure 2 *The interplay between tasks and questions*

☐ asking about the difficulty the learner had experienced in carrying out the
task, with a response on a five-point bipolar scale of degree;
☐ an assessment of problem areas, with Yes/No responses;
☐ asking how the learner went about doing the task;
☐ comparing the learner's work with that illustrated in the task.

The tasks used authentic material and texts concerned with sociology at
undergraduate level, and themselves followed the line of development of
assignment writing, using a specific assignment title and related reading text. As
the tasks proceeded, there was an increase in task complexity, semantic difficulty
and the degree of interdependence between later and earlier tasks. The earlier
tasks were shorter and simpler and required responses that were either non-
linguistic or were words or phrases. The reading text was introduced through a
scanning task, followed by tasks that required close reading. Selecting the
preferred set of notes on the text and writing a guided summary required
understanding of the text. This final writing task was the most open, and the
process of planning and writing the paragraph provided as much information to
the tutor for diagnostic purposes as the product, not only about the learner's
writing skills but about their understanding of the topic gained from the text and
from work done in previous tasks.

In wording the tasks and questions, care was taken to use language that should be clear to the learner. This applied both to the level of English and to the avoidance of technical vocabulary or jargon, such as 'blurb' and 'skim'. Focusing the entire procedure on a realistic student activity, rather than abstract notions of language skills, ensured a greater measure of accessibility.

Trialling and evaluation

The questionnaire was trialled with six students, two from overseas and four locally, resident bilinguals, in one-to-one situations at Bradford College, and also with a class of seven overseas students at Leeds University.

Validation of this type of self-assessment activity is complex and problematic. Validation procedures as used on more traditional tests cannot easily be transferred to self-assessment because of the differences in nature and in aims. It appears possible to establish face (or perceived) validity, and to investigate construct validity at different levels (Cameron, 1987).

Evaluation of the procedure employed data from notes made as learners completed the questionnaire, from their responses to the questions and tasks, and from the learners' own evaluations of the process. Recordings were made of a class discussion and of individual interviews held to discuss learners' answers and plan programmes of work. In the Leeds case, results of other tests taken by the students were used to investigate validity.

Evaluation required separate consideration of the diagnostic aims and the pedagogic aims. Thus it was necessary to look both at what had been learnt by the learner and at the information acquired about the learner's proficiency and study habits.

In terms of identifying needs and goals, the procedure was successful in two respects. First, it was shown clearly that in both class and one-to-one situations, the outcomes, in terms of information acquired about the learner, were differentiated for each student in terms of content and level. For example, two students identified problems with extracting the main points from texts, written or spoken. For one, this lay mainly in her lack of confidence in her ability to do this and resulted in a reluctance to scan or make brief notes. The other had more problems with listening and note-taking. A third student located a source of difficulty in the planning stage, in selecting and ordering points to include in an essay.

It was also clearly demonstrated (Cameron, 1987) that the inclusion of tasks led to a more complete picture of skills and needs than would emerge from questions and discussion alone, and that each of the three parts of the process is necessary. For example, in answering the questions, one learner stated that he had problems getting his subject tutor to understand him at times. From Task 1, he appeared to have difficulty identifying the elocutionary force of some utterances. From the discussion, it became clear that he was aware of having difficulties finding the appropriate word when under the stress of participating in a conversation and that one strategy he had adopted to help with this was noting down new words in a book. He also tried not to translate from his first language when speaking. The tutor, armed with this information, could advise on further strategies that might be helpful and could provide work on understanding and using spoken English in relevant situations.

This individualized and detailed information on learning needs can be used to define learning goals and to design individual programmes of work. The extent to which study skill needs emerged as different for each individual, even in a class of students placed as being at a similar language level, would reinforce the view that students' needs are best served by a large proportion of individualized work.

Short-term evaluation of successful learning (ie pedagogic rather than diagnostic aims) can be attempted by looking at the opinions of learners as expressed both in discussion and on the evaluation questionnaire. These were overwhelmingly positive in attitude and provided further evidence that learners had few serious problems identifying what they felt they had learnt from the procedure. This identification of what has been learnt is an important step in the acquisition of autonomy by the learner, which is one of the aims of such learner-centred activities.

The use of content material from sociology undergraduate courses had mixed results. For some learners the use of familiar material had the desired effect of being immediately relevant and of avoiding problems with new concepts. For others, the familiarity was demotivating; the material was seen as 'last year's' and no longer relevant, or came from a subject area a student did not feel comfortable with. The passage dealng with Marxism was politically too uncomfortable for a few overseas students. A potentially less controversial subject, less specifically related to one subject area, might remove these distractions. An alternative could be a bank of texts, so that an appropriate one could be selected for each student.

Conclusion

The procedure described here started from an activity, writing an assignment, that learners were or would have to become familiar with, and used it to examine current strategies and abilities. The information gave a broad, shared base of knowledge on which future learning could be designed and built.

It would seem that the more knowledge we have about how individuals study their academic subjects and how they use language for study, the more we are forced to question the desirability of teaching those individuals as a class and the clearer become the advantages of incorporating learner-controlled learning into class-based courses. This could be done by using the outcomes of the task-linked questionnaire to group learners with similar needs, by providing materials that cater for the range of needs and by the tutor taking on at different times the roles of advisor, trainer in learning techniques, and facilitator.

At the same time, the process described in this case study, of sharing information in order to work out a learning programme, appears to render the power distribution in initial interactions less unequal and more conducive to true learner control of the learning process.

References

Blue, G (1987) Individual needs analysis and self-assessment: the limits of learner independence *Paper given at SELMOUS conference, University of Durham* March 1987

Cameron, L (1987) The Role of Self-diagnosis in English for Academic Purposes: the development of a task-based procedure *MA Dissertation, Department of Linguistic Science, University of York, UK*

Cameron, L (1990) Staying within the Script: personality and self-directed learning *System* January 1990

Haertel, E (1985) Construct Validity and Criterion-referenced Testing *Review of Educational Research* 55, 1, 23–46

Low, G (1986) Storylines and other developing contexts in use-of-language test design *Indian Journal of Applied Linguistics* 12:15–38 (Special Ed. on Testing)

Oskarsson, M (1978) *Approaches to Self-assessment in Foreign Language Learning* Pergamon Press, Oxford

Oskarsson, M (1982) *Self-assessment in Foreign Language Learning* a report on progress of work, Language Testing Research Center, University of Goteborg, Molndal, Sweden

Rea, P (1981) Formative assessment of student performance: the role of self-appraisal *Indian Journal of Applied Linguistics* Vol VII, 1 and 2:66–88

6. Some implications of student choice of course content for the processes of learning, assessment and qualification

Dr Robert Kowalski

Introduction

Great changes are taking place in vocational education in the UK. By far the most significant of these is the advent of the National Council for Vocational Qualifications (NCVQ) with its emphasis upon criterion-referenced assessment. At the same time the decline in the 16–19 age group is placing considerable pressures on colleges of further education in regard to recruitment of students. Furthermore, in the agricultural sector, three-year sandwich courses for diploma qualification are still being maintained with the requirement of at least one year's pre-college experience, causing attainment of the qualification to occur later than for diplomates in other vocations.

As a prelude to the resubmission of a Business and Technician Education Council (BTEC) National Diploma in Agriculture course at the college where I was teaching, a number of changes were introduced. These revolved around the introduction of a set of optional units to be taken in the third year of the course. The option units were rated by means of a system of stars according to the amount of work thought to be involved. Thus there were four three-star options, five two-star options and two one-star options. Each star was to represent 15 hours of student time and the students were expected to undertake options to the value of eight stars (120 hours), with at least one three-star option as compulsory.

Associated changes were the removal of project work currently undertaken in the third year to provide space in the timetable, adjustment to the weightings of the final examinations to provide more value to the assessment of the opinions, timetable adjustments to free an entire morning for the activities associated with option studies and the freeing of staff as necessary.

The delivery of the options was very much a student-centred approach, with visits, tutorials, seminars, investigations and private study forming the bulk of the teaching/learning strategy. Assessments were also made more flexible, with the staff concerned with each option devising a scheme frequently based upon project reports, practical work and oral examinations.

The reasons for the introduction of optional material into the course were numerous. The course managers viewed it as an opportunity to tackle an over-full syllabus, to put in some effort on modularizing the course as part of the long-term development of the course, to help to make the course more responsive to both the students and to the developing needs of the industry locally, to increase student motivation and to help market the course. Some of the course tutors had additional motives for supporting the initiative. They viewed it as an opportunity to extend the students' control over the course by giving choice, by using student-centred methods and by introducing or extending the use of less traditional assessment methods. Prior to the introduction of options, most assessment was by phase test, examination and project work, with an aspect of employer appraisal of work-based performance during the sandwich year. The introduction of options was also seen as an opportunity to develop the teaching of common skills and the introduction of more integrative assignments, both of which were part of the agenda for the resubmission.

In addition to the above I also viewed the innovation as an opportunity for extending evaluation procedures in curriculum development in the college, so as to help raise awareness of techniques and issues which I felt were probably being neglected.

The evaluation

In addition to gathering the above information about the reasons for the innovation by informal and unstructured interviews with the staff, I also designed two structured interview instruments for use with the students and the staff. At first I had considered the questionnaires to be the best means of gathering information, but after trying to draft questions which were of sufficient precision to elicit reliable responses I decided that structured interviews would prove more reliable in their administration.

Student evaluation

The student group comprised 26 students. As a preliminary to the construction of the instrument I undertook an unstructured group interview with a representative subset of the class to discover their views on the important issues to be probed. Five students were selected such that at least one of them had experienced each of the 11 options. Other than that requirement the selection process was a random one.

The timing of the interview with the student group and the administration of the instrument to the whole class was probably crucial to many of the outcomes. I felt that in terms of my time and their patience I would trawl opinion only once. Thus it was inevitable that I should conduct the structured interviews as close to the end of the course as possible and that the group interview would have to be some time ahead of this.

The instrument contained 30 questions, four of which were based on Likert scales. Nineteen were of a Yes/No type, nine of which had follow up questions associated with one type of response. Three questions called for purely factual information and four questions were open ended and called for opinion to be expressed. A final section was included to provide an opportunity for students to cover ground that they felt was outside the scope of the questions so far asked.

I was unable to pilot this instrument with the students as I felt that the group was unique and I didn't want to expose any of them to the questions more than once. I did pilot it with colleagues who were not involved with the course, and amended it accordingly. The interviews took place in the two weeks prior to the end of the course and before the assessment results were known. Each interview took approximately 30 minutes.

Staff evaluation

The structured interview for the staff was based upon the student one, so that comparisons of responses could be made. There were six fewer questions. Eight staff were interviewed during the first week after the end of the course.

The results of the assessments for the various options were available and were extensively analysed during interviews.

The outcome of evaluation

The students

All 26 students welcomed the introduction of options. The majority of options taken had been enjoyed 'quite a lot' and the most frequently mentioned reasons for enjoyment were that it was new material and that it was interesting. These reasons coincided with those most often given by the students for taking the options.

The students called for changes in the weightings of the various options, as they felt that the workloads did not always match the star rating. They complained of encountering problems with the uneven distribution of work over the three terms and expressed the fact that they had expected, and would have liked, more formal delivery of the material.

A substantial majority would have liked greater control over the content of the options, but they also expressed the view that on the whole the options had measured up to their expectations.

Thirteen individuals indicated options that, with hindsight, they would not have pursued – a 12.5 per cent dissatisfaction rate. There was also a positive feeling of achievement among the students, with only 11 per cent of responses recording options as achieving 'not well' or 'poorly'. General comments about the scheme were 'Alter the weightings', 'Improve the process of choosing' and 'Devote more time to options'.

The staff

The staff also called for an adjustment in the weightings of the options. Most staff had experienced difficulties over timing of the option work, for example clashes between options and with other commitments. Half the staff would have liked more time to deliver their option.

The majority of staff did not wish to see student control over the options extended.

The staff felt that the students had achieved less well on the options than the students perceived their performance to have been. They felt that assessment was a grey area that needed attention.

Analysis of results

In addition to the structured interview returns I had the assessment marks for each student and option. A factor analysis was performed using a mixture of data from the student interviews and assessments. Thus the data from the Likert scales were used on their sense of achievement (ACHIEVEMENT), the degree of enjoyment of the option (ENJOYMENT), the degree to which the options had met their expectations (OUTCOME), and how much influence they felt they'd had over the option (INFLUENCE), together with the marks they had received and the number of students in each option group. The results of that analysis are given in Table 1.

Enjoyment, achievement and outcome were major contributors to factor 1 and so appear to be interrelated. Influence was unrelated to this variable and was the sole major contributor to factor 3. Factor 2 was made up by the numbers of students in the option groups and the marks awarded. The negative relationship between numbers and marks, and the lack of significant relationship between marks (the tutors' assessment of achievement) and achievement (the students'

	ROTATED FACTOR LOADINGS		
VARIABLE	FACTOR 1	FACTOR 2	FACTOR 3
NUMBERS	0.07	0.93	-0.12
MARKS	-0.19	-0.91	-0.12
ENJOYMENT	0.97	0.09	0.03
ACHIEVEMENT	0.86	0.36	-0.28
INFLUENCE	-0.02	0.00	0.99
OUTCOME	0.97	0.04	0.10
PERCENTAGE VARIANCE	44.38%	30.54%	18.30%

The higher the FACTOR LOADING the more significant the contribution. The most important features are underlined.

Table 1 *Factor analysis of student responses about option outcomes, and numbers of students in each option group and the marks given*

STUDENTS IN RANK ORDER	ORIGINAL MARKS	ADJUSTED MARKS	NEW RANK POSITION
1	74%	80%	1
2=	73%	77%	2=
2=	73%	77%	2=
4=	71%	72%	4=
4=	71%	70%	6
6	70%	72%	4=
7	68%	65%	11
8=	67%	69%	7
8=	67%	61%	15=
8=	67%	58%	17
11=	66%	68%	8
11=	66%	52%	22
13	65%	66%	9=
14=	64%	66%	9=
14=	64%	61%	15=
14=	64%	56%	20=
17	63%	63%	13
18=	62%	62%	14
18=	62%	56%	20=
20	60%	64%	12
21	58%	56%	20=
22	57%	57%	18=
23	56%	57%	18=
24	50%	49%	24
25	44%	48%	25
26	34%	35%	26

Table 2 *The rank order of students for the option-scheme part of the course together with the marks that they were given, contrasted with marks determined after the conflation of t-scores adjusted to the same mean percentage as the original class of marks and a new rank order established*

assessment of their achievement) was considered of importance to the evaluation.

All marks for each option were converted to t-scores, in order to take into account the discrepancy between the spread of marks given by individual option tutors, and the results reconflated to obtain marks for each individual student for the option element of the course. The resulting marks and new rank order positions for the class are given in Table 2.

In a class of 26 students, five had their marks adjusted down by more than five per cent and one adjusted up by a similar amount. Changes in rank order were more considerable but of less significance than the students' final marks. The cause of these adjustments was the effect of receiving the lowest marks in high-marked options and vice versa.

Of course, since all students were not marked by each tutor the above procedure may not be strictly valid. Making allowance for high marks and low variance may not be justified if the marks were reflecting a real difference in performance rather than a difference in marker, and the procedure is undoubtedly influenced by the degree to which the marks within each option conform to a normal distribution and by the small number of students. Nevertheless this process did raise significant questions about the assessment procedure for the evaluation.

Discussion

The evaluation raised a number of issues, some of which were only of direct relevance for this course and its team of staff. One or two issues, though, are of more general applicability and I would like to use these pages as a forum for discussing them.

The options were very successful from the students' point of view. The increase of relevance and the introduction of choice were the main reasons for this. This points towards the modularization of courses, with students being able to pick and choose what to study, as one way forward in the search for the 'responsive college'. However, there is a sting in the tail. By insisting upon the students undertaking an equivalent of eight stars' worth of option units we had created two distinct categories of students.

The first category was of students who had positively chosen an option. Almost certainly the options with few takers were studied by, on average, a more motivated group of students. The second category was of students who chose the topic because they had to do something to make up the required number of stars. Popular options may have been seen as 'easy' options, and the level of motivation lower as a consequence.

This may be one of the reasons for the negative relationship between group size and the mean mark for the option. This is the clash between learning and qualifying. Learning really stems from internal motivation, but qualification invariably demands that some elements of a course are undertaken as a result of external coercion in an attempt to see that all students do an equivalent amount of learning. As Green, P (1983) argued:

The curriculum is created out of conflict: the opposition between a curriculum structure and the opportunity for students to learn for and by themselves.

For the second usage of 'curriculum' we may use 'assessment' instead since, as Rowntree (1977) argued, the spirit and style of student assessment defines the de facto curriculum. This was reflected by the generally expressed desire to alter the weightings of the options and the desire of the students to have more influence over the option content and delivery.

The second issue is the effects the vagaries of the marking system have on the final mark of the student, where the selection of options taken can itself play a part in determining the outcome of assessment. In order to be fair to the students we must either develop a means of adjusting marks or abandon the use of norm-referencing and introduce criterion-referenced assessment. I have argued for such a move in other courses with options and put forward the results of this evaluation as evidence for this need. A unit-based course where each unit is founded upon competence would enable the students to select options from internal motivation and to be credited with each option completed, thereby obviating the need to undertake uninteresting options as well. This has the added advantage that it would enable future employers to see just what has been undertaken in any unit.

Of course these proposed changes are coincidental with the competence-based assessments being introduced by the NCVQ. Nevertheless we must accept that criterion-referenced assessments are also imperfect instruments in their turn. Norm-referencing has its advantages too. It generates competition in the student group. Passing or failing can motivate to a degree, but being able to show that you excel over your contemporaries can be a great incentive within limits. Indeed it must not be forgotten that the process of qualification is not merely an indication of competence, it is also a means of discrimination. What, I wonder, is likely to happen when numbers of students are produced with equivalent NVQs? How will an employer select for interview? I fear that references and their hidden criteria will take on an increased importance in the wake of purely criterion-referenced qualifications.

Thus I would argue that hand-in-hand with such developments a system of profiling should be introduced, especially of the affective domain, undertaken as a process negotiated with the student – an element of self-assessment. It is also possible that assessment instruments can be developed which look more objectively at the ability of the student to process information at different levels, from such ideas as the SOLO taxonomy (Briggs and Collins, 1982).

The value established for the course team was the identification of the amount of information available about the performance of courses simply in the assessment data that we collect on a regular basis throughout our courses – but which we analyse not at all. That the options were successful in achieving many of our objectives was obvious to all. So were many of the shortcomings over timings, weightings and content issues. But it was the comparison of perceptions and marks which opened up the whole issue of assessment criteria and practices.

Acknowledgements

The evaluation was undertaken as part of an MA(Ed) course of study and I would like to thank my course tutors Dr D Edwards, Peter Scrimshaw and Phil

Clift for their help and guidance. I also need to thank the staff and students of the college whose support made the whole thing possible. My colleagues at the Polytechnic who gave helpful criticisms need to be mentioned, especially Tony Crocker and Bob George.

References

Briggs, J B and Collis, K F (1982), *Evaluating the Quality of Learning*, Academic Press, London
Crocker, A C (1981), *Statistics for the Teacher*, (3rd edn). NFER-Nelson, Windsor
Green, P (1983), 'Chalk circles: the curriculum as an area of conflict', in Galton, M and Moon, R (eds) *Changing Schools . . . Changing Curriculum*, pp 144–168, Harper & Row, London
Rowntree, D (1977), *Assessing Students: How Shall We Know Them?*, Harper & Row, London

7. Assessment issues in relation to experience-based learning on placements within courses

Nigel J Nixon

Summary: This chapter is concerned with assessment issues in relation to in-course placements. It draws heavily upon a number of Council for National Academic Awards (CNAA)-funded projects in the area of experience-based learning. These are listed in the acknowledgements at the end of the chapter. The main focus of the chapter is undergraduate sandwich degree courses with reference to two themes in particular: the aspects of supervised work experience that should most properly be assessed, and the most appropriate forms of assessment available. Discussion of the two themes is informed by references to recent relevant developments in both further and higher education. Finally, the three appendices provide examples of a supervised-work-experience (SWE) assessment typology, a suggested logbook system, and a competence-based scheme for specifying learning objectives.

The higher education context

A number of current and impending developments in higher education are likely to have an impact on the assessment of in-course placements. These include the establishment of more flexible and responsive delivery systems based on modularized courses, credit accumulation and transfer and experiential modes of study, changes in the nature of the student body and the establishment of closer links between higher education and industry.

More flexible delivery systems

Of particular importance in this respect is the increased salience in recent years of credit accumulation and transfer schemes. Programmes of study under such schemes are no longer almost exclusively determined by the providers. Rather, they offer 'customers' (students) the opportunity, within certain defined parameters, to select topics best suited to their interests and needs and to study these at their own pace. Courses (and their sub-components) are linked to one another through a system of 'ladders and bridges', such that the achievement of one qualification provides a necessary and sufficient basis for some subsequent activity. Schemes of credit accumulation and transfer are greatly facilitated if courses are planned in a modular way and expressed in terms of expected learning outcomes incorporated into a transcript. Moreover, the specification of clear objectives and defined outcomes for particular programmes of study makes it possible to interpret coherence more broadly than in traditional academic terms through, for example, the inclusion of accreditation for vocational and professional activities frequently undertaken in the workplace.

Impending changes in the nature of the student body

Between 1984 and 1996 the 18- and 19-year-old population in the UK is projected to fall by one-third. The consequences for higher education of this demographic downturn are unlikely to be very dramatic since the decline in the 18-plus cohort is greater among lower social classes, whereas higher education recruits disproportionatly from the higher ones. However, it is reasonable to assume that there will be more places available than school leavers qualified to fill them.

This concern, together with widespread recognition that industry and commerce require a greater supply of highly qualified and educated manpower, underpins many of the current initiatives aimed at securing increased participation in higher education. This need is tersely stated by the Council for Industry and Higher Education in its 1987 paper *Towards a Partnership*: 'To compete in the international arena, educated brain-power and applied ingenuity, twin offspring of higher education, must become the UK's most distinctive assets.'

To meet this challenge, emphasis is being given to the creation of a more open, flexible and attractive system of higher education, one in particular which can cater responsively for the needs of mature and 'non-standard' entrants. The polytechnics and colleges sector has traditionally sought to offer a comprehensive range of provision in terms of level of course and mode of study, the aim being to facilitate access. Reflecting this ethos, deliberate efforts have been made in recent years by validating bodies such as CNAA to encourage the recruitment of mature and 'non-standard' entrants. Support has, for example, been given to the development of procedures for the formal assessment of prior experiential learning. Again, studies have been undertaken comparing the degree results of standard and 'non-standard' entry students on CNAA courses (eg Bourner and Hamed, 1987), the outcomes of which have indicated that, on average, those with non-standard entry qualifications fare at least as well as those more conventionally qualified.

These findings have led some commentators (eg Robinson, 1988) to argue that the debate about 'non-standard' entrants and mature students may be based on false premises and that concern should be with exit, rather than entry, standards. Finally, and more recently, a framework has been set up for the national recognition of access courses, ie courses designed to facilitate entry to higher education, particularly for those lacking formal qualifications and from groups currently under-represented in higher education. It is noteworthy that such courses are intended to be student-focused and androgogic (as distinct from pedagogic) in their orientation, and that one of the listed criteria for consideration in validating and recognizing such courses is that they should incorporate:

a range of modes of assessment, including self-assessment techniques with an emphasis on the learning aspects of assessment, and attention to appropriate certification, including profiles or records of achievement. (CNAA/CVCP, February 1989)

Nor should it be assumed that developments in course structures, teaching methods and assessment practices of the kinds mentioned above are simply determined by the need to respond to a more variegated student body than hitherto. The majority of 18-year-olds entering higher education in the 1990s will have undergone vastly different experiences from their present counterparts who have followed 'traditional' GCE O- and A-level routes. They will, for instance, have been exposed to the National Curriculum, will be familiar with Records of Achievement (which are to include the recording of practical and social skills as well as academic achievements) and may have followed predominantly vocational programmes of study such as Technical and Vocational Educational Initiative (TVEI). The net result is likely to be the possession of less subject-specific knowledge but greater understanding and skill in the application of knowledge. Also likely is an enhanced appreciation of context, coupled with experience of a range of individual and group coursework and (possibly) some structured work-related experience.

Higher education/industry links

Concern over graduate shortages, together with growing evidence about sustainable standards, has prompted industry to press for, and government to commit itself to, an expansion of the participation rates in higher education over the coming decade (DES, 1987; CIHE, 1987). Expansion of the system, however, is to be based on courses which, while eschewing too narrow a vocationalism, are perceived to be industrially and commercially relevant – the aim being to produce graduates equipped to be versatile and adaptable to changing work demands. It is this thinking which underpins developments such as the Enterprise in Higher Education initiative – coordinated by the Department of Employment, and launched in December 1987 – the proclaimed aim of which is to assist institutions to develop 'enterprising' graduates in partnership with employers.

Such initiatives derive from a concern, shared by a number of agencies (eg NAB/UGC, 1984; CIHE, 1987; RSA 'Education for Capability' campaign), to develop students' non-specific practical abilities alongside subject-centred knowledge. These all stress the importance of student-centred learning designed to enhance key generic competencies such as communication, teamwork, problem-solving, creativity, decision-making, risk-taking and leadership, and the need to develop these as an integral part of the existing curriculum.

Links between higher education and the world of employment are also being fostered by employers' growing recognition (itself partly precipitated by the likelihood of shortages of appropriately skilled and educated personnel) of the importance of providing all staff with carefully structured programmes of continuing professional development. Of particular importance in this respect is the collaborative development of schemes which seem to integrate in-company training programmes and employment-based projects with college-based course components – each part being formally validated and assessed for credit towards a nationally recognized award. Another similar development is that of Employment Learning Contracts. These comprise an agreement between employer, employee and academic institution in designing a learning programme for the employee that is work-based, and, hence, of likely direct benefit to the employer (in terms of enhanced employee knowledge, motivation and skill) but which is also eligible for credit towards a higher-education qualification.

Developments such as these are particularly important for two reasons. First, they recognize that knowledge and skill may be acquired in a variety of forms and contexts without necessarily being attested by formal paper qualifications. Secondly, they involve employers directly in the negotiation of programmes and the design and implementation of appropriate forms of assessment.

Supervised work experience and sandwich courses

Supervised work experience (SWE), defined as applied learning in a work environment, is not, of course, confined to sandwich courses. Practical placements, widely differing in length and form, make up an important and increasing part of a wide range of courses, including teacher education and health care. Nonetheless, most of the literature on the nature and purpose of in-course placements has been concerned with sandwich courses and these provide the main reference point for what follows.

CNAA's definition of a sandwich degree is that of a course extending over four years and incorporating 'not less than 48 weeks of supervised work experience' (CNAA, 1988, C 1.4, p 51). The CNAA Handbook goes on to state that:

> The period of supervised work experience must form a compulsory element of the programme of studies: its objectives must be specified and related to the objectives of the whole programme; the performance of students must be assessed; and satisfactory completion of and performance in the period of supervised work experience must be a requirement for the award.

In 1987–88 some 29 per cent of CNAA-registered students were enrolled on sandwich-degree courses. Not surprisingly, given the original advocacy of the sandwich principle, firstly by the National Council for Technological Awards (NCTA) in 1955 and later by the National Council for Industry and Commerce (Crick Report) in 1964, the majority of these students were following courses in engineering and technology (37 per cent) and business and management studies (27 per cent).

The Crick Report characterized the sandwich principle as being founded upon 'an interaction of academic study and practical applications such that each serves to illuminate and stimulate the other.' More recently this has been elaborated upon by George Tolley (Tolley, 1982) who analysed sandwich courses in terms of a number of long-standing ambiguities or 'tensions', which they served to throw into relief. These were:

☐ **Teaching versus learning** 'In sandwich courses there is an intrinsic recognition of the need to base learning upon experience and to provide opportunity for ordered reflection upon that experience.'

☐ **Abstraction versus application** 'All knowledge must have a base of abstraction. . . . But abstraction without application . . . cannot sustain the real world or the aspirations of most students.'

☐ **Detachment versus involvement** 'If detachment becomes an end in itself, then education becomes both suspect and lacking in purpose'. Involvement, it is alleged, enhances 'learning and competence' and should typify the non-university sector of HE, one of whose founding principles was that it should be 'directly responsive to social needs' (Crosland, 1965), thereby helping to counter the secular trend towards what Wiener has termed 'intellectual de-industrialization' (Wiener, 1981).

☐ **Generality versus particularity** 'The sandwich course emphasizes the particular, set within the context of application, so that the limits of generalization may be explored and defined.' As such, it provides a potent antidote to the seemingly ineluctable academic-led drift towards, on the one hand, specialization and, on the other, generalization on the basis of concepts intrinsic to the discipline.

Experience-based learning: what should be assessed?

Despite widespread acknowledgement of the benefits of work experience within sandwich courses, it remains comparatively rare for formally assessed SWE to contribute to a student's final degree classification. The typical focus continues to be on formative techniques for monitoring and recording the placement experience to ensure that students fulfil the minimalist CNAA criterion of *satisfactory completion* and that the placements themselves afford *suitable experience*. Survey evidence suggests that most course teams feel uncomfortable when faced with the difficulty of how to assess multidimensional social, interpersonal and communication skills, and the need to allot credit for these, alongside more conventional cognitive skills measured through discipline-based assessment strategies. Moreover, factors such as placement variability, and variability among employers, both in the form and quality of their appraisals, only serve to reinforce this reluctance. On the other hand, funding agencies note that sandwich education entails additional costs compared with shorter full-time courses, and the onus must be on its proponents to demonstrate that the output from such courses is of commensurately higher quality. Part of the evidence for this must lie, as the RISE Report (DES, 1985) intimated, in the effective integration of practical with theoretical course components, and this will need to be reflected in assessment techniques and weightings.

Reasons for assessing experience-based learning within courses

As mentioned earlier, it is a central platform of present UK government policy to ensure that every person pursuing a higher-education qualification should acquire competencies and aptitudes relevant to the workplace. Initiatives such as the RSA's *Education for Capability* campaign and the Training Agency's *Enterprise in Higher Education* initiative highlight the importance of project-based work, properly integrated into the overall curriculum, but undertaken in a real working environment and subject to joint assessment by employers as well as academic staff in the institutions. Work placements in general and sandwich education in particular are clearly key elements in this reorientation, as is evident from the development of a framework for National Vocational Qualifications intended to facilitate recognition of the ability to use skills and apply knowledge within defined contexts (DE/DES, 1986). This emphasizes that performance standards 'need to be defined', with their achievement 'verified by assessment' and adds the rider that 'some essential competences can only be assessed in the workplace' (NCVQ, 1987).

The development of more formal assessment schemes for placement-based course components is clearly consistent with a view of higher education that is responsive to changes in the work environment and to the needs of business and industry. It would also be in line with much industrial practice and would provide feedback to employers about work-related tasks while at the same time accrediting students for the abilities that they have developed.

Moreover, as Ashworth and Saxton (1989) have suggested, there are other, no less powerful, reasons for assessing in-course placements. First, by giving due weight to placement-based learning, it offers 'a more balanced profile of the abilities of the student – so that not only is academic capacity recognized, but also those practical skills and personal qualities that make for effective action in the workplace' (p 10). Second, rigorous assessment of placement performance signals the fact that placements are not 'a peripheral, soft and dispensable adjunct to the solid core of the degree, but [are] rock-hard and genuinely educational' (p 13). Student, visiting tutor and employment supervisor alike are thus able to see that their efforts have as central a place in the philosophy of the degree course as do more purely academic aspects. A third reason is that assessment of placement performance can help enhance the integration of theory and practice by, for example, encouraging students constantly to balance the practical application of theory against the theoretical implications of their placement experience.

Finally, and perhaps most significantly, assessment has a developmental, formative function and can make a major contribution to the learning process throughout the placement period. By setting a series of short-term goals for students on placement and by regularly assessing the extent to which these are being met, it is possible for students more realistically to evaluate their own strengths and weaknesses in the light of agreed objectives. In short, it provides a means of 'facilitating experiential learning, by providing relevant feedback on performance to the student, and negotiating goals for the future' (p 12).

Features of supervised work experience

The salient features of SWE, serving to distinguish it from other aspects of a course, would seem to be the linking of practitioner knowledge and theorizing, role change and locational change. Locational change is clearly of central importance as the following definition of work experience in the report of the *Review of Vocational Qualifications* makes clear:

> [the] placement of a student or trainee with a company or organization to give experience of the working environment. (de Ville, 1986)

Moreover, CNAA's explication of supervised work experience emphasizes the fact that the SWE component is an *integral* part of the course overall. As such, SWE and its assessment should not be considered in isolation from broader curricular issues, but rather as part-and-parcel of the total curriculum process. Chatterton, Roberts and Huston (1989) emphasize the importance of embedding SWE in a total curriculum-review process (with specific reference to business studies courses):

> ... there tends to be greater specificity in curriculum intentions in respect of the content and methods of college-based teaching and, to a lesser extent, learning than there is about the intended learning outcomes of work-placement periods. Moreover, there is generally only a poorly specified account of how college and work-based learning environments interact. SWE might be better incorporated into the overall curriculum through the use of a model which concentrates on the learning experiences to which students are to be exposed rather than treating SWE as an environment where the theory of the taught curriculum can be seen in application.

The focus here on learning and learning experience is commendable, but it does beg a number of questions concerning the quality and nature of work-based experiences. As Dewey pointed out over half a century ago, the view that all genuine education comes about through experience does not imply that all experiences are equally educational. Moreover, the term 'experience' has frequently received insufficient elaboration. Steinmaker and Bell's (1979) definition of experience as 'a hierarchy of stimuli, interaction and activity and response within a scope of sequentially related events' is useful in this respect since it highlights the fact that individuals, when reviewing events, tend to perceive the experience holistically in terms of a sequence of related activities having personal significance. The fact, however, that activities may be personally important does not necessarily mean that they constitute a valuable experience: practical activites can, as Dewey noted, be 'intellectually narrow and trivial' (Dewey, 1916).

Learning from experience

As Evans has indicated (Evans, N 1983; 1988) in the context of prior learning, what is important is not experience *per se* (however defined), but learning derived from the experience:

> The insistence throughout must be that the experience of a student is significant only as a source of learning. The intellectual task of moving from a description of experience to an identification of the learning derived from that experience is demanding. But if it cannot be accomplished there is no learning to assess, however important to the individual that experience may have been. (Evans, N 1988, p 7)

The point is equally relevant in the context of in-course work-based placements: SWE assessment should focus upon learning derived from experience. Learning, moreover, can only be identified through 'systematic reflection on experience'; academic knowledge (theory) has a central part to play in providing students with an interpretive resource for comprehending experience. Conversely, experience has little to contribute to understanding unless it is raised to the level of reflection. Ashworth and Saxton (1989) make the point neatly:

> The whole point of theory is to aid reflection on experience; and only

experience which is raised to the level of reflection (and therefore open to theoretical treatment) really counts as experience. (p 27)

This shift of focus from descriptions of experience to the identification of learning derived from specific experiences has affinities with Kolb's four-stage cyclical model of experiential learning based on an iterative process involving concrete experience, reflective observation, abstract conceptualization and active experimentation (Kolb, 1984).

Reflection, then, is central to the identification and, hence, the assessment of experience-based learning. But what precisely is reflection and how may it be facilitated? Reflection implies distancing oneself – at least momentarily – from one's actions and attempting to discern in a systematic fashion the relationship between what one has done and what has happened in consequence. This requires the development of an ability to provide detailed and 'thick' (Geertz, 1973) descriptions of events, to categorize, analyse and evaluate experiences, and to drawn out lessons for the future. A battery of methods to aid structured reflection have been used, such as diaries of various types, questionnaires and structured checklists, structured discussions, peer appraisal, video and audio recordings, 'shared time' and 'mutual interviewing', and the provision of 'models' of reflection (FEU, 1988). Many of these are relevant to SWE assessment.

Thus, systematic reflection on experience, using appropriate methods, is necessary if the learning derived from the experience is to be identified. At the same time, account needs to be taken of the fact that experienced practitioners sometimes encounter difficulty in formulating what they do in terms of theories, rules and procedures. There is not infrequently an ineffable component at the heart of a particular skill. The implication is that what students may be expected to learn from experienced practitioners during placement may be limited and the assessment of SWE will need to make allowances for this.

Learning objectives

Acknowledgement that what should be assessed on in-course placements is the significant learning derived from experience, and identified through a process of systematic reflection, gives rise to a further question: according to what criteria does one decide whether a particular facet of SWE is significant or not? Given the variety of phenomena to which assessors might direct their attention, an appropriate framework for assessing learning outcomes is required and this presupposes the prior formulation of aims and objectives for placement-based learning. In so far as CNAA-validated sandwich courses are concerned, these have typically been expressed in general terms, eg to imbue students with an informed awareness of industrial and professional situations or to enable students to acquire skills which are a normal requirement of careers to which their courses relate. What course teams need to do is to specify, within this broad framework, learning objectives for placements for their particular course so that students may be guided concerning the types of learning that they should seek on placement. A particularly illuminating example of this (formulated by Jones (1987) with reference to public administration degrees) is reproduced here.

LEARNING OBJECTIVES OF PLACEMENTS

☐ Obtain the benefits to be derived from the symbiosis of theory and practice by relating the knowledge and insights acquired during the course to the practical aspects of administration.

☐ Gain general work experience (including experience of the role conflicts, stresses and strains which the work process entails).

☐ Perform a job of work which is of practical value and benefit to the employing authority.

☐ Gain insights into their own abilities, aptitudes, attitudes and employment potential.

☐ Enter into professional relationships with practitioners in the field of public administration.

☐ Develop professional attitudes (in this context, the term 'professional' embraces the concept and ethos of public service in addition to the specialized interests and skills required in the public sector).

☐ Gain knowledge and experience of the work done by, and the special problems and characteristics of, a specific type of public organization.

☐ Gain experience of administration within specific functional areas (eg personnel, finance, planning, housing, supplies, etc).

☐ Relate and apply the knowledge gained during the placement period to the subjects studied during the final year of the course.

☐ Make more informed choices between the functional and service areas available to them after graduation.

Competence statements

The trend towards the development of more flexible forms of course provision, often built upon the principles of credit accumulation and transfer, has already been alluded to. Flexibility implies enabling learners to proceed through a range of learning experiences with a degree of choice over mode of learning and pacing, but this must be balanced against the need to maintain a sense of coherence and progression within course programmes. It is this concern which is prompting course designers to be more explicit in stating course objectives in terms of the particular learning outcomes that the course is intended to bring about. In the domain of vocational education in particular, this is leading to a competence approach to course design involving the specification of standards of competence, defined in terms of learning objectives and performance criteria, and the elaboration of appropriate assessment techniques and methods.

The development of competence-based learning and certification is also being driven by government in its endeavours to promote efficient, cost-effective and systematic vocational education and training which is regarded as crucial to improved economic performance and individual job satisfaction. Elements of competence and performance criteria are the written expression of the standards, based on employment needs, that were identified as a key objective for vocational education and training by the then Manpower Services Commission in *A New Training Initiative* (MSC, 1981). The approach has subsequently been elaborated upon through a series of reports and policy statements, for example, *Competence and Competition* (MSC/NEDC, 1984), the White Paper *Working*

Together - Education and Training (DE/DES, 1986). It also underlies the establishment of the National Council for Vocational Qualifications (NCVQ) in 1986. The NCVQ framework aims to produce vocational qualifications at a number of levels based on 'employment-led standards of competence'. These qualifications comprise a statement of competence recognizing the ability to use skills and apply knowledge within the context defined by the qualification.

In similar vein, the Training Agency, through its Technical Advisory Group, has produced a series of guidance notes aimed at developing national assessable standards based on competence - defined as 'the ability to perform the activities within an occupation . . . [embodying] the ability to transfer skills and knowledge to new situations within the occupational area.' In so far as higher education is concerned, a competence-based approach underlies a number of initiatives designed to produce a more coherent, nationally recognized system of assessment and interlinked awards for business and management studies. These include studies commissioned by the Council for Management Education and Development (CMED) to explore the feasibility of establishing a hierarchy of appropriate awards (certificate, diploma, MBA) within an overall competence-based framework, and pilot projects, sponsored by the Training Agency and CNAA, to develop a new initial award in management education. From this perspective, it is evident that government accords high priority to workplace performance and its assessment through the development of a workable and credible system enabling individuals to secure credit for performance in skills and competence tests carried out in industry.

Despite the general drive towards the adoption of a competence-based approach, at least in relation to vocational courses, it should not be assumed that the term 'competence' is unproblematic. One issue concerns the balance between skills and knowledge in definitions of vocational competence. As the Training Agency definition cited above and the NVQ 'Criteria and Related Guidance' make clear, knowledge and understanding, no less than skills, are considered to underpin performance in employment. It is noteworthy, however, that this has not always been the case. For example, in its original (1981) definition of competence, the MSC referred simply to the development of skills and their deployment to a prescribed standard in a specific context. Moreover, the inclusion of knowledge and understanding in definitions of competence gives rise to further difficulties. These are due to the fact that competence-based approaches are derived from the behavioural objectives' movement with its emphasis on 'observation statements' based (ideally) on direct and measurable observations of particular instances - whereas knowledge and understanding are mentalistic concepts, the existence of which can only be inferred on the basis of surface behaviour.

To return to competence statements, ideally these should have the following characteristics:

☐ involve clearly identified skills and knowledge;
☐ incorporate a range of work-based activities;
☐ employ work-based mastery assessment;
☐ be based on outputs rather than inputs;
☐ be capable of being observed or demonstrated or reflected upon; and
☐ be capable of standing alone.

Such statements are typically expressed in terms of broad sets of competencies that are subsequently 'unpacked' into more specific types of behaviour or attainments required to demonstrate those competencies. The degree of specificity in these behavioural statements will reflect different thinking on the concept of competencies and also differing views on the feasibility of assessing demonstrable outcomes of competence development. The term competence itself, moreover, comprises a number of interrelated components. Levy (1987), for instance, refers, in the context of the Youth Training Scheme (YTS), to four dimensions of occupational competence, viz:

☐ competence in a job and/or a range of occupational skills;
☐ competence in a range of transferable core skills;
☐ personal effectiveness; and
☐ ability to transfer skills and knowledge to new situations.

Implicit in this breakdown are two categories of competencies: those which are general and transferable and those functional competencies which tend to be job- or profession-specific. Since functional competencies are more prone to becoming obsolete, most emphasis is frequently given to the generic personal and interpersonal competencies as the following FEU definition makes clear: 'the possession and development of sufficient skills, knowledge, appropriate attitudes and experience for successful performance in life roles' (FEU, 1984). Thus, competence-based learning focuses upon the application of knowledge and skills through involvement in real and purposeful – as opposed to simulated – activities.

The assessment of individuals' competence is of particular concern to NCVQ: it 'must be demonstrated and assessed under conditions which are as close as possible to those under which it will normally be practised' (NCVQ Accreditation Procedures, 1988). An NVQ statement of competence comprises three parts: a definition of the area of competence and its level, a number of units of competence (each being a coherent group of elements having employment value), and elements of competence (the smallest specification of competence) each having its own performance criteria. Specification of this kind makes possible the accumulation and transfer of credits for demonstrated competence through the NCVQ's National Record of Vocational Achievement. It is, moreover, as pertinent to higher as to further education, particularly in the context of the development of more flexible forms of study through initiatives such as CNAA's Credit Accumulation and Transfer Scheme and similar analogues (eg the South East England Consortium (SEEC) and the Manchester-based Consortium for Advanced Education and Training (Contact)). Having said that, it is important to emphasize that much remains to be done in relation to the development of performance descriptors which can be used in the assessment of competencies. One such scheme, relating specifically to personal/social objectives, has been developed by the Huddersfield Polytechnic research team and is reproduced in Appendix A.

Despite the need for considerable technical refinement, competence-based models of assessment clearly have much to offer. To use such a model as the exclusive basis for assessment would, however, be unwise, particularly in the context of SWE. This is because in-course work placements at degree level are not simply concerned with the attainment of learning objectives, specified in behavioural terms, but with fostering the development of problem-solving capacities and practical reasoning abilities. The focus is on individuals' purposive and intentional actions as they attempt to reconcile apparently conflicting choices and seek to redefine situations and events. In this respect learning *processes* are at least as important as learning *outcomes*.

Thus, SWE assessments need to be devised so as to be able to take account of factors such as the extent to which students are developing a critical awareness of themselves and their actions (thereby enhancing their ability to learn from experience), the ways in which modifications are introduced into plans of action in the light of circumstances, the determination of strategies for clarifying problems, and the meanings with which students imbue their actions.

Types of knowledge

If enhanced knowledge and understanding, as well as skills development, are essential outcomes of SWE, then the question arises as to the nature of the knowledge acquired in the workplace. Cameron-Jones (1987), writing in the context of teacher education, refers to 'craft', 'practitioner' or 'clinical' knowledge which she defines as 'the knowledge which practitioners *acquire* in the course of their practice, *use to act* in practice, and *test* in the context and the process of such use' (pp 148–9). This action-orientated knowledge is clearly very different from propositional knowledge which is concerned with knowledge of facts or truths expressed in terms of propositions that are either true or false. Until comparatively recently (see below pp 93–4) this practitioner knowledge has had low status, at least in higher education, relative to theory-based forms of knowledge.

A further useful distinction may also be made between these knowledge forms and what may be termed experiential knowledge acquired through sustained acquaintance and interaction with an entity of whatever kind (person, place, thing or process). Experiential knowledge is particularly problematic since for experience to be made meaningful it needs to be communicated and for this to occur it requires verbal expressions which, in turn, reduces experiential knowledge to propositional knowledge. One particularly common form of placement assessment exemplifies this, namely that which involves students in the production of a report or presentation on their practical experience. Such reports or presentations possess advantages – for example, they enable assessors to share in the experience and they have the potential to offer students learning opportunities through systematic reflection on experience. Nonetheless, they 'reduce' experience as a 'lived-through' multifaceted process, and, consequently, are probably best used in conjunction with other forms of assessment.

The theory–practice interrelationship

The relationship between theory and practice has traditionally been viewed as relatively unproblematic. Practice has been regarded as subordinate to theory with the latter being applied to the former. From such a perspective, 'knowing-how' (practice) becomes equated with mere technique, lacking the status of 'knowing that' (scientific knowledge). In point of fact, the theory–practice link would appear to be much more complex than is implied by this viewpoint, with the balance between learning through doing and learning through the acquisition of formal knowledge varying according to context. Barnett, Becher and Cork (1987), for example, have illustrated this complexity with reference to three areas of initial professional education at degree level: pharmacy, nursing and teacher education. According to their analysis, pharmacy courses are based 'almost entirely on theoretical understanding', with the emphasis on scientific knowledge. Pharmacy graduates are required to undertake a separate pre-registration year in a professional setting in order to qualify. College lecturers do not perceive this practically oriented pre-registration year as part of their responsibilities. On the other hand, such a degree of academic–practitioner apartheid is not apparent in nursing. For degree courses in nursing it is seen as crucial that theory should be 'generated from' and 'critically inform' practice. The nurses' knowledge-base must be 'developed from and underpin practice' in a complementary relationship. As for teacher education, 'the significance of theory stemming from, and illuminating, practice is shown by the way in which abstract theory is giving way to professional studies and to opportunities to discuss and reflect on practical experience.'

The relationship between academics and practitioners in the case of teacher education would appear to be characterized by detailed collaboration and not simply a generalized cooperation. Barnett (1987 has termed this a *partnership* model of professional preparation, and it has much in common with Schon's designation of 'the reflective practitioner' and a form of professionalism based on 'reflection in action' (Schon, 1983). This requires a distinction to be drawn between formal theory and practice-derived or practitioner theory. Whereas formal theory is generated through conceptual representations of an abstract nature and accords priority to explanatory models, practitioner theory would result from 'situational thinking' (Usher and Bryant, 1987). It is a device for understanding and validating the choices confronting the practitioner and the judgements that need to be made about how to act. From this perspective, the process of theorizing incorporates a repertoire of reasons for acting and may entail the eclectic borrowing of concepts and model constructs from formal theory. The importance of formal theory, therefore, lies in the fact that its representations and explanations can give assistance to practitioner theory 'not as directly applicable to the problem of the moment but as a source of metaphor and sensitizing concepts with which to view in a different way and to reformulate the problem'.

This notion of a complementary and dynamic relationship between two types of theory, the one gained through practical experience in the workplace and the other based on propositional knowledge acquired in academic settings, has implications for the importance to be attached to in-course placements. If the potential of 'reflection in action' for generating theory during placements is accepted, there is a *prima facie* case for the formal assessment of students on placement. This assessment should, moreover, focus upon the following:

☐ ways in which students' judgements and understanding are enhanced by conceptual representations and explanatory models;
☐ ways in which students review their practice in the light of theory; and
☐ the extent to which students explore the interdependence and interpenetration of theory and practice.

At the same time, however, account will need to be taken of certain situational impediments such as the fact that the day-to-day 'reality' of the workplace may well inhibit reflective practice, or the frequent difficulty experienced by students (and, indeed, their employment supervisors) in reflecting upon and articulating what they are doing (see above, p 88).

Ways of assessing experience-based learning

The issue of how to assess in-course placements raises questions concerning who is responsible for what, to whom and when during the placement. It will also be affected by the ability and willingness of employment supervisors to involve themselves in the assessment process. The following paragraphs discuss the part played by the principal participants in the assessment process – college-based tutors (placement tutors and/or visiting tutors), employment supervisors and the students themselves.

Participants in the assessment process

COLLEGE-BASED TUTORS
Most sandwich courses include some form of visiting tutor report as an important ingredient of the assessment. The visiting-tutor perspective is important since it bestows some comparability, and hence objectivity, on the assessment, given that tutors will normally be involved with more than one placement student. Visiting tutors also have a key role to play as moderators of the appraisals made by employment supervisors who necessarily have a more partial and limited view of students and placements. They are also uniquely well placed to assess students' ability to relate their practical experience to academic issues. Nonetheless, the intensity of visitor tutors' involvement in student assessment should not be such as to subvert some of their other functions, in particular: diagnosing students' needs, supporting students in self-evaluation, generally counselling students, and evaluating placements in terms of their overall suitability.

EMPLOYMENT SUPERVISORS
Employment-supervisor input to student assessment is vital since only the employment supervisor is in close and continuous contact with the student during the placement. Whatever form this may take ('closed', pro formas, appraisal records based on 'open' interviews, etc), it is important to be aware of the sorts of problem which typically occur. These include:

☐ varying standards by which student performance is assessed due to uncertainty concerning the level of work the student can reasonably be expected to attain;
☐ stereotyping and/or personality conflicts which may distort an employer's view of a student;
☐ a tendency to assess student performance highly so as not to have an

adverse effect on students' degree chances (or, indeed, because a poor performance record may reflect negatively on their own supervisory skills);

☐ difficulties in ensuring that the supervisor (or supervisors) directly involved in observing students in a range of employment situations actually complete the appraisal report (as opposed to training personnel or higher management);

☐ a tendency to highlight personal qualities, such as communication skills, with insufficient attention being paid to technical competence (possession of which may be taken for granted).

Also, given that the developmental process inherent in the placement is no less important than the performance outcomes, employment-supervisor assessment should ideally embrace formative feedback on a regular basis, eg through two-way appraisal interviews, in addition to the summative assessment.

STUDENTS

Students are also key actors in the assessment process, in that perhaps the prime objective of assessing work-based learning is to inculcate in students the ability to undertake their own continuous self-appraisal, subsequently developed throughout their professional career. Students are, moreover, best able to evaluate what they have learnt in the course of the placement, and to relate that learning to other parts of the course.

Care, however, needs to be taken in interpreting student self-assessments given students' widely reported tendency to be over-critical. Logbooks (see below), as a means of recording and reflecting on the placement period, can act as a major stimulant to such self-evaluation, encouraging students to identify the learning potential of their placement and ways of further improving their work performance.

The extent to which each of the key actors becomes involved in the assessment process, and the nature of the interlinkages between them, will have evident ramifications for reaching decisions upon an appropriate general assessment framework for SWE. Whatever the framework finally adopted, it will need to take into account factors such as the following:

☐ the development of criteria for selecting appropriate opportunities for students to demonstrate their competencies;

☐ the development of marking/grading schema, including the determination of relative weightings for different aspects, eg reflection and analysis, communication skills;

☐ mechanisms for reporting competencies acquired in the workplace.

Appendix B details one assessment framework developed by Chatterton, Roberts and Huston (1989) as part of a CNAA-funded project. The proposed framework serves to highlight three particularly important issues:

☐ the need to view placement assessment as a *process* rather than a discrete event;

☐ the need to regard placement assessment as a *corporate* endeavour, with each of the three main participants making important inputs;

☐ the importance of granting placement assessment *equal* status with other forms of course assessment.

The focus on *process* involves decisions concerning what information is relevant, how it is to be gathered and how it is to be reported upon. The potential afforded by *task-based logbooks* in this respect is highlighted, and appendix C provides details of one such logbook system (that devised by the Huddersfield Polytechnic research team).

The need, however, to make decisions concerning what constitutes relevant information implies the prior establishment of criteria by which to judge such information. Criteria of relevance will usually be established in relation to the kinds of achievements it is considered worthwhile to report upon; these achievements will normally be assessed in terms of levels or standards of performance. This tends to be particularly problematic in the case of placement assessment for a number of reasons. First, as is evident from the discussion of profiling below (pp 98–9), it is not always easy to achieve a consensus viewpoint on which qualities are to be appraised. Secondly, many of the qualities deemed appropriate are not amenable to the mechanical application of prescribed standards but require assessment in terms of more elusive, judgemental criteria. Thirdly, questions arise concerning the extent to which those assessing students in the workplace are able accurately to perceive the evidence on which their judgements are based (Ashworth and Saxton, pp 17–24). It should be added, however, that these do not constitute an argument for abandoning the assessment of in-course placements. Indeed, many of the points raised may be applied with equal force to college-based assessments. Rather, they emphasize the importance of reliability and validity and the development of assessment techniques designed to enhance these.

Validity and reliability issues

It is axiomatic that forms of assessment should be designed to reflect the objectives that a course (or a particular sub-component) is designed to achieve. This principle is reflected in the concept of validity, which refers to the fact that what is being assessed demonstrably indicates students' attainment of the objectives in question. The fact that placement assessments tend to be context-dependent enhances their face validity. Nonetheless, this has implications for the design of such assessments, which need to ensure that appropriate opportunities and critical experiences are sampled and relevant observations made. In common with the ethnographic research paradigm, multiple sources of evidence should be drawn upon, permitting a wide range of issues to be addressed. One way of implementing this idea in the context of SWE is to involve a variety of assessors with different perspectives and (possibly) different expertise in the assessment of a particular student in the workplace. This will highlight the degree of convergence or divergence of the assessments, thereby helping to produce a more balanced and comprehensive profile of student attainment.

Sustained reflexivity on the part of assessors may also enhance the validity of the assessment. In the context of placement assessment this might involve:

☐ being explicit about the conditions under which observations are made, as

is generally the case for statements of competence;
- ☐ identifying factors that constrain the assessor's interpretation of student's work;
- ☐ describing the intentions behind a particular assessable item (especially important in relation to project-based work);
- ☐ verifying with others involved in the assessment process the evidence on which the assessments are based;
- ☐ offering a clear rationale for generalizing about a student's competence based on a sample of observed performance;
- ☐ relating placement assessments to course assessments overall;
- ☐ prompting students to reflect upon, and participate in, the assessment of their competence and to provide them with full access to the assessment.

Reliability refers to the consistency and precision of assessment procedures. Would the same assessors on a different occasion – or different assessors on the same occasion – arrive at the same judgement in a specific instance? In the context of placement assessments, divergence may arise from two sources in particular: variations in the tasks students are set and idiosyncratic differences between assessors.

To overcome some of the problems of reliability common to most forms of 'open' assessment (including SWE) a number of strategies have been devised. Three in particular (originally proposed in relation to naturalistic research methods, eg Guba and Lincoln, 1981; Kirk and Miller, 1986) are pertinent in relation to the assessment of placements. The first involves adopting standardized procedures for the gathering and recording of information. The second requires that the procedures used should be documented with particular reference to how conclusions may be drawn, making replication possible (at least in theory), and, hence, check reliability. Thirdly, by encouraging assessors to reflect on the tasks they are undertaking and the perspectives they bring to bear, it is possible for their observations about students to be brought into sharper focus and perspective.

Above all, attention needs to be given to means of eliciting consistent observation-derived information at a specific point in time as a basis for a particular assessment, the intention being to maximize the likelihood of all parties involved reaching a consensus. Even so, it has to be acknowledged that such a consensus may well be spurious, merely reflecting the fact that all involved have similar standards in relation to the assessed work rather than that the work is in some objective manner of a particular standard. This matter of assessment objectivity is, of course, common to all forms of assessment, and underpins much of the debate on norm- and criterion-referencing. In the context of SWE assessment, it may be said that, provided assessment criteria have been identified, agreed and pre-specified, there is some claim to objectivity and some basis for comparability.

Nonetheless, the difficulty of ensuring reliability should not be underestimated. Students on degree-level courses are unlikely to be assessed at the workplace on vocationally specific tasks for which it is relatively easy to specify and apply consistent standards. Rather, assessment is likely to involve complex tasks requiring understanding, reflection and the application of high-order general vocational abilities such as decision-making, creativity and teamwork.

This renders the prospect of achieving consensus among assessors more difficult. Again, one expectation of sandwich placements is that students' competence will develop over time; consequently, desirable change rather than consistency is sought. This clearly has implications for reliability expressed in terms of the preservation of consistency over time.

Profiling

While assessment profiles have received scant attention in UK higher education, their use (generally as a supplement to a final degree classification) is not entirely unknown (Klug, 1975; 1977) and their potential is considerable in respect of placement assessment. Profile reporting is a *systematic* procedure for recording personal development and achievement. It has been used, for example, in the assessment of prior learning for credit and is assuming increasing prominence in the secondary sector with the proposed introduction of National Records of Achievement by 1995.

One of the virtues of profiles is that they facilitate the reconciliation of assessments of different types of student ability. The aim of the profile document or transcript is to describe as accurately (but succinctly) as possible the range of knowledge, skills and experience of an individual in relation to a particular curriculum (FEU, 1984). Profiles attempt to provide a more broadly based and balanced portrait of a particular student, drawing on observations over a period of time and referring to personal, as well as academic, qualities (EC, 1984). Profiles, thus, appear capable of remedying what employers of graduates perceive to be a major deficiency of more traditional forms of assessment (such as single-grade examination results), namely the fact that many qualities and skills esteemed in the workplace are given short shrift.

Since the information contained in a profile is presented in disaggregated form, profiles offer considerable potential both for diagnostic purposes and for monitoring students' progress. The development and use of profiling instruments are not, however, straightforward matters. O'Hara (1987), in his study of a profiling system in action, has enumerated some of the issues that compilers and assessors have to address. First, the profile must be seen to be valid by all concerned. It has to confine itself to qualities that ought legitimately to be appraised, and these key qualities require explicit definition in terms that *all* users can understand. This is particularly important in the context of SWE, given the significance attached to the assessor's construction of 'reality' at the workplace and the fact that this construction tends to be in terms of expectations and assumptions concerning personal qualities and intricate abstractions of student activity such as 'initiative', 'relationships with others', 'dependability' and 'personal effectiveness'.

Secondly, the profile instrument needs to be used reliably. This implies that assessors are experienced in matters relating to appraisal more generally and that they are confident in their ability to use the particular profile in question. Confidence in the merits of the profile and confidence in their own judgement will help ensure that differences in judgements derive exclusively from differences of the evidence concerning performance and competence, and not because of significantly different perceptions on the part of assessors. A third factor relates to more practical matters. The utility of the profiling system (which, in turn, will influence the amount of valid data generated) will be determined by aspects such as the amount of time required to complete the instrument in relation to the time available to the assessor, the number and frequency of assessments that need to be made, and the number of assessors involved. Failure to take account of such matters not infrequently results in the adoption of a checklist mentality among assessors (Evans, M, 1988).

Finally, it is important that profiling systems are criterion-referenced, ie gradings should be bsed solely on the student's ability or level of performance in relation to explicitly defined graded levels. The problem, with reference to workplace assessment, is that assessor perceptions, particularly of behavioural attributes, tend to be context-sensitive, with implicit contrasts being made, eg with the attributes evinced by other students currently or in the past, or by other employees.

There are also major technical difficulties surrounding profiling systems (many of which are common to index construction more generally). Nuttall and Goldstein (1984) have sought to address a number of these, particularly those relating to the scaling, weighting and combining of items. Profiling systems incorporating rating scales (in an endeavour to provide quantitative assessments of learning outcomes) are considered technically weak for a number of reasons including:

- [ ] **Halo effects** (arising from the assessor's failure to distinguish between conceptually distinct and independent attributes). A high or low grading on one criterion comes to influence others occurring later in the profile.
- [ ] **Leniency or severity errors.** Higher or lower ratings than are warranted by the evidence are assigned.
- [ ] **The central tendency error.** Extremes of the rating scale tend to be eschewed.
- [ ] **Restricted range.** Ratings become clustered around a particular point on the scale.

Difficulties also arise in differentiating clearly between items so that there is no perceived overlap or redundancy and, above all, in formulating statements which succinctly but unequivocally define levels of attainment.

Notwithstanding the difficulties enumerated above, profiling systems are currently being incorporated into the assessment schemes (usually as an adjunct to more 'standard' methods) of a number of work-based education and training schemes. These include the Training Agency's schemes for Youth Training and Employment Training and Further Education schemes operating under the auspices of examining bodies such as the RSA and validating bodies such as The Business and Technician Education Council (BTEC). Even more significantly, profiling systems are being increasingly employed for the detailed reporting of assessment outcomes, both at the level of specific competencies and at that of individual course units or modules.

Student self-assessment

Student self-assessment is a natural outgrowth of student-, as opposed to subject-centred, approaches to course design. Moreover, it accords with the development of assessment profiles which, by providing more detail about a student's work and indicating progress and achievements in a range of areas, encourage systematic reflection on the student's part and so provide a basis for self-assessment. Student-centredness highlights the learner and the process of learning. It stresses the importance of negotiation and cooperation both between students and lecturers and within the student group itself. Learning from this perspective is an active process and implicit in this is '. . . the idea that students should learn to manage their own education' (Abercrombie, 1981). Student self-assessment, whether taking the form of self-evaluation by the individual student or involving evaluation by student peers, is normally an adjunct to lecturer-based assessment with students negotiating the final grade with tutors.

In the context of work placements, the value of self-assessment of this kind is considerable. It is likely to foster the development of self-confidence and self-esteem among students. It also encourages critical self-reflection and motivates students to become self-initiated and self-directed learners – attributes held to be essential to the enterprising graduate. Self-assessment does, however, have the disadvantage of being demanding in time and effort if issues relating to validity and reliability are to be seriously addressed.

Accreditation and certification

Accreditation involves the presentation of a formal statement of achievement based on a collation of the various assessment items for each placement student. As mentioned above (p 85), because of perceived deficiencies in terms of validity, reliability and objectivity, this traditionally involves a statement as to whether a student is deemed to have passed or failed the placement – a pass being a prerequisite for progress to subsequent stages of the course. One danger of this minimalist approach to assessment is that the placement receives scant emphasis, and, hence, has poor visibility, within the broader curriculum. This means that potential employers may not be alert to the fact that a particular course incorporated a placement component, let alone be able to inform themselves concerning the applicant's performance in this aspect of the course. From the student's standpoint, without a properly elaborated representation of assessment, feedback concerning task performance and work attitudes is unlikely to be adequate.

One way of overcoming this is to provide separate certification of the SWE component of the course. Such a procedure has affinities with practices on a range of four-year professional courses in areas such as social work, teaching and nursing which lead to two parallel qualifications: a degree and professional status involving a licence to practise. While this might help to allay fears concerning potentially adverse effects on students' degree performance arising from allegedly subjective work-based assessment, it reinforces the separation of academic and practical course elements. As such, it runs counter to the view expressed in this chapter that SWE (in any of its numerous guises) should be an *integral* part of the course in question. SWE as a designed component to enable students to acquire knowledge and skills through work experience which complement those gained in college is affected by what precedes it. In turn, it affects what follows.

There are, moreover, difficulties concerning the design of a certificate, particularly in terms of its external credibility to potential employers. Many placement tutors consider numerical scores to be inappropriate to the assessment of something as varied, complex and subjective as a placement. One suggested way forward would be to provide a transcript of activities incorporating a profile of achievements. Despite some of the technical problems associated with profiling (see pp 98–9), there is much to be said for representing performance in this way. However, unless the overall assessment for the course comes to be based on a profiling system, rather than degree classifications derived from numerical scores, the result will be that the methods used for placement assessment will continue to differ from those employed elsewhere on the course, with consequential adverse effects in terms of overall course integration.

Problems arising from too much emphasis on placement assessment

At the end of a chapter devoted to assessment issues in relation to experience-based learning within courses, it is worth recalling Ashworth and Saxton's (1989) observation that the effects of formally assessing placements are not necessarily always beneficial. For example, the placement experience may become distorted due to assessment, with students concentrating on assessable aspects of the placement (usually those most open to measurement). Again, intangible skills and motivational dispositions are central to the benefits of placements; yet it is precisely these factors that are so difficult to assess quantitatively. Thirdly, it is widely acknowledged that visiting tutors have an important pastoral role to fulfil; this is likely to be placed under severe strain if they become too closely involved in the detailed assessment of placement performance. Fourthly, the relationship between employment supervisor and student tends to have a major effect on the way the student experiences the placement. It is, however, subject to almost unlimited variation, with the consequence that any assessment of the student's performance will draw upon evidence which is outside the control of the student. A fifth factor relates to the legitimacy of assessing students on their placement performance when comparability of placements cannot be presumed. Finally, there is the fact that sophisticated (and arguably more valid) assessment techniques tend to be expensive in terms of their calls on resources.

Acknowledgement

Though the responsibility for this chapter rests with me, it owes a great deal to insights developed by those involved in the following CNAA-funded projects.

1. *Learning from Experience. Assessing Supervised Work Experience* (Chatterton, Roberts and Huston, Ealing CHE, 1986–88).
2. *The Primary Placement Project* (Cameron-Jones, O'Hara, Moray House College of Education, Edinburgh, 1986–89).
3. *A Process Evaluation of the Supervised Work Experience Component of a Sample of Courses at Huddersfield Polytechnic* (Bennett, Jackson, Lee, Huddersfield Polytechnic, 1987–89).

References

Abercrombie, M L J (1981) 'Changing Basic Assumptions about Teaching and Learning', in D Boud (ed), *Developing Student Autonomy in Learning* (London: Kogan Page)

Ashworth, P and Saxton, J (1989) *Experiential Learning During Sandwich Degree Placements and the Question of Assessment*, Sheffield Papers in Education Management 82, (Sheffield City Polytechnic)

Barnett, R A (1987) 'Teacher Education: A Changing Model of Professional Preparation', *Educational Studies* vol 13, no 1, 57–74

Barnett, R, Becher, T and Cork, M (1987) 'Models of Professional Preparation', *Studies in Higher Education*, vol 12, no 1, 51–63

Bourner, T and Hamed, M (1987) *Entry Qualifications and Degree Performance*, CNAA Development Services Publication 10 (London: CNAA)

Broadfoot, T P (ed) (1986) *Profiles and Records of Achievement: A Review of Issues and Practice* (Holt, Rinehart and Winston)

Cameron-Jones, M (1987) 'Improving Professional Practice in the Primary School', in S Delamont (ed), *The Primary School Teacher* (Brighton: Falmer Press)

Chatterton, D, Roberts, C and Huston, F (1989) *The Assessment of Work Experience: Issues Arising from a Survey of CNAA Business Studies Degree Courses*, CNAA Development Services Briefing paper 18 (London: CNAA)

Council for Industry and Higher Education (CIHE) (1987) *Toward a Partnership, Higher Education–Government–Industry* (London: CIHE)

Council for National Academic Awards (CNAA) (1988) *Handbook* (London: CNAA)

Council for National Academic Awards/Committee of Vice-Chancellors and Principals (1989) *Access to Higher Education: A Framework of National Arrangements for Recognition* (London: CNAA)

Crick Report (1964) *A Higher Award in Business Studies*, Report of the Advisory Sub-Committee on a Higher Award in Business Studies, National Advisory Council on Education for Industry and Commerce (London: HMSO)

Crosland, C A R (1965) Speech at Woolwich Polytechnic, 27/4/1965, quoted in J Pratt and T Burgess (1974), *Polytechnics: A Report* (London: Pitman), 203–7

Department of Education and Science (DES) (1985) *An Assessment of the Costs and Benefits of Sandwich Education* (The RISE report) (London: HMSO)

Department of Education and Science (DES) (1987) *Higher Education: Meeting the Challenge*, Cm 114 (London: HMSO)

Department of Employment (DE)/Department of Education and Science (DES) (1986) *Working Together – Education and Training* (London: HMSO)

de Ville, H (1986) *Review of Vocational Qualifications in England and Wales* (MSC/DES, London : HMSO)

Dewey, J (1916) *Democracy and Education* (New York: Free Press)

European Community (EC) (1984) *New Developments in Assessment: Profiling* (Working Document, Action Programme)

Evans, M (1988) *Practical Profiling* (London: Routledge and Kegan Paul)

Evans, N (1983) *Curriculum Opportunity* (FEU)

Evans, N (1988) *The Assessment of Prior Experiential Learning*, CNAA Development Services Publication no 17 (London: CNAA)

Further Education Unit (FEU) (1984) *Profiles in Action*

Further Education Unit (FEU) (1988) *Learning by Doing. A Guide to Teaching and Learning Methods*

Geertz, C (1973) 'Thick Description: Toward an Interpretive Theory of Culture', in C Geertz, *The Interpretation of Cultures* (New York: Basic Books)

Guba, E G and Lincoln, Y S (1981) *Effective Evaluation* (San Francisco: Jossey Bass)

Jones, R (1987) 'The Evaluation and Grading of Placement Performance', *Teaching Public Administration*, 7, 31–43

Kirk, J and Miller, M (1986) *Reliability and Validity in Quantitative Research* (Beverly Hills: Sage)

Klug, B (ed) (1975) *A Question of Degree* (London: The Nuffield Foundation, Group for Research and Information in Higher Education)

Klug, B (1977) *The Grading Game* (London: National Union of Students)

Kolb, D (1984) *Experiential Learning* (Englewood Cliffs, NJ: Prentice-Hall)

Law, B (1984) *Uses and Abuses of Profiling* (Harper Row)

Levy, M (1987) *The Core Skills Project and Work-based Learning* (MSC)

Manpower Services Commission (MSC) (1981) *A New Training Initiative*

Manpower Services Commission (MSC)/National Economic Development Council (NEDC) (1984)

Competence and Competition (Report prepared by the Institute of Manpower Studies, Sussex University)

National Advisory Body (NAB)/University Grants Committee (UGC) (1984) *Higher Education and the Needs of Society* (A joint statement by the National Advisory Body and the University Grants Committee)

National Council for Vocational Qualifications (NCVQ) (1987) *The National Vocational Qualification Framework*

Nuttall, D and Goldstein, H (1984) 'Profiles and Graded Tests: The Technical Issues', in *Profiles in Action* (FEU)

O'Hara, P (1987) *A Study of a Profiling System in Action* (Primary Placement Project, Technical Report no 2), (Moray House, Edinburgh: unpublished)

Schon, D (1983) *The Reflective Practitioner: How Professionals Think in Action* (London: Temple Smith)

Steinmaker, N W and Bell, M (1979) *The Experiential Taxonomy, a New Approach to Teaching and Learning* (The Academic Press)

Tolley, G (1982) 'Some Reflections on Education and Training' in Science and Engineering Research Council, *Future Patterns in Education, Training and Work* (London: SERC)

Training Agency (1988–89) *Development of Assessable Standards for National Certification, Guidance Notes 1–6* (Sheffield: Training Agency)

Usher, R S and Bryant, I (1987) 'Re-examining the Theory–Practice Relationship in Continuing Professional Education', in *Studies in Higher Education*, vol 12, no 2, 201–12

Wiener, M J (1981) *English Culture and the Decline of the Industrial Spirit 1850–1980* (Harmondsworth: Penguin Books)

Appendix A The specification of learning objectives for personal/social skills (Huddersfield Polytechnic)

To formulate clear performance criteria and to identify and assess the potential for learning at the place of work, it is necessary to formulate a set of personal/social objectives applicable to *all* placement students and a set of technical objectives that are specific to a subject area. The following set of personal/social objectives was drawn up by the research team at Huddersfield Polytechnic and is based on analysis of a wide range of data including employers' appraisal forms, interviews with students and employers, and students' industrial training reports.

Personal/social objectives

COMPETENCE AREA A (TECHNICAL KNOWLEDGE AND SKILLS)
All placements should provide students with opportunities to learn to:

A1 – Demonstrate appropriate breadth and depth of technical knowledge and skills acquired from the course.

A2 – Rapidly and efficiently acquire additional knowledge and skills required by the tasks to be undertaken.

A3 – Keep up to date with latest developments in the field.

A4 – Learn from people with greater technical knowledge and skills.

A5 – Deal with problems of appropriate technical complexity.

COMPETENCE AREA B (BUSINESS KNOWLEDGE)

B1 – Demonstrate appropriate breadth and depth of business knowledge acquired from the course.

B2 – Rapidly and efficiently acquire additional business knowledge required by the tasks to be undertaken.

B3 – Identify the people and parts of the company involved in and/or affected by the student's work.

B4 – Learn from people with greater business knowledge.

B5 – Take account of the broader business implications of her/his actions.

COMPETENCE AREA C (PROFESSIONAL CONDUCT)

C1 – Adopt the standard practices of an organization in terms of:

- ☐ dress
- ☐ hours of work
- ☐ punctuality
- ☐ company policies and procedures.

COMPETENCE AREA D (MOTIVATION)

D1 – Demonstrate application to tasks, however routine or long term.

D2 – Carry through a task from inception to completion.

D3 – Demonstrate self-motivation and enthusiasm.

D4 – Complete tasks in an accurate and thorough manner.

COMPETENCE AREA E (COMMUNICATION)

E1 – Present information/argue a case either orally or in writing in a clear, concise and accurate manner.

E2 – Display tact, discretion or assertiveness to inspire respect and confidence in a colleague, user or customer.

E3 – Conduct information-gathering interviews in an analytical and perceptive manner.

E4 – Participate constructively in meetings.

COMPETENCE AREA F (INITIATIVE)

F1 – Think and act effectively and independently.

F2 – Progressively require less supervision.

F3 – Contribute creative ideas and proposals to improve task management and the success of a project.

COMPETENCE AREA G (WORKING WITH OTHERS)

G1 – Demonstrate and maintain cooperative and helpful relationships with all employees.

G2 – Accept the authority of others and criticisms of work or ideas.

G3 – Display some leadership qualities.

G4 – Seek help and guidance from colleagues when required.

G5 – Offer help and guidance to colleagues when appropriate.

COMPETENCE AREA H (SELF-ORGANIZATION)

H1 – Plan and prioritize own work.

H2 – Ensure that such plans/priorities accord with corporate objectives and the needs of other employees/customers.

H3 – Organize workload to achieve maximum effectiveness and efficiency of resources.

H4 – Consistently meet deadlines.

COMPETENCE AREA I (JUDGEMENT)

I1 – Demonstrate a logical, objective and methodical approach in analysing the key aspects of a problem.

I2 – Make appropriate decisions with assurance and accept responsibility for them.

I3 – Recognize when *not* to make a decision.

I4 – Develop a self-critical awareness.

COMPETENCE AREA J (ADAPTABILITY)

J1 – Grasp readily new ideas, concepts and situations.

J2 – Change at short notice procedures, technology, responsibilities or assignments.

J3 – Develop new skills rapidly.

J4 – Undertake more than one task or play more than one role at a time.

COMPETENCE AREA K (CONTRIBUTION/COMMITMENT TO THE ORGANIZATION)

K1 – Accept responsibility to operate within timescale and budgets of projects.

K2 – Identify and act on opportunities to secure benefits for the organization.

K3 – Accept pressure/personal inconvenience by working overtime when required.

K4 – Represesnt the organization at various functions.

ONE POSSIBLE SYSTEM FOR RATING STUDENT PERFORMANCE IN RELATION TO AN AGREED SET OF LEARNING OBJECTIVES

This is based on a pro-forma reflecting the agreed set of learning objectives. The pro-forma would be completed by employment supervisors and may be used to appraise students both formatively and summatively. It provides for entries at the level of competence area, alongside which the employment supervisor is required to write comments and give a grade. Two pro-formas are required, one covering the PERSONAL/SOCIAL COMPETENCE areas and one which is course-specific relating to the relevant TECHNICAL COMPETENCE area.

GRADING

It is suggested that grades be allocated to each competence area based on a four-point scale. The advantage of a four-point scale is that it is one with which many employers are familiar since it is used on many existing staff appraisal schemes. The grades are intended to reflect the student's performance in relation to the employment supervisor's *perception* of the requirements of the job. One possible definition of grades would be:

0 *Does not meet the requirements of the job.*
The student fails to meet most of the job requirements for a specific competence area.

1 *Meets the requirements of the job.*
The student does what is expected at a normal pace but may not meet all the requirements of the job all of the time in relation to a particular competence area. For more complex problems the student requires considerable direction.

2 *Meets the requirements of the job and exceeds them in some areas.*
The student does what is expected rather more quickly, with more imagination and some anticipation in some but not all areas of the job. The student is learning from previous experience but, for more complex tasks, the student still requires some guidance.

3 *Consistently exceeds the requirements of the job in most areas.*
Basic objectives are achieved with ease and excellence. For complex tasks little guidance is required. The student anticipates and adapts, and, on occasion, is creative. Above-average results can be expected on any given task.

WEIGHTING
Given that each competence area may vary in importance for different jobs, there is a need to specify a weighting for each grade. These entries are suggested as follows:

1 = less important
2 = important
3 = more important

To arrive at a score for the appraisal the grade is multiplied by the weight and all the weighted grades for each competence area are summed. This enables a score to be calculated that represents a measure of performance against the highest possible score (defined as $3 \times$ summed weightings for each competence area).

The authors emphasize that the proposed performance-rating scale is just one way of tackling an inherently difficult problem. They recognize that it is open to many of the criticisms raised in relation to indicator construction more generally, in particular that it attempts to encapsulate in a quantitative measure complex concepts such as motivation and initiative which are not amenable to direct measurement.

AN APPRAISAL PRO-FORMA FOR PERSONAL/SOCIAL OBJECTIVES
This could be set out as shown opposite:

Competence Area	Comments	Grade	Weighting	Weighted Grade
A			2	
B			3	
C			1	
D			1	
E			1	
F			1	
G			2	
H			3	
I			1	
J			2	
K			3	
Maximum score (3 × weightings) =			60	
Actual score (= sum of weighted grades) =				

WEIGHTINGS 1 = less important
2 = important
3 = more important

Appendix B

Types of assessment available

Chatterton, Roberts and Huston (1989) propose the following typology:

ASSESSMENT TYPE	PURPOSE	ASSESSOR/EVALUATOR
Formative assessment	To provide feedback and to facilitate reflection on learning by the student	Student/Visiting Tutor/ Employment Supervisor
Summative assessment (i) Direct (simple)	To provide a profile of competencies of the student	Employer/Employment Supervisor
Summative assessment (ii) Indirect (elaborated)	To provide evidence of learning and a capacity to use it within the college-based curriculum	College Lecturers (including visiting tutor)

FORMATIVE ASSESSMENT

The development of *task-based logbooks* can provide a framework for formative assessment involving the three main partners in the placement process (student, visiting tutor and employment supervisor). In particular, they can:

□ encourage systematic reflection on learning, one aim being to develop students' ability to transfer competencies;
□ provide a context within which an employer's profile of competence might be judged;
□ help structure industrial visits;
□ provide fresh data for use in presentations, assignments and projects in the final year, ie have a washback effect on the curriculum overall.

DIRECT SUMMATIVE ASSESSMENT

The development of a profile of competence for use by employers to assess student performance in the workplae is desirable provided that a 'share culture' for assessment can be negotiated between employer and educational institution. A *profiling* system is to be preferred to more conventional forms of assessment since it enables a broader spectrum of abilities to be encompassed (Law, 1984; Broadfoot (ed), 1986). Existing appraisal schemes used by employers may usefully be taken into account in developing the profile which should include examples of actual tasks to illustrate how well each competence has been performed. An added advantage of profiles of competencies is that they require companies to formulate explicit performance objectives and so provide institutions with a measure for gauging placement quality.

INDIRECT SUMMATIVE ASSESSMENT

A set of criteria appropriate to SWE learning needs to be devised. This should be derived from a review of student logbooks and the profiles of competence. The criteria may then be used as part of the assessment objectives for grading projects, written assignments and oral presentations, thereby facilitating the *integration* of workbased learning into the curriculum more systematically.

☐ Assessment should take explicit account of oral presentations and communication skills, given the perceived potential of SWE for developing interpersonal and communication skills.
☐ Assignments need to be designed which highlight that learning from SWE is a *group*, not merely an *individual* process.

Appendix C

Suggestions for a logbook system

The following logbook system has been proposed by the Huddersfield Polytechnic research team. It comprises four parts as follows:

PERIODIC RECORD AND ANALYSIS
A periodic record of work done constitutes the framework which enables the student to reflect critically on the work being done. It is recommended that this should be completed at regular intervals (fortnightly or monthly for a thick sandwich placement depending on the variety and amount of change in the placement). The preferred vehicle for this analysis is a brief pro-forma covering:

☐ achievements during the period under consideration;
☐ plans/targets for the following period; and
☐ ways in which the placement might be improved.

TWO ACTIVITY ANALYSES
This involves the student in reflecting upon a completed activity about which some conclusions may be drawn. It requires the student to step back from the placement in order to appraise part of it. This activity analysis should be undertaken twice during a sandwich placement: once during the first half and once during the latter part. It is suggested that this should take the form of a report, having predefined sections.

The total length should probably not exceed 3000 words. The following is a suggested structure for the activity analysis:

Section a: Defining the activity.
Use the question box to define the activity.

What?	Why?
Who?	Why?
How?	Why?
When?	Why?
Where?	Why?

Identify the information needs of the activity, the processes involved, the outputs produced, the decisions made.

Section b: Defining the learning objectives involved.
What technical skills were required?
What personal/social skills were required?
What knowledge was required?
How was the new knowledge and skills needed acquired?

Section c: Identifying what has been learnt.
What problems were encountered?
How were they overcome?
What have you learnt? Why?
Relate what has been learnt to the course aims.

ORGANIZATIONAL ANALYSIS
The purpose of this part is to set the activities/tasks/projects into context by encouraging students to describe and analyse the organization in which they are employed. It is suggested that this should be completed about two-thirds of the way through the placement. The report should not exceed 6000 words and should be in free format. Recommended content should include:

Section a: Defining the organization.
Involving analysis and comment on the:

- ☐ nature of the business;
- ☐ objectives of the business;
- ☐ clients;
- ☐ products;
- ☐ suppliers;
- ☐ structure;
- ☐ financial data.

Section b: Defining your position in the organization.
In terms of:

- ☐ an organization chart;
- ☐ structure of department;
- ☐ jobs and titles of colleagues;
- ☐ tasks to be undertaken;
- ☐ way in which the tasks relate to the organization's overall objectives.

Section c: Defining the environment of the organization.
In terms of:

- ☐ its relationships with government and other central agencies;
- ☐ the political environment;
- ☐ the market place;
- ☐ technology;
- ☐ the legal position.

SUMMARY REPORT
The fourth and final part takes the form of a summary report of the value of the

placement set against its objectives. This is primarily a synthesis of items covered in the other three parts and should probably be not more than 3000 words in length.

The whole logbook would be handed in at the end of the placement and would constitute a major element of the assessment of the student while on placement. The focus would be on the extent to which the student has achieved the learning objectives identified for the placement. Though the logbook system described above is designed for one-year sandwich placements, it is capable of modification to accommodate shorter placements.

Responsibilities of the different SWE participants in relation to the logbook
The student

☐ To keep the periodic record up to date.
☐ To attempt to be critical and analytical rather than descriptive.
☐ To use the learning objectives as the basis for the evaluative sections of the periodic and other reports.
☐ To complete the activity analyses, organizational analysis and summary report on time so that they can be perused by both the employment supervisor and visiting tutors.
☐ To treat the placement as a learning opportunity and to exploit the vehicles for review (logbook, employment supervisor and visiting tutor) to obtain the best out of the placement.
☐ To be candid, but also careful, in criticizing the organization or the supervision.

The visiting tutor

☐ To make sure that the various parts of the logbook are being completed according to the agreed schedule.
☐ To help students be self-critical in their analysis, drawing their attention to the use of the learning objectives as a vehicle for evaluation.
☐ To exploit the logbook as the basis for discussion of the student's progress (both with the student and the employment supervisor).

Employment supervisor

☐ To allocate time to the student to complete the various parts of the logbook.
☐ To treat the logbook seriously by taking a close interest in the periodic record and analysis.
☐ To sign the periodic entries as testimony of having read them, and to discuss with the student any aspect of the analysis which might suggest the need for change or improvement in either the programme of work or the student's performance.
☐ To read and comment upon the various reports which together make up the logbook.

8. Performance measurement in higher and continuing education

Tom Schuller

Summary: Performance measurement is an issue of increasing significance within the public services generally. The chapter derives from the experience of an attempt to construct a set of performance indicators for continuing education. It briefly reviews the wider debate, and relates this first to higher education and then to continuing education. The author argues against the orthodox view of performance indicators as quantitative, unambiguous measures developed without regard for the institutional or professional context in which they are to be applied. He concludes by suggesting a number of guidelines for policy in the area, stressing the need to see performance measurement as a process of institutional self-development.

Introduction: public services and the politics of performance measurement

Wittgenstein said, 'Whereof one cannot speak thereon one must remain silent'. With reference to public services today this might be paraphrased as follows: 'Where one cannot quantify results one must remain apprehensively silent'. Or must one? In this paper I shall relate discussion of performance measurement to higher education, suggesting that the notion and the techniques of performance measurement are increasingly recognized as significant but problematic. Within higher education I shall then focus on continuing education and show how practical consideration of the application of performance measurement calls into question some of the existing definitions and approaches. The substance of this chapter derives from a practical initiative taken at Warwick University in developing means for measuring institutional performance in the area of continuing education. The initiative has resulted in the production of a draft instrument – the Warwick Indicators on Continuing Education – but in this paper I am concerned not with the practical outcome but with the issues which have been raised. The core of the argument is that while the question of performance measurement and the use made of public resources cannot be ignored, nor left exclusively to internal dialogue among professionals within a particular service, exclusively quantitative and externally imposed approaches not only suffer from technical limitations but are inherently dangerous to proper accountability.

Underlying the emergence of enthusiasm for performance measurement has been a general concern with accountability and value for money within the public sector of the economy, and particularly within the non-traded sector –

that is, services which are not paid for directly at the point of delivery. In the UK the context for this has been set by the particular stance adopted by the Conservative administration towards the public sector and public expenditure in general as part of its economic strategy, and by its political disagreement with several local government authorities. But the impetus behind this approach has fed off a more widespread concern with the use of public money and the accountability (or lack of it) of public services both to the specific groups which they are intended to serve and to the wider population of tax-payers and electors.

There are several dimensions to this concern. One relates to who decides what should be the goals and priorities of a service; an example of this is the natural tendency of medical professionals to wish to have at their disposal expensive high-technology equipment for use in such areas as heart transplants, to be set against the alternative use of the same resources for preventative medicine or more labour-intensive caring services. Secondly there is a desire to ensure that whatever resources are devoted to a particular end are efficiently used and pack the biggest public service punch possible. Thirdly there is the question of the mechanism for improving performance where it has been shown to be deficient in some respect, whether or not blame is in any sense to be attached to the practitioners involved. All impinge on the complex relationships between professionals and other employees within the service, managers and administrators, the elected representatives at national and local level who are formally responsible for the setting of priorities and the use of resources and finally the actual or potential consumers.

Public services are becoming increasingly familiar with the notion of performance measurement. The list of potential areas of application is extensive. Mayston, for example, refers in a relatively brief article, to the Post Office, British airports, motorway repairs, the National Health Service, education, local government and the Civil Service (Mayston 1986). Pollitt (1986) takes up three of these (the NHS, local government and education) and provides a critique of the trend to narrow the scope of measurement, especially in the health sector. Whittington (1988) draws the attention of social workers to what is happening elsewhere in the public sector. Other authors go into depth on single areas. Education is obviously a key area; the post-school sector is the subject of what follows, but the school sector has naturally been a major focus (see, for example, Hartley and Broadbent 1986; Jesson, Mayston and Smith 1987). A particularly fertile breeding-ground is local government, on which the Audit Commission has concentrated much of its effort (McSweeney & Sherer, forthcoming). The treatments not only cover a wide range of service areas; they also vary in the degree to which they offer a critique of current practice. There is consensus on the fact that existing measurement techniques are inadequate, but not on the extent of their inadequacy.

Many areas of the public sector grew very substantially in the 1960s and 1970s in terms both of resources and the number of people they employed, and this created its own strains. The decline of the economy as a whole, rapid social and technological change and the restrictions and uncertainties of government funding have combined to put further strains on management, practically and ideologically. The judgement is obviously a loose one; many public services have been and continue to be efficiently, effectively, economically and quietly managed. Not only does the private sector have no monopoly of virtue, but it is increasingly apparent that the supposedly objective measures of the market place are often inadequate when it comes to assessing the performance of a trading company. (The recent unsettling wave of merger bids has raised serious questions about the way information is generated and used in company dealings.) But the problems of being seen to be virtuous, of gathering and disseminating information which is both useful for managing and improving performance and for demonstrating to the outside world that this is happening, are perhaps greater for public services, especially those that operate in the non-traded sector. There is fairly widespread acknowledgement that public sector institutions are now obliged to make more explicit the basis on which they use the resources committed to them and the level of success they achieve in meeting the objectives they set for themselves. There is, too, a fair measure of agreement that progress needs to be made in developing the instruments appropriate for this.

It is the inadequacy of those instruments that is worrying. Evaluation of any kind is potentially threatening. The apparent menace is multiplied if it is seen largely in negative terms: the best that can be hoped for is escape from punishment. In the present climate this is too often the case. Fears of this kind are all the greater if the process of information-gathering is clouded in uncertainty and people do not understand or accept as both valid and relevant the type of information sought. As Kenneth Baker, the ex-Secretary of State for Education, observed in a speech to the Committee of Vice-Chancellors and Principals:

> The use of the word 'accountability' sounds negative and grudging, and I am not surprised that it has produced reactions ranging from negative to defensive or even superficial and dismissive. We have to achieve a better understanding of our different roles and agreement on common objectives. The terms on which extra funding is provided, and the joint commitment to monitor the delivery of what is agreed will, I hope, help to establish that mutual confidence (Baker 1986).

(It is worth at this stage only noting that Baker refers to *extra* funding; this becomes significant in the light of subsequent government publications which have promoted the idea of 'contracts' as the basis for all higher education funding.) Much of what is currently presented under the rubrics of accountability and value for money rely too heavily on narrow and easily quantifiable measures which do not capture the essence of an institution's purpose nor the quality of its service.

Higher education and performance measurement

Conceived of as a business, higher education in the UK has a multi-billion pound turnover, a labour force of many thousands and a huge customer population. Its performance clearly affects the future of the country as a whole, not only for the resources it consumes but also for the results of its labours in relation to the economic and cultural life of the nation. So much is common ground to everyone; the implications for accountability are much less clear. The complexity of the issue is well demonstrated by Pollitt (1987) who identifies ten different purposes for which performance assessment schemes have been implicitly or explicitly introduced. These include clarifying an organization's objectives, evaluating outcomes, indicating areas of potential cost saving, providing an input to staff incentive schemes, and enabling consumers to make better choices. His argument, he says,

> has *not* been against the establishment of systems to maintain efficiency. These will always be needed. Rather it has been against collapsing other, distinctive and important aspects of performance into one, efficiency-dominated set of appraisal procedures (p96).

The vocabulary of performance measurement is becoming increasingly complex. The issue is, of course, not a new one (see, for example, Sizer 1979; Ball and Halwachi 1987), but it has only recently attracted attention beyond a relatively small circle. A recent review points out:

> The indicator movement is in full swing despite the fact that at the national level the indicators used are only now becoming explicit, and the extent to which they were used by the UGC in its past rankings is far from clear (Cave *et al*, 1988, p16).

Some readers will already have been offended by my lack of definitional precision and apparent willingness to conflate performance indicators with performance measurement and evaluation more generally. The reasons for this will become apparent later. For the moment it is enough to quote the same authors, who provide a thorough account of the different types of indicators and the use to which they are put:

> The problem of interpretation and use of performance indicators is quite as complex as that of measurement itself (Cave *et al*, 1988).

It is precisely this interdependence that I wish to stress.

The debate on performance measurement in higher education, as elsewhere, has two major dimensions which are often confused. *Ideologically* there is a good deal of resistance at a general level to the idea of performance measurement because of its use as a device to restrict public expenditure wherever possible. Reactions range from an outright refusal to countenance the development of performance indicators through to a regret that more has not been done before to pre-empt the issue by evolving a more appropriate set of techniques. On this dimension the arguments cover such issues as professional autonomy, the acceptable level of state intervention in matters of higher education, the quality in their own field of the advocated private sector techniques and the contribution of public spending on higher education to both economic performance and social justice. The other dimension is the *technical*. Assuming that the need for performance measurement is accepted, how adequate are the instruments which currently exist? How and by whom should they be developed? And over what timescale should they be implemented?

The two dimensions are obviously closely interrelated – inextricably so, as I shall argue later. I shall deal first with the former, and review the criticisms that have been levelled against current practice. The Jarratt Committee on efficiency in universities recommended that a range of performance indicators should be developed, covering both inputs and outputs, designed for use within individual universities and for making comparisons between institutions. Reaction to the Jarratt Committee's report has been mixed. It is difficult to sort out how far the criticisms of its approach and recommendations derive from hostility to outside interference and reluctance to attempt institutional change, from a general condemnation of its rationale, or from specific consideration of its conclusions. In the background is the confusion caused by the difficulty universities have in sustaining their long-term planning capabilities because of the uncertainties of government funding policy. But the merits or demerits of the particular exercise have not undermined the case for more explicit accountability; what they have done is highlight the need for appropriate measuring instruments, and for an appropriate policy on the application of whatever measurement approaches are adopted.

A joint working group of the Committee of Vice-Chancellors and Principals was set up to respond to the Jarratt recommendation. It agreed that the availability of sound management information is necessary for the running of any large organization, adding that 'among such management information, performance indicators, as an aid but not a substitute for judgement, are essential' (CVCP/UGC 1986). The CVCP/UGC group defined its conception of performance indicators as 'statements usually quantified on resources employed and achievements secured'. Initially it listed 16 indicators in general use in universities in the UK, noting that a further 70 were used by one or more universities. A second effort resulted in a list of 37 indicators. The 1988 CVCP/UGC document on University Management Statistics includes a further 15.

Oh for the simplicity of a bottom line, a single figure twice underlined giving the overall results of the company's performance over the last year, with the previous year's smaller figure deferentially alongside to lend it added lustre. But apples and oranges are difficult to add together, and this veritable fruitstall of incommensurable products defies unification. It is not merely that the indicators have no common unit of currency; they refer to different parts of the process. Wagner (1987) makes the general point:

> Most. . . indicators are measures either of inputs or more usually of outputs without any attempt to relate the two. The only indicators which make such an attempt are staff/student ratio and possibly also institutional income and expenditure' (p 16).

He goes on to warn that:

> the danger is that managers, administrators or decision-makers will seek ever more sophisticated measures of inputs *or* outputs separately and believe, wrongly, that they are learning something about productivity (p17).

Other, similar admonitions abound. Sizer (1982), for example, notes the partial nature of the measures used and asks:

> Do those who develop and employ such partial performance indicators always remember that optimizing the parts does not necessarily optimize the whole? (p69).

and warns later against oversophisticated research designs that will prove both too expensive and impractical for administrators to cope with. In a comparative review of experience with quality measures for universities in the UK and the US, Bourke (1986) concludes:

> it is precisely this unexplained mix of inputs, outputs and processes, the combination of broad aggregate indicators and individual performance measures which made the British deployment of quality indicators so divisive (p6).

Yet the more convincing critiques are those accompanied by a different type of warning – that the issue of performance measurement and accountability will not disappear. The leaden inadequacy of existing techniques is not enough to sink it. In the first place it is politically unlikely to evaporate; and on moral grounds it would be an exceptionally thick-skinned claim to professional autonomy which rejected the case for a legitimate public interest in how higher education uses the resources committed to it. As Wagner (1987) concludes:

> It does not follow that pointing out all the problems involved in productivity analysis will simply lead to managers and policy-makers sadly shaking their heads and walking away agreeing it is all too difficult (p17).

The Further Education Unit recently commissioned a research project on the feasibility of developing a set of criteria to provide a valid and viable framework for an educational audit of further and higher education. Although it was not concerned specifically with continuing education, the project report is worth quoting on the nature of the task. First, it identifies several reasons why evaluation techniques have not kept pace with the growing need for information on institutional performance: the complexity of the concept of evaluation; the difficulty of defining 'quality' as an outcome; the complications of attempting to relate educational processes to society's needs; and the problem of trying to relate particular dimensions to an overall model of institutional performance (FEU 1986 p 86). All of these apply to the issue under consideration here; to them may be added the critical problem of changing the criteria for evaluating performance, as policy objectives change. The report concludes its survey of the literature as follows:

> Conceptualizations of the dimensions of institutional performance prolifer-ate but are fragmented, unrelated and require coordination... Present techniques and judgement procedures are inadequate to produce totally valid and reliable data ... current pressures for evaluation, both from within the education system and beyond it, are irresistible. The limitations on the capability to measure the performance of education institutions are no justification for refraining to do so. It is naive to assume that if educators eschew their responsibilities in this area, others will not undertake the task for them. The intelligent way forward is a cautious and thoughtful identification of the best available evaluative techniques and procedures, giving due consideration to their potential for further refinement, their strengths and their limitations, so building and extending the diversity of good practice that currently exists (pp101–2).

Where does all this leave us? Two key points emerge from the CVCP/UGC working party's report but with general applicability to a discussion of performance indicators. The first is the assumption that performance indicators must be expressed in terms of quantity. It should be noted that in the preamble quoted above the group referred to 'statements *usually* quantified. . .' and observed that PIs should be used as an aid but not a substitute for judgement. The question that this immediately raises is how performance indicators are to be kept in their desired servile state and prevented from assuming magisterial powers. Even in the most abstract and academic of contexts numbers tend to assume magical properties; when it comes to policy-relevant information which will presumably be used in the process of resource allocation it is essential to construct very firm fences to keep simple numbers in their appropriate place, and to define their relationship to other kinds of information. Not to do so is not just to do only part of the job; it leaves the numbers dangerously unsecured, like loose cargo sliding around on the deck of a ship.

It is of course possible to resolve this particular question definitionally, by disallowing any type of indicator that is not quantitative. No number, no validity. The case for this has its attractions, most obviously that of clarity. Performance indicators would make no claim to make up the basis for an adequate evaluation of institutional performance; they would simply be one of a number of inputs into the decision-making or resource-allocation process. But not only does it run the very real risks – just referred to – of the numerical driving out the substantial; it also means, ironically, that the whole notion of evaluation may encounter more resistance and criticism, since members of the institution and other interested parties will show their opinion of the adequacy of indicators to measure the service that they are involved in offering. It is notable that although most proponents of performance indicators in this sense acknowledge that their instrument cannot measure the full range of the institution's inputs, outputs or processes, they usually remain completely mute on the subject of what the rest of the measurement operation should contain, or on the relative weighting which they expect to be afforded to their own proposals.

The second point was made by my own university in its response to the working group's first statement. The Vice-Chancellor of Warwick noted that the indicators selected by the group contained no reference to performance in relation to continuing education, post-experience work or mature students, as well as earned income and industrial support. He commented that failure to include such activities will give a false public image of the universities' activities and fails to mirror national priorities for the university system. The comment points to an important weakness in current approaches to performance measurement. Objectives are not only often difficult or impossible to define in quantitative terms. They are also – or should be – subject to change, so that past practice may have only a partial bearing on desired future behaviour. Indicators need to be able to accommodate such changes, both in aspiration and practice. This is not to suggest that universities have or should forsake their established goals. But there must be ways of allowing the introduction of significant changes in purpose and orientation. The growth in significance of continuing education as a mainstream objective for universities should not be ignored when we consider the development of performance indicators. Yet a recent paper from a DES official to an OECD conference on Performance Indicators in Higher Education is not untypical in making no mention of continuing education, even though it is subtitled 'Progress and Prospects' (Cullen 1986).

Many of the issues referred to above can only gain in significance if the government proceeds to implement some or all of the proposals it has published for promoting contracts as the basis for funding higher education. The mechanics of this are as yet very unclear, but it is certain both that new forms of information will be required and that the generation and use of that information will raise a series of highly political issues. At present one can only speculate about the eventual outcomes, but to give concrete illustration of the kinds of issue that are foreshadowed I turn in the next section to the results of a working party convened at the University of Warwick to consider the development of performance indicators for continuing education. Before doing so it is worth noting that there are significant differences to be found in other countries in the way performance indicators are conceived of and applied, especially in their implications for the relationship between central authorities and individual institutes.

> In Finland, the 1987 legislation incorporates PIs as part of a revised structure for financing universities but, starting from a system in which central control has been detailed and prescriptive, the authorities claim that PIs will enhance rather than reduce the freedom of universities. This claim is echoed in proposals made for FRG and for the Netherlands. The argument seems to be that to apply objective indicators will both free universities from the more traditional, detailed and subjective processes of making a case for funds and establish clear rules of the game and a structure of incentives within which HEIs [Higher Education Institutions] can operate: (Cave *et al* 1988, p54).

In a more general discussion of evaluation in Swedish higher education Bauer (1988 p 26) observes that 'Decentralization of powers entails greater responsibility for quality and efficiency and with it for the evaluation of one's own activities. One can see therefore that the implications of the growth of measurement for institutional autonomy are highly dependent on the political context.'

Performance measurement and continuing education

In 1986 the University of Warwick made a small grant from its Research and Innovation Fund to the Department of Continuing Education for the development of a set of indicators for assessing institutional performance on continuing education. The object of the exercise as originally stated was to establish a common framework or set of benchmarks which could be used to gather information on what institutions of higher education are actually doing in the field of continuing education. This information would serve to monitor performance across institutions and over time.

The outcome has been a draft set of indicators, accompanied by a statement of the philosophy underlying their production (Schuller 1987). The indicators are divided into two parts. The first deals with numbers, primarily of continuing education students in various categories. It asks for the numbers of students on courses specifically designated as continuing education, of mature students on regular degree courses, of 'occasional' students sitting in on courses, and of distance students. These basic categories (and sub-categories within them) can then be cross-classified with a range of other items, to give the picture across subject areas, or the significance of modular courses, or policy on admissions and qualifications. The second part of the 'instrument' (the set of indicators) deals with policy positions taken by the institution, which cannot be expressed in simple numbers. Some of these are referred to later on.

The character of the exercise changed significantly over time. The initial approach was to treat the construction of the indicators as an independent exercise, the finished results of which could then be applied to gather information about the delivery of continuing education. Several problems emerged which made such an approach look increasingly implausible.

First was the difficulty of producing a set of indicators which could in any sense purport to be comprehensive, allow sufficiently for institutional variation and at the same time stay within the realm of practicality. Adequately to cover even this subsector of higher education meant the generation of a mass of possible questions, easily enough to discourage even the administrator with the most high-tech database and the firmest grasp of policy. For example, one indicator of an institution's commitment to continuing education might be the extent to which it makes courses available on a part-time basis. To gather accurate information on this requires a stipulation as to what is meant by part-time, a decision on whether it is important to distinguish between evenings only, daytime only and mixed mode provision, and some indication of the significance of the numbers of part-time students relative to full-timers. It also requires, ideally, information on the resources devoted to a part-time programme, and an indication of the degree of staff preparedness for teaching on the programme.

All these types of information have eminently concrete implications for policy-makers and practitioners. The funding of part-time provision is only just beginning to be approached on a basis of explicit rationality, and there is no agreement on how its costs and the financial support required should be estimated. If equity is one of the broad goals of the programme it would be very useful to know how far part-time provision caters for groups hitherto under-represented in higher education. There are many other important areas of information which could be reasonably put forward for consideration under this single heading alone. The probable result would be the consignment of the enquiry to the bin, or at best a cursory and unsatisfactory reply. The CVCP/UGC group quite rightly argued that indicators must be both as simple as possible and acceptable. The type of information which an academic researcher or a policy analyst concerned with longer-term issues might wish to get their hands on would not appeal to the instincts of the continuing education practitioner or administrator with a programme to organize for the next half-year. The approach to performance measurement must therefore recognize that there is an inherent tension between the information needs of the different agents involved – even where there is no actual conflict of interest, which may not infrequently be the case. An externally imposed demand for information may succeed if the demander is powerful enough to impose their requirement, but it is unlikely to generate the most productive climate for institutional development.

There is a further significant aspect to this. It is unreasonable simply to ask for significant amounts of extra information on a one-way basis. On the other hand part of the rationale for performance measurement is to encourage institutions to commit themselves effectively to improving their practice and to be able to present a coherent account of what they are doing in the field of continuing education. There are obvious resource implications in the collection of information, but it is in the long run in the institutions' interest to collaborate in the development of a coherent framework for the collation and dissemination of relevant information. The process can best be seen as a bargaining one, without implying either that there is equality of power between the negotiating agents, nor that the process is necessarily overtly conflictual.

The probable quality of the information elicited is a further consideration. There is some evidence from the health service that where the respondents, or those involved in feeding the required information to them, do not understand the reason for the request or are suspicious of the motives behind it, the information generated is often of poor quality if not downright misleading (Harley and Yates, 1987). This is particularly likely where the sole or chief motive for the operation is to uncover areas for reducing expenditure or cutting services. To find such reactions understandable is not to condone deliberate falsification. It is to recognize the inevitably political character of information gathering – political both in the general sense and in how it affects the internal decision-making of the organization.

Perhaps the most contentious point is the inclusion of non-quantitative information, discussed above. The Warwick group agreed unanimously that the exercise should not be restricted to the gathering of quantitative information only. At the same time it considered that this should not be taken as disqualifying the work from the field of performance measurement. A prime example here is the need to understand the extent to which an institution shows itself aware of the implications for teaching methods of a growth in mature students or a shift towards short course work. What steps have been taken to help the teaching staff in this direction? To what extent is specialized help available? Answers to these questions are highly relevant in two respects: they will tell us something about the quality of provision, but they will also tell us about the commitment to institutional change, for without some measure of staff development progress will be harder to achieve. Other headings to be found in the Warwick indicators under the non-quantitative heading refer to the inclusion of a contribution to continuing education as a formal criterion for promotion, the location of responsibility for continuing education within the insititution (ie an indication of organizational marginality) and the extent of collaboration with external agencies, educational and non-educational.

Obviously such a departure from purely quantitative aspirations has implications for the whole approach. It is worth stressing that there is no simple polarity between quantitative and qualitative, but a spectrum running from easily quantifiable and standardized data to information which is very much a matter of personal opinion. In between there is a range of possible facts and positions which fit with varying degrees of ease and certainty into a common mould. The crucial point turns around the provision of a context for the information. It is hard to see how a balanced statement can be achieved without context, yet there are many crucial institutional characteristics which are simply not reducible to figures.

One possible way out of the dilemma is to identify separate sets of indicators for separate purposes. Thus a minimum set of purely quantifiable data could be construed as acceptable for certain purposes, for example annual returns to the appropriate government department. A more detailed and contoured account would be required for the institution's own governing body and a still more complex sheaf of information would be used for internal discussion among those responsible for the actual management of provision. This may indeed be one way forward, but in itself it does not answer the twin questions of how the information is to be generated and how it is to be used. The significant reversal of approach which took place in the course of the Warwick work was to move away from a sequential and mechanistic model – devise the instrument, apply it, analyse the results – and towards a cyclical and collaborative model.

The latter can be characterized as a five-stage process, but with constant backwash and iteration of the kind that cyberneticists delight in sketching. The first stage is the development of the instrument or set of indicators, and concomitantly of the rationale for it. Second is negotiation with individual institutions, groups of institutions, or policy bodies on its use. This may entail differentiating between several types of application, and the different conditions under which they are to be undertaken. Third is the actual application of the indicators to gather information in whatever detail has been agreed. Fourth is the interpretation of the information. This may be a purely internal matter, for members of the institution alone; or outsiders may be involved in some kind of consultancy role; or it may be an expression of relationships between the institution and national or local government. Fifth is the implementation of any changes that flow from the interpretation, with the same range of possible participants.

At any stage of this process the indicators may be refined or the rationale modified. But even to insist on this, and on the overlaps between the various stages, it is not enough to remove entirely the mechanistic flavour. The key feature is the acknowledgement that the use of performance indicators involves a series of power relationships between the different agents involved: the promoters of the measurement activity, the measurers, the members of the organization being measured and their clients. Once this acknowledgement is made and recognized it opens the way towards a very different approach to performance measurement from that which currently predominates within the UK.

We cannot evade the question of outcomes. I referred earlier to the confusion between inputs, process and outputs which characterizes many of the current approaches to performance measurement. It would be odd to ignore output, yet the measurement of it poses peculiarly intractable problems. In the case of higher education as a whole, there are several measures proposed. Probably the most prominent are (for teaching) the numbers of graduates and their employment records, perhaps classified by subject, and (for research) the amount of published material, again classified by department. Each of these has obvious weaknesses. The quality of degrees obtained should presumably be related to the level at which students entered the course, and this has led to the introduction of 'value added' as a concept. This allows for institutions that take less qualified entrants to claim credit for bringing their students up to a certain overall level, even if this is lower than another institution with a higher level intake. Even so, the weakness of A level scores as a predictor of degree class raises questions about the validity of such an approach. Employment records are also dubious, in that jobs are easier to find in some areas than others; much depends, moreover, on when the measurement is made – immediately after graduation, six months on, or later still. Income level is the standard economist's measure of value added, yet the structure of the labour market makes this dubious, and it says nothing about wider notions of job satisfaction, still less about the effectiveness of higher education in endowing elite citizens with civilized notions and values. (See Cave *et al* 1988 for further discussion.)

If output measures pose problems for higher education, they pale into insignificance when one confronts continuing education in all its diversity. For one segment of continuing education, it is true, evaluation can up to a point be left to the market. Vocational and full-cost provision can be judged by whether it finds takers, and by whether these takers continue to put their money on the table. Yet even here there are difficulties. Commercial companies tend to prefer to assess training not at the end of the course but at a time when the skills supposedly acquired during it have been put into practice. Apart from the obvious problems of choosing an appropriate moment for the assessment and of devising appropriate techniques, there is the major difficulty of distinguishing the course itself from the factors which affect the individual's ability to put into practice what he or she has learnt. Some small research of my own into the effectiveness of shop steward training showed how dependent this was on the attitude of the senior steward in the company from which the steward came; irrespective of the quality of the course, where the convenor was supportive of the value of the training the likely impact was far greater than where he or she regarded training as little more than a ritual (Schuller & Robertson 1982).

Quality is a far more slippery concept when it comes to the range of non-vocational courses that are to be found in most institutions (Freeman 1987). A common motive for participation is the desire to rethink things at a point in the life-cycle when some more or less significant change is occurring – what Havighurst has referred to as the teachable moment. Domestic strains are often associated with the re-entry into education of one partner; are these to be attributed to the education, and if so on which side of the ledger do they fall? Given that many people participate in classes as much for social as for strictly educational reasons, what criteria are to be applied? These are familiar issues to any adult educator. As with the issue of measurement as a whole, the fact that they allow no easy solution does not mean that they should be ignored. Arguably, however, we should, while not forgetting the need for a constant concern with quality and with outcomes, focus for the time being more on inputs and process, not because they are more easily measurable but because under present circumstances the primary need is to remove the constraints on continuing education.

The diehard external assessor will greet this with a sceptical snort as a piece of blatant self-justification. As a tactic it holds out little hope for justifying the allocation of resources to continuing education in the face of competing services which purport to put their output clearly on show. My defence is not just a bluff-calling appeal to the rhetoric which commends an increase in the continuing education effort. I would argue simply that by beginning the measurement process with a primary focus on inputs and process we will at the same time get closer to an adequate grasp of output measures than if we busy ourselves directly with whatever the end product is supposed to be. (Even this position accepts too readily the input-process-output model, but that is another story.)

The way ahead: performance measurement as process

Where does this leave performance measurement as an instrument of educational policy? To reiterate: the issue will not go away; the debate is over how and not whether it should take place. Secondly, because it involves relationships of power it cannot be conflict-free and consensual, especially in the current climate. This does not mean that the conventional political groupings will appear in opposition to each other: there will be strange bedfellows as well as unfamiliar opponents. But in so far as there are productive conflicts as well as unproductive ones we can try to ensure that whatever friction is generated produces light as well as heat.

I shall conclude by constructing a number of pairings whose combinations make up contrasting approaches to performance measurement. Before that, I should like to glance briefly across the Atlantic – almost as far as the Pacific, in fact. Policy analysts in the state of California have been actively discussing the issue of performance assessment throughout the education system, partly in response to a resolution from Congressman Hayden that 'talent development, value-added and performance-based budgeting approaches to measuring and improving the quality of education' should be reviewed. (Hayden, it should be noted, is on what can be considered the left of the American political spectrum.) The Californian Post-Secondary Education Commission (C-PEC), a high-powered quangoish group of policy analysts, produced a report in response to this initiative. The report focused specifically on the financial implications of performance measurement. It noted, first, that approaches which base themselves on the assessment of student outcomes suffer from major defects. They are necessarily simplistic and too narrow in their focus; they tend to assume an easily definable causal relationship between education and change in the student; and the implementation of formal and rigorous assessment procedures needed to produce the requisite data are themselves educationally discouraging, notably to disadvantaged groups.

All of these points can be readily applied to the issue discussed earlier in this paper. But the CPEC report has more to it. It distinguishes between two basic strategies linking performance measurement to budgets. *Performance-based funding* ties budget appropriations directly to measurable outcomes; its aim is to fund *results*. *Good institutional practice*, on the other hand, is supported by setting funds aside to encourage desirable behaviour in the assessment area, for example through better data collection and staff development; its aim is to shape the educational *process*. The report comes down firmly in favour of the latter approach. It concludes by enunciating five principles conducive to effective measurement:

☐ funding for evaluation should be *supplementary* to the budget;
☐ *cooperation* should be encouraged between institutions, to improve the education system's aggregate performance, rather than setting institutions against each other in competition for a specific sum;

☐ measurement should recognize the *multiplicity* of the goals and functions involved;

☐ measurement instruments should be developed *over time*;

☐ it should be recognized that measurement is *only one* component of a policy for ensuring an institution's effectiveness.

To repeat, these points are drawn from an analysis which had as its focus the relationship between budgetary policy and more effective measurement. Yet given the American preoccupation with educational bangs for their bucks, the conclusions are striking in the emphasis they put on process rather than outcome, and on the need to tie the assessment process into a net of other mutually supporting activities.

There is, I would argue, one overriding principle that should govern the use of performance measurement; it is a good servant, potentially, but a bad master. We should, in other words, always be ready to challenge and revise the criteria and the techniques employed, aware of the pitfalls of teaching to the test. Given that guiding principle the debate should focus around the appropriate balance to be struck along the following dimensions:

☐ between the qualitative and the quantitative;

☐ between the encouragement of institutional diversity and innovation, and the need for some common framework for comparison;

☐ between the need to involve practitioners in the measurement process and the legitimate requirement of external accountability;

☐ between the formative, objective-setting, future oriented functions of performance measurement, and its summative and retrospective modes.

The pairings, it should be clear, are not simple antitheses. They offer practitioners and policy-makers scope for a productive debate, internally among themselves and between themselves and other interested parties. Judgements on where an institution or system should locate its approach on any of these dimensions is likely to vary over time. Such variance is probably one sign of a healthily innovative character; it does, of course, suggest a fifth dimension, between keeping a measurement approach constant to allow strict monitoring, and permitting variation in order to allow for fresh ideas and technical refinement.

References

Baker, K (1986) Speech to CVCP residential conference, September

Ball, R and Halwachi, J (1987) Performance indicators in higher education *Higher Education* 16, pp 393–405

Bauer, M (1988) Evaluation in Swedish higher education: recent trends and the outline of a model *European Journal of Education* Vol 23 Nos 1/2

Bourke, P (1986) *Quality Measures in Universities* (Belconnen, A C T, Commonwealth Tertiary Education Commission)

Cave, M, Hanney, S, Kogan, M and Trevett, G (1988) *The Use of Performance Indicators in Higher Education* (London: Jessica Kingsley)

Cullen, B (1986) *Performance indicators in UK higher education: progress and prospects* paper to OECD Programme on Institutional Management in Higher Education, Paris

FEU (1986) *Towards an Educational Audit: Feasibility Study* Research Project 304, Further Education Unit, London

126   T. SCHULLER

Freeman, L (1987) *Quality in Continuing Education* (San Francisco: Jossey-Bass)
Harley, M and Yates, J (1987) Performance indicators in the health service *Public Finance and Accountancy* 6 November, pp 9–12
Hartley, L and Broadbent, P (1986) Assessing teacher performance *Journal of Educational Policy* **3:1** 39–50
Jarratt Committee (1985) *Report of the Steering Committee for Efficiency Studies in Universities* (Committee of Vice-Chancellors and Principals: London)
Jesson, D, Mayston, D and Smith, P (1987) Performance assessment in the education sector: educational and economic perspectives *Oxford Review of Education* **13:3**, pp 249–266
Mayston, D (1986) Performance indicators: are they performing? in Mayston, D & Terry, F (eds) *Public Domain 1986* (London Public Finance Foundation/Peat Marwick, Mitchell), pp 39–53
McSweeney, B and Sherer, M Value for money auditing: some observations on its origins and theory in Cooper, D and Hopper, T (eds) *Critical Accounting* (London: Macmillan, forthcoming)
Pollitt, C (1986) Beyond the managerial model *Financial Accountability and Management* **2:3**, pp 155–70
Pollitt, C (1987) The politics of performance assessment: lessons for higher education? *Studies in Higher Educaion* **12:1**, pp 87–98
Schuller, T (1987) *Towards A Continuing Education Audit: Warwick Indicators for Performance Measurement* Department of Continuing Education, University of Warwick
Schuller, T and Robertson, D (1982) *Shop Stewards, Members and Trade Union Training* Discussion Paper 6, Centre for Research in Industrial Democracy and Participation, Glasgow University
Sizer, J (1979) Assessing institutional performance: an overview *International Journal of Institutional Management in Higher Education* **3:1**, pp 49–77
Sizer, J (1982) Performance indicators for institutions of higher education under conditions of financial stringency, contraction and changing needs in Robert McCormick (ed) *Calling Education to Account* Heinemann, pp 66–77
Wagner, L (1987) The concept of productivity in institutions of higher education: analytic report – Europe (University of Quebec/OECD conference, May)
Whittington, L (1988) The efficiency and performance assessment debate *British Journal of Social Work* **18:2**

9. Evaluation: a problem-solving activity?

David Clemson

Introduction

Formal educational evaluation is a comparatively new undertaking and like any new venture is still in the period of rule definition, refinement and development. In the UK, evaluation can be seen to be rooted in the early work of the Schools Council in the 1960s. At that time the concern was to improve what was being offered to pupils in schooling through the provision of curriculum materials and courses. Evaluation was seen as being primarily concerned with the quality of materials, and value for money. The influence of evaluation work in the USA was evident with its emphasis on measurement and the close definition of aims and objectives. But while this influence was ever present there was already a growing appreciation of the complexities of real classroom work and the ways in which materials were 'interfered with' by teachers and children. This appreciation led to major attempts by some developers, notably Lawrence Stenhouse (1975), to engage teachers in the process of curriculum development. Quite quickly there developed a separation of approach to evaluation based upon, on the one hand a centralized learning outcomes approach, and on the other a classroom process, discovery centred approach. This bifurcation, despite numerous attempts by some evaluators to resist the polarization, is still with us. And it is still with us for a number of reasons which are to do with research paradigms, political pressures, and the status of formal education in the UK.

In this chapter it is the intention to review the state of play in educational evaluation and to attempt to indicate some of the issues we now need to address in the further development of evaluation in the 1990s. This will be done through a consideration of some of the tensions which exist between educational research and evaluation together with a brief exploration of the most significant change to the educational landscape in the UK since the introduction of compulsory schooling, viz The National Curriculum. The basic tenet of the paper is that the word 'evaluation' is used as a catch all and evaluators need to become more analytical in their use of the word. There are a range of philosophies and expectations used in evaluative activity, only some of which should actually be labelled evaluation, with all that it implies about the exposure of and commitment to human values.

128   D. CLEMSON

Evaluation and research

Educational research has its roots in scientific approaches to enquiry and interpretation. In the early days of educational research there was an almost universal adoption and acceptance of scientific method. The use of control groups, the accumulation of statistical data and the formulation of generalizations and new hypotheses characterized research in education well into the mid 1950s. Indeed the use of quantitative data and the design of research based upon scientific method still continues. While there is a clear place for the collection of statistics in education there has been a growing appreciation over the last 30 years that there is also a need for well designed and thorough qualitative research. The development of qualitative research had a great influence on the development of evaluation exercises. As more techniques in qualitative research have been legitimized they have been added to the portfolio of the evaluator. At times this may have led to the idea that evalution is easy or amenable to countless treatments. A sort of 'have evaluation techniques – will travel' mentality; however, this does not invalidate the use of such techniques in evaluation. Indeed without the exploitation of available qualitative techniques evaluation by and with teachers would never have progressed at all and the idea that practitioners might actually study their own classrooms may never have emerged.

Alongside the development of qualitative approaches there has also grown an awareness that practitioners may be rather well placed to conduct research for themselves. The whole of the action-research movement can be seen as a real attempt by professional researchers to empower classroom teachers (Nixon 1981, Hopkins 1985, Walker 1985). Evaluation work has fuelled this power. This evaluation work is often described as self-evaluation and it is hard to see how classroom-based action research and teacher self-evaluation differ in either intent or effect. They are characterized by being context dependent, value laden, and centrally concerned with human relationships (Clemson 1985). The terminological distinctions are there primarily for the research community. The implicit rejection of 'evaluation' by the action-research movement is to do with a rejection of non-participative approaches and external accountability and monitoring with predetermined criteria. But this has only served to muddy the waters. Alongside the action-research movement there is a group of like-minded evaluators. Simons (1987) points this up in her concern for participatory, democratic evaluation. She is concerned that external, bureaucratic evaluation is excluding and overpowering other, more democratic, evaluation stances. If she is right, and there would now seem to be ample evidence to support her conjecture, then it would seem a pity if we appear divided within the evaluation and action research communities.

Given that there is a set of tensions affecting the conduct of evaluation it would be fruitful for us to re-examine evaluation in the light of the pressures upon us. Both research and evaluation are driven through a common set of techniques which are influenced by the prevailing scientific culture of the Western world. This culture is well represented by the current preoccupation and concentration of discourse and policy development on notions of problem solving.

Problem solving

Ours is a problem-solving culture, with the scientific and technological communities holding a central position in determining government policies and national priorities. The notion of the 'technological fix' has considerable sway over all of our lives. Science and scientific method seems unassailable, although it remains to be seen whether international pressures regarding environmental issues bring about a shift in emphasis. But even if this is to happen there is no doubt that science will continue to be at the centre of our thinking and our thinking is commonly defined in terms of our capacity to solve problems.

Typically approaches to problem-solving have four main phases:

- ☐ the definition of a problem, its relative importance and components;
- ☐ ideas for solutions are generated and decisions are made about how to initiate first attempts;
- ☐ the implementation of the chosen courses of action is then undertaken and the effects 'evaluated';
- ☐ the solution is reviewed and improvements are made if possible.

A problem is seen as essentially being about obstacles and objectives to overcome these obstacles (Instone 1988). These steps, and the order in which they are presented are very familiar to evaluators in that they are found in a number of models of evaluation activity (*see*, for example, Harris, NDC *et al* 1981). It is possible to clearly map the chosen order of progression onto the traditional scientific approach. In the same way much work which is identified as evaluation is clearly scientific and problem-solving in nature and philosophy. However, it is quite clear that in complex human activities such as learning and teaching it is not possible to meet the requirements of scientific method. Variables cannot be controlled, the parameters of experiment are often impossible to define, and many factors are not amenable to measurement of a transferable and external kind. Yet evaluation has often been justified on the grounds that its outcome is the improvement of a package in much the same way that designers and technologists claim improvements through problem-solving.

Eisner (1985) makes some potent distinctions between artistic and scientific approaches to qualitative research. He does so in the context of evaluation through educational connoisseurship and criticism. The major points to be drawn from his work for mention here are those to do with human relationships and situational uniqueness. While continuing the metaphor from art we might see that, though at any time, there are schools of thought and style prevailing in educational matters it is important to recognize and respond to individual portrayal and mastery of the art of teaching. House (1979) made a similar point in considering teaching as a craft and seeing this as part of a subjectivist rather than objectivist epistemology. The messages here are clear: if we are concerned with curriculum evaluation in the unique context of each and every classroom we have to abandon a scientific approach. But in so doing we therefore have to foreswear notions of problem-solving! This means that we must reconsider the role and function and legitimacy of much activity currently labelled evaluation.

Alternatively we may be able to offer a more sophisticated analysis of evaluation through a consideration of differences of kind when we associate 'evaluation' with such things as assessment and accountability. In order to fully appreciate the misuse of the word evaluation when used in relation to accountability and assessment it is useful to look at an example. The National Curriculum in England and Wales offers an appropriate and highly significant example for such a consideration.

The National Curriculum in England and Wales

The emphasis in this section will be on the National Curriculum as it affects children of primary age. This is for two reasons: first, there is nothing more important than the education of young children and, second, it is in primary classrooms that the National Curriculum will have the most immediate and probably longest lasting effect.

The introduction of the National Curriculum can be seen as the almost inevitable outcome of the modern history of education in this country. Following the reorganization of the education system in line with the requirements of the 1944 Education Act and the consolidation of the system in the 1950s we entered a boom time for educationalists. However, 'boom' is only a relative term for it might be argued that we have never really given the system its fair share of the gross national product. The sixties were characterized by rising rolls, comprehensive schooling and the demise of the 11+. The Schools Council was formed and rapidly embraced a liberal approach to curriculum development. Plowden and the so-called Progressive Primary Schools were upon us. At the time it seemed that all things were possible. But the seventies brought the first hints of detailed, and critical, accountability and by the mid-seventies we were witness to increasing criticisms of our schools and schooling. This culminated in Callaghan's launch of the 'Great Educational Debate'.

The eighties have been a period of increased central control of the curriculum although this would be denied by government as the 1988 Education Reform Act contains provisions for the movement of financial control and curriculum delivery to the individual school level. However, the content of what is to be taught, and the co-ordination of its assessment, is now firmly within central control under the auspices of the National Curriculum Council and the Schools Examination and Assessment Council.

The National Curriculum has been constructed using two main planks; subject divisions and the application of a set of aims and objectives for those subjects. Mathematics, English and Science have been the priority areas and these will be followed by History, Geography and Design and Technology. Other subjects will follow in due course. In all documents to date a similar pattern has been followed for layout and ordering of information. Each subject is broken down into a set of Attainment Targets (learning goals) and each Attainment Target is further broken down into Levels (up to 10). Children will be assessed at four points, known as Key Stages, during compulsory schooling. Key Stages 1 and 2 occur in the Primary phase and correspond to ages 7 and 11 years. Typically Key Stage 1 will assess children in respect of Levels 1–3 and Key Stage 2 Levels 2–5/6. Variations do occur on Levels within the subjects. Teachers will contribute their assessments at Key Stages and will be responsible for administering the external Standard Assessment Tasks. (See Clemson and Clemson, 1989, for more detail.)

From this brief description of the structure of the National Curriculum documents it is easy to see the models being operated. They are based upon an objectivist epistemology and are seen as providing a 'solution' to the problems of our schooling system as seen by some. It is easy to identify the scientific and problem-solving approaches upon which the National Curriculum has been developed.

It is quite clear from the manner in which the National Curriculum was constructed, using tight deadlines and nominated working parties, that no authorized evaluation was possible. Justification for the National Curriculum has been given in terms of national concerns for low 'standards'. Further there is no evidence to suggest that curriculum evaluation is on the agenda for the future. All of the use of 'evaluation' is in the context of accountability and assessment. Suggestions have been made, for example, that the National Curriculum will help to get rid of poor teachers. Schools will have to report Key Stage assessments to parents, and governors will have to hold open meetings. School governors will have enhanced monitoring powers and functions. Authorized evaluation of the National Curriculum and its assessment is objectives-based and summative in nature. So where does this leave evaluators and evaluation?

Evaluation in the Nineties

There is no doubt that the delivery and assessment of the National Curriculum is the major agenda item for those concerned with schools and schooling. It is equally certain that centrally controlled 'evaluation' exercises will be proscribed very tightly and will be geared to given aims and objectives. In such a climate it is vital that evaluators who do not subscribe to the notion that evaluation is a problem-solving activity offer an alternative view. Such evaluators must assume guardianship of both 'evaluation' and, in this case, the provision of a critique of the National Curriculum in action.

The values and judgements of teachers and children need to be given proper emphasis in any discussion of curriculum matters. The process of learning and associated teaching activity cannot be judged through problem-solving approaches. This is not to say that other forms of empirical knowledge than those arrived at through particular classroom practices cannot inform those practices, rather it is that the interplay in the classroom can exploit or reject external knowledge in order to further develop the curriculum for given children and their teacher. This means, essentially, that evaluation is about self, and self in relation to both others and selections from knowledge and culture. This might be envisaged as an equilateral triangle in the classroom where the corners of the triangle are child, teacher and task. The sides of the triangle represent the interactions between teacher and child, child and task, and teacher and task (Clemson & Clemson 1989). This triangle is subject to changes in its equilibrium through external forces. These forces act upon the teacher, the child, and elements of a task. It is these forces together with the day-to-day dynamic of the triangle which the evaluator must seek to make available to to the teachers and children. This is best done through participative enquiry and enquiry which is not trapped in a problem-solving mould. Evaluation is not research, although research can serve evaluation. Evaluation is not circumscribed by scientific approaches or methods. Genuine advances in curriculum development and delivery come through staff development which, in turn, is a product of self-evaluation. It is this set of connections we need to concentrate on rather than the seductive catch phrases to do with 'value added', 'efficiency' and 'performance indicators'. Let us consign these phrases to the areas to which they are best suited and get ourselves back to our real business, helping educators offer more fulfilling learning opportunities through real evaluation.

References

Clemson, D W (1985) Supporting evaluation in Kenya: a reflection on experience with the Kenyan adult literacy programme *International Journal of Education Development* 5(3)

Clemson, D W & Clemson, W (1989) *The Really Practical Guide to National Curriculum 5-11* Cheltenham, Stanley Thornes

Eisner, E W (1985) *The Art of Educational Evalution: a personal view* London & Philadelphia, The Falmer Press

Harris, N D C, Bell, C D & Carter, J E H (1981) *Signposts for evaluating: a resource pack* London, Council for Educational Technology

Hopkins, D (1985) *A Teacher's Guide to Classroom Research* Milton Keynes, Open University Press

House, E R (1979) Technology versus Craft: A Ten Year Perspective on Innovation in Taylor, P H (ed) *New Directions in Curriculum Studies* London, The Falmer Press

Instone, I (1988) *The Teaching of Problem Solving* York, Longman

Nixon, J (1981) *A Teachers' Guide to Action Research* London, Grant McIntyre

Simons, H (1987) *Getting to know schools in a democracy: the politics and process of evaluation* London, The Falmer Press

Stenhouse, L (1975) *An Introduction to Curriculum Research and Development* London, Heinemann Educational Books

Walker, R (1985) *Doing Research: A Handbook for Teachers* London, Methuen

10. Evaluating large-scale, computer-related educational activity: an example from The Netherlands

Betty Collis

Summary: Some special problems and characteristics distinguish the evaluation of large-scale computer-related educational activity from other educational evaluation situations and may serve as constraints to the conduct of an evaluation. Nonetheless, systematic evaluation is important. This chapter discusses some of these problems and characteristics, describes a general approach to such evaluation that can accommodate computer-related educational activity, and illustrates this approach through commenting upon its application to the evaluation of a national educational-software-development project in The Netherlands. The article concludes with an evaluation of the evaluation approach, paying particular consideration to its generalizability to other large-scale computer-related educational activities.

Problems in the evaluation of large-scale computer-related educational activity

Very often, decision-makers involved with computer-related educational activity – especially at the regional or national level – express the conviction that it is 'too early' or otherwise inappropriate to evaluate these sorts of activities. Various characteristics of computer-related educational activities underlie this conviction:

1. Evaluation is often seen as a summative, endpoint activity. Most computer-related educational activity, in contrast, is preoccupied with start-up and implementation decisions. In most cases, the endpoint is nowhere in sight or is not even defined.
2. Computer-related educational activity is still predominantly at the exploratory level. Evaluation is often seen as incompatible with exploration. It is felt that evaluation will somehow deflate the momentum or inhibit the activity of those who are being encouraged to develop experience in an area.
3. Computer-related educational activity is continually changing because of the rapidly changing nature of the field, both in terms of technology and experience. Evaluation of a 'moving target' is often felt to be unproductive and inappropriate. Traditional evaluation methodologies require too long a timespan to execute. Therefore, the recommendations generated from such evaluations will be outdated before they can be disseminated.
4. Computer-related educational activity is distinguished from most other

types of educational activity in that it is predominantly 'belief-driven' rather than objectives- or goal-driven (Baker, 1988). Policy for computer activities in education is often unrelated to specific outcomes, but instead is 'motivated by a more general desire to improve educational quality' (Baker, 1988) or by equally diffuse motivations to 'better prepare students for the future' or to 'improve students' thinking,' or even, somehow, to prevent a country from falling further behind other countries with respect to global competitive advantage (Collis & Oliveira, 1989). Evaluating progress with respect to visionary and vague beliefs is methodologically (and politically) difficult.

5. Even when a computer-related educational activity has distinctly stated goals, these goals are often aimed at a date far in the future (ie, develop software that will eventually be in frequent use in schools; change the role of teachers; through experience with computer use in a particular curriculum area, make changes in the curriculum in that area), which again makes traditional evaluation seem inappropriate.

6. No budget has been provided for evaluation (probably because of the above five reasons and also because all available money needs to be directed toward the never-ending task of adequate hardware and software provision).

All these are components of real-world practice and policy with respect to computer-related educational activity. Each of the six points can be argued as a logical reason for postponing the implementation of specific evaluation studies in the context of computer-related educational activity. In addition, large-scale activity by definition involves many different people and can involve many different smaller bureaucracies, each with its own way of doing things. Evaluative comment that criticizes subgroups as not operating efficiently, for example, can place great strains on attempts to coordinate cooperation between groups for the sake of the overall project. Constraints on implementation that relate to human idiosyncracies or to past experience among participants in the activity may be considered too sensitive to clarify in the context of an evaluation study. The relatively small amount of systematic evaluation of computer-related practice or policy, particularly at the large-scale or national level (in practice or in the literature), is probably a result of this human complexity as well as of the six points mentioned above.

Motivation for the evaluation of large-scale computer-related educational activity

Despite the constraints to systematic evaluation of computer-related educational activity listed above, there are important reasons why such activity should nonetheless occur. These reasons relate to both the specific situation and to the advance of knowledge in the overall field.

For the specific situation, systematic evaluation can serve various helpful roles. It can function as a coordinator and interpreter of different experiences within the activity, identifying trends and interactions. This sort of identification is just as important at the start-up phase of large-scale educational activity, where insights gained can be funnelled immediately into the project, as it is at some sort of 'summative' point. Because of the inevitable changes which will occur in a large-scale computer-related educational activity, both in terms of the characteristics of the personnel and of the computer-related resources available, evaluation can serve the role of interpretive historian, helping practitioners to learn from past experiences. And because goals and objectives are often so vaguely stated, evaluation can serve as the stimulator of consideration about these goals on a periodic basis. Through such consideration, a gradual refinement of goals and realistic expectations can occur.

Evaluation is important not only to the specific situation, but also to the general cause of better understanding of computer-related activity in education. Research studies which focus on a controlled situation and a limited set of variables are often difficult for the practitioner to apply to their large-scale situation. A better representation in the literature of evaluation studies, including a more realistic range of real-world factors that constrain or shape computer-related educational activity in practice, could facilitate a synthesis of experience in a way that is as pertinent to the decision-maker in the field as to the researcher. Planning and expectations can be improved if decision-makers have a more informed sense of the predictable problems which constrain implementation of computer-related innovation in the field. Such better understanding can lead to savings in time, energy and cost, as well as preventing the build-up of overly simple expectations among initial participants in a computer-related initiative.

What can be valuable therefore is an approach to evaluation that embodies the above benefits but also directly acknowledges the six constraining areas mentioned earlier.

Strategies for the evaluation of large-scale computer-related educational activity

It is clear that evaluation activity should acknowledge and accommodate the characteristics of large-scale computer-related activity rather than presuppose a situation where the problems associated with these characteristics are not pertinent. What seems to be needed, relative to the six points listed above, is an approach to evaluation that:

- ☐ emphasizes the formative aspect of evaluation;
- ☐ is perceived as a constructive contribution rather than as a judgemental commentary and is seen to be stimulating to those involved in exploratory activities;
- ☐ is able to provide, in a timely manner, comments about an existing situation, but also able to reorient itself quickly to new realities in the situation (this means that an iterative approach relative to the parameters of the evaluation is necessary);
- ☐ has as part of its contribution the possibility of stimulating the sharper articulation of intentions and goals for the computer-related activity, but is also able to proceed when goals are only vaguely formulated;
- ☐ is able to predict progress toward long-range goals by using interim evaluative benchmarks; and
- ☐ can be done in a relatively casual and inexpensive manner.

In addition, the approach must be executed in a way that respects the sensitivities involved in trying to foster cooperation among sometimes disparate groups of people. In the next section, we describe a framework for an evaluation approach that meets these requirements.

A general framework for the evaluation of large-scale computer-related educational activity

A simple framework, based on Robert Stake's (1973) concepts of congruency and contingency and his (1977) concepts of preordinate and responsive evaluation, can meet the above requirements and has been used in a number of large-scale, computer-related evaluation studies. The framework can be represented by the diagram in Figure 1.

As can be seen, the framework consists of six boxes in two columns, interconnected with various arrows. The left hand column represents the intentions, or plans, of an activity, and the right hand column represents what actually happens. It is important to note that the content of the boxes can change many times during the course of the evaluation. This is due to the other aspect

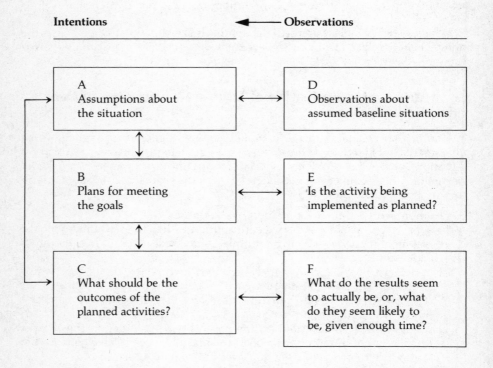

Figure 1 *A framework for evaluating computer-related educational activity, adapted from* Stake, (1973)

of the framework: the arrows. The arrows describe the different paths of evaluative analysis possible with the framework. The first analysis-set interrelates boxes A, B and C. At any point in the project, but especially before events have progressed very far, analysis can be made of what Stake calls the 'logical contingencies', or logical relationships, between the assumed baseline characteristics of the system, the outcomes that are hoped for, and the activities that are planned to move the basic elements of the system toward the intended goals.

A second analysis focus relates to a comparison of boxes A and D, boxes B and E, and boxes C and F. Stake calls this an assessment of the congruencies in the system. A congruency assessment between boxes B and E can occur at any time when the activity has moved beyond the planning stage. An intelligent 'guess' or appraisal of the congruency between boxes C and F can also occur at any time once execution of activities of the project have begun. (It is this congruency, taken at the endpoint of a project, which is typically the basis for summative evaluations.) A congruency assessment between boxes A and D usually occurs after the interpretive analysis described in the next paragraph.

A third analysis focus in the system relates to the interpretation of incongruencies between boxes B and E, or between boxes C and F. It is at this point that the system is particularly powerful. When incongruencies exist, and they seem to be inevitable, it is important to be able to categorize them as relating to 'theory or planning breakdown' or to 'execution breakdown' (Suchman, 1976). Do the incongruencies arise because some aspects of the logical planning of the activity should be reconsidered? In particular, do some of the assumptions about the baseline characteristics of the system (such as the capabilities or motivations of the people involved) need to be modified? (This is where a careful consideration of the components of boxes A and D often occurs.) Or do the incongruencies arise because of execution deviations from what was intended? If so, how can these deviations be rectified? If they cannot realistically be rectified, there is a 'theory' or intention problem in the system.

The last analysis focus relates to making recommendations that can change the state of the system. If theory breakdowns have occurred, or if outside events urge a change in the intentions or initial parameters of the activity, or if the participants in the project themselves make changes in the intentions of planning of the activity, then a new iteration of the status of the system must occur, with new contents in at least some of boxes A, B or C. It is important that the evaluator keep track of the various alterations in the intentions of the activity, partly because it is useful on occasion to remind the project participants of how far they have deviated from their original intentions, and partly because this sort of information – relative to unrealizable aspects of intended activities – can be very important for others beginning a similar project themselves.

Once there is a new appraisal of the intentions of a project or activity, the cycle of analysis can begin again. Thus the framework represents an iterative system.

How does the framework function relative to the six criteria for the evaluation of computer-related educational activity listed earlier?

☐ The framework is an appropriate tool for formative analysis. The assessment of logical relationships (contingencies) among boxes A, B and C, and the assessment of congruence between boxes A and D, B and E, and, on an interim or predictive basis, boxes C and F, and the iterative recasting of the first column of the system are all activities most productive in the domain of formative evaluation.

☐ The approach can be presented with an emphasis on the iterative refinement of the planning of the activity rather than with a judgemental focus relative to specific persons or activities. This approach does not suggest personal judgements about individuals so much as it suggests changes to overall considerations and planning. As such, it can mute the usual connotations involved with 'being evaluated', particularly in the context of exploratory activity.

☐ Quick applications of the framework can occur, in that it can be used in reference to particular and even 'small' aspects of the system as well as to larger perspectives. The iterative nature of readjustments to the 'intention column' of the framework accommodates the fact that computer-related educational activity is always changing in its characteristics even in the midst of careful planning.

☐ The iterative aspect of the approach provides the opportunity for various reconsiderations of the goals of a project. The process of attempting to contribute to the logical analysis of the relationship between boxes in the first column can also be a useful stimulus for the clearer articulation of goals by those involved in the activity.

☐ The strategy of considering box F in terms of prediction of how likely it is that intended outcomes will occur given the current status of the planning of a project and the way in which execution decisions are evolving provides a way to extrapolate from the current state of the system toward the likelihood of eventual success in the future. What comprises 'success' and what intermediary steps are likely to precede it can be fruitful objects of discussion among those involved in the computer-related educational activity. It can also be a useful approach relative to better goal specification (see the previous point).

☐ A particular benefit of the framework is that its flexibility allows it to be used in a 'modest' manner as well as in more extensive ways. A single 'expert', for example, from outside the project of activity can be asked to give opinions on the local premises of the project (logical contingencies between boxes A, B and C). This activity can take place at any time within the project, and can be reasonably quick and inexpensive. The insights obtained can be valuable, particularly if the project team is oriented toward the value of a specific reconsideration of the intentions and assumptions of their project.

To illustrate these points with a practical example, an application of the framework to the evaluation of a national educational software development project in The Netherlands will be described.

Evaluation of the POCO project: an application of the evaluation framework goals of the POCO project

A national educational-software-development project began in The Netherlands in the summer of 1987. This activity, called the 'POCO Project' from its

Dutch name *Programmatuur Ontwikkeling voor Computers in het Onderwijs* (Software Development for Computers in Education), was established by the ministry of education in The Netherlands under the framework of another national initiative called the INSP (the Dutch Informatics Stimulation Programme (see the section by Scheerens in this volume for a report on the evaluation of this overall project). The POCO Project had as its goal the development of educational software:

> that can be used by teachers in a meaningful way during their regular teaching activities, and that can be used with such frequency as to strengthen the teachers' perceptions that using such packages is an effective and efficient response to an educational need. (Policy Note, Minister of Education, June 11, 1987, p 2, English translation)

The project was also given the organizational goal of completing a first set of 18 software packages in 18 months ('Cycle 1', to be completed in December 1988) and a subsequent set of approximately 25 more packages during 1989 and 1990 ('Cycle 2'). For political reasons, the minister stressed that the project must involve collaboration with the established commercial educational publishers in The Netherlands, to minimize the fears of the publishers and of private enterprise more broadly that a subsidized government project would compete with their own business initiatives.

A final goal for the project emerged during the initial elaboration of the minister's directive:

> The POCO project has to promote products that are marketable, both to the internal Dutch market but also in foreign countries. Through the incomes of these 'saleable' products (both the software and the approach used for developing the software) the project can become a self-supporting activity. (Moonen, 1987a, p 3, English translation)

Motivations for an ongoing evaluation of POCO

A critical point for the project was to be the transition between Cycles 1 and 2. At that point, a decision about continuation of the project under its current management would be made by the ministry. With approximately $12 million committed to the overall project, the seriousness of preparation for the ministry's post-Cycle-1 evaluation can be appreciated. The director of the group given the management of the project for at least its first cycle felt it desirable to include evaluation activity throughout the first period. It was also decided to engage an external evaluator to be responsible for this activity in order to avoid reflecting the biases of any of the installed educational groups within The Netherlands who were either involved in some way in the project or who felt some concern that they were not involved in the project. The tasks given to the evaluator were to provide regular information to the director and the project-management team for ongoing readjustments and continuous quality control during Cycle 1 and to predict the level of eventual attainment of the goals of the project based on the evolution of implementation decisions during Cycle 1. In particular, it was felt to be important to focus on the procedure for software development being used for the project. Both logically and in practice, it was important to consider the procedure, as planned and as implemented, in terms of the likelihood that it would yield software that would eventually meet the ambitious goals of the project. When the procedure deviated in execution from what was planned, it would be important to analyse these deviations in terms of either the intentions of the project or the ways in which the intentions were implemented in order better to anticipate what sorts of modifications should be made both during Cycle 1 and the hoped-for Cycle 2.

Design of the POCO evaluation

The adaptation of Stake's model described earlier in this report was chosen as an appropriate framework for the ongoing evalution of Cycle 1 of the POCO project (Collis and Moonen, 1988; Moonen, 1987b), particularly because of the way its iterative orientation allows for continual reassessment of both planning and execution decisions within the project. An evaluator was appointed for the project (the evaluator was external to The Netherlands during the first 14 months of the 18-month evaluation period) and presented a plan for the evaluation structured around a design with the following components (Collis and Berger, 1987);

- ☐ evaluating the logical fit between the assumptions and goals of the POCO project and the plans developed to meet those goals;
- ☐ observing actual implementation of the plans and interpreting deviations from the intended plans for the project;
- ☐ reassessing the intended assumptions and goals of the project and the plans developed to meet those goals;
- ☐ predicting periodically the likelihood that the project will meet its long-range goals; and
- ☐ making recommendations for project adaptation.

In addition, the following issues were identified as being of ongoing importance to the evaluation study:

- ☐ Can the project, within the resources and time available to it, develop software that is likely to be in frequent use by Dutch teachers?
- ☐ Can the project develop, implement, and manage an innovative model for software development that will involve collaboration among a large number of different groups, such as commercial software developers, commercial educational publishers, the ministry, teachers, various established educational support groups, and the group chosen to manage the project?
- ☐ Can classroom teachers be meaningfully involved at appropriate places in the decision process relating to the software packages?
- ☐ Can written material be developed that effectively supports the use of the software by teachers and students?
- ☐ Can a widespread and positive public image be developed, both within and outside The Netherlands, for the software, the approach used to develop the software, and the team involved in managing this approach?

Data were accumulated through the continual exchange of ideas and observations, through either personal or telecommunications-mediated communication, between the external evaluator and an assistant working within the project. In addition, the evaluator visited the project regularly, conducted interviews, and had access to all internal and external material produced by the project. Ongoing feedback was accomplished through having evaluation reports produced at approximately two-monthly intervals. The eight evaluation studies produced for the project are outlined in the Appendix.

Because the POCO evaluation was ongoing, its interim reports could focus on the distinction between intentions and implementaton relative to specific aspects of the project at the times the aspects were most pertinent to the project. The major evaluation focuses were:

- [ ] organization of the infrastructure for the project;
- [ ] development of a priority list of software topics for Cycle 1;
- [ ] development of product descriptions;
- [ ] development of lines of communication and responsibility within the project;
- [ ] interactions and arrangements with commercial educational publishers;
- [ ] technical development of the software;
- [ ] development of the print materials to support the software;
- [ ] field testing of products;
- [ ] ongoing field involvement ('field confrontations'); and
- [ ] ongoing information dissemination about the project, nationally and internationally.

Relationship of the POCO evaluation to the general framework for the evaluation of large-scale computer-related educational activity

Earlier in this report, the general framework for evaluation of large-scale computer-related educational activity shown in Figure 1 was discussed in terms of how it could produce pertinent short- and long-term recommendations for a project as well as for the educational community at large. The framework was also discussed in terms of how it related to six typical characteristics of large-scale computer-related projects. How does the POCO evaluation relate to all of these considerations?

Specific challenges of the evaluation

The fifth of the six problems described at the beginning of this section presented the major challenge to the POCO evaluation. This problem relates to the evaluation of progress towards goals that can only be directly assessed long after a project is completed. In the POCO example, goals about developing software that will eventually be 'in frequent use' by teachers and profitable in the educational market both inside and outside The Netherlands. The director of the group managing the project felt that the development of regular feedback loops (or 'confrontation' opportunities) between representatives of those eventual target groups (classroom teachers from within The Netherlands and educational decision-makers from within and outside The Netherlands) would be an effective means by which the project could anticipate the long-range response from those groups (Moonen, 1987a).

Having frequent 'confrontations' would also allow adjustments to be made to the packages during the design and development phases in order further to enhance their eventual market appeal. In consequence, a major focus of the ongoing external evaluation of the project was the degree to which these sorts of confrontations took place (Collis & Berger, 1987). In each of the eight evaluation reports some attention was given to the current level of field-project interaction. The difficulties involved in trying to organize meaningful interaction between teachers and professional software developers working under severe time restraints were never resolved.

Fit of the POCO evaluation to the general framework

The POCO evaluation reflects the general framework illustrated in Figure 1 and discussed earlier in this report. Assumptions of the project were frequently examined, particularly in relation to the implications of the substantial involvement of educational publishers, but also in relation to the time and resource allotment given to the project. The logical relationships between the intentions of the project and the activities chosen to meet those intentions were often appraised, in particular with respect to the various conferences sponsored by the project to promote awareness of its activities.

A major focus of the evaluation involved interpreting project slowdowns. In a project of the scope and complexity of POCO – involving, in various ways, hundreds of people in diverse groups (educational publishers, teachers, curriculum specialists, educational technologists, commercial software houses) working on, in effect, 18 different projects – it is inevitable that project implementation will not always proceed as planned. However, it was perceived to be highly valuable both in an immediate sense in Cycle 1 and for planning relative to Cycle 2 that a distinction be made between slowdowns rooted in theory and slowdowns rooted in implementation specifics. When implementation decisions formed the major basis of project showdowns, the evaluator could offer comments on alternative implementation strategies. Relative to theory or logical slowdowns, however, the evaluator could also help the management team identify elements of their basic planning which might be modified either directly or in Cycle 2. Also, the evaluator could elaborate more globally on basic implications of the original assumptions and goals of the project.

As an example of this, a fundamental tension existed between the goal of actively involving educational publishers in the project and the goal of creating products of interest to buyers outside The Netherlands. Involving Dutch publishers meant creating products that reflected existing Dutch textbooks and methodology, thus limiting the portability and innovation of the software and the international aspects of its marketability. It would be inappropriate to indict the POCO management for not meeting the dual goals of publisher accommodation and external saleability when this is more a logical consequence of the project's initial assumptions than it is something that could be related to project-management decisions. Thus the continual application of the framework shown in Figure 1 allowed the evaluator to categorize interpretations of ongoing project activity and to offer constructive suggestions based on those interpretations (Collis & Moonen, 1988)

Contributions of the evaluation

The evaluation contributed both short- and long-range value to the project (Collis and Moonen, 1988). Various recommendations made in the eight evaluation reports were implemented or at least considered carefully during Cycle 1 itself. The ministerial evaluation at the end of Cycle 1 awarded the continuation of the project in its second phase to the same management team. The extensive documentation provided by the evaluation during its first cycle was used during the planning for its second cycle.

The evaluation also made at least one other global contribution to the project. The periodic appearance of the evaluator, with the mandate to ask individuals about their planning and their interpretations of the goals and activites of the project, served as a catalyst to better project self-awareness. This is the benefit of an external evaluation – to be sufficiently outside a system to ask specific questions about implementation decisions and intentions in the way it could not as part of the project staff. The stimulus of the evaluator's reports ensured the project had regular periods of self-inventorization, something it might not have taken time to do, at least on such a regular basis, without such a stimulus.

It is more difficult to claim that the evaluation contributed to the advance of more general experience with regard to large-scale computer-related educational activity or even national software-development projects in a more specific fashion. This is because of an inherent characteristic of evaluation studies: their confidentiality. Projects may be mature enough to welcome feedback and comment within their ranks, but most do not feel that the public exposure of these interim comments is to their advantage. This is understandable; however, it creates a definite problem with respect to the better dissemination of experience throughout the field.

Fit of the POCO evaluation to the evaluation criteria associated with the framework

With respect to the fit of the POCO evaluation to evaluation criteria associated with the six characteristics of large-scale computer-related educational activity discussed at the start of this report the following observations can be made:

- ☐ The evaluation was related to ongoing formative evaluation.
- ☐ The major orientation of the evaluation was to reassess the totality of project assumptions and planning, rather than to make judgements about the adequacy of performance of any particular participant in the project, minimizing the chance that any individual felt uncomfortable or inhibited by the feeling that he or she was being personally assessed.
- ☐ The framework was used not only for the overall evaluation but also for each of many 'small evaluations' that occurred on an ongoing basis throughout the project relative to component activities within the general project. Continual and quickly delivered recommendations were provided

through the mechanisms of eight evaluation reports, each representing one or more iterations of the framework.

☐ The evaluation made it clear that the original planning for the project had to be clarified in many ways. In this project, however, the goals were quite specific, so the evaluation did not have to deal with the need for better articulation of the goals of the project itself, as is often the case with less product-oriented educational activity involving computers.

☐ The evaluation helped the project management to consider more closely how their ongoing implementation decisions may affect the eventual attainment of the goals of the project, particularly with respect to field confrontations and quality assurance for support materials to accompany software products.

☐ The evaluation was relatively easy to implement and tolerate, with the cost to the project relatively small.

Conclusion

The adaptation of Stake's model shown in Figure 1 appears to be a useful approach to the evaluation of large-scale computer-related educational activity. Its application to the evaluation of the POCO project is only one of many examples of its flexibility and usefulness. The accommodation of the approach to the particular characteristics of computer-related educational activity, characteristics which deter many decision-makers from initiating evaluation studies of such activities, offers a particularly strong support for the approach. Thus, in conclusion, the experiences of the POCO project evaluation support a recommendation to managers of comparable projects that they include similar evaluation projects as essential parts of their projects. In such a way the evaluation study will have more value to the project than if it were attempted in a summative framework. Too often evaluation studies have only a minor influence on projects because critical observations appear too late to be incorporated into ongoing project activity and the results of the study will be unlikely to be used for new projects because each project creates its own circumstances and contextual conditions. The evaluation procedure described in this report allows for ongoing implementation adjustments as well as goal respecification, and as such is recommended for other large-scale computer-related educational projects.

References

Baker, E L (1988) *Sensitive Technology Assessment of ACOT*, paper presented at the annual meeting of the American Educational Research Association, New Orleans

Collis, B A and Berger, L (1987) *Evaluation Design: POCO Project Cycle 1*, Enschede, The Netherlands: ECC (Educational Computing Consortium)

Collis, B A and Moonen, J (1988) *Designing an External Evaluation of a Large-scale Software Development Project*, paper presented at the annual meeting of the International Association for Computers in Education, New Orleans

Collis, B A and Oliveira, J (1989) *Models for Computer-related National Policy: An International Perspective*, paper presented at the Third International Conference, Children in the Computer Age, Sofia, Bulgaria

Minister of Education (1987) *POCO Policy Note (English translation)*, Den Hague, The Netherlands: Ministry of Education

Moonen, J (1987a) *POCO Plan of Action (English translation)* Enschede, The Netherlands: ECC (Educational Computing Consortium)

Moonen, J (1987b) *Applying a General Evaluation Model to a Seminar on the Evaluation of National Policies for Educational Computing*, paper presented at EDITE 87, Evaluation and Dissemination of Information Technologies in Education, Luso, Portugal

Scheerens, J (1989) *The Evaluation of the Educational Section of the Dutch Informatics Stimulation Programme (INSP)*, Enschede, The Netherlands: University of Twente. Paper submitted for publication

Stake, R E (1973) The Countenance of Educational Evaluation, In B R Worthen and J R Sanders (Eds), *Educational Evaluation: Theory and Practice*, Belmont, CA: Wadsworth Publishing Company, pp 106–125

Stake, R E (1977) *To Evaluate an Arts Programme* unpublished report, University of Illinois at Urbana-Champaign

Suchman, E (1976) *Evaluation Research* New York: Russell Sage Foundation Press

Appendix: POCO evaluation reports

(Date submitted given in parentheses.)

1. Evaluation of the September 1989 'Working Conference' (October 14, 1987).

    ☐ Evaluation of the working conference relative to its intentions.
    ☐ Recommendations for Cycle 2.

2. Evaluation of the 'Priority Determination Phase' (December 4, 1987).

    ☐ Evaluation of the determination of priorities.
    ☐ Implications from the implementation period, September–November 1987, for the remaining components of Cycle 1.

3. Planning for 1988 (December 31, 1987).

    ☐ Critical issues relating to the Product Description Phase.
    ☐ Issues relating to the Product Development Phase.
    ☐ Strategies for broad support in the educational field.

4. Evaluation Report – January–May, 1988 (May 13, 1988)

    ☐ Current status of the 18 POCO products.
    ☐ Implications of current status for the remainder of Cycle 1 and for Cycle 2.
    ☐ Follow-up to recommendations made in Report 3.
    ☐ Evaluation of the POCO infrastructure.

5. Evaluation Report 5 (August 19, 1988).

    ☐ Current status of the 18 products.
    ☐ Major issues relating to the products.
    ☐ Recommendations for Cycle 2.
    ☐ Field input and confrontations.

6. Evaluation Report 6 (September 28, 1988).

   ☐ Evaluation of the 'POCO After 1 Year' Conference.
   ☐ Evaluation of POCO-field interaction.
   ☐ Evaluation of current field response to POCO products.
   ☐ Recommendations for Cycle 2.

7. Evaluation Report 7 – Product Status and Field Testing (December 20, 1988).

   ☐ Current status of products.
   ☐ Field tests.
   ☐ Publicity and public relations activities.

8. Evaluation Report 8 – Recommendations for Cycle 2 (December 31, 1988).

   ☐ Assessment of congruence between the original POCO 'Plan of Action' and project status as of December 23, 1988.
      – Goals of the project.
      – Developing a criterion for 'frequent use'.
      – Anticipating the saleability of the products.
      – Taking advantage of already-existing products.
      – Assessment of educational impact.
      – Ongoing evaluation.
      – Time schedule.
      – The 'White Papers' and setting priorities.
      – Field confrontations.
      – Product Description Phase.
      – Technical Realization Phase.
      – Relationships with the Dutch educational publishers.
      – Relationships with the Dutch educational community.
   ☐ Summary, and recommendations for Cycle 2.

11. The evaluation of the educational section of the Dutch Informatics Stimulation Programme (INSP)

Jaap Scheerens

Introduction

In this section, the context, methodology and results of two evaluation studies concerning the Dutch Informatics Stimulation Programme (INSP) are discussed, the educational section of the programme being the main focus of interest. The first was an 'evaluability analysis' and the second was a 'sober, future-oriented evaluation'. Each study was conducted within a period of roughly six months. The strengths and weaknesses of the evaluation approach used in the second study are discussed, the conclusion being that the proactive, improvement-oriented and partly analytic (as well as empirical) nature of this study was warranted by the stage of development of the programme to be evaluated and by contextual constraints.

The most striking findings are the recognition of the importance of education and training for all elements of IT stimulation in society and the seriousness of the problem of how to organize and control large-scale IT stimulation in education.

The Dutch Informatics Stimulation Programme

The Dutch Informatics Stimulation Programme (INSP) was launched in 1984 as a joint venture between the Departments of Economics, Education and Agriculture. Its overall aim was to stimulate the introduction of information technology and to compensate for the supposed lagging behind in the Netherlands in comparison with other industrialized countries. The stimulation programme has run for a period of five years and was terminated in December 1988. Its total budget amounts to 1.7 billion Dutch guilders (approximately $950 million).

Figure 1 shows the division of funds over fields of application and over sponsors. The subprogrammes of the INSP cover the areas of *information and guidance* (1 per cent of the total budget), *education* (22 per cent), *research* (17 per cent), *stimulation of the market sector* (51 per cent) and *stimulation of the administrative use of the computer in government agencies* (9 per cent). It is clear from Figure 1 that the market sector was the major funding area and that the Department of Economic

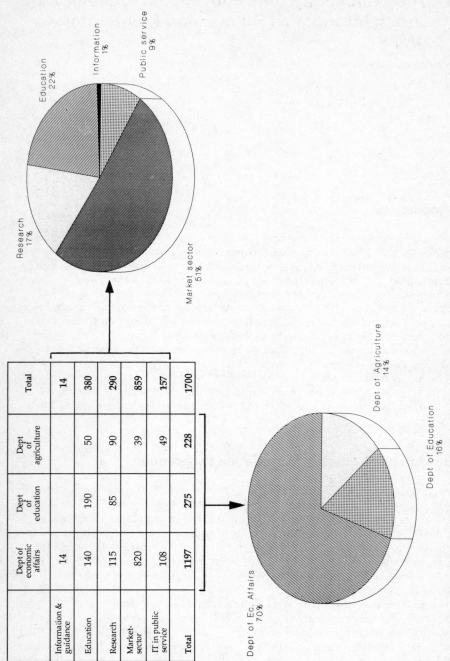

Figure 1 *INSP as financed by participating departments*

	Dept of economic affairs	Dept of education	Dept of agriculture	Total
Information & guidance	14			14
Education	140	190	50	380
Research	115	85	90	290
Market-sector	820		39	859
IT in public service	108		49	157
Total	1197	275	228	1700

Affairs was the major sponsor. Figure 1 also shows that Economic Affairs took care of no less than 37 per cent of the total budget for stimulation of informatics in education. This illustrates the priority that was given to human capital development as a means to stimulate the supply-side of the economy. Other important features of the INSP as a whole that are not shown in Figure 1, are the following:

☐ No less than 45 per cent of the total budget for the INSP consisted of already existing funds and stimulation measures that were subsequently brought under the control of the INSP.

☐ Almost 60 per cent of the INSP funds were directed to the stimulation of the supply-side of informatics applications (eg development and supply of hard- and software) as opposed to the stimulation of the demand for informatics applications.

☐ Each main area of INSP stimulation (the areas shown in Figure 1) was divided into numerous projects and subprojects. As a whole all these subprojects made up a fragmented and not very well integrated whole. Many projects came into existence in a 'bottom-up' fashion and in general there were no powerful coordinating structures to integrate all these projects. When the prospect of evaluation of the INSP took on a more definite shape several features – like the number of subprojects (several hundreds), the unclear boundaries between INSP and other government stimulation measures with respect to information technology, and the relative lack of central control and coordination over this conglomerate of activities – were seen as specific difficulties for carrying out an overall evaluation.

The aims of the *educational section* of the INSP were: to make young citizens familiar with information technology, eg by enhancing 'computer literacy' in secondary education; to create human capital in the field of information technology, eg by means of specific courses in vocational schools; and to improve the quality of education by integrating the computer in the curriculum (computer-assisted instruction). The overall structure of the educational section of the INSP consisted of school-sector-specific subprogrammes (programmes

Elementary and special education	15
Secondary education, phase 1	25
Secondary education, phase 2	10
Lower and intermediate vocational education	75
Higher vocational education	43
Agricultural education	56
Adult education	43
Infrasture ed. software development	40
Teacher training and retraining	53
Educational research	10

Table 1 *Budgets for educational subprogrammes of the INSP for the period 1984–1988 (in millions of Dutch guilders).*

for elementary schools, secondary schools, lower and middle vocational schools, higher vocational schools, and adult education) and supportive subprogrammes, namely: the provision of an infrastructure for the development of educational software, teacher training and retraining and educational research. Figure 2 shows the budget for each of the educational subprogrammes.

Table 1 gives an impression of the division of priorities over the various educational sectors and computer applications. Among other things it shows the relatively low priority of computer assisted instruction in elementary and special education. It is important to note that no less than 80 per cent of the total budget for the educational section of the INSP was spent on hardware (50 per cent) and software (30 per cent) provision.

Like the INSP as a whole, the educational section too was further divided into several hundreds of subprojects. To coordinate all these educational projects a management structure was set up that was more articulated than comparable structures for the other major INSP areas. This management structure consisted of a special taskforce at the Ministry of Education (outside the 'regular' structure of the various directorates in the ministry) and external 'cluster-managers' for each of the subprogrammes mentioned in Table 1. Another feature of the educational section of the INSP is the effort that was required to develop and implement all these new projects within a relatively short timespan. The accounts show that the proportion of the budget actually spent over the successive years was far less than in the initial years of the programme, causing an uneven spread. Since, within the framework of this paper on the *evaluation* of the INSP, the description of the actual programme should be limited to a rather general picture of the overall features of this 'evaluation object', I would like to refer to other sources (eg several contributions in Plomp, Van Deursen and Moonen, 1987) for further details of the INSP education programme.

Context of evaluation

Several authors have underlined the importance of contextual factors in relation to evaluations (eg Cronbach and Associates, 1980; Scheerens, 1985). In order to promote a better understanding of the choices and decisions related to evaluation approaches, evaluation management and the utilization of results, several contextual factors need to be taken into consideration. Here, we would like briefly to examine the following factors:

☐ the need for the INSP evaluation;
☐ certain generic characteristics of the INSP programme as an evaluation object;
☐ organizational and institutional arrangements.

The need for INSP evaluation

The decision to evaluate the INSP, preferably before its termination in December 1988, was made by the Council of Ministers in late 1988. It seems highly likely that the political motive of some of the members of the cabinet in having the INSP evaluated was to obtain further positive publicity for a spectacular *demonstration project*. From the beginning, it was made clear that the evaluation should be sober (not expansive) and quick. The agency within the central bureaucracy that was to operationalize the concept of an INSP evaluation was the directorate of science policy at the Ministry of Education, which played a coordinating role between the three departments involved in the INSP. One of the other special fields of interest held by the directorate of science policy is 'programme evaluation', and for this an independent committee of experts, the Committee for Programme Evaluation (CPE) was called into life. It was this committee that advised the directorate of science policy to attack the 'problems of how to evaluate the INSP' first of all by means of an evaluability assessment.

The taskforce that managed the educational section of the INSP at the Ministry of Education was initially somewhat reluctant about the idea of further evaluation activities; they said that many educational subprojects were already being evaluated both internally and by the inspectorate. Without additional guesswork about the motives of the various government agencies involved in the shaping of the INSP evaluation, it seems safe to conclude that the 'coincidence' of the involvement of the directorate of sciency policy in both the INSP and programme evaluation determined the way the INSP evaluation was tackled. When, after the evaluability-analysis, the INSP reached its second stage, there was a lot of debate concerning its proactive rather than retrospective 'summative' nature. Initially differences arose between the various ministries involved with the INSP. This debate was settled in favour of giving a more proactive role to the limited evaluation to be conducted.

Certain generic characteristics of the INSP as an evaluation object

To refer back to the description of the INSP programme in the previous section, it must be concluded that the INSP education programme formed a *complex* evaluation object: both sector specific and supportive subprogrammes, a great number of projects and subprojects, and a somewhat complicated management structure (both external 'cluster-managers' and coordinators at the Ministry of Education).

A second general characteristic of the INSP education programme of relevance to its evaluation was the inherent scope for innovation in terms of the intensity of changes in routine educational practice that were implied, combined with the *relatively short period of time* (five years) that was available. In addition, it should be noted that several parts of the programme sought to apply technologies that are really still in their experimental stages (eg the more advanced types of computer-assisted instruction) and that other parts demanded completely new organizational arrangements (eg the subprogramme aimed at the creation of an infrastructure for the development of educational software).

A final characteristic of the INSP evaluation programme to be considered here is its *rational structure*. Although explicit plans were drawn up for most of the subprogrammes, in many cases it would be hard to reconstruct the deductive logic behind the choice of projects and subprojects within a particular subprogramme. Had this been clearer, it would have been easier for evaluators to infer the overall success of a subprogramme by means of aggregating the evaluative results of the projects and subprojects. However, this was not the case, so a hierarchy of goals and methods could only be discerned to a limited extent in this particular programme (plans were altered during the course of a particular subprogramme, central planners were dependent on local initiatives to a certain degree, and procedures to implement projects lasted longer than was expected).

In summary, the INSP education programme can be characterized as a complex and dynamic ('moving target') evaluation object, where the factor of the required lead-time for the intended innovation should be given due consideration.

Organizational and institutional arrangements surrounding the evaluation

The first phase of the INSP evaluation was conducted under the auspices of the Committee for Programme Evaluation (CPE), an advisory committee of the directorate of science policy at the Ministry of Education. Three professors, representing the fields of economics, technology policy and educational evaluation were asked to conduct this evaluability analysis. They worked completely independently from the departments involved and presented their final report to the CPE.

The second phase of the INSP evaluation was again conducted by a committee of three members (two of whom had also conducted the evaluability analysis). The committee was supported by a bureau of organizational consultants of international repute and, in addition, six studies were contracted out by the committee to private bureaux and universities. The committee had complete control over its own budget. Observers from each of the three departments involved in the INSP attended the committee meetings.

These organizational arrangements surrounding the INSP evaluation are quite different from the normal situation, as far as educational evaluation in the Netherlands is concerned:

☐ The evaluation was conducted outside the 'educational province' and formed an integral part of the multi-sector and multi-disciplinary overall INSP evaluation.

☐ Secondly, control by officers from the Ministry of Education over educational evaluation programmes at national level is usually much stronger than was the case in the INSP evaluation.

☐ The fact that an external committee was given a 'lump sum' over which it had complete budgetary control is quite exceptional.

☐ In the Netherlands there is an elaborate structure of several types of institutes that all have certain stakes in educational evaluation; usually lengthy procedures are required to divide tasks within major evaluation projects over these institutes. In the case of the INSP evaluation these time-consuming manoeuvres of distributive justice could be dispensed with and a new source of prospective evaluators, private research and consultancy agencies, could be used alongside the more traditional research agencies (for example universities).

In my opinion, both the independence and managerial effectiveness (lack of red-tape) of the INSP evaluation were served by these unconventional arrangements.

Evaluation approach and methods: evaluability analysis and proactive, formative evaluation

So far the evaluation of the INSP has consisted of two phases: an evaluability analysis which was conducted during the first half of 1987 and a 'sober, future-oriented' evaluation, carried out from November 1987 until July 1988.

Evaluability analysis

As indicated previously, the idea of starting evaluative activities concerning the INSP using an evaluability analysis originated from the Committee for Programme Evaluation, an advisory committee of the Directorate of Science Policy. The idea of an evaluability analysis was motivated by uncertainties as to how and by whom the INSP evaluation should be tackled, given the overall complexity of the programme and the relatively short time that policy-makers would allow for the evaluation. The task force that was asked to carry out the evaluability analysis consisted of three members, W Zegveld (expert in technology policy), J S Cramer (econometrician) and the present author. The evaluability analysis was to answer the following questions:

- ☐ To what extent is an overall evaluation of the INSP feasible?
- ☐ How should such an evaluation if feasible be carried out?
- ☐ By whom should the evaluation be carried out; how should the evaluation be organized?

The evaluability analysis was structured by determining, first of all, which basic questions ought to be answered in programme evaluation. The task force state that policy programmes can only be evaluated if their aims are known. When this is indeed the case, programme evaluation should try to establish:

- ☐ whether the programme's aims have been accomplished;
- ☐ whether this result can indeed be attributed unequivocally to the policy programme; and
- ☐ whether the same result could have been reached in another, faster or more efficient way.

Evaluability analysis might lead to the conclusion that, for instance, only the first question can be answered, and that answering the two additional, more refined questions, would not be feasible (too difficult, too expensive or too time-consuming).

The analytical framework used in the evaluability assessment further comprised a division of the total INSP into four aggregation levels and the establishment of a set of evaluation perspectives. The four levels used were:

- ☐ *level 1*, the INSP as a whole;
- ☐ *level 2*, the five main substantive target areas of the programme (information and guidance, education, research, stimulation of the market sector,

and the use of information technology in government agencies);
- [ ] *level 3*, about 30 subprogrammes divided over the five main substantive areas;
- [ ] *level 4*, project-level.

The taskforce chose *level 3* as the main focus of the evaluability analysis, since the first two levels were deemed rather general and the fourth too specific.

The evaluation perspectives used by the taskforce were threefold. They held that traditional evaluation uses a *policy-imminent* perspective, drawing heavily on the aims and means of policy-makers and programme staff. A broader evaluation perspective also questions the logic and the underlying assumptions of the policy programme; this was termed a *policy-analytic* perspective. Finally, since several projects of the INSP had already been evaluated, or were being evaluated at the time, the taskforce discerned a *meta-evaluation perspective*, from which overall evaluation could be seen as an aggregation and reinterpretation of the evaluation results available.

In carrying out the evaluability analysis at the level of subprogrammes (level 3), these perspectives were used as feasible, alternative ways of evaluating certain subprogrammes. To determine the evaluability of each subprogramme the taskforce used a checklist, based on the following main categories:

- [ ] description of the subprogramme or project in terms of aims and means;
- [ ] general statements of the evaluation problem, choice of the most feasible evaluation perspective;
- [ ] evaluability in terms of the three basic questions in programme evaluation (assessability of effects, attribution of effects to programmes and efficiency considerations);
- [ ] the scope of the evaluation ranging from the control of accounts and distribution of funds (is the available budget used for the purpose intended, is the program that is actually being carried out congruent with the programme plans?), to the establishment and attribution of programme effects;
- [ ] general outline as to how each programme could be evaluated, the required expertise, budget and time needed for the evaluation.

Proactive, formative evaluation of the INSP

One of the 'procedural' recommendations – to be distinguished from the substantive results that will be summarized in the next section – that followed from the evaluability analysis, was to start the evaluation of the INSP with a first phase that would be proactive, rather than retroactive, both analytic *and* empirical and with an overall formative orientation (ie to yield information that could help in shaping the ongoing decisions in the work).

The reasoning behind this recommendation ran as follows. The evaluability analysis had yielded an extensive list of subprogrammes, of which evaluation was thought to be both relevant and feasible. If only because of budgetary limitations further selection from this overall list was deemed necessary. The taskforce that carried out the evaluability analysis concluded that such further selection should be based on an analysis of those areas that were of strategic importance to the further 'informatization of society'. This analysis could then yield two types of outcomes: a further shaping and selection of evaluation activities and tentative evaluation conclusions about the main features (like policy mix, choice of priorities, overall programme organization) of the INSP. When this analysis/evaluation gradually took shape, the first objective almost disappeared and the second predominated. In this way the cabinet's original wish to have a 'sober' substantive evaluation of the INSP completed before the termination of the programme in December 1988 could be realized.

The project structure to carry out this sober and future-oriented evaluation of the INSP was described in the previous section. The core of this structure was a committee, chaired by Professor Zegveld, and two members, Mr Stehouwer (with a background of information management and managerial consultancy) and the present author. Before embarking upon any further reflection on the specific evaluation approach that was used in this project, a brief overview of the sequence of concrete steps in the analysis/evaluation will be given.

First of all, the project organization for this evaluative study was negotiated with the funder (the budget was controlled by the directorate of science policy at the Ministry of Education).

During an introductory period the specific orientation of this evaluative study was discussed with the contractors (the three ministries involved) and with the executive bureau. It took quite some time to get all parties concerned to agree on the specific mixture of policy-analytic and evaluative activities that was finally chosen. In addition, about 25 stakeholders in various types of information-technology application, both from within the public sector and from industry, were interviewed in order to establish bottlenecks and areas of strategic importance in the development and further application of IT.

This introductory period resulted in a concrete plan of action for the actual evaluative study. Only when this plan was ready was the formal assignment given to the committee; it proved to be in line with the committee's plan of action.

An important part of the plan of action and a direct result of the orientation-phase was the selection of six topics considered to be of strategic and exemplary importance for the future stimulation of IT. These topics were: production automation, logistics, the software industry, courseware, the introduction of complex systems and the relation between regular/independent education in meeting the demands of a labour market that is becoming more and more permeated with applications of information technology.

For each of the six topics a study of two or three months was contracted out to specialized agencies and research institutes. All the reports appeared on time. The committee and its executive staff selected core issues that ran through each of the problem areas covered by the six topics, these were: the problem of training, standardization, legal aspects, organization and management of IT stimulation, the priorities given to technology 'push' (the stimulation of the supply-side of the economy) versus technology 'pull' (stimulation of the autonomous demand). In addition the committee consulted international and national panels of experts.

The committee's final report appeared on time and consisted of a general problem analysis, evaluative conclusions and recommendations, as well as the reports of the six areas of study. From an evaluation-theoretical point of view the approach chosen in this evaluation study has several interesting features.

First, the approach purposely went beyond the specific aims and methods of the INSP programme and looked at the INSP from a wider perspective of trends and developments in information technology and societal aspects of IT application. In terms of the three perspectives used in the evaluability analysis, this implied a policy-analytic rather than a policy-immanent approach.

Secondly, even in the more specific studies dedicated to each of the six selected topics, the emphasis was on global characteristics rather than specific facts. Interviewing key figures was the predominant method of data collection (altogether over 600 people were interviewed). The advantage of this approach was that the evaluators did not become lost in all kinds of details and that an attempt was made to reflect on the main issues. The weakness of this method of evaluating is, however, that when gathering opinions one is likely to miss the sharp edge that may result from the collection of detailed factual evidence. A similar comment can be made with respect to the generality versus specificity of the committees' recommendations. In seeking to induce the general strategic and organizational issues from a very divergent field of IT applications, more elaborated and field-specific recommendations had to be sacrificed.

Thirdly, it is important to note that, notwithstanding a certain emphasis on analysis and strategy formation, the evaluative aspect was certainly present in this study. Each of the six part-studies gave inventories of how the INSP had tackled the problem area concerned, and evaluated this from various perspectives, such as developments in other countries, experiences in other sectors of society, and the point of view on the matter that was developed on the basis of personal expertise or the informed opinions of respondents. In the final report, the committee, too, drew clear evaluative conclusions on several major aspects of the INSP.

Fourthly, the fact that the committee was supported by a bureau of organizational consultants made its mark on certain important aspects of the execution of the study. The way the committee insisted on a clear assignment that was supported by the various contractors was certainly enforced by the consultants' standard never to accept assignments to which contractors gave different interpretations. Other beneficial influences of this arrangement were a strictly planned and monitored progress of the study and a businesslike style of presentation. (Although from the academic point of view this preference for brief and 'catchy' statements sometimes goes against the grain due to the accompanying lack of detail and depth.)

In the fifth place, an important feature of this study was that it was led by an experienced committee chairman, who had easy access to officials of the highest rank at the various ministries. Apart from the fact that this arrangement made for a very well managed study, it will probably also enhance the use that is made of the evaluation: for instance, due to the fact that evaluation results were communicated to high-ranking officials personally, at points in time (even before the appearance of the final report) when they needed the results for important meetings on the follow-up of the INSP. The specific – and for the Dutch situation, remarkable – organizational features of this evaluation study have been described above.

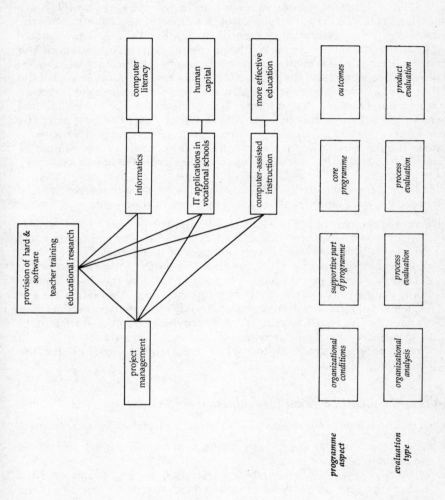

Figure 2 *Structure of the education part of the INSP and evaluation types*

Results

Results of the evaluability analysis

The evaluability analysis led to the conclusion that the level of the (about 30) subprogrammes of the INSP was the best level at which to answer the question of evaluability. Here, I will only summarize the results of the educational section of the INSP. The (ten) subprogrammes within this part of the INSP are summarized in Table 2 in the first section of this paper. Figure 2 summarizes the main aspects of the educational sections of the INSP with respect to management structure, the supportive part of the programme, the core programme and intended outcomes. It also mentions feasible types of evaluation for each aspect.

The overall conclusions of the evaluability analysis of the education part of the INSP were that an organizational analysis of the project-management structure was relevant and feasible, that outcomes like computer literacy and educational effects on the labour market are measurable but at a point of time after the termination of the INSP, that process evaluation of the supportive subprogrammes is quite feasible and relevant and that the contribution of computer-assisted instruction to the overall quality and effectiveness of education is very hard to assess.

In addition, general evaluation proposals for those sections that were thought to be evaluable were designed. The most important of these were:

- ☐ Process-oriented studies to establish whether the INSP core and supportive subprogrammes were carried out as intended. It was recommended that the inspectorate should carry out most of these studies.
- ☐ Effect-evaluation of the NIVO project – a large project in secondary education – aimed at enhancing computer literacy, by means of international comparison geared to the IEA (International Association for the Evaluation of Educational Achievement) study on computers in education.
- ☐ Various longitudinal studies aimed at determining educational attainment in specific vocational sectors where IT is of major importance.
- ☐ Organizational analysis of the INSP management structure for the education programme.

Results of the proactive formative evaluation of the INSP

The main conclusions of the evaluation of the INSP as a whole were as follows:

- ☐ IT development and the societal changes surrounding it are still in the initial phase of development.
- ☐ In parts of the INSP the required transition from a supply-oriented 'technology push' to a more user-oriented approach is not getting off the ground and this is detrimental to the otherwise attainable effects of IT stimulation.
- ☐ The various parts of the INSP show a lack of coherence and coordination which has reduced its effect.
- ☐ Neither of the previous two remarks applies to the agricultural sector of the INSP – here programme elements are well planned and coordinated.
- ☐ A large number of activities in the field of IT in various sectors would not

have occurred, or would have taken place at a much slower pace, without the INSP.

☐ The actual effects of important parts of the INSP will only be apparent in future years. If good management and the adaptation of policy in line with experience so far is implemented, it is to be expected that the INSP-investments will contribute to the positive balance of the Dutch economy.

The major recommendations of the evaluation committee were:

☐ to continue IT stimulation;
☐ to centralize strategy formation and process control of post-INSP activities and to decentralize the implementation of subprogrammes to existing institutes with a clear mission;
☐ to emphasize stimulation of the demand-side (training, demonstration projects, organizational aspects);
☐ to gear IT-stimulation policy to existing platforms for international cooperation;
☐ to give extra attention to legal aspects with respect to standardization, privacy, copyright, etc;
☐ to see to it that vital parts of IT stimulation, such as the stimulation of the so-called irregular educational system (private training centres, etc) are continued.

As for the educational section of the INSP, the evaluative committee stated four main conclusions:

☐ The implementation of computers in education appears to be a complex innovation, where many aspects must be taken care of simultaneously and, what is more, must be integrated (hard- and software provision, curriculum development and training and guidance of teachers). Such complex innovations take a great deal of time and are difficult to manage. The results that have been reached so far correspond to this level of difficulty.
☐ The NIVO project, executed in cooperation with various industrial firms, contributes favourably to the enhancing of computer literacy at the level of secondary education.
☐ The problem of gearing educational supply to the demands of the labour market remains a problem area. Educational institutes (the official, government-financed, educational system) lack the information and flexibility to adapt to the fast changes in functions and professions. Nor does the independent system work systematically in gearing supply to demand, but this system could operate in a more flexible way.
☐ The POCO project (consisting of a specialized executive structure for the development of courseware) is a satisfactory organizational form for developing courseware in the Netherlands. The actual application of computer-assisted instruction within the various school sorts is still incidental. (See the section by Collis in this edition for further details of POCO.)

The committee's recommendation for future IT stimulation in education were:

☐ IT stimulation in education should be closely geared to national technology and science policy (which implies that the strategic decisions on these technological developments concerning education should not only be made within the boundaries of the educational province).

☐ The regular educational system should focus on basic skills, whereas the independent system should be stimulated to adapt to the more job-specific changes in functions and professions. Both systems could be interrelated by means of regional centres based on the idea of community colleges.

☐ Ensure that the management structure for the post-INSP education programme can operate with sufficient autonomy and power.

☐ Give educational research concerning IT applications and experimental developments a higher priority than it had during the INSP period.

Discussion

The experience with the INSP evaluation has been described both with respect to evaluation methodology, evaluation management and substantive results. Evaluability analysis proved to be a helpful approach in getting an evaluation of a complex and dynamic innovation programme like the INSP off the ground.

From a methodological point of view the proactive, 'formative' evaluation contained strong elements of analysis, expert judgement and reflection, as well as empirical facets. Also the overall evaluation approach was improvement-oriented rather than accountability-oriented which also meant that, apart from 'looking back', the evaluation and analysis had a proactive orientation. The way the evaluation was conducted and managed corresponded to some extent to evaluation approaches that have been specifically designed to enhance relevance and usefulness to the relevant parties, namely 'utilization-focused evaluation' (Patton, 1978; Alkin, Daillak & White, 1979) and 'stakeholder based evaluation' (Cohen, 1983). Aspects of the INSP evaluation that correspond to these approaches are the timeliness of the evaluation report, communication of results to key persons at the time they needed the results (somewhat before the publication of the final report), and the intensive orientation period when stakeholders from various parts of society were interviewed.

The most important critical question that should be asked with such a smooth and user-friendly evaluation approach, is whether one of the most vital elements of evaluation, its critical edge, is not being lost in the process. Undoubtedly, the phase of the INSP evaluation described here has not yielded hard empirical evidence on the effects of INSP subprogrammes, not has it produced future-oriented numerical analyses that unequivocally point to the feasibility or otherwise of certain approaches to IT stimulation. Yet, in my opinion, the 'softer' approach that has been used is quite defensible, given the stage of development of the programme that was the evaluation object, and given the constraints on the evaluation's budget and lead-time. It will be quite interesting to investigate what future use will be made of the evaluation results that this evaluation phase has yielded. At the same time there is no doubt in my mind that future empirical effect-evaluation of major INSP subprogrammes is both necessary and feasible.

With respect to the usual organizational conditions that surround large-scale educational evaluation programmes in the Netherlands, the INSP evaluation has been a refreshing experience. Because of the fact that the evaluation of the educational section of the INSP was an integral part of an overall evaluation that covered all the five main areas of the programme, the complicated network-structures that usually have to be developed for each major educational evaluation programme could be dispensed with.

Hopefully, this experience will inspire the funding agencies of follow-up educational evaluations to design flexible and efficient organizational and management conditions for these activities. As for the substantive findings of this evaluation I think two demand further reflection. The first is the importance of education and training to all aspects of IT development and application. Hence the evaluation committee's recommendation to continue to stimulate all types of IT uses in education both in the regular and in the independent educational system. It should be noted, however, that further policy analysis and development is required as to how this should best be accomplished. Particularly the question of how the stimulation of the independent system should be directed and accomplished is a complicated matter.

The second finding in the educational section of the INSP evaluation that is particularly intriguing is the importance of the problem of effective coordination and organization in the process of a large-scale implementation of new applications of computers in education. On this matter the evaluation committee has taken the position of a centralized approach to strategy formation and overall monitoring and decentralization of operation planning and implementation to institutes with a clear mission. I think the way this overall approach could be applied to the particular structure of the Dutch educational system requires further study.

References

Alkin, M C, Daillak, R and White, P (1979) *Using Evaluations* Beverly Hills: Sage Library of Social Research

Cohen, D K (1983) Evaluation and reform in *Stakeholder-based Evaluation*, (New Directions for Program Evaluation no 17) pp 73–81, San Francisco: Jossey Bass

Cronbach, L J and Associates (1980) *Toward Reform of Program Evaluation*, San Francisco: Jossey Bass

Patton, M Q (1978) *Utilization-focused Evaluation*, Beverly Hills: Sage

Plomp, T J, Van Deursen, K and Moonen, J (eds) (1987) *Call for Europe Computer Assisted Learning for Europe* Conference of European Commission on Development of Educational Software, Amsterdam: North Holland Publishing

Scheerens, J (1985) Contextual Influences on Evaluations: The Case of Innovatory Programs in Dutch Education, *Educational Evaluation and Policy Analysis*, 7, 309–317.

12. The Italian school system

Maria Ferraris and Donatella Persico

Structure of the Italian school system

The Italian educational system includes five major types of school as shown in Figure 1:

- ☐ kindergarten (age 3 to 6);
- ☐ primary school (age 6 to 11);
- ☐ middle school (age 11 to 14);
- ☐ high school (age 14 to 19);
- ☐ university (age 19 to 25).

Only primary and middle schools are compulsory, although at both high-school and university level, attendance has increased during the past two decades (Figure 2).

Kindergarten is the only type of school not controlled by the central government; some are run by local authorities, while many others are private institutions often run by religious orders. The children's activities are not based on any pre-defined curriculum, nor are they aimed at providing knowledge within academic disciplines; rather, they target the development of social skills and teamwork attitudes.

Primary school is the first stage of compulsory education. Its curriculum has recently been renewed and now includes: Italian language, history, science, geography, mathematics, music, arts and gymnastics. In addition, the basic elements of a foreign language should be taught, although in practice this is not yet widespread. Typically, primary school engages children four or five hours a day, six days a week, with one teacher who remains the same from the first to the fifth grade. The full-time schedule (eight hours a day, five days a week and two teachers), however, is becoming more and more popular, probably due to the growing number of working mothers. The new curriculum provides for a weekly school schedule of a minimum of 30 hours with more than one teacher for each class.

Middle school lasts three years and its present organization dates back to 1979. In addition to the subjects studied at primary school, the students approach 'technology' and study natural sciences in more detail. All teachers (eight for each class) have a university degree in a discipline related to the

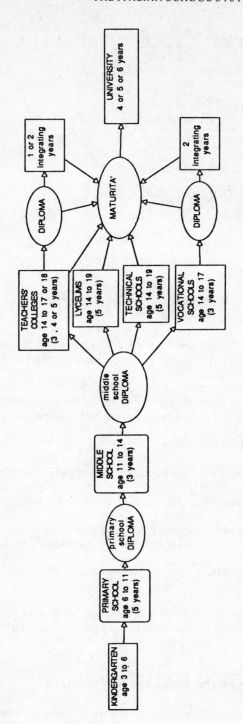

Figure 1 *The Italian school system*

Rectangular boxes: non-compulsory school
Rounded boxes: compulsory school
Ellipses: exams

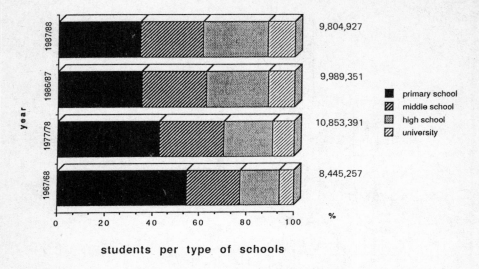

Figure 2 *Student attendance per type of school*

subject(s) they teach. The schedule provides for 30 hours over a six-day week. Like primary schools, however, many middle schools have adopted the full-time schedule.

Students with a middle-school diploma can enter high school, choosing among various types of specializations, as indicated in Figure 1. This choice, made at the age of 14, is quite critical since it is not very easy to move from one school to another later on.

High schools can be grouped as follows:

Lyceums offer students a basic cultural background without any professional emphasis (although there are different types of lyceums with different foci, for example the humanities or sciences). This kind of school is typically chosen by students who intend to go to university.

Technical schools give students different specializations with reference to employment in the industrial, business, accounting, agronomic, building and construction sectors etc.

Teachers' colleges place emphasis on professional and technical skills in different fields.

The high-school diploma (*diploma di maturita*) obtained after five years' high school allows access to any university faculty, regardless of the kind of high school attended.

Management structure of the Italian school system

The Italian school system has, at least as concerns primary and secondary education, a centralized structure under the control of the Ministry of Education. (Universities are now controlled by the Ministry for Research.)

Curricula and timetables for schools are centrally agreed and any experimentation involving their modification has to be authorized by the minister. Decisions made by the minister are transmitted to the *Provveditorati agli Studi* (ie local bodies supervizing schools in a particular area) and then to the head-teachers. Teachers enjoy a wide autonomy as far as teaching strategies and methodologies are concerned: this helps explain the wide variety of educational results.

State schools, which make up the majority of Italian schools (over 90 per cent), are financed by the government, which pays teaching and non-teaching employees.

Compulsory education is free. Fees for non-compulsory education are quite low, expenses for books being the highest cost.

For each type of school (primary, etc) there is a separate administrative body within the Ministry for Education – the *Direzioni generali* – which is in charge of funding, curriculum modifications and the control of the functioning of individual schools through a network of central and local inspectors.

Such centralization of the school system has been partially reduced since 1974 by establishing new forms of school self-government: class councils which decide on their classes' syllabus; school councils, made up of elected teachers and parents (in high schools, student representatives too); and other elective bodies at provincial and national level provided with formal rather than real powers.

In 1974, new bodies were set up for research in the field of education and for in-service teacher training:

☐ Twenty regional bodies for educational research, experimentation and teaching training (IRRSAE). These coordinate initiatives concerning experimentation and teacher training in the Italian regions.

☐ The National Education Library (BDP – *Biblioteca di Documentazione Pedagogica*) in Florence, with the specific task of collecting, storing, documenting and gathering information at a national level.

☐ The European Centre for Education (CEDE – *Centro Europeo Dell'Educazione*) in Frascati (Rome), dealing with documentation on educational systems in other countries and with comparative research at a national level.

All these bodies enjoy complete administrative autonomy and their functions are similar or almost overlapping with those already performed by the ministry and the *Provveditorati*. The integration of these new structures with the old ones does not appear to be an easy task.

Teacher training

Initial teacher training is one of the most disputed and confused aspects of the whole Italian school system. The existing regulations require that all teachers have completed a university course and obtained, inside the university, a teaching qualification diploma (*diploma di abilitazione all'insegnamento*) through specific courses and postgraduate specialization schools.

Such regulations, which became law in 1974 and 1982, are not operative yet;

in practice the situation is very different. In particular there is a gap between the qualification of middle- or high-school teachers (*professori*) and that of kindergarten or primary school teachers (*maestri*). To become a *maestro* it is sufficient to get specific high-school diplomas (*Scuola Magistrale* – three years – and *Instituto Magistrale* – four or five years). As a consequence, it is possible to take part in national examinations required to obtain the teaching qualification and then a permanent post as a *maestro* at the age of 17 and 18.

On the contrary, a university degree (in maths or physics or humanities etc, which takes a minimum of four years after the high-school diploma) is necessary to teach a specific subject in middle and high schools. Unfortunately, no university faculty includes systematic courses devoted to the teaching of a particular subject, nor are there postgraduate specialization courses for teacher training. Young teachers, therefore, though competent in their specific disciplines, often lack pedagogical competence.

According to the law, candidate teachers should qualify through an examination (*abilitazione*) aimed at ascertaining their competence. After such qualification, to get a permanent job in the national school system, they are supposed to pass a national examination (*concorso*). In practice, many derogations of this procedure are made.

The lack of initial competence and the modifications to primary- and middle-school curricula have led, in the past few years, to the proliferation of many training courses for in-service teachers, organized by different bodies (ministry, provincial authorities, IRRSAE, individual schools with the approval and financial support of the local school authorities, university institutes and research bodies interested in promoting experimentation in school).

Generally speaking, however, the participation in updating courses is not compulsory, nor are the contents and organization of the updating system planned at a general level. Teachers are simply required to devote at least 40 hours per year to updating activities. This fragmentary and casual system has recently been partially overcome by launching two national plans: the first concerns the introduction of computer sciences in high school, the second the implementation of the new curricula for primary school. Both plans envisage compulsory updating for thousands of teachers and introduce the concept of recurrent training, thus creating a new professional figure: the 'trainer'.

Assessment system

The assessment methods of students' learning change according to the school level. In compulsory schools (primary and middle schools) qualitative descriptive assessment is used, expressing a judgement on the capacities acquired by the student and on their personality and behaviour. At the end of each year the student is admitted to the following year or, in the case of a negative judgement, made to repeat the same grade.

In secondary education (middle and high school) assessment results are expressed by means of marks (1 to 10 with a pass-mark of 6) assigned by each teacher on the basis of written and oral tests held during the year. At the end of the school year, all marks are summarized by subject in a global judgement, another figure. Students obtaining a pass-mark in all subjects are admitted to the following year; those who fail to reach such a mark in five or more subjects must repeat the grade. Other cases have to take a catching-up examination in the subjects where they are deficient, held before the beginning of the following school-year.

On average, the percentage of students failed in compulsory education is low. On the other hand, in secondary education – and in particular in the first two years of technical schools – the percentage is high, sometimes reaching 50 per cent.

At the end of each school cycle (primary, middle, high school) students must take an examination to get the related diploma and to be admitted to the following school cycle.

Primary- and middle-school final examinations (at 11 and 14 years respectively) are held by the teachers of the school itself and provide a global assessment, expressed in qualitative form, of the student's performance with respect to the curriculum.

The high-school examination (at 19 years) – the *esame di maturita* – is held by an external commission, comprising teachers from other schools who give a global assessment expressed in sixtieths. The written tests, the material and the performance modes of this examination are decided at national level by the Ministry for Education and are therefore the same for all Italian schools, even though the examination subjects (apart from the written test in Italian which is always present) change according to the type of high school.

There is, however, no national standard as concerns the assessment criteria to be adopted in the *esami di maturità*. As a consequence, even though the examinations are formally the same everywhere, there are many differences in the difficulty and in the assessment criteria adopted by the various examining commissions.

The lack of well-defined and homogeneous assessment criteria and tests (by subject and educational level) is typical not only of the final examination but also of the whole school system. It leads to greatly differing levels of competence being exhibited by students who attend the same type of school, following the same curriculum. In fact, especially as far as high school is concerned, reference cannot really be made to the curricula at all, since these are theoretically the same, being established at central level by the Ministry for Education, with respect both to the timetables and to the contents and targets.

Student assessment is a particularly critical aspect of the Italian school system (though this is probably true for any school system). The following papers analyse this issue and offer (without any claim to exhaustivity) examples of studies and experiences presently under way in Italy. They illustrate:

☐ the qualitative assessment system introduced in Italian compulsory education a few years ago (Frabboni);
☐ a procedure to distribute students in different classes at the beginning of middle school (Ferretti & Laviosa);
☐ an analysis of the assessment problems in the field of physics with particular reference to the understanding of commonsense knowledge (Mayer); and
☐ an analysis of objectives and methodologies for assessment in history education (Calvani).

13. Class-group constitution procedure based on student assessment

Maria Ferretti and Lorento Laviosa

Introduction

The example of the procedure for 'class-group constitution' reported here has been applied in the experimental middle school 'Don Lorenzo Milani' in Genoa. Middle schools are included in compulsory education and attended by students between 11 and 14 years of age, who, after five years' primary school, can enrol from any part of the town. Within middle schools, year groups (or grades) are organized in *sezioni*. These are groups of mixed-ability classes, each identified by a letter. Within each *sezioni* there may be up to three grades. Generally, once a student enrols he or she is assigned to the first grade of a given *sezione*; during the following years they will be assigned to the following grades of the same *sezione*. Since each *sezione* is characterized by a constant group of teachers, this procedure generally prevents a student from changing teachers and classmates.

Curricula subjects are taught to each classgroup simultaneously, therefore providing a certain degree of uniformity of curriculum among *sezioni*. One of the problems of all Italian middle schools at the beginning of the school year is the constitution of the first grades and in particular the criteria by which students are grouped inside each *sezione*. No official instructions provide precise indications on how the students are to be subdivided into the various *sezioni*. One of the strategies often followed is to take into account the requests expressed by the families on enrolling their children (such preferences may concern a particular section, and therefore a particular set of teachers, or the foreign language to be taught). This is followed by holding more or less controlled 'draws' aimed at satisfying the largest possible number of families. This procedure, however, means that classes tend to be very unbalanced with a high concentration of low-level students in one class and high-level ones in another. Such lack of homogeneity is increased by the different instructional level of the students entering middle school, due to their coming from different primary schools.

Don Milani is one of the seven Italian experimental schools. As such it is able to make structural modifications, within the state curriculum, which may concern staff and/or aims. In particular, changes may be made to planning, assessment and the application of new educational technologies. In order to experiment with a uniform curriculum for all first, second and third grades, class-groups need to be heterogeneous inside but homogeneous (and therefore comparable) with each other. This need for heterogeneous class-groups is understood at Lorenzo Milani as:

☐ a guarantee of a valid comparison between different class-groups of the educational procedures used (comparable methodologies, verifications, assessments, etc);
☐ a guarantee that each class is representative of the actual school population; and
☐ a guarantee that all students are able to gain experience in a diversified environment and to compare them with experiences and habits different from their own.

Procedure

In an attempt to find a solution to the problem of an equal distribution of students among the first grades of the various *sezioni*, a number of significant variables have been identified.

Type-A variables are knowledge and skills acquired during previous schooling:

Logical–linguistic skills:

☐ (L1) rich vocabulary and its uses;
☐ (L2) rapid logical–verbal operations;
☐ (L3) reading comprehension level.

Logical–mathematical skills

☐ (M1) technical knowledge of the four operations and their use;
☐ (M2) logical skills.

Type-B variables denote social and cultural level of origin:

☐ parents' educational qualifications;
☐ parents' work activities.

Type-A variables aim at establishing level bands. Type-B variables subdivide each level band into three subgroups on the basis of socio-economic status. These data cannot be inferred from the assessment papers of the final grade of the previous school. Therefore pre-enrolled students are called to the Lorenzo Milani School to undertake tests to ascertain type-A variables while parents are asked to complete a questionnaire to ascertain type-B variables.

The testing of students' skills (Test A)

The test consists of 150 questions grouped into five types of defined skills. Students have two hours to answer them. (Table 1 shows some examples of the test items.)

These tests were used for the first time in the school year 1972/73 and later

L1>	Person who is learning a job a) juggler b) specialist c) expert d) apprentice e) technician
L2>	When we lived in the countryside, we knew many birds. My favourite one woke me up . . . on my window sill. a) stopping b) walking c) singing d) barking e) talking
L3> 1)	Once upon a time there was a huge box, full of money. All of a sudden the box rose by some metres spitting fire and smoke. Then the people looking at the box started to run away. What was there inside the huge box? a) Sweets b) Nothing, because it was empty c) Money d) Books
2)	What did the people looking at the box do? a)They got into the box b) They ran away c) They rose inside the box
M1>	A runner covers 245km in 7 hours. How many km does he cover in one hour? a) 245 + 7 b) 245 × 7 c) 245 –7 d) 245 ÷ 7
M2>	In the following series there is a wrong number: 1–7–2–7–3–7–4–7–5–7–6–7–8–7 If you discover their order, you will find it easily As soon as you find it, underline it and write the right number in brackets

Table 1 *Examples of the items used to test logical–linguistic maths skills*

adjusted to our school situation with the help of a team of psychologists and pedagogic experts. The starting point was a model developed by the teachers of the Lorenzo Milani school themselves during an in-service teacher-training course, based on a battery of tests prepared by a research group at the Institute for Psychology of the University of Milan and Pavia.

The students (about 100 per year) are subdivided on the basis of alphabetical order into groups of ten; two teachers are in charge of each group and take care to administer the tests according to modes and paces which are the same for all students. Afterwards, the tests are marked by means of predefined grids, one or two points being given for each correct answer. Males' and females' data are analysed separately because each first grade is intended to reflect the total percentage in respect to this variable too. As mentioned above, the aim of this phase is to subdivide the students into four bands with respect to the abilities assessed by the test.

The adopted criteria do not refer to standard values of competence (ie the test is not a criterion-referenced one, since the 'threshold' values which delimit the bands are calculated each year on the bases of the test results). To achieve this, several ordering types are carried out and compared for each set of items. In particular, the procedure adopted includes:

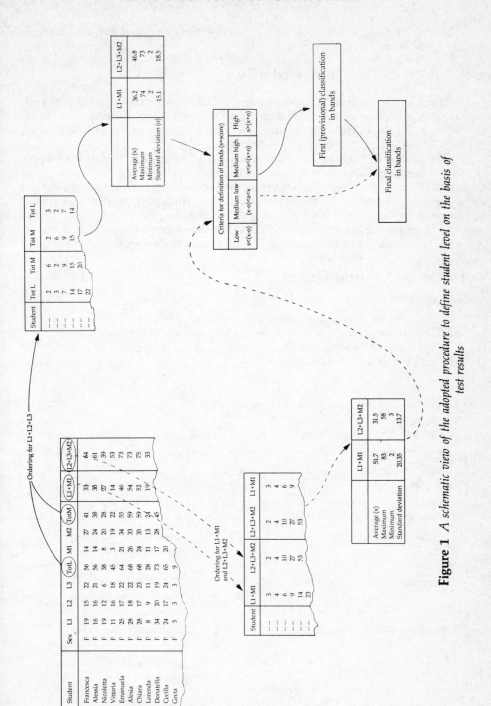

Figure 1 *A schematic view of the adopted procedure to define student level on the basis of test results*

☐ ordering of the total literary-skill answers as compared to mathematical-skill ones;
☐ ordering of the M1+L1 total requiring technical skills, in respect to M2+L2+L3 (requiring logical skills).

Through the analysis of the averages and of the standard deviation of each ordering, the division into four bands is performed (low, medium-low, medium-high and high). As shown in Figure 1, to assign each element to its final band, both orderings are taken into consideration.

Due to the relatively low amount of data (from about 100 students per year), the procedure requires empirical adjustments. However, the results are adequate enough to describe students' test performance. Students showing a great gap between technical and logical skills and students presenting contradictory data are more thoroughly analysed by comparing the papers of the fourth year (penultimate year) of the primary school or by meeting their primary-school teachers. After these further enquiries, contradictory students are fairly distributed in the four bands.

Parents' questionnaire (Test B)

The test asks parents a series of questions concerning:

☐ family composition (eg number of children);
☐ the student's possible psychological and physical problems;
☐ the student's sports and hobbies outside the school environment;
☐ parents' school qualifications;
☐ parents' work activities.

PARENTS' SCHOOL QUALIFICATION	POINTS	PARENTS' JOBS
illiterate or primary school	0	unemployed
primary school certificate	1	disabled/pensioner
middle school certificate	2	unskilled worker/craftsman/housewife
incomplete secondary school	3	skilled worker/shopkeeper/low office worker
secondary school certificate	4	teacher/office worker
degree	5	professional/industrialist/manager

Table 2 *Parameters used to define the family socio-economic status*

Information concerning the first four points is used as a support and completion, if necessary, of the general outlines of the students, without being codified in specific parameters. Information concerning the last two points is codified in numbers using Table 2.

Table 2 is used to deduce the socio-economic status of the family by giving a specific score to the school qualification and jobs of both parents. Each student's status is the sum of the scores of the individual items. The minimum score is zero, the maximum 20. This range is divided into three main subgroups:

☐ a 'low' socioeconomic status (from 0 to 6);
☐ an 'intermediate' one (from 7 to 13); and
☐ a 'high' status (from 14 to 20).

By way of example, a child whose mother attended high school for two years (three points) and is a housewife (two points), whose father has a high-school diploma (four points) and is an office worker (four points) will get a status score of 13. This corresponds to the highest value of the 'intermediate' socio-economic status.

Class-group composition

At the end of the test analysis process, both the female and male student populations are grouped in four bands on the bases of their knowledge (assessed through Test A). Inside each band, a further division reflects the socio-economic status (based upon the parents' questionnaire results). To a certain extent, such distribution reflects the heterogeneity of the newly enrolled student population and it may therefore be used to subdivide the students among the *sezioni* in such a way that the first grade are equally heterogeneous.

For example, let us suppose that the population (about 100 students) comprises 60 per cent females and 40 per cent males and that Test A on logical skills resulted in 25 per cent low-level students, 20 per cent medium–low students, 40 per cent medium-high students and 15 per cent high-level students. A first criterion for subdividing this population into class-groups (usually five class-groups out of 100 students) is to reflect these percentages in sex and competence bands. In our example, therefore, in the first place five class-groups are formed consisting of 12 females and eight males; five students out of 20 (25 per cent) belonging to the low-level band, four to the medium–low, eight to the medium–high and three to the high. The second stage of the class-constitution procedure is an adjustment of the class-groups to reflect the distribution of the socio-economic status of the actual population. Finally, the end result is analysed and, possibly, modified to meet the families' requirements.

Notwithstanding this schematic description, in practice the class-constitution procedure is not so clear and deterministic, since it requires an interactive process of stepwise refinements and mediations to solve a series of problems which are not of a purely statistical nature.

Once the student subdivision is finalized, all class councils are called to be informed by the 'class-constitution commission', about the students' group and the particular cases present. They are also informed about the number of students belonging to each band (eg 25 per cent L; 20 per cent ML; 35 per cent

MH; 20 per cent H) without any names being mentioned. The students whose difficulties are signalled by the psychopedagogic advisory bureau are discussed in more detail.

Conclusion

Of course, the variables taken into account up to now cannot include or highlight factors concerning each student's personality (in the assessment paper of the fourth grade of the primary school there are only references to the student's behaviour and diligence) and even less to the dynamics which will be activated within the class-groups. The variable of personality, which cannot be checked, involves several problems which we have not been capable of solving by codifying it; this has led us to regard the first 15 schooldays as a period for monitoring the class-group dynamics and the attitudes of the individual students. During this period, students can be moved inside the same band from one *sezione* to another. This possibility, however, has rarely been used because there is a big difference between working with abstract names and data and deciding these changes after meeting the students. Such changes are often experienced by the teachers as a sign of their inability to integrate the class-group. There is also a tendency not to subject the student to a situation which he/she might experience as a form of rejection.

During the first school month, all the teachers work out entrance tests taking into account prerequisite skills for the various subjects. These tests concern not so much knowledge as skills – and can therefore be used by several teachers (in close connection with entrance tests). At the end of this period, the 'class-constitution' commission asks the various councils for a distribution of the students in four level bands, similar to the initial ones. The comparison with the initial distribution (performed for at least the past six years) has highlighted that the results are reliable even though there are some variations in the distribution, widening the gap between the high and low bands (ie the intermediate bands lose elements in favour of bands A and B). As we see it, the differences in results between the two assessment procedures cannot be eliminated because they are due to factors not considered by the tests employed, such as the influence of the emotivity factor (which affects the initial test more than the one performed in the class situation) and the deeper knowledge between teachers and students (which favours a better discrimination of the student's real skills).

14. Diagnostic testing in formative assessment: the students as test developers

A Di Carlo and G Trentin

Summary: By acting as authors the students are more responsible as to what they learn and how they learn it; this leads them to test their knowledge through a critical revision. The experience described in this chapter was based on a particular role played by students, who created an assessment test working on a personal computer. The test was developed using the DELFI system in connection with a methodology based on a hierarchical model of contents. For this purpose the students have constructed the hierarchy of test contents and formulated the specific queries in an exhaustive way.

The results of this particular approach were: self- and peer-assessing about the internalization of contents; mastering the appropriate language of the subject matter; becoming aware of topic mastering.

Introduction

One of the main objectives of the teaching/learning process is deepening knowledge by focusing the attention on what is learnt and how it is learnt (Laurillard, 1987).

In the research literature, knowledge has often been described as cognitive structure (Ausubel *et all* 1968), semantic memory (Tulving, 1972) or schemata (Rumelhart and Ortony, 1977).

Knowledge attainment is a dynamic process, based on a net (cognitive structure) logically connecting the key concepts (Pask and Boyd, 1987), which determines a restructuring of the net itself as it expands or as pre-existing knowledge is modified by new elements. Ausubel *et al* (1968) assert that students can *meaningfully* learn concepts by actively linking the new ideas to *anchoring ideas* in their cognitive structure which will be modified in the process; he contrasts this meaningful form of learning with *rote* learning.

Knowledge structuring does not follow a unitary scheme or one which can be predefined: when a new knowledge quantum is introduced into the net, its logical connections with the pre-existing elements must be identified. In this stage, research points out the difficulties resulting from the gap between the common-sense understanding of phenomena and the scientific theories.

These difficulties can be ascribed to the presence of mental images not coherent with scientific theories, to the resistance of such ideas against change, or to the fact that transferring scientific knowledge to the level of common experience is not always an easy task (Tall, 1986).

To explain the non-coherence between theoretical contents conveyed by the teacher and what the student learns in terms of personal knowledge, Tall uses the term *concept image*

to describe the total cognitive structure that is associated with the concept, which includes all mental pictures and associated properties and processes. . . As the concept image develops it need not be coherent at all time. . . We shall call the portion of the concept image which is activated at a particular time the *evoked concept image*. At different times, seemingly conflicting images may be evoked. Only when conflicting aspects are evoked simultaneously need be any actual sense of conflict or confusion (Tall and Vinner, 1981).

These remarks underline the need to stress two particular moments in the learning process: the awareness of the acquired knowledge and internal assessment or self-assessment.

The adopted learning-process model

The learning-process model adopted in the experience described below is a cyclic one (Di Carlo, Galizia Angeli and Trentin, 1988), which proceeds in successive steps and where each individual step can be schematically illustrated as shown in Figure 1.

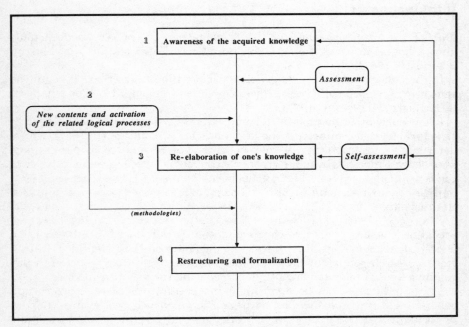

Figure 1 *The adopted learning-process model*

Each individual step in the learning process is therefore subdivided into the following phases:

1. Awareness of the acquired knowledge: this is a moment of balance, the achievement of a target in the cognitive process.

   This target is satisfactorily achieved if the student a) perceives themself as builder of their own knowledge, b) is aware of their knowledge; c) can manage the acquired knowledge.

   The assessment, performed by the teacher, aims at verifying the mastery of the subject with the prospect of dealing with the subsequent knowledge steps through the introduction of new contents, the activization of logical processes and the use of methodologies which are either new or already at the disposal of the student.

2. Acquisition of new contents and activation of the related logical processes.

3. Reflection on the relations between the new information and pre-existing knowledge: thought-producing processes are activated in this phase.

4. Formalization of new contents, revision, and updating of the cognitive net: the ability to organize and structure knowledge is mostly involved in this phase.

   It is in this phase that students may find difficulties activating themselves and consequently too often accept the proposal of the textbook or of the teacher: this is the moment when it is interesting to intervene with proposals which stimulate internal assessment (self-assessment) by the student.

The aim of the experience: the control of one's learning

In order better to organize learning, it is necessary to consider the various phases into which the teaching activity can be subdivided: design of an instructional path within the curriculum, presenting new contents, assessing the students' learning.

In each of these phases the teacher must be convinced that the students and their learning strategy play a basic role since knowledge is built by each learner autonomously and according to their individual learning process. In this learning situation, teachers must not limit themselves to providing information but must, first of all, induce and stimulate internalization (Larsen, 1986). Only when feeling responsible for their learning do students focus attention on what is learnt and how it is learnt. In other words 'the student is given control over what the content can be, as well as control over their access to and experience of it' (Laurillard, 1987). Such control refers to the learning strategy, contents handling and contents description.

The main objective of the work described below is in helping the students become used to handling and describing knowledge. The student plays an active role; in scientific subjects, it is very important to help the students become masters of their own knowledge and know how to use it when necessary, avoiding imposing repetitive calculation exercises on them and usage of formulas that we don't think meaningful from the cognitive point of view. It is necessary to stimulate creative handling of the contents, as well as the use of the correct terminology in describing such contents. The purpose of this kind of learning situation is to lead the student to give personal sense to the knowledge used (Comiti, 1988).

The debate in class on particular aspects of the topic can be stimulating and productive but each student can be really involved in the classwork only if they have internal motivation or if assigned a task they are capable of inducing such motivation. Such a task may be, for example, producing an *original object* for use by other students.

The psychological mechanisms connected with the production task are not dealt with here, but it can probably be maintained that student motivation increases if they have to produce something, because they feel that their work will be evaluated not only by the teacher, but also by other people, and best of all other students: it is not the mark which is important, but the quality and effectiveness of the work (Di Carlo and Trentin, 1988).

In dealing with the development of any learning material regarding a specific knowledge domain under study (a short lesson, a course, an assessment test), students are stimulated to organize the information they have, seeking the most correct and effective way to use and state it. In this phase student-authors must, on the one hand, transform their own knowledge (what has been learnt as a result of an instructional intervention) into adequately organized information, and on the other they must treat the communication of the information by means of a correct structural setting of the contents and the correct linguistic formulation of this contents.

It is clear, moreover, that in order to develop any learning material, a certain mastering of the related topic is necessary (consider, for example, the formulation of the queries for an assessment test). During the design, assessment and development of the material, students have the opportunity of self-verifying their learning level with regard to that specific content and successively of becoming aware of the acquired knowledge.

Any doubts, uncertainties or difficulties related to the knowledge necessary to perform the work inevitably hinder performance. Doubts, uncertainties and difficulties therefore represent a useful guide for the student to identify the knowledge lacking and to study the corresponding topics thoroughly.

Two crucial moments can therefore be identified in the process of developing the work, corresponding to two specific aims: self-assessment and consolidation:

☐ *Self-assessment:* while developing the work, the difficulties which occur often help students identify the unknown topics necessary for the complete and correct performance of the work (formative assessment).

☐ *Consolidation:* If students identify the gaps, they re-examine the knowledge domain, thoroughly studying unknown topics responsible for the difficulties which occurred while developing the work, and may suggest a new version of the work itself.

The five phases of the experiment

The experience described below is based on the role played by the students, who were asked to devise the instructional material themselves. The experiment was carried out, within a mathematics course, in the first year of a scientific lyceum with 14-year-old students.

The experiment was divided into the following phases:

- [ ] choice and specifications of the material to be produced;
- [ ] design and production of the material;
- [ ] analysis of the produced material;
- [ ] use;
- [ ] debate between users and authors about the material produced.

Choice and specifications of the material to be produced

The students were encouraged to create an assessment test working on a personal computer, related to a subject of study included in their mathematics course. The exercise was intended to satisfy the two main objectives of the whole experiment, ie:

- [ ] stimulate the students to reflect on their state of knowledge on the specific topic;
- [ ] motivate the students with the prospect of assessing, by computer, their peers' learning with reference to a common subject of study.

After a preliminary analysis of the topics treated in the mathematics course, 'order relations' were chosen as test contents. The subject was chosen because it had recently been introduced into the curriculum (Nuovi Programmi; 1986) and also because it is sufficiently complex to allow the construction of a hierarchy of the concepts involved.

After going into the details of the theoretical aspects through lectures and individual study focusing on the specific topic, the students, subdivided into working groups, went on to the second phase: designing the material.

Design and production of the material

In this phase the students were introduced to some typical features of instructional material design, stressing content structuring. The aim was to make the students aware that the production of any educational unit must be preceded by a detailed structuring of the topics, in order to define prerequisites, modes and display sequences. For this reason the students were asked, as first step, to structure the contents schematically under test by means of a hierarchical representation. The basic assumption was that the ability to represent one's knowledge is one of the keys to using it (Donald, 1987).

On hierarchically ordering the contents under test, the students were asked to:

- [ ] Analyse the subject domain in order to clarify the least understood aspects focusing the main topics involved:

  - – total/partial order;
  - – order and pre-order relations;
  - – all relations' properties;
  - – relations on a set;
  - – relations between elements of two sets;
  - – A X A and A X B.

☐ Define the bounds of the topic; in other words, recognize what distinguishes order relations from other kinds of relations, putting aside non-essential concepts.

　　For example A X A, A X B, relations *between elements of two sets and symmetrical property* don't intervene in the definition of order relation if they also constitute a prerequisite knowledge of them.

☐ Identify the key concepts.

☐ Describe each key concept through the specific mathematical language.

☐ Graphically represent the contents structure by making explicit the interconnections among the various topics.

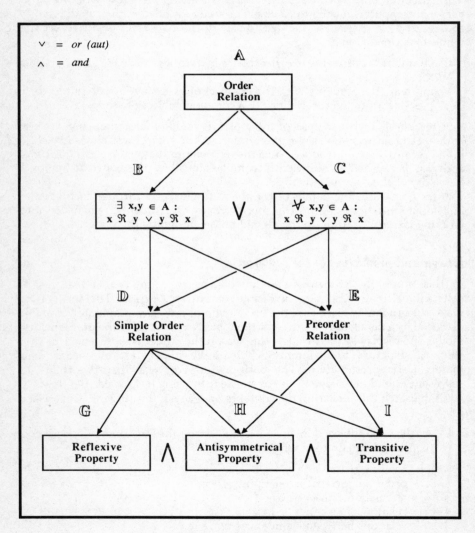

Figure 2 *A hierarchical model of contents*

To develop these activities, the students organized themselves into work groups and each group elaborated a hierarchy of contents. The hierarchies produced were discussed in a class debate, reaching a unified version that was subsequently used to develop the test. This activity confirmed that the representations of a contents structure reflect the analysis method used to produce it and that various versions are possible (Donald, 1987). The working groups agreed on the following hierarchical model.

THE DEVELOPMENT TOOL USED

When developing learning material on computer, either the author knows and uses a programming language or relies on systems usually called *authoring systems*. When carrying out an experiment with 14-year-old students it is difficult to find classes skilled at programming, and it is therefore necessary to rely on systems which allow the development of lessons, practice or, in this case, tests on computer, without the need to deal with the specific language used to programme the machine.

For this experiment only authoring systems allowing the development of diagnostic learning tests were taken into consideration and the DELFI system was chosen.

After defining the contents structure, therefore, the students provided DELFI with the corresponding hierarchy and the output was information on the number of queries to be asked as well as on their structure.

THE DELFI SYSTEM

The DELFI system is based upon a specific methodology to develop diagnostic tests (Ferraris, Midoro and Olimpo, 1983). The system gives assistance and support to the author in performing most conceptual phases of test design and fully automates the production of the code for test delivery, so freeing the author from a complex task devoid of conceptual content and extremely error prone (Ferraris, Midoro, Olimpo and Trentin, 1984).

The input to the system is the hierarchy representing the content domain, interactively supplied by the author. On the basis of the hierarchy and of the logic links supplied by the author, the system generates the item table, that is, the table indicating the number of test items necessary for the assessment of the hierarchy nodes and, for each of them, the nodes (skills) to be involved in the corresponding questions.

For instance, the node A, the highest in the hierarchy, has two distinct items associated with it, A1 and A2. A1 should involve the subnodes A, B, D, G, H, I while A2 should involve A, C, E, H, I. The purpose of the item table is to help the author to define the structure and the content of each individual item.

This activity, together with the hierarchy construction, is the only phase which cannot be fully automated and requires the author to select the item type suitable for verifying the skills involved by a given node and the formulation of the item on the basis of the skills involved.

The last phase of test development concerns the automatic generation of the code for actual test delivery according to a top-down strategy. It should be noted that the code produced by DELFI also includes the storage of test results in a file which can be subsequently used by suitable programs to provide individual feedback, course feedback or individual diagnosis.

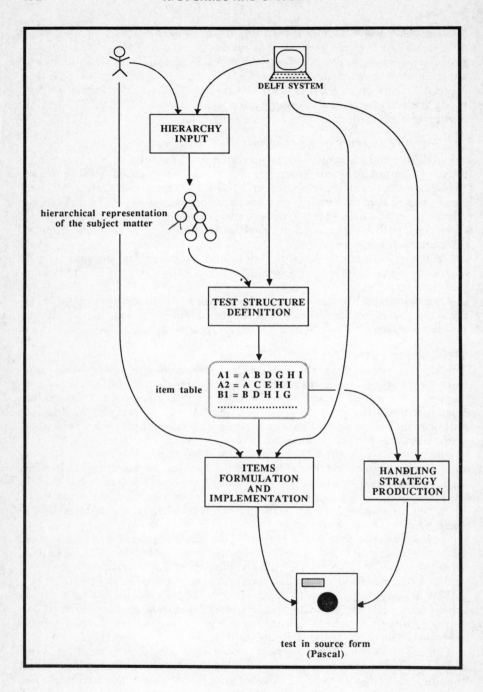

hierarchical representation
of the subject matter

item table

Figure 3 *The phases of test design*

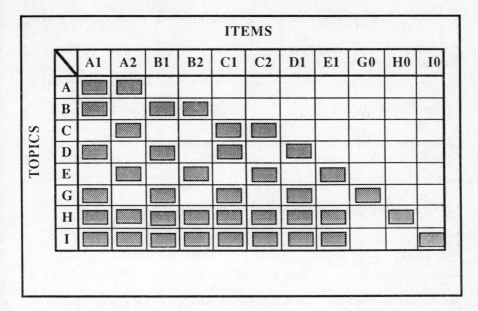

Figure 4 *The item table for the hierarchy related to order relations*

The second activity performed by the students was formulating the queries. In structuring the contents, the aim was the organization of one's knowledge, in formulating the queries the focus was on communication. In the course of their work the students came to appreciate the value of a high-quality computer/user interaction, the importance of which grew with the specificity of the contents involved.

In this sense, beside using the specific mathematical language properly, the main task for the students was devising the most appropriate formulation of the queries in order to make them effective, non-ambiguous, non-misleading, non-self-explaining, concise and correct from the point of view both of the contents and of the terminology used. In particular, on preparing a multiple-choice test, much attention was paid to the alternative answers to the questions, particularly because of the specific features required: at least four, similar structure, strictly related to the contents, non-self-explaining, likely though wrong, respecting the convention that only one answer in a group could be right (Ferraris, Midoro, Olimpo, Persico and Trentin, 1988).

Each group of students prepared the individual items; the items for the final draft of the test were then chosen during class discussion. Queries A2 and C2 are noted below as examples.

Analysis of the material produced

The aim of the analysis, performed by the student authors themselves with the help of their teacher, was to verify the test flow and the effectiveness of communication. For this reason the first users of the test were the authors

---

Question A2

Complete the following definition: "the relation R, on the set S, makes S completely preordered if"

---

1. there exist x,y ∈ S,   x,y : x R y   and   R is reflexive and transitive,

2. there exist x,y ∈ S,   x,y : x R y   and   R is not transitive,

3. for all x,y ∈ S,   x,y : x R y   and   R is transitive and antisymmetrical,

4. for all x,y ∈ S,   x,y : x R y   and   R is reflexive and antisymmetrical,

0. I don't know

Choose your answer (0-4):

Question C2

Which of the following orderings makes the done set well ordered ?

---

1. $R°$: x = y / k,   k ∈ N,   x,y ∈ D,   D ={ 2, 3, 6, 7, 11, 13 },

2. R'' : x ≤ y,   x,y ∈ C,   C = { 1, 3, A, S, 5, T },

3. R : x = ky,   k ∈ N,   x,y ∈ A,   A = { 2, 3, 5, 6, 8, 9 },

4. R' : x ≥ y,   x,y ∈ B,   B = { 1, 2, 3, 4, 5, 6 },

0. I don't know

Choose your answer (0-4):

Table 1 *Questions A2 and C3*

themselves, who, after identifying any weak points (ambiguity in formulating the queries, misspellings. . .) made any necessary changes.

Use

The real test on the spot was performed by a class in the first year which followed the same program. The student users were explicitly asked to perform a critical analysis of the test as regards the correctness of the contents, the symbols used and the mathematical language, as well as the clear formulation of the items.

Debate between users and authors on the produced material

The final phase of the work was a meeting between the student authors and the student users in order to perform a critical analysis of the work done from the various points of view. During the meeting:

☐ The student authors answered users' criticism by motivating their choices with self-assurance and mastery of the topics. They explained the formulation of some questions – for example, the reasons that determined the requirement of individualizing the right definition between multiple choices, instead of applying the definition to individualize the kind of property or order relation. Asserting that, for what concerns the property, generally it is easier to give the definition than being able to understand if it has been applied, but you can't recognize an order relation if you aren't able correctly to apply the properties.

☐ The work developed in the test realization, the habit of comparing ideas and the teacher's corrections about the language used appeared evident during the debate. Student authors gave a rigorous and spontaneous usage of the set language, in comparison with that of the student users.

Instructional remarks on the specific approach adopted and conclusions

Developing something for possible users may help students become aware of the learning level reached with regard to a specific topic, allowing them actively to intervene when inadequacies were noticed. In this way it is the students themselves who create and strengthen their own knowledge by developing a net of connections between concepts, ideas and information.

The kind of approach followed requires particular care by the teacher in the choice of the topic, which must be sufficiently complex (ie, though defined by exact limits, it must provide the possibility of being structured in various ways). This remark, in particular with mathematics, points above all to theoretical topics with different applications (in this case algebraic and geometrical topics) as subjects to be processed.

In general terms, it can be stated that the teamwork, focusing on specific aspects of the knowledge domain, imposes a twofold commitment on the students: on the one hand the close investigation of the theoretical concepts which must be thoroughly mastered and on the other hand, the ability to express themselves clearly to other people in the team.

Generally speaking at a pedagogical level, the students showed serious commitment to the work and remarkable enthusiasm for a topic difficult for the abstraction level required and not particularly fascinating for 14-year-olds. They attained remarkable self-assurance which came out in the contacts with the designers of the experiment. The student authors illustrated the work performed and provided reasons for each of the choices made.

Reading the final report of the students, the teacher could verify that the aims, in terms of knowledge structuring and representation, had been achieved. Some particularly significant passages are quoted below:

'This work is more useful for the authors of the test than for its users, because it has made it possible to criticize what was being done and thus to correct it.'

'Only those who have already mastered the topics can build the contents hierarchy.'

'By building the hierarchy we have understood what the minimum knowledge required is.'

'The habit of building hierarchies might also be extended to other subjects.'

'The work path followed has allowed us to understand that the textbook follows a path too, something we recognized only after building a few hierarchies.'

'Order relations, we'll never forget them!!!'

To sum up, we can state that the experiment has achieved its aims, though some problems still exist; in particular: *Can it be repeated? Is it productive?* Of course, for reasons of time, it cannot be expected to extend this kind of work to all curricular subjects. Each year, however, one topic might be thoroughly studied, parallel to the ministerial curriculum, producing the related test of courseware: this would also help the students acquire a working method.

References

Ausubel, D P, Novak, J D and Hanesian, H (1968) *Educational Psychology: A Cognitive View* (2nd edition 1978), Holt, Rinehart and Winston, New York

Comiti, C (1988) *A Proposal for a Process Organizing the Role of Teacher and Students to Allow the Learners to Construct their own Knowledge*, communication presented at the 6th ICME, Budapest

Di Carlo, A, Galizia Angeli, M T (1988) 'Un test di valutazione per produrre pensiero matematico: un'esperienza', *Proceedings of 8th National Didactical Congress*, Cagliari, Italy

Di Carlo, A, Galizia Angeli, M T and Trentin, G (1988) *Diagnostic tests in learning evaluation: an alternative use in the knowledge organization*, short communication presented at the 6th ICME, Budapest

Di Carlo, A and Trentin, G (1988) 'Le Reti di Petri nella didattica della matematica', *Proceedings of the 12th CIIM-UMI*, Sorrento, Italy

Donald, J G (1987) 'Learning Schemata: Methods of Representing Cognitive, Content and Curriculum Structures in Higher Education', *Instructional Science, 16*, 187–211

Ferraris, M, Midoro, V and Olimpo, G (1983) 'Diagnostic testing and the development of CAL remedial sequences', *Proceedings of 4th Symposium of Educational Technology*, Winnipeg.

Ferraris, M, Midoro, V, Olimpo, G, Persico, D and Trentin, G (1988) *DELFI: Manuale d'uso*, ITD-CNR technical report, 69

Ferraris, M, Midoro, V, Olimpo, G and Trentin, G (1984) 'DELFI: un sistema per la valutazione diagnostica dell'apprendimento.' *Proceedings of the Annual AICA Congress*, vol 1, 435–51

Larsen, S (1986) 'Information can be transmitted but knowledge must be induced'. *PLET (Programmed Learning & Educational Technology), 23, 4*, 331–36

Laurillard, D (1987) 'Computers and the Emancipation of Students: Giving Control to the Learner', *Instructional Science, 16*, 3–18

Nuovi Programmi di Matematica per il biennio della scuola Secondaria Superiore [New Mathematical Programs for the biennium of High Schools] (1986), Bollettino UMI XII, 2

Pask, G and Boyd, G (1987) 'Conversation Theory as Basis for Instructional Design', in D Laurillard, *Interactive Media: Working Methods and Practical Applications*, Ellis Horwood Chichester/J Wiley, New York

Rumelhart, D E and Ortony, A (1977) 'The Representation of Knowledge in Memory', in R C
    Anderson, R J Spiro and W E Montague (eds), *Schooling and the Acquisition of Knowledge*, Laurence
    Erlbaum Associates, New Jersey
Tall, D O (1986). 'Building and Testing a Cognitive Approach to the Calculus using Interactive
    Computer Graphics', PhD thesis, University of Warwick
Tall, D O and Vinner, S (1981) 'Concept Image and Concept Definition in Mathematics, with Special
    Reference to Limit and Continuity', *Educational Studies in Mathematics*, 12, 151–69
Tulving, E (1972) 'Episodic and semantic memory', in E Tulving and W Donaldson (eds), *Organization
    of memory*, Academic Press, New York

15. Assessing and understanding common-sense knowledge

Michela Mayer

Assessment in school is generally concerned with the *effects* of the teaching process. Whether it is carried out in a traditional way (in Italy through colloquia or written essays) or through objective tests, assessment is intended to test the *knowledge* acquired and its *applications*. Only in a few cases is the mastery of methods and procedures tested. Thus, the assessment tools are almost always used in school in order to test and evaluate students' achievement, not to know and understand the students' way of thinking. Teachers accept, often implicitly, a 'behaviourist paradigm' of the teaching process and consider students as 'tabulae rasae', empty blackboards where 'school knowledge' has to be written.

This old assumption has to be revised in the light of the 'constructivist' theory of learning, and greater importance has to be given to the previous knowledge students have, as authors like Ausubel claim:

> If I had to reduce all of educational psychology to just one principle, I would say this: the most important single factor influencing learning is what the learner already knows. Ascertain this and teach him accordingly (Ausubel, 1968).

Common-sense knowledge and scientific knowledge

In the last ten years several research projects have been undertaken all over the world on 'previous knowledge' and its importance, especially in science-learning processes. Some researchers prefer to call it 'misconceptions' (Za'rour, 1975) or 'preconceptions' (Novak, 1977); others speak about 'children's science' (Gilbert, Osborn and Fensham, 1982) or 'alternative frameworks' (Driver and Easley, 1978). I prefer to use the item 'common-sense knowledge' in order to stress that school science and science teaching have to cope with a different, but consistent, kind of knowledge rather than with 'mistakes'.

Bachelard indicated in 1938 that scientific knowledge is built up through a progressive differentiation of common-sense ideas and therefore that learning takes place by overcoming everyday knowledge. What changes, in general, is not the experiences but the 'theories', often the implicit or 'tacit' theories (Polanyi, 1966) used to give meaning to the experiences.

How are these theories built? In spontaneous common-sense theories, differences matter, not similarities. Moreover, they do not aim at simplicity, coherence and generalization, as scientific theories do. As reality is a complex matter, scientific knowledge is a way to simplify it just as the intersection of a plane with a complex n-dimensional solid reduces dimensionality. On the other hand, the common-sense knowledge is sometimes nearer to the complexity of the real world.

Scientific knowledge and common-sense knowledge correspond to different 'levels' of representations of reality. In order to pass from one level to another, a change in the system of rules which give meaning to experiences is necessary. This change between systems of rules belongs to a different logical type as compared to a change within a system of rules. As Watzlawick *et al* (1975) pointed out, the change can take place only by considering the tacit or implicit rules and by being aware of their existence. In this case it is possible to use this meta-knowledge in order to obtain meaningful learning, where the previous, common-sense thinking is not removed but reinterpreted from a different point of view.

This theoretical perspective proposes new aims for the assessment process, and new aims mean new contents and new methodologies. For instance, not only is it impossible in this perspective to assess a concept asking a single question, it is also impossible to isolate a concept from the complex network or 'conceptual map' (Novak and Gowin, 1984) to which such concept belongs.

CEDE research: conceptual maps

Within this theoretical framework, a research project on common-sense knowledge in secondary-school students (compared with scientific knowledge) was carried out at CEDE* (Mayer, 1987).

The aim of the research was to provide teachers with a tool allowing a deeper, and relatively rapid, understanding of students' common-sense conceptions, schemata or theories on five different physics topics: light/vision, inertia, forces, pressure/weight/gravity, electric circuits.

For every concept or group of concepts taken into account, the research compared a scientific conceptual map with a common-sense knowledge map. These maps are general rather than 'individual'. The scientific conceptual map was derived from current textbooks while the common-sense-knowledge map was derived from previous research using individual or group interviews.

Figure 1 shows the common-sense map for one of the chosen topics; pressure/ weight/gravity. As other researchers pointed out, these three concepts can be linked together by students in many different ways:

☐ gravity and weight may be conceived as separate entities (Gunstone and White, 1981; Watts and Zylbersztain, 1981; Vicentini, 1982);
☐ weight may be considered as a characteristic property of bodies, and therefore weight may be confused with the concept of mass;

* CEDE, European Centre for Education, is the Italian institute devoted to comparative educational research and is associated to the IEA. (International Association for the Evaluation of School Achievement.)

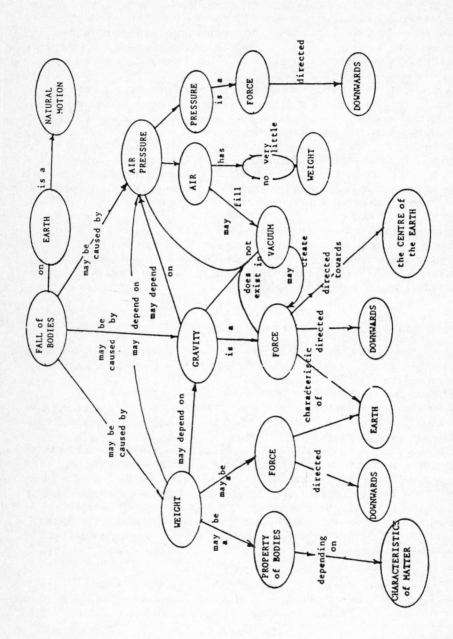

Figure 1: *A common-sense conceptual map for the topic pressure/weight/gravity*

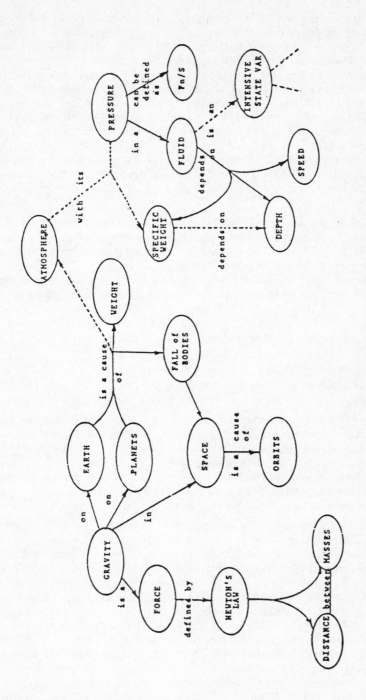

Figure 2: *A textbook conceptual map for the same topic*

- [ ] gravity is often seen as the 'falling down' property of a body, where down means 'downwards', in a 'vertical' direction. Sometimes gravity is a characteristic only of the Earth, linked to the presence of the atmosphere, which implies air pressure (Ruggiero *et al*, 1985);
- [ ] pressure in everyday language is related to a force. For atmospheric pressure, this force is conceived as directed only downwards;
- [ ] pressure, and the related concept of vacuum, are for common sense undetermined concepts, as recent research pointed out (Engel and Driver, 1981: Ruggiero *et al*, 1985). Moreover in Italian (as in Greek and Latin) a single word, *vuoto*, is used both for 'vacuum' and for 'empty space'. Therefore, in everyday language *vuoto* means a space 'empty of things' but 'filled with air'. When the word is used in describing special situations, as for instance interplanetary space, 'no air' is, implicitly or explicitly, linked with 'no gravity'.

According to the *present* scientific view, represented in Figure 2 many of these links implied by common-sense are absurd. However in the *past*, opinions about movement, falling bodies and vacuum were very different from today, and in some cases very similar to present common-sense knowledge. For instance Galileo and Gassendi considered gravity as an effect, and not a cause, of weight; they linked the absence of air to the absence of forces and movement.

CEDE research: questionnaires

By comparing the two maps – the common-sense and the scientific – one notices a lot of differences. On the basis of these differences, a questionnaire was constructed for every topic we dealt with. Each quesionnaire comprised:

- [ ] free-response questions on the meaning of the 'key words' used in the questionnaire (for instance, for the topic described above, the meaning of the words: weight, gravity, pressure, *vuoto*);
- [ ] multiple-choice or free-response questions on the 'critical differences' between the scientific and the common-sense knowledge highlighted by the two conceptual maps. For each multiple-choice question, students were asked to give explanations for their choice.

Not all the topics were equivalent: forces, inertia and electric circuits were more 'school topics' and the questionnaires were more directed to assess the presence, or absence, of scientific concepts or schemata. On the other hand, light/vision and pressure/weight/gravity reflected the spontaneous links established by common-sense knowledge. However, in both cases the questions proposed were not ordinary ones, as in the IEA achievement tests, but were specifically designed to 'activate' the common-sense point of view. Many questions were adapted to the Italian context and language from other research.

The five questionnaires were constructed in two different versions, suitable to be administered before and after physics instruction. The two forms were designed to be very similar in order to allow a comparison between the answers. The whole sample consisted of 600 secondary school students, aged from 14 to 18 years, and coming from three types of secondary schools (humanistic,

	TOPIC				
	L	I	F	P	E
Number of Students	179	369	544	518	292
Number of common items	21	12	20	18	16
Mean	7.83	4.05	7.45	5.62	8.44
Standard deviation	4.0	2.4	3.1	3.3	2.7
Cronbach alfa	.80	.64	.64	.74	.64

Table 1 *Results of the five questionnaires. Letters refer to the topics. L-light/vision, I-inertia, F-forces, P-pressure/weight/gravity, E-electric circuits*

scientific and technical) which differ in the number of hours of physics and in the school years in which physics is taught.

Table 1 shows the results obtained in the five topics, for those items common to the two versions. Letters refer to the topic (L for light, I for inertia, and so on). Every scientific answer supported by a *correct explanation*, scored one point.

The mean value and standard deviation, when compared with the number of items, show how difficult it is for the students to master a coherent and meaningful scientific view of reality, even after studying physics courses. Even more interesting are the results of an analysis of variance, calculated for different variables gathered by means of a background-information question-naire. It seems that the results on the two questionnaires more closely linked to common-sense knowledge are *less* dependent on gender differences and more dependent on the family's level of education. Physics teaching, of course, improves the performance, and the significance of the variance for 'year of course' is high, but it does not eliminate the initial difference.

The questionnaires: main factors and results

A qualitative and quantitative analysis was undertaken for each questionnaire. From the former point of view, using free responses and multiple-choice answers, it was possible to check the hypothetical common-sense map previously drawn and to find other unforeseen relationships.

The ambiguity of the language was confirmed as a crucial obstacle to the understanding of a scientific statement or of a mass-media item of information. For instance, the percentage of students who declare 'to take air out of a given space means that the objects in this space will float' increases with schooling (from 11 per cent to 20 per cent), because no books actually point out that 'no air' doesn't mean 'no gravity'. Gravity for some students can be a 'force which keeps objects from falling' and this statement was explained by a student as follows: 'I saw it on TV during the shuttle launch . . . with the engines out the rocket was kept in orbit *by gravity*'.

From this qualitative analysis two general conclusions can be drawn:

☐ Scientific definitions are difficult to remember and to master. Only a minority of students (ranging from 10 per cent to 40 per cent after a physics course) are able to give a meaningful explanation of the key words proposed.

☐ Students' common-sense definitions before teaching are rich in terms of imagination and references to everyday situations. After teaching, their variety decreases, as do the relationships which pupils are able to establish between the scientific definitions and everyday life examples.

From a quantitative point of view, a factor analysis confirmed the importance of different conceptual schemata. So the more important factor for the forces questionnaire, explaining more than 15 per cent of the variance, is the *impetus* (McCloskey, 1984) or the *capital of force* (Viennot, 1979) naive theory. Students used the idea of an 'inner force', consumed by friction during a movement, in order to explain the movement of a thrown object where no external forces but gravity are visible. Inertia is interpreted, within this naive but very consistent theory, as a force which is needed to explain uniform movement; textbooks often strengthen this idea by reference to 'inertia force'. A 'Newtonian theory' of movement is mastered by less than 5 per cent of the students *after* the physics course. These results are confirmed by a similar questionnaire proposed to students who attended the basic physics course at the University of Rome.

For the light/vision questionnaire the two more important factors were a *Lux* naive theory contrasting with a *Lumen* scientific theory (19 per cent of the variance explained) and a *visual rays* naive theory (15 per cent of the variance explained). For the first one, light is a property of space which permits vision (La Rosa *et al*, 1984). It is a static situation in the sense that light is present everywhere when one has a *light source* and when *vision* is possible. In the quesionnaire we asked, for different light sources, 'how far from the source will you find light?' For scientific knowledge there is only one answer: 'light will travel until it finds an obstacle'. But from a common-sense point of view the distance covered depends on the type of light source (a lamp, a candle,. . .) and on external conditions (day or night). In Figure 3 the distribution of answers before and after the physics course is reported for the case of the light source being a 'lighted cigarette in the night'.

Although the question stressed that the lit cigarette was 'visible', almost no student chose the D answer: 'light comes out as far as you but no further', or the C: 'light comes out about half way towards you'. The majority of the students before the physics course decided that 'light stays around the cigarette' and also after the physics course more than 40 per cent of the students preferred the B answer to the scientific one (E).

This 'decoupling' between vision and light is confirmed by the questions, adapted from one of Jung's investigations (1981) and presented in Figure 4.

Only 5 per cent of the students gave the scientific answer, 'no one can see both

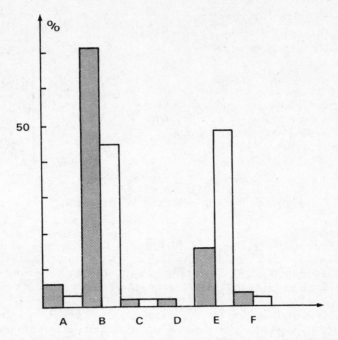

Figure 3: *Results before (dotted columns), and after, the physics course to the 'cigarette in the night' question. Answers were: A: no light comes out from the cigarette; B: light stays around the cigarette; C: light comes out about halfway towards you; D: light comes out as far as you but no further; E: light comes out until it hits an obstacle; F: other answers or no answers*

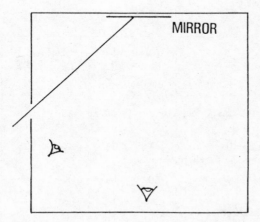

Figure 4: *Students are asked: 'In a completely dark room with perfectly black walls a collimated beam of light enters the room in the direction indicated and hits the mirror placed on the wall. Which one of the two people in the drawn positions could see the light? Which one could see the mirror?'*

Interviewer to pupil: Suppose that someone dug a hole all the way through the earth and dropped a rock into it.

On the pictures below, of a make believe earth, four different children (a,b,c, and d) drew a line showing the way a rock would move as it falls. . . . Which drawing best shows what would really happen to the rock? . . . Why do you think so?

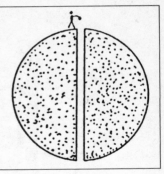

Figure 5 *The 'hole in the Earth' original question*

light and mirror', while the majority think that 'if they have eyes and light is there, of course they can see both', showing in this way an implicit scheme of visual rays where light is only a necessary condition. Again students seem to reproduce the historical path: Euclid's geometrical optics was built on 'visual rays'. And it works!

The most important factor for the pressure/weight/gravity questionnaire, accounting for 15 per cent of the variance, emerges from the three items on 'the hole in the Earth'. The question shown in Figure 5 was originally proposed by Nussbaum and Novak (1976) and modified at the University of Rome (Dupré *et al*, 1981) by adding two more items, where the hole does not pass through the centre and is drawn both 'inclined' and 'horizontal'.

The results are shown in Table 2. There were four categorizations of students responses:

Catagories of responses	Vertical		Inclined		Horizontal	
	P1	P2	P1	P2	P1	P2
	%		%		%	
Goes out the hole or stands (flat Earth)	17	8	25	10	49	35
Goes through the Earth (geographically spherical Earth)	24	11	40	35	14	8
Stops in the centre (physically spherical earth)	50	59	31	40	36	40
Oscillates around the centre (scientific scheme)	1	18	1	15	1	16

Table 2 *Results to the 'hole in the Earth' question. P1 and P2 refer respectively to the pre-instructional and to the post-instructional form of the questionnaire*

☐ *flat earth*, where the force, and the fall, is only downwards;
☐ *geographically spherical earth*, where bodies fall toward the centre only *outside* the Earth surface (inside the hole, bodies fall down on the other side);
☐ *physically spherical Earth*, where the rock stops at the centre of the Earth;
☐ the *scientific scheme*, where, taking inertia into account, the rock oscillates.

A flat-earth scheme dominates when the hole is drawn 'horizontally'; in this case common life experience suggests that 'a body on a horizontal table will not fall'.

A geographically spherical scheme is particularly attractive when the hole is inclined. Often in this scheme, the cause of gravity is ascribed to air pressure that presses from outside towards the Earth's surface.

A physically spherical Earth scheme is the most popular – but not very consistent: about 20 per cent of students change their mind when the position of the hole changes.

School teaching is not very effective: the scientific scheme is mastered only by about 15 per cent of the students, even after the physics course.

It has to be noticed that school teaching itself sometimes leads to confusion. Pictures in textbooks, maps and the globe, all support a scheme where 'up' and 'down', 'vertical' and 'horizontal', are absolute and not relative concepts. A very good student answered the question 'why does the Moon not fall on the Earth?' in this way: 'the Moon goes round the Earth on a horizontal plane, so if it fell down, it would fall along a vertical line and would not impact on the Earth, but would be lost in space'.

Similar results were obtained in the electric circuits questionnaire; in this case the main problem derives from a 'sequential reasoning' (Closset, 1983) where the electric current is conceived as a 'river' – a water current where what happens 'in the valley' does not affect the flowing of the river 'on the mountain'. The basic idea of a closed circuit is not stressed enough in textbooks and 'water analogies' are often used in the teaching process, so that sequential reasoning is strengthened by the physics courses. Thirty-four per cent of students before teaching and only 26 per cent after teaching gave correct and consistent answers for the current intensity in two simple circuits. Students after teaching are often able to solve circuits more complex than the proposed ones, but what was required in the questionnaire was not calculus but a semi-quantitative estimation, which probably 'activated' common-sense analogies.

Conclusions

The results of the questionnaires show that difficulties still persist even after instruction and the scientific conceptual map has not been built. On average, only from 5 per cent to 10 per cent of the students show a consistent use of the scientific concepts in eight or more items for each questionnaire.

The questionnaires therefore represent a useful tool for physics assessment but, more important, they also represent a useful tool to investigate students' thinking (ie their common-sense knowledge, before, during and after instruction).

These types of tools are indispensable. The same research showed that teachers ignore the meaningful but common-sense concepts and networks pupils already have when they come into the classroom

The teachers of the students' sample were, indeed, asked to anticipate the results their students would achieve. Their *expectations* were then compared with the *observed* performance. More than 50 per cent of the teachers' expectations for more than 50 per cent of the students are significantly ($p < 0.05$) different from the achieved results. Looking at teachers' predictions, it is easy to observe that they do not take account of either the obstacles or the potential help that common-sense knowledge could offer for a meaningful understanding of scientific concepts. Quoting Bachelard (1938), teachers don't understand that the students' problem 'is not to acquire an experimental knowledge but to change their experimental knowledge' already acquired from everyday experiences.

The questionnaires allow teachers to be aware of the common-sense knowledge their students have, and therefore to act by consequence. In addition, the questionnaires proved to be a useful 'learning tool': when students are obliged to explain and make explicit their common-sense schemata, they become aware of their previously implicit knowledge and their ability to recognize and criticize inconsistencies and incoherences improves. After writing their explanation some students remarked: 'now that this stuff is written down I'm no longer convinced it is right'. And doubt is a first step towards conceptual change and meta-knowledge.

References

Ausubel, D P (1968) *Educational Psychology: A Cognitive View*, Holt, Rinehart and Winston, New York

Bachelard, G (1938) *La formation de l'esprit scientifique*, Librairie Philosophique J. Vrin, Paris

Closset, J L (1983) *Le raisonnement sequentiel en electrocinetique*, PhD thesis, Université de Paris VII

Driver, R and Easley, J (1978) 'Pupils and Paradigms', *Studies in Science Education*, 5, pp 61-84

Dupré, F, Noce, G and Vicentini-Missoni, M (1981) 'I modelli fisici prenewtoniani nella conoscenza degli adulti', *Scuola e Città*, no. 2, pp 53-64

Engel, E and Driver, R (1981) 'Investigating Pupils' Understanding of Aspects of Pressure', *Proceedings of an International Workshop on Students' Representation*, Ludwigsburg, Germany

Gilbert, J K, Osborne, R J and Fensham, P J (1982) 'Children's Science and its consequences for teaching, *Science Education*, 66(4), pp 623-33

Gunstone, R and White, R (1981) 'Understanding of Gravity', *Science Education*, 65(3), pp 291-99

Jung, W (1981) 'Conceptual framework in elementary optics', *Proceedings of an International Workshop on Students' Representations*, Ludwigsburg, Germany

La Rosa, C, Mayer, M and Vicentini-Missoni, M (1984) 'Commonsense Knowledge in Optics: Preliminary Results of an Investigation into the Property of Light', *European Journal of Science Education*, vol 6, no. 4, pp 387-97

Mayer, M (1987) 'Conoscenza Scientifica e Conoscenza di Senso Comune', PhD thesis, Universitá di Roma 'La Sapienza'

McCloskey, M (1984) 'Cartoon Physics', *Psychology Today*, April, pp 53-58

Novak, J D (1977) 'An Alternative to Piagetian Psychology for Science and Mathematics', *Science Education*, 61, pp 457-77

Novak, J D and Gowin, D B (1984) *Learning How to Learn*, Cambridge University Press, Cambridge, USA

Nussbaum, J, Novak, J D (1976) 'An Assessment of Children's Concepts of Earth Utilizing Structured Interviews', *Science Education*, 60(4), pp 535-50

Polanyi, M (1966) *The Tacit Dimension*, Italian Version: Armando Armando (1979), Roma

Ruggiero, S, Cartelli, A, Dupré, F, Vicentini-Missoni, M (1985) 'Weight, Gravity and Air Pressure:

Mental Representation by Italian Middle School Pupils', *Eur J of Sci Education*, vol 7, no. 2, pp 181–94

Vicentini-Missoni, M (1982) 'Earth and Gravity: Comparisons Between Adults' and Children's Knowledge', *Proceedings of an International Workshop on Students' Representation*, Ludwigsburg

Viennot, L (1979) *Le raisonnement spontane en dynamique elementaire*, Hermann, Paris

Watts, M and Zylbersztain, A (1981) 'A Survey of some Children's Ideas about Forces', *Physics Education*, 16, pp 360–65

Watzlawick, P, Weakland, J and Fisch, R (1975) *Change*, Norton & Co, Italian version: Astrolabio, Roma

Za'rour, G I (1975) 'Science Misconceptions among Certain Groups of Students in Lebanon' *Journal of Research in Science Teaching*, 12, pp 183–94

16. The area of social history: what to assess and how to assess it

Antonio Calvani

The teaching of social history has always raised significant problems for experts in evaluation as well as teachers who seek criteria and instruments capable of assessing the effectiveness of their educational work. This is because, within what is generally defined 'learning history', a wide range of cognitive activities can be identified, including both general and more specific activities.

On a theoretical level epistemologists and philosophers who study the nature of historical knowledge have underlined its many and various characteristics: on the one hand, history can be regarded as a language, with the features of a plot or a report; on the other, its imaginary and hypothetical character is stressed. In addition, it involves logical–deductive processes and concepts involving models and theories.

Since historical knowledge or thought as engaged in by specialists (ie historians) presents a wide range of aspects, history in an educational context should also take on a range of characteristics. These characteristics variously intersect activities in other fields of education. In the past few decades in particular, innovators who – in various ways and usually spurred towards 'activism' – aimed at breaking the verbal repetitive model typical of traditional history teaching, contributed to revealing the substantial heterogeneity and diverse characteristics of educational work in history.

In a field like this, the need for a significant educational method taking into account the wide range of aspects related to the presentation of historical topics does not easily proceed side by side with the need for 'objective' assessment. When dealing with assessment in a field like history, one of the main risks is concentrating on purely technical measurement requirements (eg having a sufficiently large number of homogeneous items necessary to get a 'valid' score). These practical requirements match a notional view of the learning of history which usually leads to the widespread use of multiple-choice tests.

When considering assessment in the field of social history, the following aspects must be defined:

☐ the skills necessary;
☐ the degree of extension and generality of the skills involved; and
☐ the margin of error tolerable in assessment tests.

SKILLS	TYPICAL QUESTIONS
1) NOTIONAL: strict dependence on specific contents	
1.1. Verbal repetition	'When did it happen?'
1.2. Identification	'Place in chronological order . . .'.
1.3 Ordering	'Who is referred to?'
1.4 Space-temporal association	
2) PROCEDURAL: Strict dependence on algorithmic sequences	
2.1. Selection	'Consult the file'
2.2. Consultation	'Calculate the rate, the percentage . . .'
2.3. Quotation	'Draw the graph . . .'
2.4. Calculation	
2.5. Compilation	
2.6. Use of equipment	
2.7. Graphs	
3) CONCEPTUAL: Use of concepts according to classificatory and deductive criteria	
3.1. Definition	'Give an example of a revolution.'
3.2. Comparison	'All these cases are examples of . . .'
3.3. Classification	
3.4. Exemplification	
3.5. Causal relation	
3.6. Application	
3.7. Extrapolation	
4) EVALUATIVE: Use of assessment criteria	
4.1. Estimate	'How much time must have been
4.2. Contextualization	necessary for Z to happen?'
4.3. Relativization	'Compare X's opinion with Y's.'
4.4. Counterbalancing	'Compare the effects of event X in the
4.5. Criterion assessment	short and long run'.
5) SEMANTIC: Integration and transfer of meanings	
5.1. Inference	'Behind these documents (graph, etc.)
5.2. Heuristic research	a problem hides . . .'
5.3. Translation	'From this document the attitude of
5.4. Interpretation	this author should be understood . . .'
5.5. Explication	'These materials should make it
5.6. Paraphrase	possible to advance an hypothesis.'
5.7. Synthesis	
6) IMAGINATIVE: Imaginative, little conditioned expression	
6.1. Construction of historical scenarios	'Draw a scenario set in . . .' 'Devise a story . . .'
6.2. Dramatization	'Dramatize . . .'

Table 1 *Skills involved in learning of history*

Defining the skills

Facing assessment problems in history without a preliminary analysis of the various and significant forms which learning in this field may take means favouring a repetitive and mnemonic vision of history.

The experiments performed by innovators in accordance with the principle of 'activism', together with the need for a clear view of the skills which may play a role in the 'educational work with history', have led to the definition of taxonomic frames which can be used as flexible instruments to help direct the teacher's work.

Table 1 shows one of these 'large-spectrum' frames resulting from the integration of various grids collected from primary and secondary-school teachers in various parts of Italy and later synthesized. It includes a subject index of the most relevant activities (or skills) which appear to be involved in educational work with history. The skills are listed according to class, and some typical assignments are indicated beside them.

Table 2 shows an outline of each class. The general classification criteria are provided by the relation between test type and necessary pre-knowledge: from the 'notional' and 'procedural' classes where the relation with pre-knowledge is mechanical and rigid, towards the 'semantic' and 'imaginative' classes where it is significantly more flexible and integrative.

NOTIONAL:
A notional knowledge content is drawn from memory (of the date, name type, etc) and is then applied in the test (or exercise) in a relatively static way.
It is based on the fact that history concerns a framework of facts and events.
It includes skills placed under 'knowledge' in Bloom's taxonomy.
This sphere includes the traditional view of history teaching, according to which history is a mass of verbal knowledge to be repeated orally.
'Notional' skills can also however, be connected to educational applications others than those of 'read/repeat' type.

Example:

- ☐ The students can use images and short passages mixed together, trying to arrange them in chronological order or to relate each element to a corresponding context (type of society, etc).
- ☐ The students can be assigned to discover a mysterious event (or historical character) by gradually discovering maps or questioning a file which provides progressive clues (as happens with a computer in the case of John Nicols' Prolog games).

PROCEDURAL:
The information the mind draws from memory takes on the character of procedural criteria, similar to algorithms. It concerns the fact that history learning also implies 'ability to do things', eg being able to consult an index, calculating an average (percentage, etc), drawing a graph, consulting a file (on paper or electronic).
Some operations are more strictly linguistic: being able to write a footnote, a quotation, etc.

In some cases the procedural modality is linked to other modalities.

Example:

- ☐ Constructing a database: this implies the intervention of the 'conceptual' dimension.
- ☐ Selecting passages according to non-literary criteria or taking notes: this implies also the intervention of the semantic modality.

CONCEPTUAL:
Characterized by the retrieval, from memory, of conceptual categories, which can be logically organized.

Concerns the logical aspect present in historical knowledge.

Includes operations such as definition of a concept, exemplification, cause–effect relation, application, extrapolation (in Bloom's sense).

Typical operations for this skill are the selections which can be performed by means of logical operators in a database and the extrapolations which can be modelled by means of an electronic sheet.

It is assumed that the categories have limited boundaries, that it is possible to ascertain whether specific cases belong to a determined category, that deductive logic can be applied to historic reasoning and that there are definable cause–effect relations.

EVALUATIVE:
Assessment criteria are looked for in memory.

It concerns the fact that historical thought also implies expressing judgements.

In this sphere more or less complex situations can also be found – from a simple estimate (eg about the life of a phenomenon) to operations more typical for historical thought, such as activities indicated by means of terms like contextualization, counterbalancing, relativization.

The formative effectiveness of this dimension can be connected to Piaget's concept of 'decentring'.

SEMANTIC:
These allow a hidden meaning to emerge, and are looked for in memory. This is the 'going-beyond-data' dimension.

The analysis must be performed in a flexible way, searching for possible connections among several elements, with references and feedbacks between data and pre-knowledge.

This sphere includes operations connected to the search for a global meaning as well as of an interpretation (circumstantial reconstruction, explication of the 'implicit' part of a text, translation, paraphrase, etc).

IMAGINATIVE:
Recollections, images, sensations are retrieved from memory in a flexible way. This is the dimension of associative thinking and creativity.

The relation with memory is neither the application of specific pre-knowledge to the data of the problem-raising situation (mod 1–4) nor research to discover a hidden sense (mod 5); emotional behaviour is allowed to come to the surface, free from constraints.

The production acquires an imaginative and aesthetic character.

Table 2 *Classification of the skills involved in learning history*

Before designing the assessment, it is necessary to know what is to be assessed. The purpose of these frames is to raise questions in the teacher's mind such as: 'What is the sphere of my way of working with history?', 'Which skills do I manage to activate and which are neglected?'

Defining the degree of extension and generality of the skills involved

The second aspect to consider concerns the assessment of the extension of the skill in question and its degree of generality. By 'extension' we mean the number of opportunities offered by the working unit actually to use and apply a particular skill. Any working hypothesis in this sphere necessarily leads one to envisage a varied and heterogeneous scenario. It must be taken into account that, in many cases, the skill in question will be activated in a purely casual form.

Educational work in the field of history offers a wide range of stimuli, with the drawback that only rarely will any particular skill be totally developed. It is theoretically possible to undertake a unit with the explicit purpose of developing, for example, the skills of 'extrapolation' or 'judgement counter-balance' etc. In these examples, *ad hoc* methods to develop the desired skill could be devised; however, if systematically applied, these would lead to a total historical nonsense by forcing the teacher to extract the examples used from their specific context. However, educational work in history requires that an event is always placed in its context and that the need to do this is always in the foreground. Furthermore it requires that the internal coherence and unity of the topics are not subordinated to the development of specific skills. As a result, a working method appears reasonable if it both safeguards the unity and coherence of the subject and provides operational characterizations in accordance with the opportunities granted by the type of problem and the historical topic.

The degree of specificity/generality of the skill involved and its possible intersection with different subjects is next considered. From this perspective, we can place knowledge and skills along the following scale:

- ☐ specific knowledge;
- ☐ historical knowledge;
- ☐ specific skills;
- ☐ encyclopaedic knowledge of the world;
- ☐ linguistic and conceptual instruments.

The structure and content of assessments will be different if strictly historical knowledge and skills within the subject can be reached in a short time rather than if a general knowledge of the world or –even more so – linguistic and conceptual instruments of a general character are required.

Many of the tests used by teachers do not take the difference between these levels sufficiently into account. Asking for a correct quotation, or consulting a table of contents, for example, may be regarded as specific skills within the subject area which are obtainable in a short time. The question, however, is different when the learner is asked to make a simple comparison (eg between the situation studied and today's reality) or some extrapolation starting from known data. In these cases, recourse is made to the student's encyclopaedic knowledge which is usually quite independent from the specific acquisitions provided by the teaching unit in question.

Similarly, when a teacher decides to use a document with comprehension questions, he or she should consider that what is being assessed is mainly the student's linguistic comprehension, a skill quite independent of the teaching activity performed and which can be improved only in the long term.

It seems reasonable to keep different working modes separate. It is important to profit from stimuli and problem-raising/solving situations, exploiting general formative opportunities (eg interpreting a document, synthesizing etc) without the need to submit these components to short-term summative assessment.

Defining the margin of error tolerable in the assessment

The choice of test largely depends on the balance between two often conflicting requirements: the tolerable margin of error and the educational and formative value attached to the test itself.

There are a number of objective tests with a reduced assessment error. These include:

Operative tests with intrinsic performance criteria

The introduction of computers into school has considerably widened the opportunities available for this type of test. Thus, for example, the chosen criteria may be getting a score in a game, retrieving data from or inserting data into an electronic file, managing to print a table etc.

Multiple-choice tests on paper

The most common type of test, which best meets the need to achieve a score by means of a sufficiently high number of homogeneous items within the shortest time. The response-time per item is usually short (40–50 seconds); therefore in less than an hour a class can complete a test including over 80 items.

In the case of history, the use of this technique is traditionally linked to a notional concept (see Table 2), but it is worth remembering that it can also be used at other levels. Learners can, for example, be asked to choose among different possible interpretations, among different levels of acceptability for one hypothesis etc.

Lexical verifications, which may take on various forms (definition, fitting an example into the appropriate category, choice of a synonym, choice of an antonym, association of a term to a semantic area etc) appear to be particularly useful.

The main trouble with an extensive use of this kind of test is the low involvement of the learner. Though very useful as a technique for summative assessment, the educational potential of such tests is low.

Other 'closed' paper-based tests

A variety of other styles of test can also be used:

☐ correspondence (associations among objects, events, characters, concepts, short passages, etc);
☐ ordering (chronological, logical, hierarchical, information);
☐ highlighting (eg elements of a passage suitable to support a hypothesis);
☐ completion (Cloze type).

Open questions

At the opposite extreme there are 'open' questions; having a very wide range of possible answers, these inevitably leave much room for arbitrariness if the answer is to be transformed into a measurement.

Open questions can be very useful during the educational process itself, especially if they are followed by immediate feedback (ie formative evaluation). Regarding the improvement of the quality of the educational activity, it is important for the teacher to devote more attention to stimulating, rather than assessing, the learner (ie to devising significant questions, capable of involving the learner regardless of strictly metric measurement problems).

In some cases, a compromise can be reached between the meaningfulness of the question and measurement requirements, by defining the approximation

---

The students have passages from manuals, some documents, quantitative data and passages of historical criticism already known to them, at their disposal.
They are instructed as follows:

'After re-examining the materials relating to topic X, write a short report, following the outline below. Some quotations taken from original documents or from historical literature, if relevant, will improve the quality of your work.:

Example of outline:
In the years . . .
We get information from . . .
The obtained data can be graphically illustrated . . .
The causes lying at the basis . . .
The resulting consequences . . .
The historical evaluation of the event . . .

In the assessment, three general skills plus two specific skills are taken into consideration; there is a five-level scale for each variable:

☐ clarity;
☐ exhaustiveness;
☐ differentiation of speech levels (evidence, personal opinion, historical interpretation);
☐ correctness in quotations and notes;
☐ correctness in the graphical illustration of the data.

Table 3 *Example of a complex test, resulting from the integration of general and specific skills*

margins for the variables in question. The most common procedure is to define a grading scale (three or five points are common) adequately specifying the classification criteria by means of some typical examples. For example, 'practically worthless or poor; partial; adequate or good'.

In this way, within certain limits, it is possible to reduce the arbitrariness of the measurement and deal with the quantification of 'complex' tests (such as the one shown in Table 3 by way of example) in reasonable terms.

Conclusions

The assessment of learning in the field of history will still cause difficulties to experts in docimology and to the protagonists of 'objective' evaluation. The existence of a tension between the needs of measurement and the requirements of history education may be a positive element in so far as it means that history education is not deprived of its particular connotations in favour of external requirements – such as those associated with the need to quantify the results of learning.

History knowing and thought are first of all to be taken as they are, without rejecting their wide-ranging components (notional, logical, problem-raising/solving etc) and their stimulus to aggregate wide-ranging skills (more or less general or specific ones) which, according to the particular case, can enrich a purely notional corpus.

The 'scoring' obsession, in the sphere of history teaching, inevitably entails aspects of the following consequences:

☐ privileging a purely notional (and therefore rote) view of history;
☐ isolating specific aspects (eg skills) from their surrounding context.

In the first case, history is badly debased, thus depriving it of meaning; in the second, through an abstraction, it is decontextualized. This conflicts with the very nature of historic thought.

This does not mean, however, that assessment in the field of history is to be abandoned to a total subjectivism, to the kind of intuitive assessment which prevailed in many schools in the past. It is however to be acknowledged that, to a certain extent, a qualitative component cannot and should not be eliminated.

The solution can only be a sort of 'strategic wisdom' which leads the teacher to avoid the two extremes of subjectivism on the one hand, and of the distortion of the discipline on the other hand. This 'strategic wisdom' should enable the teacher to identify both the significant components to be assessed and the measurement tools which make assessment possible within acceptable error margins. Such a 'wisdom' implies a clear awareness of the choices made (ie the ability to weigh up the pros and cons of the various possibilities which arise according to the particular case).

In order to choose the criteria and tools for assessment, we believe that the strategy involves taking into particular consideration three aspects of basic importance:

☐ the skills at stake;
☐ their degree of extension and generality; and
☐ the error margin tolerable in the assessment.

In training teachers for this discipline, particular attention should be paid to developing the ability to integrate and adequately proportion the various components, with reference both to the materials and information techniques and to the objectives and assessment tools themselves.

17. Aptitude tests as the predictor of success in the Israeli matriculation

Elchanan I Meir and Nurit Adler

Summary: The purpose of this paper is to show the predictive validity of a battery of pencil-and-paper psychometric aptitude tests administered to eighth or ninth graders in Israel. The criterion of validity was achievement on matriculation exams administered at the end of the twelfth grade.

The main issues of this paper are:

- Success in the matriculation exams in Israel is a necessary requirement for admission to almost all higher education options. Only about 40 per cent of the Jewish elementary school graduates passed these exams in 1987. (Parallel figures for the non-Jewish population cannot be presented due to ambiguity in the definitions). This paper presents findings on the validity of the aptitude tests which serve as the basis for guidance and admission to high schools in Israel.
- The criterion of matriculation, in spite of its importance, was found to suffer from low reliability. Nevo (1980) found that the correlations between two teachers independently assigning scores to matriculation exams vary between .42 (on composition) and .94 (on maths), with a median of about .75. Also, grades achieved in school showed only moderate correlations with the national matriculation scores (see 'method'). The incongruence in the assessment of achievements limits the potential predictive validity of any suggested variable. The study will show the aptitude tests to be of significant predictive power despite the limitations of the criterion.
- A prediction of any variable throughout the period of adolescence suffers from outside influence related to the biological and psychological characteristics of this stage of development. The relations which were found between prediction and criterion indicate the possibility of basing adolescents' guidance on valid data.
- Data indicate the relative predictive power of psychometric aptitude tests in comparison with other predictors (eg motivation, socio-economic conditions, health). This issue is interesting both for theoretical and practical implications.

Method

Subjects

All of the 1097 subjects in the follow-up study were Jewish Israeli pupils. The sample consisted of: (a) 164 and 113 pupils who were tested in the eighth or ninth grade, respectively, and who studied in the general high school programme; and (b) 399 and 421 pupils who were also tested in the eighth or ninth grade, respectively, but studied in the high school vocational programme (this programme includes, beside the usual subjects of maths, languages etc, an emphasis on a chosen vocational subject, eg, electronics, electricity, technical drawing).

Due to dropout and failure, the correlations between the psychometric tests and the criteria were based on smaller sample sizes. The issue of this range restriction will be discussed later.

The study did not include Arab pupils since, at present, there are no adequate psychometric tests in Arabic and there is no demand for administering psychometric tests and/or predicting pupils' achievements in Arab high schools.

Instruments – the psychometric tests

The battery of psychometric tests used in the research consisted of 12 to 14 aptitude tests developed at the Jerusalem Hadassah Vocational Guidance Institute. The tests' text and instructions were in Hebrew. The split-half reliability of these tests ranged between .80 and .94 depending on the test content, probability of guessing correct answers, length, etc (see Meir and Vardi, 1972).

The aptitudes measured were:

☐ *Verbal:* analogies, word antonyms, sentence completion;
☐ *Numerical:* number series, problem solving, exercises;

☐ *Figural:* figure series, partition, spatial perception, copying;
☐ *Motor:* drawing, cutting with scissors, bending an iron fibre;
☐ *Other:* word and number comparisons, mechanical comprehension.

The test batteries differed according to the testees' educational level and sometimes as a result of idiosyncratic decisions.

Raw scores on these tests were transformed to stanine scores based on adequate samples of eighth or ninth graders of the Jewish population in Israel. The same norms were used for boys and girls.

Criterion

Deciding on an adequate criterion was not simple. There were three options: (a) the scores assigned to the national matriculation exams (the mean of the two evaluators), (b) the final school scores assigned by teachers, and (c) the final matriculation scores which were the means of (a) and (b). For more details see Adler and Meir, 1985; Adler and Meir, 1989.

As expected, many school teachers try to 'defend' their pupils from failure by assigning scores higher than the scores these pupils would have deserved based on their achievements in the national exams. To illustrate: in the Bible exam, the teachers' means score exceeded the national mean score by 5.8 and 14.5 points (in the 0–100 scale) for the 257 and 498 general and vocational high school pupils, respectively; and by 8.4 and 14.6 points on the English language exam (similar population). The correlations between the teachers' scores and the national matriculation scores on the Bible and English exams were .70 and .93 in the general programme, and .45 and .69 in the vocational programme. The median correlations between teachers' scores and national scores for all exam subjects in the general and vocational programmes were only .55 and .45, respectively. It should be noted that, generally, teachers' scores are based on acquaintance with pupils for at least one year, during which several interim exams and a final exam are administered; while a national exam, by its very nature, consists of a single assessment which is, presumably, more carefully standardized than most teachers' exams.

Because of its better standardization and greater objectivity the decision was made to adopt the national matriculation exam as the criterion for the present follow-up.

Results

Data was analysed by Pearson correlations between the psychometric tests as predictors and the matriculation scores as criteria. Separate correlations were computed for each of the psychometric aptitude tests and for their combinations (eg, 'verbal aptitude'). These correlations were calculated separately for aptitude tests administered in the eighth and ninth grade, and in the general and vocational program.

Table 1 presents a selection of such correlations. Due to limitations of space

High School Programme	Predictor: Aptitude	Criterion: Matriculation	Prediction at 9th grade		Prediction at 8th grade	
			r	n	r	n
General	Verbal	Hebrew	.44	112	.43	163
		English	.53	112	.38	163
		Weighted mean	.46	112	.35	163
	Numerical	Maths	.56	107	.35	159
		Weighted mean	.46	113	.38	164
	Mean aptitude	Weighted mean	.52	113	.42	164
Vocational	Verbal	Bible	.10	320	.38	337
		English	.38	310	.38	354
		Weighted mean	.49	119	.39	116
	Numerical	Maths	.57	178	.48	251
		Weighted mean	.57	119	.61	116
	Mean aptitude	Weighted mean	.62	119	.59	116
	Figural perception	Technical drawing	.56	159	.57	225
		Electrical theory	.37	61	.36	114
		Mean electronics	.41	164	.25	149

Table 1 *Selected correlations between psychometric exams administered at 8th and 9th grade and matriculation scores at 12th grade*

(and presumably also the readers' motivation to observe) not all correlations are presented here. (The table can be found in Adler and Meir, 1985, and in Adler and Meir, 1989, or obtained by request.)

The findings confirm the hypothesis that matriculation scores can be predicted by means of psychometric aptitude tests administered 3.5 to 4.5 years ahead. This prediction is not only statistically significant, but also efficient as indicated by the correlation coefficients. The 'stars' conservatively assigned to note the level of confidence were not included because the main issue here was not significance in comparison with an absolute relationship. The mean aptitude score assigned to pupils in the eighth or ninth grade showed correlations of .42 and .52, respectively, with the weighted mean matriculation scores in the general programme of the secondary education. The respective correlations for the vocational programme even exceeded these coefficients: .59 for the eighth grade and .62 for the ninth grade.

Discussion

A basic question emerges from the findings: is the confirmation of the predictive validity of the aptitude tests strong enough for guidance and admission decisions? The correlation coefficients between the mean aptitude scores and the weighted mean of the matriculation scores ranged between .42 and .62, depending on the pupils' ages at the time of their aptitude measurement and programme (general or vocational) of studies in grades 9–12. The sample sizes were large enough so that even much lower correlation coefficients would be considered as highly significant on the conservative confidence levels. Yet in many follow-up studies (eg, analyses by Ghiselli, 1966; Hunter, 1986) one can find evidence that aptitude tests were correlated with 'training' criteria in coefficients that exceeded those found in the present study.

The main reason why the predictive validity of the aptitude tests in the present study did not exceed .62, may be related to the reliability of the criteria. As indicated above, the agreement between two teachers who scored the same matriculation exam was moderate – the median correlation of the matriculation exams being about .75, and the correlations between scores given by the high school teachers and the scores on the national matriculation exams were even lower – median correlations of .45 and .55 for the general and vocational programmes, respectively. In other words: the reliability of the criteria indicates a maximum of only 56 per cent common variance between two independent assessments. The prediction by aptitude tests 3.5 to 4.5 years ahead was found to be 20 per cent to 36 per cent of the common variance for the general and vocational programmes, respectively. This means that all the non-aptitude variables together (including motivation and interest in studies, need of achievement, health, socioeconomic conditions and prior achievements) can predict only 20 per cent to 36 per cent of the total variance. Thus, the importance of aptitudes in predicting achievements in high school cannot be over-emphasized.

The reported correlations were neither corrected for range restriction nor for attenuation. Such corrections, if made, would yield even higher coefficients of correlation. The effect of the range restriction in the present study was significant: only about 60 per cent of the Jewish graduating class sat for matriculation exams and only about 40 per cent of the term passed these exams. There is an indication of the effect of the range restriction in the findings: the validity of the same test battery was significantly higher in the vocational programme than in the general programme, perhaps due to the fact that in the vocational programme only 45 per cent of the examinees passed the matriculation exams while in the general programme 71 per cent passed.

The aptitude tests varied in content and consequently in the criterion which they predicted best. To illustrate: the figural test given at the eighth and ninth grade correlated by .56 and .57, respectively, with the technical drawing score in the matriculation exams (see Table 1), but only .35, .37 and .22 with English, Maths and Bible, respectively in the general programme, and .24, .35 and —.07 in the vocational programme.

As the criterion was the national matriculation scores and not the high school teachers' scores, it was impossible to ascribe the aptitudes – achievements correlations to teacher prejudice.

Psychometric aptitude measurement in Israel is implemented in the educational system with the instruction to use the data as a tool to promote achievements among *all* pupils. It is believed that appropriate differential usage of counselling and teaching methods in a curriculum congruent with the pupils' interests will lead to a higher probability of success than that predicted by psychometric tests. We challenge the systems: 'Spoil our valid predictions!' Thus, aptitude measurement can foster the achievements of all pupils, especially those whose success depends on non-aptitude variables.

References

Adler, N and Meir, E I (1985) Prediction of success in matriculation exams by means of psychometric aptitude tests. *Studies in Education, 41*, 35–50 (in Hebrew)

Adler, N and Meir, E I (1989) Prediction of matriculation achievements in vocational high schools. *Studies in Education, 49–50*, 191–208 (in Hebrew)

Ghiselli, E E (1966) *The Validity of Occupational Aptitude Tests* New York, Wiley

Hunter, J E (1986) Cognitive ability, cognitive aptitudes, job knowledge and job performance. *Journal of Vocational Behavior*, 29, 340–362

Meir, E I and Vardi, M (1972) *Reliability and Validity of Aptitude Tests* Jerusalem: Hadassah Vocational Guidance Institute (in Hebrew)

Nevo, B (ed) (1980) *High School Matriculation Examinations*. Tel Aviv: Am Oved Publishers (in Hebrew)

18. An unbiased, standardized method for quality in student assessment at the post-secondary level

Claude N Kennedy

Summary: Tertiary educational institutions have various methods of assessing their students' performance. Ideally, formal summative student assessment should consist of two parts: first, the setting of examination papers which reasonably reflect both the content and difficulty level of the course in question; and secondly, based on the examination results, the assignment of student grades which give a fair and meaningful representation of students' academic performance. It is imperative that both parts meet so that an unbiased and standardized assessment can be achieved.

This chapter proposes a system that takes the set of raw numerical scores (R-scores) from a properly constructed examination paper and statistically maps them on to a set of standardized adjusted numerical scores (A-scores). The A-scores are then mapped linearly on to a semi-extended letter grade scale which is suggested as the most meaningful way in which to represent the students' academic achievement. Implications of the proposed system on the numbers of failures and distinctions, staff/student morale and academic standards are discussed.

What is assessment?

Summative assessment is an absolutely essential component of the educational process which determines if the process has been effective or not. *Effective* assessment can determine, to a reasonable degree of accuracy, the depth of knowledge and understanding a candidate has attained in a particular course of study.

Assessment is a form of measurement and, as with any other type of measurement, an assessment of student knowledge in a particular course of study has an error associated with it. Thus no particular assessment result can be thought of as being absolute. However, we can label an assessment result as being either *valid* or *invalid*.

Finally, and most importantly, any assessment method used must be able to be fully justified on sound pedagogical grounds.

The critical importance of using valid assessment methods

In the modern world, educational institutions have become not only places of learning but, more than ever before, vehicles for certification. Government, business, the public and private sectors in general and society as a whole – all have come to rely and depend upon tertiary educational institutions as official certifiers of that most important product of modern advanced society: the knowledgeable, educated individual. This is why it is imperative that the assessment processes employed are legitimate and valid. To accept anything less does a great disservice not only to the taxpayers who fund the institutions but also to society as a whole and to the individual students.

The assessment process is intimately connected with the achievement and continued maintenance of standards of academic excellence, and as such its importance to the educational process cannot be overstated. We would be seriously failing in our duty as professional educators if we stood silently by and permitted a valid assessment process to be compromised by arbitrary demands such as 'There can be no more than X% "A" grades in their course' or 'The failure rate in this course cannot be greater than Y%'.

The 'excellence in teaching' which administrators and managers are so fond of emphasizing to their teaching staff is undoubtedly critical in the achievement of quality education. However, human nature being what it is, the effect of even the best teaching will be severely mitigated vis-a-vis student performance if not complemented by an honest and effective process of student assessment. Too often the best efforts of teachers are compromised by externally imposed assessment criteria which may be expedient from a political or administrative point of view but which have little or no sound pedagogical basis.

The impact of a less-than-honest, biased or compromised assessment process on the tertiary institution in question is often far reaching and always negative; a dangerous level of student cynicism regarding the whole assessment process resulting in a less than responsible attitude towards their studies, significant staff demoralization, and an overall general malaise and lack of positive spirit among staff and students alike.

General requirements for an assessment process to be valid

While it is acknowledged that some courses may not have any final examination, for the large majority of post-secondary subjects the assessment process should ideally comprise both a significant continuous assessment component and a final examination covering the entire subject syllabus. Since this final examination is usually the only opportunity to assess the candidates on the entire subject material, in most cases it is suggested that it should be weighted not less than 50 per cent of the overall subject grade. On the other hand, keeping in mind the importance of continuous assessment, it is suggested that the weight of the continuous assessment component be no less than 30 per cent.

The assessment process must be uniformly applied across the whole institution. Applying the process to only particular courses or certain departments violates the principle of universality which is essential not only for fairness but also in establishing and maintaining a common standard of academic excellence across the entire institution.

The *only* deviation from universality that should be entertained is the case of a department which has a formal affiliation with a recognized professional body external to the institution. Such a body may require its own particular standard.

In such a case we would make the argument for a uniform standard across the whole of the department in question.

The process must be based on sound pedagogical grounds.

The process must be applied in an unbiased fashion to each and every candidate. No single candidate or group of candidates can be allowed preferential treatment over the population of candidates as a whole.

The process must above all be *honest* and *uncompromised*. It must at all cost be able to resist the natural inclination of power centres both within the institution and without who may try to distort it for their own purposes. In short, the assessment process must be 'tamper proof', beyond the reach of those who would compromise it to suit their own parochial interests.

The valid assessment process

The valid assessment process consists of two parts: first setting valid examinations/assignments and then correctly mapping the raw exam/assignment scores on to a *meaningful* grade representation. This mapping should produce not only a legitimate number of 'A' grades but should also allow certain students the 'right' to fail.

Setting of valid examinations

Characteristics of valid examinations include:

☐ Accurate reflection of the subject syllabus with the more important topics given correspondingly more representation over the more ancillary ones.

☐ An ability to measure whether or not the student has attained sufficient knowledge and/or skills to have met the objectives of the course in question.

☐ A level of difficulty in the questions which closely corresponds to the level of difficulty at which the subject was pitched.

☐ An ability to discriminate between the candidates in accordance with their individual understanding of the concepts and ideas embodied in the material being examined.

☐ Revealing the relative knowledge of the candidates most clearly. This desired effect of maximum discrimination amongst the candidates will usually be manifested by a distribution in the raw exam grades which is more or less Gaussian (normal) in shape and which will have a mean value around the 50 per cent mark.

☐ Allowing enough time such that the large majority of students (say three out of four) can complete the paper with at least 15–20 minutes to spare for final checking of solutions.

Characteristics of invalid examinations include:

☐ Allotting too little time. Speed tests are not a good way to test subject knowledge. Any testing situation is stressful. The degree to which this stress affects performance varies significantly from person to person. The added stress of an *unrealistic* time constraint will tend to distort test scores unevenly thus resulting in an unfair assessment process. Remember that what we want to test is the candidates' knowledge of the subject in question, not how well they can handle stress. A deliberate effort should be made to minimize all possible sources of stress.

☐ Setting the difficulty level of the questions well below the level the subject was pitched at, in an attempt to ensure a low failure rate. Setting an unrealistically simple examination makes it difficult to discriminate between the good students. As a result the raw marks distribution will tend to be significantly skewed to the top of the marks scale. Worse still, once this practice becomes common, word quickly spreads through the student community that the examinations are being set at an artificially low level of difficulty. This knowledge tends to have a negative impact on the work and study habits of a significant number of students. Human nature being what it is, if you demand the minimum from a person you are virtually assured of getting the minimum.

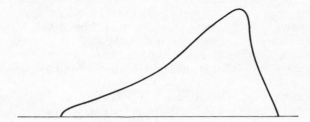

☐ Deliberately leaving out specific subject topics because of fears that students do not understand them well enough.
☐ Giving students a choice of questions to do. By letting students choose say 'any five out of eight questions' you have actually set not one examination but rather $^8C_5 = 56$ different examinations. This is a violation of one of the cardinal rules in most examination processes that *all* candidates attempt *exactly* the same examination. We would thus strongly argue against any question choice being practised in the lower, basic level subjects where mastery of the entire syllabus is essential.

Notwithstanding this general prescription, it is acknowledged that examinations in many advanced subjects do offer question choice. In some cases this practice can even be seen as enhancing the educational process. For example, an advanced subject syllabus may contain seven distinct topic areas with the institution declaring mastery of any four topics sufficient to qualify for a pass in the subject. In such situations a question choice (eg, answer any four out of seven questions) can certainly be justified. Moreover, from a pedagogical viewpoint, encouraging the advanced student to make knowledge-based choices as to which areas they wish to specialize in can be seen as enriching the educational process.

Mapping of raw examination scores

Having set and given a valid examination, one must then correctly map the raw exam scores onto a *meaningful* grade representation. This grading scale should have intuitive meaning not only to the students and teachers, but also to potential employers. That is, one should have an intuitive feel as to what a grade of 'X' really represents.

The mapping should be reasonable in that it not only produces a legitimate number of 'A' grades but also allows certain students the 'right' to fail.

The right to fail

In virtually every advanced nation in the world today, government has taken on a major role in the funding of tertiary education. With its increasing fiscal interest has come an ever-growing sensitivity to the quantity (if not as much to the quality) of the product from those tertiary education systems.

In many nations, education has become a burning political issue with all classes of society demanding their children be allowed their fair share of the tertiary education pie. These demands not only refer to equal access to the institutions in question but often also encompass a desire that graduation rates be high.

It would be naive in the extreme to assume that the political sensitivity of this issue has not had some effect on the autonomy of government-funded institutions and on the administrators and teachers employed therein when it comes to the question of what is an acceptable upper limit in the failure rate of students.

Be that as it may, responsible professional educators cannot ignore the salient point of this issue. Pushing a student through a course in order to meet some arbitrary quota of passes, even though the student has clearly demonstrated an inability to master the course material to even the most minimal extent, is doing a great disservice not only to those who legitimately passed the course but even more so to the said student.

A 'failure' is in itself a very important learning situation and is often the catalyst for significant success later on. A result of 'Failed' is critically important information for the student concerned that should not be covered up by an artificial 'Pass'. Success in life demands that individuals know not only where their best aptitudes lie but also for which areas of endeavour they have little or no aptitude.

In addition to the most obvious possibility, bad teaching, a result of 'Failed' has two primary causes; either an absence of a reasonable level of effort on the part of the student or simply a lack of adequate ability to cope with the course material.

In the former, the student is forced to recognize a basic law of the real world – you cannot get something for nothing. Recognition of this fact will enhance the maturation process and encourage a more responsible attitude to future activities.

In the latter, students will hopefully draw the inference that their abilities and talents may well lie in other areas of endeavour and will stop wasting time trying to master a field of study for which they have little aptitude.

For some students 'failure' can indeed be a very positive experience in the long run for it may well open up new avenues of endeavour that might otherwise have been closed to them forever. Covering up clear and obvious failures to meet some arbitrary pass quota has very negative connotations not only for the particular student concerned but also for society as a whole. You cannot force feed an education system and expect it to produce the kind of quality product that the society is demanding from it.

Grade representations

There are a number of different grade representations in common use in academia today but all fall into two primary classifications, numerical grades and symbolic grades.

1st Class	75–100	90–100	80–100
2nd Class	66–74	80–89	70–79
3rd Class	60–65	70–79	60–69
Pass	50–59	60–69	50–59
Fail	0–49	0–59	0–49

Table 1 *Typical numerical grade representations*

There are three major reasons why numerical grade representation schemes are a less than adequate way in which to represent student achievement.

Firstly, in any testing situation we can at best only select a representative sampling of the total subject material. While candidates may be able to answer all the questions on the test correctly and thus obtain a grade of 100 per cent, this does not mean that they know the entire subject material. Yet, by its very structure a percentage grade representation *implies* that a score of 100 per cent corresponds to complete knowledge of the entire subject material. The representation is thus quite misleading in this respect.

Second, in two of the most commonly used representations, passing students are assigned grades from 50 to 100 inclusive, resulting in 51 different levels of passes. Measurement error alone precludes the possibility of being able to discriminate so finely amongst the passed candidates. The implication that this system makes, that the '78 per cent' student has superior subject knowledge to that of the '76 per cent' student is clearly invalid. Measurement error alone could hide the fact that the 76 per cent student may have a somewhat better grasp of the subject material than the 78 per cent student.

Third, possibly the most important argument against numerical grading schemes is that they tend to impart little intuitive feeling as to what they represent for those for whom they are most intended: employers, parents, and the students themselves. While it may be obvious that the 75 per cent student clearly has a relatively better grasp of the subject material than the 60 per cent student, it is by no means clear what that grade of 75 per cent is actually meant to represent.

The symbolic grade schemes overcome some of the deficiencies of the numerical grade schemes in the following ways.

Firstly, the most outstanding candidates may achieve grades of A or A+. While these grades quite clearly and correctly signify outstanding knowledge of the subject material, they by no means imply 100 per cent knowledge of such.

Letter grade	Extended letter grade	Semi extended letter grade
A	A+	A+
B	A	A
C	A–	B+
D	B+	B
F	B	C+
	B–	C
	C+	D+
	C	F
	C–	F–
	D+	
	D	
	D–	
	F	
	F–	

Table 2 *Symbolic grade representations*

Second, the presence of measurement error is taken into account as the number of passing categories is reduced from 51 to 4, 8, or 12.

Third, a letter grade has more universally intuitive meaning. People tend to associate a grade of A with excellence, B with superior ability, C with average ability, etc.

Lastly, specific definitions of what each letter grade should represent in terms of student achievement can be clearly spelled out to the assessors, thus making the assessment process more standardized and less biased.

Which symbolic grade representation is best?

LETTER GRADE
Having only four pass categories usually results in too gross a discrimination amongst the candidates. Even with our measurement error, a finer discrimination amongst passing candidates is certainly possible.

Also, this particular scheme tends to foster 'grade inflation'. It is often the case that with a full grade difference between the individual passing categories, a very good B student will be given an A, there being no category to distinguish the superior B student from the minimal B student. Similar situations hold with the superior C and D students.

EXTENDED LETTER GRADE
Here, as with the numerical schemes, we again have too many passing categories, a total of 12.

Another problem arises with the presence of the negative passing grades: A–, B–, C–, and D–. A grade of A– should imply an outstanding student. Yet psychologically (in addition to literally), there is a definite negative connotation to such a grade. In addition, negative grades also tend to engender a degree of ambiguity. Is an A– really a first-class grade, or is it something less than a first-class grade?

SEMI-EXTENDED LETTER GRADE

This scheme overcomes many of the shortcomings of the others.

There are no 'negative' passing categories. Having only LETTER and LETTER+ passing grades results in a very positive connotation psychologically. Both A and A+ are definitely seen as 'first class' and 'superior first class' grades respectively, B and B+ as 'second class' and 'superior second class', etc.

There are enough passing categories (8) to allow a finer discrimination amongst the passing candidates yet not so many as to overflow measurement error bounds and thus render the grade assignments meaningless. Having eight passing categories also tends to mitigate against grade inflation.

| | Calculation of Averages | |
Letter grade	Grade point (GP)	Grade point average (GPA)
A+	9	8.5–9
A	8	7.5–8.49
B+	7	6.5–7.49
B	6	5.5–6.49
C+	5	4.5–5.49
C	4	3.5–4.49
D+	3	2.5–3.49
D	2	1.5–2.49
F	1	0.5–1.49
F–	0	0–0.49

Table 3 *Semi-extended letter grade scale*

The definitions of levels of achievement for grade assignments are as follows:

A+	OUTSTANDING	Thorough knowledge of concepts and/or techniques and exceptional skill or great originality in the use of those concepts and/or techniques in satisfying the requirements of an assignment or course.
A	EXCELLENT	Thorough knowledge of concepts and/or techniques together with a high degree of skill and/or some elements of originality in satisfying the requirements of an assignment or course.
B+	VERY GOOD	Thorough knowledge of concepts and/or techiques together with a fairly high degree of skill in the use of those concepts/techniques in satisfying the requirements of an assignment or course.
B	GOOD	Good level of knowledge of concepts and/or techniques together with considerable skill in using them to satisfy the requirements of an assignment or course.

C+ COMPETENT   Acceptable level of knowledge of concepts and/
                         or techniques together with considerable skill in
                         using them to satisfy requirements of an assign-
                         ment or course.

C   FAIRLY COMPETENT   Acceptable level of knowledge or concepts and/
                         or techniques together with some skill in using
                         them to satisfy the requirements of an assign-
                         ment or course.

D+ PASSING   Slightly better than minimal knowledge of
                         required concepts and/or techniques together
                         with some ability to use them in satisfying the
                         requirements of an assignment or course.

D   BARELY PASSING   Minimum knowledge of concepts and/or
                         techiques needed to satisfy the requirements of
                         an assignment or course.

F   FAILURE
F – SEVERE FAILURE

Test	Weight	Individual Subject Grade	Grade point	Weighted grade point
Test 1	20%	B+	7	1.4
Test 2	20%	B+	7	1.4
Final exam	60%	C	4	2.4
			Final total grade point =	5.2

Table 4 *Example of calculation of grade average*

A final GP of 5.2 lines in the C+ range (4.5–5.49). Thus the candidate is awarded a final subject grade of C+, and a final subject GP of 5.

Subject	Year's course work Final grade	Grade point
1	C+	5
2	B	6
3	A	8
4	A	8
5	C	4
6	B+	7
	Total grade points =	38

The year's course GPA is thus 38÷6 = 6.33 which is in the B range (5.5–6.49). Thus the student's course average for the year is B.

Mapping of raw test scores to letter grades

Raw test scores, particularly in the sciences, tend to be numerical. How then should these raw numerical grades be mapped on to the semi-extended letter grade scheme in order to produce an unbiased distribution of grades for a particular assignment, test or examination?

For smaller courses of less than about 40 students the instructor should know the students well enough by the end of the course to be reasonably confident of taking the raw scores and assigning the correct letter grade to each individual student. However, for larger classes this becomes less feasible and an unbiased, standardized, statistically based mapping is called for.

It should be noted that this genre of procedure has for many years now been internationally accepted as valid. It manifests itself in such well-known assessment vehicles as the Cambridge 'O Level' and 'A Level' scoring, GRE scoring, SAT scoring, etc.

Assumptions

The validity of this method for a single subject at a particular institution is based on the following *a priori* assumptions:

- ☐ The sample size is statistically significant, ie a subject enrolment greater than about 50 students.
- ☐ The population of candidates in the subject is reasonably homogeneous.
- ☐ The examination in question reasonably reflects both the content of the subject being examined and the level of difficulty at which the subject was given.

If the above conditions are satisfied, then in general we expect:

- ☐ The distribution of raw scores should be more or less Gaussian in form, with mean value around the 50 per cent mark.
- ☐ As the higher level subjects have in general a more homogeneous student population, we should expect to see the standard deviation (σ) of the raw marks distribution decrease in the more senior years. Thus, for the raw marks distribution of a second-year subject as compared to that of a first-year subject, we should expect to see that $\sigma_2 < \sigma_1$. In general, for the standard deviation in first-, second- and third-year subjects we expect to see that $\sigma_3 < \sigma_2 < \sigma_1$.

Mapping procedure

The procedure consists of two consecutive mappings. First, the candidate's numerical raw test score (R–score) is mapped on to a universal adjusted test score (A–score) which is normally distributed and can range from 0 to 100. This A–score is then mapped onto the semi-extended letter grade score.

R–score	Mapping	A–score	Mapping	Grade	GP
		90–100	$\longrightarrow$	A+	9
		80–89	$\longrightarrow$	A	8
		75–79	$\longrightarrow$	B+	7
		70–74	$\longrightarrow$	B	6
Raw	$\longrightarrow$	65–69	$\longrightarrow$	C+	5
score		60–64	$\longrightarrow$	C	4
		55–59	$\longrightarrow$	D+	3
		50–54	$\longrightarrow$	D	2
		35–49	$\longrightarrow$	F	1
		0–34	$\longrightarrow$	F–	0

NOTE: If the test in question is not of out 100 points, then the corresponding percentage scores become the R–score values.

Table 5 *Mapping procedure*

Details of procedure for mapping R–score to A–score

EXAMPLE FOR A 1ST-YEAR ASSIGNMENT, TEST OR EXAMINATION

1. Calculate the mean (μ_R) and standard deviation (σ_R) for the raw marks (R–score) distribution.
2. For the adjusted marks (A–score) distribution set $\mu_A = 65$ and $\sigma_A = 15$. Then + $1\sigma_A$ is mapped onto 80 and – $1\sigma_A$ is mapped onto 50.
3. For each student calculate a Z–score – the number of standard deviations their R–score is from the μ_R. From the maximum and minimum R–score values, R_{max} and R_{min}, the values of Z_{max} and Z_{min} for the R–score distribution are then obtained.
4. Perform a tri-linear mapping on the data as follows:[2]

   Z–score from Z_{min} to –1 mapped onto A–score from R_{min} to 50
   Z–score from   –1 to 0 mapped onto A–score from   50 to 65
   Z–score from   0 to +1 mapped onto A–score from   65 to 80
   Z–score from +1 to Z_{max} mapped onto A–score from   80 to 99

   It is very important to note that after the initial mapping the A–scores are compared to the R–scores. Then any students having A–score < R–score will have their A–scores adjusted upwards to equal their R–scores. Thus, *the mapping can never lower a student's score, only raise it!*

In practice the procedure might work as follows. A class of first year university students is given a test with a total of 100 points available. The resulting R–score distribution is roughly Gaussian in shape, but with some discernible negative skew. It has mean μ_R = 55, standard deviation σ_R = 20, minimum score R_{min} = 20, and maximum score R_{max} = 96.

Following the four-step algorithm detailed above, a Z–score is calculated for *each* student in the class using the formula:

$$Z\text{–score} = \frac{R\text{–score} - \mu_R}{\sigma_R}$$

Consider three of the students in this class:

Alan scored 78 points. His Z–score is thus given by:
(78 – 55)/20 = +1.15 .

Betty scored 45 points and thus has a Z–score of:
(45 – 55)/20 = –0.5 .

Colin had the lowest score of all the students, 20 points. His Z–score is thus: (20 – 55)/20 = –1.75 .

Next we obtain the values of Z_{max} and Z_{min} as follows:

$$Z_{max} = \frac{R_{max} - \mu_R}{\sigma_R} = \frac{96 - 55}{20} = +2.05$$

and

$$Z_{min} = \frac{R_{min} - \mu_R}{\sigma_R} = \frac{20 - 55}{20} = -1.75$$

Then, according to step 4 in our algorithm, Alan's score will fall into the range of the third linear mapping (Z–score from +1 to Z_{max} mapped onto A–score from 80 to 99). Alan's A–score is thus calculated as:

$$A\text{–score} = 80 + \frac{Z\text{–score} - 1}{Z_{max} - 1} \times 19$$

$$= 80 + \frac{1.15 - 1}{2.05 - 1} \times 19$$

$$= 80 + 3$$
$$= 83$$

Betty's score falls into the range of the second linear mapping (Z–score from –1 to +1 mapped onto A–score from 50 to 80). Her A–score is thus:

$$A\text{–score} = 50 + \frac{Z\text{–score} + 1}{2} \times 30$$

$$A\text{–score} = 50 + \frac{-0.5 + 1}{2} \times 30$$

$$= 50 + 8$$
$$= 58$$

Finally, Colin's score will fall into the first linear mapping (Z–score from Z_{min} to –1 mapped onto A–score from R_{min} to 50). His A–score is thus:

$$\text{A-score} = R_{min} + \left[\frac{Z\text{-score} - Z_{min}}{-1 - Z_{min}} \times (50 - R_{min}) \right]$$

$$= 20 + \left[\frac{-1.75 - (-1.75)}{-1 - (-1.75)} \times (50 - 20) \right]$$

$$= 20 + (0 \times 30)$$

$$= 20$$

The grades awarded to Alan, Betty and Colin are A, D+ and F– respectively. The final A–score distribution for the class has mean $\mu_A = 63$, standard deviation $\sigma_A = 17$, 18 per cent failure, 14 per cent A/A+, $A_{max} = 99$ and $A_{min} = 20$.

Notice that μ_A, σ_A, percentage F/F– and percentage A/A+ grades are not exactly 65, 15, 16 per cent and 16 per cent respectively. This is because the original R–score distribution was not exactly Gaussian in shape.

For an R–score distribution which is very close to Gaussian in shape, setting the 'A' grade threshold at $Z = +1$ and the failure threshold at $Z = -1$ will result in a *minimum* of 16 per cent A/A + grades and a maximum of 16 per cent failures for the first-year subject. Thus the mapping puts an *upper limit* on the number of failures at 16 per cent. However, it should be clearly noted that *there is absolutely nothing in this scheme to prevent the failure rate being 0 per cent*! Indeed, if the lowest R–score on a particular test is 50 per cent or greater, then the failure rate for that test will be 0 per cent.

In this very important way the proposed system is not strictly 100 per cent norm-referenced. Let us say for example, as happens from time to time, that we have an exceptional group of first-year students. Suppose a first-year test given to these students produced a more or less normal R–score distribution with mean $\mu_R = 70$, standard deviation $\sigma_R = 14$, 21 per cent A/A + grades and a failure rate of 6 per cent. Remember that our mapping procedure can never lower a student's score. Thus, after applying our mapping procedure we would find none of the raw scores altered and the A–score distribution would have $\mu_A = 70$, $\sigma_A = 14$, 21 per cent A/A+ grades and 6 per cent failures.

Rationale for setting first-year failure rate at not more than 16 per cent

Aside from poor teaching, a situation which can and should be corrected by the institution concerned, there are three primary reasons for first-year failures. With these three sources of failure in mind, the rationale for setting the first-year failure rate at not more than 16 per cent is as follows:

9–11%   Imperfect selection criteria for new students resulting in students who do not have the academic ability to cope with the course being offered.

4–5%   Lack of serious effort on the part of some students resulting in an inadequate work level.

1–2%   Personal problems affecting the performance of some students.

Rationale for a minimum of 16 per cent A/A+ grades

The rationale for a minimum of about 16 per cent A/A+ comes from the *a priori* assumptions of the sample of students being assessed and the quality of the assessment instrument being used.

We are assuming that our sample size is both statistically significant and reasonably homogeneous, having been selected in the first place using valid and reasonable selection criteria. In addition we are assuming an assessment instrument which reasonably reflects both the content of the material being examined and the level of difficulty at which the material was originally presented.

Given the above assumptions it is not unreasonable to suggest that approximately one student in six should be able to perform at the level indicated from the definition of an A or A+ grade.

Second-year subjects

In the second year of a course of study we can reasonably expect the class to be more homogeneous than the first-year class and also contain better students on average. These two facts should manifest themselves in the grade distribution by a smaller standard deviation and a lower failure rate. However, the higher difficulty level of the subject should mitigate against any increase in the number of A/A+ grades.

For the second-year subjects it is thus reasonable to increase our setting for the adjusted mean from 65 to $\mu_A = 68$ and decrease our adjusted standard deviation by some 20 per cent, from 15 down to $\sigma_A = 12$. Thus for the second-year A–score distribution we will have:

Z–score from Z_{min} to –1 mapped on to A–score from R_{min} to 56
Z–score from   –1 to 0 mapped on to A–score from   56 to 68
Z–score from   0 to +1 mapped on to A–score from   68 to 80
Z–score from +1 to Z_{max} mapped on to A–score from   80 to 99

Third-year subjects

By the same reasoning we set $\mu_A = 70$ and $\sigma_A = 10$ for the third-year subjects giving an A–score distribution as follows:

Z–score from Z_{min} to –1 mapped on to A–score from R_{min} to 60
Z–score from   –1 to 0 mapped on to A–score from   60 to 70
Z–score from   0 to +1 mapped on to A–score from   70 to 80
Z–score from +1 to Z_{max} mapped on to A–score from   80 to 99

The above scheme will result in the following *approximate* grade distributions for individual first, second- and third-year assignments, tests and examinations:

1st-year subjects % of		2nd-year subjects % of		3rd-year subjects % of	
Grade	Students	Grade	Students	Grade	Students
A/A+	16	A/A+	16	A/A+	16
B/B+	21	B/B+	27	B/B+	34
C/C+	25	C/C+	32	C/C+	34
D/D+	21	D/D+	15	D/D+	9
F/F–	16 (max)	F/F–	10 (max)	F/F–	7 (max)
Class GPA (average grade):					
4.5 (C+)		5.0 (C+)		5.4 (C+)	

Suggested programme for implementation

A programme for realistic and unbiased assessment of candidates is absolutely critical in the establishment and maintenance of standards of academic excellence and achievement. In addition, for the sake of uniformity, fairness and effectiveness, any such programme must, as much as is reasonably possible, be implemented in its entirety *throughout the whole institution*. The following programme is suggested:

1. The previously described scheme for arriving at a final adjusted letter grade should be adopted. This algorithm should be applied to each individual subject assignment, test or examination independently. The weighted average of the adjusted letter grades will then be calculated to obtain the final letter grade to be awarded for the subject in question.
2. For each individual subject the class GPA should lie between 4.0 to 6.0 inclusive. Any subject having a final GPA outside these limits should have its grades scrutinized by an impartial 'standards committee' before they are accepted by the institution.
3. Students who fail one subject in their year but who have an overall course average for the year of at least D+ should be allowed to make up that one failed subject before continuing on to the next year of studies.
4. Those students who:

   ☐ fail one subject and have an overall course average of D or less for their year's work, or
   ☐ fail two or more subjects during the year,

   should have to repeat their year. However, this make-up year should consist of repeating only those subjects where a final grade of C or less was obtained. Students failing one or more subjects during this make-up year should be barred from further attendance at the institution.

In most course subjects both a continuous-assessment component and a final examination covering the entire subject material are essential for good assessment. The following scheme is suggested:

1. A final examination at academic year-end covering the entire subject syllabus.
2. In most course subjects, stipulation that the weight of the final examination be not less than 50 per cent and not more than 70 per cent thus giving a weight to the continuous assessment component of 30–50 per cent. The rationale for this is that the final examination is the only opportunity one has to examine the entire subject material. Thus it cannot reasonably be weighted at less than 50 per cent. On the other hand, a weighting of the continuous assessment mark of less than 30 per cent would tend to mitigate its effectiveness in keeping the student working at a reasonable level throughout the academic year.
3. It is a commonly accepted practice to hold supplementary examinations in those subjects where virtually all of the student's grade is arrived at through the vehicle of a single final examination. In the proposed model, having a significant portion of the course grade (up to 50 per cent) being arrived at through continuous assessment eliminates any need to hold supplementary examinations.
4. In those subjects which do have a final examination covering the entire subject material, it is perfectly legitimate that any student receiving a pass grade on the final examination *must* be guaranteed a pass grade in the subject as a whole. Students who pass the final examination but whose final average for the subject is less than D should automatically be awarded a final subject grade of D.
5. In order to

   ☐ guard against students abusing the policy stated in 4 above by doing very little work during the course of the year in the hope of being able to cram at the end of the year in order to achieve a pass on the final examination; and
   ☐ help identify and possibly eliminate those subjects who are clearly out of their depth in a particular subject;

   it is proposed that, at a certain specified point in the academic year (typically around the two-thirds mark), any student having a GPA (up to that point) in a subject of less than 1.0 (ie, less than a 'middle F') be asked to withdraw from that subject.

Acknowledgements

The author wishes to thank Dr Henry Ellington (Robert Gordon Institute of Technology, UK), and George Hutchison and Geoffrey Wilson (Ngee Ann Polytechnic, Singapore) for their reading of the manuscript and their helpful comments and suggestions.

References

1. Definitions taken from the academic calendar (1986–87), York University, Toronto, Canada.
2. Dr R Kreps, University of Toronto, Private communication (1974).

19. Optical mark reading technology in Chinese educational development

Roger Singer

Introduction

Educating the younger generation poses problems for governments all round the world, but nowhere are these problems on a more gigantic scale than in the People's Republic of China. Its school-aged population is already an enormous 200 million and increasing rapidly. The government there is determined to overcome all the difficulties it faces. It recognizes that universal education is essential for a modern state and future superpower as the twenty-first century approaches. Education is accepted as a major priority in China and the nation is determined to come to terms with the demands which administration on this scale is bound to bring. China is looking to Western technology for help.

The educational system in China

China is still a relatively poor country and it is not surprising that schools there lack some of the equipment and physical facilities that would be considered essential in the West. Nonetheless, the country compares well to other developing nations. Three out of every four pupils, for instance, can read. But perhaps the first thing which a visiting teacher might notice is that Chinese pupils are much more attentive and punctual than those at schools in the Western hemisphere. They generally behave better and playground fights are a rarity.

Chinese primary schools enroll around 90 per cent of all seven year olds in the country – no less than 140 million pupils. The course lasts six years but many children, particularly in the rural areas, drop out. Facilities are usually spartan. The teachers concentrate on single subjects. This system means a high ratio of teachers to pupils overall, but classes remain large while teaching duties remain at a low level.

Fifty million pupils in China are receiving secondary education and they graduate to it by examination. The full secondary course consists of a compulsory three years lower secondary course followed by a further three years upper secondary course of either a general nature or based on a variety of technical, vocational, agricultural and commercial programmes.

The Chinese are striving to better their secondary education and are concentrating on quality rather than quantity: improving facilities and standards of teaching. The secondary schools are better equipped than the primary, but the system was damaged by the Cultural Revolution when no less than 5,000 vocational schools were closed. Another handicap is that many of the textbooks are out-of-date and students often face difficult and outdated questions in examinations. Great efforts are now being made to update syllabuses and to revive secondary education generally.

The Cultural Revolution did even more damage to higher education in China. In one decade, the numbers enrolled dropped from one million to 50,000. Numbers are now back, if all types of post secondary education are taken into account, to near two million. But nonetheless, 20 million Chinese missed higher education as a result of the upheaval 20 years ago.

There is likely to be further reform of the Chinese educational system during the next two decades. This will demand capital investment, but China's GNP is forecast to treble by the end of the century, so the nation should be able to afford it. The scale of education in China is massive and the nation is approaching the problems it faces with urgency.

The scale of the problem

Secondary schooling is not yet compulsory and the demand for places in secondary and tertiary education in China exceeds what is presently available. It is considered essential that the best students are selected.

The need to standardize is also considered urgent, but there are few if any school inspectors to supervise this. The vastness of China and the exceptional conditions there make the organization of an inspectorate, working with uniformity, almost impossible. The Chinese situation is complicated even more because of its many regions which are totally different in character: different languages are spoken and each contains ethnic minorities.

The political and social upheavals of the 1960s have also left their mark and, together with the other difficulties faced by the education system, have left China with skill shortages in the adult population. Nonetheless, the considerable efforts being made to correct things is reflected by the fact that the nation has no fewer than thirty equivalents of our Open University.

Multiple choice examinations

China has never had a system of standardized universal education but it now regards the multiple choice examination system as a means of achieving uniformity of marking and asessment nationwide. Multiple choice offered the State Education Commission in China an examination system which is fair and brings about better selection of pupils for further education. Examination papers can be marked with absolute uniformity.

The Education Commission also recognized that it would need the latest automated educational processing systems and modern electronic document readers have already been purchased for pilot multiple choice schemes in selected regions.

The technology which makes it possible

The technology which has made the widespread use of multiple choice assessment possible is known as Optical Mark Reading (OMR). Data can be transferred directly from multiple choice examination papers completed in pencil into a computer. The pencil marks are detected by a method based on reflected infra-red light. Clean white paper reflects 80 per cent of the light whereas the pencil marks reflect only about 20 per cent. The answer papers are transported in quick succession past a stationary light read-head. They have to be designed very precisely for the highly sensitive optics of the system to ensure that scanning, and subsequent processing, is absolutely trouble-free. Sophisticated machines will not pick up two papers without failing to detect it immediately, and the paper transport has to be very carefullly designed so that each answer paper is read correctly.

Examination papers can be read by an OMR scanner at a very rapid rate. Automatic-feed machines can cope with 10,000 forms per hour, whereas smaller hand-fed machines depend on the dexterity of the operator. In the latter instance, one form per second is easily attainable.

The ability of the OMR reader to ignore erased marks, dirt or defects in the paper is due to years of technological development, and the fact that these difficulties have been overcome totally contributes to the error-free performance of this type of equipment. Any discrepancy in an answer paper is detected immediately by the system and the form is then rejected for operator intervention.

One major benefit which stems from OMR equipment harnessed to computer systems is that teachers have the time to concentrate on teaching. But there are, of course, other benefits as well. In the interests of fairness, there should be a parity of marks overall, in all subjects and between related subjects. An examination based, for example, on parity between three different mathematics papers would not be achieved if the marks for one averaged much higher than those for the other two. The computer can make the necessary adjustments needed to help ensure fairness.

The system can isolate any question to which the number of correct answers is very low. This might indicate, for instance, that the question itself is ambiguous. If, on further examination, it appears to be so, it can be eliminated from the examination entirely in order to achieve a fairer and more accurate assessment. With multiple choice examinations human error and subjectivity are eliminated from the marking process.

A computer-based system also allows statistics to be gathered with ease. Comparisons of results can be made between one region and another, or against set standards. The quality of the multiple choice questions will also improve as unsatisfactory ones are isolated and progressively eliminated from future examination papers. It is also easier to detect overall rising or falling standards: something which is almost impossible from the subjective marking of essay answers.

The Chinese experiment

Until three years ago, the State Education Commission in China was thinking of introducing multiple choice only for university entrance examinations in English language. These were to have been based on the internationally accepted TOEFL (Test Of English as a Foreign Language), for which the multiple choice examinations are used.

The Commission first begun to realize that the multiple choice system could be used much more widely in 1986 after contacts made with DRS at an educational computing exhibition in Beijing. We were invited back soon afterwards to explain to selected educationalists the latest advances in document reading technology. This led to the Chinese educational authorities recognizing that, with this technology, multiple choice systems could be adapted to examinations for many subjects at various levels and that nationwide standardization of assessment and teaching could be achieved.

The Chinese have good reason for moving forward with a certain amount of caution. The introduction of a new technology involves a high level of investment for the country. If they were to be committed long-term to an overseas supplier, they wanted to be sure that the relationship would be beneficial. For the Chinese, there is always the alternative of developing and manufacturing their own systems; but this would divert scarce engineering resources which might be better concentrated on the manufacture of high volume products, even though it would save hard currency. They wanted, therefore, to be assured that any importer of high-tech equipment would offer long-term support.

The type of OMR equipment used for the TOEFL examinations required special pencils and paper which had to be imported. The Chinese do not want systems which, for them, have these limitations. Therefore, the requirement that OMR systems should work with Chinese paper was particularly important. Otherwise the demand on limited hard currency resources would be endless. The paper used for multiple choice answers in China is made from plant fibres and not from wood pulp. This is much softer than the paper which would normally be used with OMR equipment in other countries.

Pilot schemes in two provinces

Machines have been supplied to two Chinese provinces, Guangdong and Shandong, which have more liberal economic controls than some of the others. The progressive Guangzhou Institute of Foreign Languages is in Guandong province and much of the impetus for change has come from it.

Both provinces organized a pilot scheme in 1988 involving a million pupils altogether. These schemes were successful and similar schemes are now planned for the provinces of Hainan, Henan and Anhui, and for the municipality of Shanghai. The systems used have already justified themselves by saving costs in excess of their purchase price.

The pilot schemes have shown that the equipment will work with Chinese paper; that the running costs generally are low; and that there are no environmental problems with which to contend. The machines, for instance, will work efficiently in the typically sparse Chinese office conditions.

OMR machines tend to be graded according to their reading speeds. The Chinese provinces which are running pilot schemes use DRS OMR 30 machines which read at 3000 forms per hour. This is equivalent to fifteen operators keying-in data simultaneously. It is also the fastest rate at which forms printed on Chinese paper can be put through satisfactorily. Ultra-high-speed through-put (10,000 forms per hour) would demand harder conventional paper.

DRS OMR 30 machines can be connected to any of a wide range of micro, mini or mainframe computers. Typically an IBM PC would be used, or a compatible such as the Chinese Great Wall microcomputer. Programming is straightforward and programs can be written in a language chosen by the user. In China, most of the programs are written in BASIC which can produce error messages and reports in Chinese.

The system is simple to operate after a short period of training which covers document handling, processing, editing and storing. Very quickly, novice operators are able to look after high volume throughput.

The future

With the future of pupils and students at stake, there has to be absolute trust in the accuracy, fairness and impartiality of an automated system. Many countries are now, of course, committed to use of multiple choice questions for examinations at every level, including entry into professions. China will almost certainly follow the same path and will find itself handling numbers which, compared to those of other nations, are gigantic. It is essential, therefore, that the selection process at all stages is efficient and that the State Education Commission gets the statistical feedback it needs to monitor progress.

The pilot educational schemes in China have been successful and the provinces involved are content with the level of support and commitment they have received. It is likely now that other regions will soon change over to the multiple choice system for every academic grade and will demand the high grade technical equipment needed to operate it.

20. Profiling: the role of technology

Roger Singer

The importance of profiling is becoming increasingly recognized throughout the educational sector. It has been used in business for a number of years to help evaluate job applicants and it is now, of course, beginning to be used in this country for the first time as part of the overall assessment of pupils. A graphical snapshot which highlights the strength and weaknesses of a pupil or student has long been recognized as a useful aid to teachers.

The requirement that every British school uses profiling has been given considerable impetus by the 1988 Education Reform Act. Local education authorities feel that the relationship between teacher and pupil will be strengthened if profiling documentation accompanies GCSE results, and especially if the questions which lead to assessments are answered by both together.

The conversion of answers into a graphic presentation is much more easily achieved with a computer and printer, driven of course by the necessary software. This has already spawned a competitive new market and the various software packages which have appeared so far have been developed primarily for LMS applications. But many of these packages have add-on capabilities to handle such things as documentation and records of achievements. As it uses essentially the same database, a profiling module can be added easily.

Also esssential to the efficient working of these systems is an Optical Mark Reader (OMR). This type of machine is capable of reading marks made by teachers and pupils on the assessment questionnaires and of transferring the data directly into a computer. The pencil marks made on the questionnaires are detected by an infra-red light optics system.

OMR technology can speed up the input of data very considerably. Teachers who are not necessarily trained typists or computer operators find it very time-consuming to key in the information on which profiling assessments would be based. A small OMR reader can be hand-fed at the rate of one questionnaire form every second. This means that these machines will input data ten times faster than a number of keyboard operators working simultaneously. Bigger automatic-feed machines – used predominantly by examination boards – can cope with 10,000 forms every hour.

It is difficult to believe that schools of any size can consider anything other than an automatic system in future. To prepare reports or profiles by hand will be too tedious, time-consuming and inefficient. OMR machines offer the only way of inputting data quickly and accurately enough. This is vitally important to schools as teachers will have time to prepare courses and actually teach. Otherwise they would be overwhelmed by what is going to be demanded of them by the Education Reform Act. It has already been estimated that a typical school of 1,000 pupils will generate more than one million different items of information every year!

Teachers in some secondary schools already use a computer system to compile end-of-year reports. While this is not, of course the same thing as profiling, there are important technical similarities. End-of-year reports are printed from a bank of words and phrases held in the memory of the computer, but it still depends on human keying of data. This is less time-consuming than laboriously writing every report by hand but it is likely to be more error-prone. An OMR-based system makes no errors and will separate incorrectly completed forms for scrutiny by teacher or administrator. The machines will also differentiate intended marks from erasures, smudges or dirt.

Optical Marker Readers were first introduced 20 years ago and are now widely used in commerce, local government and education. Big automatic-feed OMR machines are used for multiple choice testing in several of the more populous third world countries and also now in some regions of China where the school-aged population is, by any standards, enormous. It is only recently that the more modest needs of individual British schools have led to the development of low-cost OMR machines. They have highly sensitive optical systems, yet are robust enough to withstand the typically rigorous school environment. They are compatible with most microcomputers used for school administration.

It is almost certain that all secondary schools in Britain will find that they cannot do without Optical Mark Readers. The primary, further and higher education sectors are likely to follow suit primarily for assessment, but ultimately for a whole range of administrative tasks as well.

21. Teacher evaluation as the technology of increased centralism in education[1]

John Smyth

Introduction

Portraying teachers as a much-maligned group within the community would not be hard at all, given the draconian nature of recent 'educational reforms' visited upon them in the UK, USA, Australia, New Zealand and elsewhere. But to engage in an activity of that kind would be largely to miss the point – namely, that teachers need to be more active in deconstructing 'dominant' forms of evaluation and articulating and developing alternative ways of construing and evaluating their own and one anothers' teaching.

The last thing we need at the moment is to acquiesce to those who would paralyse teachers with externally determined and imposed forms of teacher evaluation, by focusing only on the sense of hopelessness that these engender. This is not to argue that the history or the context of current moves to impose harsher forms of evaluation on teachers is somehow unimportant; rather, it is to argue instead for a way of looking at contemporary events that takes account of the cultural, political and social circumstances that have led to the formulation of these policies in the first place. Situating events in this way enables those most affected by them – in this case teachers – to begin to see official pronouncements and reforms for what they really are: ways of constraining and inhibiting the real work of teaching. The focus needs to be shifted to ways of mounting alternatives that recognize the potential of teachers in generating purposeful alternatives to the hierarchical schemes that currently pass as teacher evaluation (Hunter, Elliott, Marland and Wormald, 1985).

Teachers need to be able to see that they are increasingly caught up in a boundless text that structures and delimits what they do to the point that 'the hell they are in remains invisible to them' (Johnson, 1988, p 313). They need to be equipped to re-read the official pronouncements so as to develop ways of seeing this 'imposing text for its contradictions', and 'deliberately incorporate them into richer more self-conscious, alternative perspectives' (Diamond, 1988, p 6). Where governments continue to insist on reacting to complex cultural, economic and social problems with simplistic solutions that use schools and teachers as the blunt implements for belabouring protracted problems, then teachers need to develop their own counter-discourse that intellectualizes the nature of the problems while enabling them to theorize in more politically informed ways about what is occurring.

What this amounts to in practice is a form of teacher-initiated evaluation. Teachers, in concert with students, parents, employers and members of the wider community, collectively determine and debate the agenda for schooling, rather than having policies thrust upon them that bear no relationship to educational or pedagogical agenda. It is not that teachers are opposed to evaluation of their work, or bent on resisting changes to their work practices *per se*, as the popular press would have us believe (Wilby, 1986) – far from it. What teachers justifiably object to is the non-consultative and inappropriate imposition of industrial modes of evaluation/appraisal, that not only bear no relationship to the nature of the work they perform in schools (Dadds, 1987), but are antagonistic to the objectives of schooling. I want to look somewhat more closely here at the nature of teachers' work, and at ways of monitoring it that are more respectful and understanding of what teachers as a professional group *do* in classrooms.

In this chapter I want to achieve several things. Firstly, to expose the chimera of educational reform for the mythical creature that it is. Second, to locate the technocratic, reductionist and managerialist processes that masquerade as teacher evaluation and appraisal, within the context of claims that such bureaucratic intrusions amount to an improvement of teaching. In doing this I want to detail the manifest shortcomings of the dominant approach to teacher evaluation, and look at the forces at work to maintain it. Finally, as a counter to the instrumentalism touted by governments (of all political persuasions) under the guise of inert, neutral, and objective teacher evaluation, I want to offer some pointers on a more collegial, inclusive approach that teachers might adopt.

The chimera of educational reform

The major justifying rhetoric used by Western governments for increasing controls over what goes on in classrooms is that the decline in competitiveness of Western capitalist economies makes it imperative that schools (and teachers) be made to do their economic work of skills formation. Accordingly, the range of so-called reform measures designed to check up on teachers are justified as a way of ensuring that incompetent teachers are removed from schools, that wastage of educational resources is eliminated, and that in the process, schools produce 'outputs' that slot neatly into industry and improve national economic performance. The argument is so simplistic and misleading as to almost be laughable (were it not that people actually believe it!).

The problem with this line of argument is that it is fundamentally flawed. Those who adhere to it want simultaneously to believe that teachers can be blamed for poor economic performance and act as the major means of escape from this economic quagmire. They can't have it both ways!

Educational reform, of which teacher evaluation/appraisal is a major component, has failed largely because the social and economic problems we face are not ones that can be attributed to schools. In reality, what we have is not a *crisis of competence* as is alleged by our schools and teachers, but rather a deep-seated *crisis of confidence* going to the heart of Western capitalism. Trying to kick schools and teachers into shape is not going to come to grips with the fundamental structural inequalities and injustices that are at the root of our economic demise. By proposing educational reforms that focus on teacher appraisal, our political masters have created alienation, demoralization.

As Jonathan (1983) put it, moves towards such a 'manpower services model of education', with measures to introduce benchmark testing, national curricula and national appraisal schemes, are all predicated on an impoverished and unsubstantiated view that somehow schools are failing to 'deliver the goods', and that teachers need to be held more accountable personally through more rigorous forms of appraisal for the 'right' sorts of learning. It is also clear that this labour-market view of education regards 'the development of internationally competitive manufacturing and service industries . . . [as requiring] . . . a more highly skilled and better educated workforce' (Diamond, 1988, p 4). Designing and implementing appropriate indicators of performance is viewed as being imperative to the overall agenda of quality control, and of ensuring that the products of schools fit easily into the national economic effort. Recent moves to mandate teacher appraisal in the UK (Walsh, 1987) need to be considered for what they really are: an interventionist desire on the part of government to extend central control over education through proceduralizing the work of teachers in the guise of rational management procedures (D'Alcan, Alexander, Machej & McCafferty, 1986). In Brtain, this has taken two main forms:

> The first is the attempt to rationalize teachers' work through influencing both the teacher-training process, notably through control of the teacher-training and in-service-training systems, and the content and output of teaching through influence over the curriculum and examinations. The second form is the attempt to formalize the employment relation, by specifying much more closely teachers' conditions of work (Walsh, 1987, p 148).

In the foreword to a collection of papers presented to the British Educational Research Association, the point was made that to date 'teacher appraisal [has been] treated as if it were non-problematic and as if all that had to be decided were procedural methods of a managerial nature' (Dockrell, Nisbet, Nuttall, Stones and Wilcox, 1986). In that collection, Wilcox argues that teacher appraisal is

> but one manifestation among several of a pervasive 'managerialist' approach to the process of schooling . . . an approach that not only conceptualizes the educational enterprise in terms of a rational management model but also seeks to ensure that individual institutions and teachers conform in practice to such a model. . . Rational management models (precisely because they are based upon a logical analysis of situations and do not take account of the complexities . . . of real classrooms, teachers and pupils) fail to embody adequate *theories* of education. As a result 'educational policy is designed to alter the practice of education without an understanding of how education actually occurs' (Wise, 1977).

This technologization and hyper-rationalization (Wise, 1977) of education has been made possible because of a dramatic reversal of labour-market conditions in teaching over the past decade, and has spurned a form of teacher–employer relationship in Britain (as elsewhere) based upon 'exchange rather than . . . trust' (Walsh, 1987, p 148; Elliott, 1989).

By silencing teachers (Dadds, 1986) and implying that some (if not all) teachers are incompetent (see Anderson, *The Times*, 9 January 1985, 'How many [teachers] are incompetent? Let me start the bidding at 76%') it becomes much easier to argue for forms of individual rationalization of teachers' work that, while managerial, hierarchical and control-oriented, nevertheless appear on the surface to be about promoting efficiency and effectiveness. The evaluation of teachers' work is never *just* about assessing technical competence – it is also ideological in the way it focuses on the distribution of power and the exercise of social control through social relations, the personality dispositions and the distribution of cultural capital necessary for the maintenance of existing social reationships.

What I want to argue here is that focusing – as we are in many Western countries – on how to improve the quality of education through improving the rigour of teacher evaluation, is to head in totally the wrong direction. Like Apple (1983), I agree that we need to turn the problem on its head by looking at how 'teaching as a labour process . . . fit[s] into changes in power relations in our society' (p 3). Apple's argument is that we can only 'fully understand the growing emphasis on teacher quality by government officials [when] we recognize that it is part of a long continuing struggle by groups of people outside of school to take both control of teaching and curricula out of the hands of teachers and to alter what education is for' (p 3).

Locating the issue of teacher evaluation in a broader context means coming to see how demands for tighter forms of appraisal are related to the fiscal crisis in Western societies, wherein publicly provided programmes of various sorts are labelled as too costly. The broader process is one in which teachers (like other educated workers) are increasingly becoming 'proletarianized'. In general terms, proletarianization refers to 'the reduction of the value of labour power . . . whereby agents have less control over their work activity' (White, 1983, p 46). As Larson (1980) put it, this becomes clear in several tendencies: a tendency to increase and rigidify the division of labour (increasing the number of routine or menial tasks); a tendency towards the intensification of labour (reducing the amount of inactivity and speeding up production); and, the tendency towards routinization of high-level tasks (intervention by expert consultants with a view to codifying operations into reducible tasks). It is becoming clear too that with moves towards standardized/rationalized curricula, teachers' work has been intensified, broken up into a series of smaller and smaller concrete components, with objectives laid out sequentially – set numbers of which are to be covered in a given time specified, and the achievement of which are monitored and policed.

Meisenhelder (1983) has raised grave reservations as to whether this 'Taylorization' of education, which has accompanied the proletarianization of teachers, and the concomitant arguments for reduced costs and standardization that accompany it, have actually produced any savings at all without harming the quality of education. According to him, the effect has been to increase management control over the working situation of teachers.

While the objective situation of fiscal shortfall created by the economic problems of late capitalism may force administrators to try to reduce costs and increase the efficiency of work, it allows them to do so in a manner that increases their own power at the expense of [teachers] (pp 302–3).

Apple (1983) claims that the deepening economic crisis has placed schools everywhere directly in the spotlight, resulting in a considerable reduction in what counts as legitimate teaching content and knowledge. The social dynamic he sees behind this expresses itself in an attempt to 'industrialize the school' (Apple, 1988, p 274) in the interests of promoting it as the agency through which to restore economic productivity and competitive advantage.

> When government (the 'state') comes under attack for not being responsive
> enough to 'economic needs' and when a fiscal crisis creates increasing
> pressures on the state to make the immediate needs of business and
> industry its primary goals, the crisis will be *exported downwards*. That is, rather
> than attention being directed toward the unequal results and benefits
> produced by the ways our economy is currently organized and controlled,
> schools and teachers will be focused on as the major cause of social
> dislocation, unemployment, falling standards of work, declining productiv-
> ity, and so on. Intense pressures will build on educators and state officials to
> respond. Very often these pressures will result in the form of attempts by
> government bureaucrats, ministry officials, and others to rationalize
> teaching and tighten control. . . . Teacher grading systems . . . need to be
> seen as part of the attempt by the larger government to solve its own
> economic and ideological problems by exporting them on to teachers
> (Apple, 1983, pp 4–5).

The fundamental problem with the notion of school reform that relies upon improving schooling through the evaluation of teacher competence, is that it is predicated on an inaccurate and misconceived notion of what constitutes quality teaching (for a good example of this see Bridges, 1986). As Hargreaves (1988) has pointed out, the traditional conception of what constitutes quality teaching is 'psychologistic' in nature, and overstresses personal qualities, attributes and technical actions of individual teachers. Defined in this way, the search becomes one of locating individual teacher deficits, and then targeting them for remediation through staff development (or in extreme cases, dismissal on the grounds of incompetence). Hargreaves (1988) notes that while this might be a politically attractive way to portray the problem because of the ease of an apparent 'solution' in the form of 'training', and the fact that it conveys an air of certainty that 'things can be done [and] be seen to be done . . . relatively cheaply' (p 215), such analyses are very wide of the mark. For these solutions to be credible we would have to accept the inevitability of an exceedingly narrow conception of teaching – one which Hargreaves (1988) calls 'frontal teaching' in which 'transmission of knowledge', 'teacher dominance', 'control', 'conformity', 'closed questioning' and 'desk work' are the most common recurring features.

While Hargreaves draws upon the studies of Tye (1985a), Tye (1985b), Westbury (1973) and Hoetker and Ahlbrand (1969) and others, as evidence of a remarkable consistency in the frontal or dominant mode of teaching, it is the interpretation he places on this evidence that is especially important. Rather than regarding it as a hallmark of the inevitability of a certain style of teaching, Hargreaves explains this kind of pedagogy as a rational historical response by teachers to the need to mobilize attention and sustain control 'among large numbers of potentially recalcitrant working-class children, while getting information and material across in an environment where resources were in short supply' (p 217). While this context-specific response has become 'habitu-ated', 'sedimented' and 'petrified' into teachers' unconscious ways of operating, it has had the added and unfortunate consequence of entrenching individualism as an all-too-convenient benchmark against which to calibrate 'good' teaching, for those who would evaluate the work of teachers. Such a view, of course, takes little account of:

> how teachers themselves understand, interpret and deal with the demands that their work situation makes upon them. Without such understandings of why teachers do what they do, it is then possible for researchers' and policy makers' own interpretations to flood into the vacuum (p 215).

Hargreaves (1988) is worth quoting at length on this:

> teachers, like other people, are not just bundles of skill, competence and technique; they are creators of meaning, interpreters of the world and all it asks of them. They are people striving for purpose and meaning in circumstances that are usually much less than ideal and which call for constant adjustment, adaptation and redefinition. Once we adopt this view of teachers or of any other human being, our starting question is no longer why does he/she *fail* to do X but why does he/she do Y? What purpose does doing Y fulfil for them? Our interest, then, is in how teachers manage to cope with, adapt to and reconstruct their circumstances; it is in what they achieve, not what they fail to achieve (p 216) . . . [Notwithstanding] . . . teaching is certainly a matter of competence. But it is competence of a particular kind. It is the competence to recognize and enact the rules, procedures and forms of understanding of a particular cultural environ-ment. What is involved is not *technical* competence to operate in a pre-given, professionally correct and educationally worthwhile way, but cultural competence to 'read' and 'pass' in a system with its own specific history, a system once devised and developed to meet a very particular set of social purposes (p 217).

The apparent prevalence of transmission (or recitation) as a way of teachers adapting to and accommodating to the 'problematic' (Dale, 1977; Hargreaves, 1978) they find themselves in, has important and far reaching effects on the appraisal of teaching. If it is true that there are substantial pressures on teachers to orchestrate dialogue and activities in their classrooms (Sachs, 1987), with the result that there is a lack of pedagogical pluralism and a remarkable uniformity in teacher culture (Sachs and Smith, 1988), then this makes the task of legitimizing and reproducing that image of the teacher through systems of evaluation and appraisal all that much easier. In an activity that has objectives as indeterminate as teaching, and where there is a clear benchmark model that appears to be endorsed by teachers themselves as to what constitutes teaching, it is not altogether surprising to find this as a centrepiece against which teaching is in turn evaluated. What goes unattended to, of course, in schemes that try to capture the surface realities or outward manifestations of teaching, is the undisclosed histories of how and why such actions were adopted in the first place and what they mean in the cultural context of teachers' and childrens' lives.

Addressing the limitations of teacher-evaluation methods that focus on observable reductionist aspects of teachers' work, Stodolsky (1984) claimed that the entire enterprise rested on the assumption that 'the characteristics of "good" or effective teaching are known and recognizable' (p 11) in terms of being present or absent to some extent in any individual. Expressing 'good' or 'poor' teaching solely in terms of a demonstrable capacity to quell what would otherwise be a 'potentially chaotic "babble" in the classroom' (Hargreaves, 1988, p 217), is to purge teaching of those dimensions that have to do with the social, historical and interpretive nature of what transpires. Resorting to context-stripping methods (Mishler, 1986) of this kind, is to work in the direction of destroying the habitus of teaching.

Intrusion of bureaucratic and corporate ideology

To understand moves to control the work of teachers through evaluation and to bring them into line with the views and agenda of the state (particularly its economic rationalist views on the role of schooling in the labour process), it is necessary to sketch the scene on a broader canvas and to look at the issue raised in the previous section about the increasing proletarianization of teachers. Like manual workers in the Industrial Revolution who lost control of their craft skills through the move into factory modes of production, teachers in Western countries are losing control of their work in precisely the same way. In the current troubled economic climate that has meant budgetary measures designed to 'rationalize' and 'streamline' work in order to reduce costs and increase productivity. The effect of this, White (1983) argues, is to bring 'mental' (ie non-manual) workers more into line with 'manual' workers through measures that 'reduce their autonomy (immediate control over the labour process), de-individualize their skill and qualifications (fragmentation of tasks), and affects their incomes in relation to the volume of work performed (downgrading of status)' (p 46). All of this has been necessitated by a marked decrease in relative expenditure on services of the public sector, including publicly provided education, with a concomitant 'emphasis in school policy . . . [on] streamlining and rationalizing the system, a restructuring which is geared to the needs of the capitalist labour market ' (White, 1983, p 50).

By way of example, in England, Hartley and Broadfoot (1986) see the establishment of the Assessment Performance Unit in 1975 and the rash of government-initiated papers that accompanied it, as concrete evidence of the government's desire to centralize educational policy decisions, and through that, identifying and implementing a core curriculum and its associated centralized teacher appraisal. The danger in this is that what started out as an initial concern to remedy 'under-achievement', rapidly gives way to calls for 'enhanced managerial control, under the convenience flag of "accountability"' (Simon, 1979, p 10). Hartley and Broadfoot (1986) draw upon Wragg's (1980) scenario of the 'slippery slope' and the escalation towards 'state-approved knowledge' that follows from a centrally determined core curriculum:

> . . . such a movement can begin with centrally prescribed aims that are broad enough for no one to be able to take exception to them in principle. This is certainly the case with the six familiar broad aims laid down in 'Framework' which are:

- to help pupils develop lively inquiring minds;
- to help pupils acquire knowledge and skills relevant to adult life;
- to help pupils to use language and number effectively;
- to instil respect for religious and moral values;
- to help pupils understand the world in which they live;
- to help pupils to appreciate human achievements and aspirations.

Next to step down the slippery slope, would be to prescribe time allocations centrally for core subjects (percentage times for core subjects are suggested in 'Framework'). A subsequent step might then be the institution of agreed syllabuses and more precise objectives. . . . A potential fourth step involving the imposition of centrally prescribed teaching methods, teaching strategies, testing techniques, remedial provison and the like, could complete the process whereby central government could lay down 'standards' identifying what a school and a teacher should be able to deliver and could take whatever action it thought appropriate it if considered they failed to do so .

Moves in other countries are not all that inconsistent with what is sketched out above. Both state and federal governments in the USA have long held the view that education ought to be tightly controlled and have vigorously pursued central policies to effect that. The kind of rhetorical flourishes we find in recent government-sponsored reports in the USA like 'Nation at Risk' (National Commission on Excellence in Education, 1983) and 'Nation Prepared' (Carnegie Corporation, 1986), make it abundantly clear that teachers are to be subjected to increasingly repressive measures in that part of the world.

A recent example might be illustrative of the extremes to which such a preoccupation with teacher evaluation can lead. In the case of *Sweeny v Turlington* (Hazi and Garman, 1988) a Florida teacher appealed against the evaluation of her performance, and in its decision the court ruled that the state had the legislative power to mandate a particular evaluation scheme (the Florida Performance Management System) which contained 121 behaviour criteria against which teachers were to be rated, and which was deemed to have been validated by research as reliable (Florida Coalition for the Development of a Performance Management System, 1983). As if the scheme itself were not oppressive enough, what is more disturbing about this case is the way in which classroom observers who are to conduct the evaluation are disenfranchised from making any judgements at all about how worthwhile the act of teaching is. Observers are required to:

... turn their coded FPMS forms over to a machine that calculates the teacher's score. Thus, a computer – not the observer – mathematically renders judgement about the teacher's lesson and identifies who is a superior teacher (Hazi and Garman, 1988, p 7).

While some of this may seem a little far-fetched, it is the trend that is important. In Australia, for example, the fashionable rhetoric being used as a smokescreen for the extensive reintroduction of hierarchical forms of teacher evaluation goes under the rubric of 'monitoring school performance' (State Board of Education, 1987). In the guise of a benign form of managerialism aimed at serving the corporate interests of the educational bureaucracy, schools and the community are being sold the idea that 'comprehensive performance indicator frameworks' (p 18) against which there can be a 'close tracking of costs, and the routine association of data on inputs, processes and outputs' (p 18), is the way to ensure efficiency and effectiveness in schools. Authorities in Victoria and other states favour a process of re-arming an allegedly apolitical inspectorate (in what is a highly charged political environment) in a move that is supposedly designed to 'inspire public confidence' in schools (State Board of Education, 1987, p 19) while winning over teachers because it will be 'close to practice'. Such moves to reintroduce, via backdoor means, schemes that have patently failed in the past, are doomed to failure.

Also speaking of the Australian scene, Preston (1987) says we should not be blinded by the 'superficial charm of "teacher appraisal for professional development and school improvement"' (p 3) because such thinking avoids a whole range of deep-seated problems that go unattended. For precisely the same reason we also need to be wary of moves that link 'teacher appraisal' and 'school improvement' (as do writers like Ingvarson, nd; Beare, 1987; & McLaughlin, 1984), because of their undisclosed and inherently conservative agenda of maintaining the status quo of existing power relationships.

In New Zealand too, the spectre of a centralized 'Review and Audit Agency' (Ministry of Education, 1988) is a very distinct possibility as educational policy makers embark down a similar path of technocratic accountability (Taskforce to Review Educational Administration, 1988). In short, in New Zealand as elsewhere, educational authorities are more concerned with control than with genuinely improving educational practice.

Schemes like those referred to above are clear evidence of the increasingly 'unequal partnership' (sic) that Lawn and Ozga (1986) portray as historically coming to characterize the work of teachers, particularly when matters of evaluation are canvassed. They see 'indirect rule' which had comprised 'sensitive systems of checks and restraints' based on broad consensus about education, being replaced as a way of managing teachers (at least in the UK and in parts of Australia), by much more direct means that make teachers 'servants of the state' (Seddon, 1988) and return them to their nineteenth-centry status of functionaries. Lawn and Ozga (1986) put this fairly bluntly:

> Equality of status is no longer on offer to teachers, and the old internal divisions of status – by sector, sex, subject and by increasing separation of 'managers' from teachers reflect the growing divisiveness of the education system where equality of access is no longer a guiding principle of education policy (p 237).

This increasingly pronounced incursion of bureaucratic and corporate norms and values into classrooms is certainly not a new phenomenon, but its enchancement in recent times is not made any easier by the general lack of acknowledgement that it is even occurring (see for example Suffolk Education Department, 1985; McGreal, 1983; Murphy, 1987; Whyte, 1986; Stenning & Stenning, 1984). Darling-Hammond, Wise and Pease (1986) are right in their claim that 'research on teacher performance and teaching effectiveness does not lead to a stable list of measurable teaching behaviours effective in all contexts. . . . [The] needs [is] for context-specific strategies for improving teaching rather than systemwide hierarchical efforts' (p 245). However, their claim about the need for balance between 'standardized, centrally administered performance expectations and teacher specific approaches' (p 245), is essentially an unconvincing one. This kind of naive arrangement flies directly in the face of existing power relationships and of the need for an extensive renegotiation of the 'unequal partnership' within such a coexistence.

Shaping the dominant form of teacher evaluation[2]

I have been arguing that there appears to be a dominant form of teacher evaluation and that it has rather an ugly face to it. It aims at *social control*, and is characterized by *technocratic rationality* (Jesson, Mayson and Smith, 1987), and endorses *authoritarian notions of pedagogy*. Seeking to harness schools to national economic goals, as is occurring at the moment, and developing methods of surveillance of performance that have the effect of strait-jacketing teachers, is a deliberate form of social control founded on the belief that it is possible to separate 'goals' from 'practice', and as a consequence, render teaching a purely technical process. As Popkewitz (1984) puts it:

> Ideally, practice emerges from the interrelation of purpose with situated actions. To separate the two is to deny that interrelationship and the interplay of thought and action (p 167).

Educational reforms that intervene in this way to prevent teachers and students *themselves* from engaging in judgements about the worth of what they do and the nature of the relationship between goals and practices, are actually 'fake' reforms which aim to produce nothing more than docility (Gitlin and Smyth, 1989). While I would not want to over-emphasize the extent of that control (it is never *complete*, due to forms of resistance developed by teachers; Smyth and Garman, in press), there can be little doubt that dominant forms of evaluation are closely aligned with certain agenda in schools that percolate through to teachers who are urged to communicate to students the virtues of 'punctuality, individual achievement, and authority relations' (Apple and Beyer, 1983). Teachers are encouraged to facilitate identified goals, rather than to debate them. What we find being celebrated, therefore, are approaches that identify and entrench technical aspects of teaching where goals are treated as if they were agreed upon, and where social, moral and political issues are put to one side. Under these conditions, evaluation becomes a utilitarian process of deciding the extent to which programmes and practices actually meet predetermined goals.

Such technocratic rationality can, of course, only be held in place as long as a substantial portion of the population believes in the myth that there are 'experts' in teaching (administrators, supervisors and researchers) who 'know what's best' in teaching, and 'inexperts' (teachers, students and parents), who need to be better informed by those who are wiser. This is a nonsense, of course, but it is used as a legitimating device for subjecting the work of teachers to supposedly rational forms of bureaucratic scrutiny, while leaving the highly contestable purposes for which schooling exists entirely unexamined. In this technocratic approach to teaching, any possibility of school change and reform that might be informed and underpinned by processes of 'on the spot surfacing, criticizing, restructuring, and testing of intuitive understandings of experienced phenomena' (Schön, 1984, p 42) by teachers themselves is lost. What is also lost, as a consequence, is the capacity of teachers to remake, and if necessary re-order the world in which they and their students live.

Embedded within the dominant form of teacher evaluation is a particular view of what constitutes teaching. The assumption is that teaching is a commodified product in which expert teachers deposit the 'right' information in the heads of students. From this authoritarian 'banking' notion it follows that school 'problems' can be remedied by changing what teachers do. The difficulty with this is that teaching is not an individual act, it is a social, relational and interactive process that depends for its success on notions of sharing and community. To deny this relational view of teaching is to endorse an individualistic approach that degenerates into a 'blaming the victim' (Ryan, 1971) strategy in which 'personal needs, personal responsibility and personal rewards' (Broadfoot, 1981, p 104) become the domain of individual teachers. The solution, so the argument goes, is to have a better system of monitoring, detecting and evaluating what teachers do so as to remove deviant behaviour from teachers' repertoires. Evaluative solutions of this kind end up actually entrenching an 'authoritarian pedagogy' (Beyer, 1985) through what is regarded as a general tightening-up of discipline in schools, through calls for enhanced academic standards, and even more measurement-oriented outcomes geared to teaching and learning. By linking evaluation with this authoritarian, commodified view of teaching there is a 'wrenching apart of the cooperative project' (Hextal & Sarup, 1977, p 157) as the social act of teaching is progressively dismembered so that value can be placed on artificially created teacher behaviour. Teachers continue to be blamed for problems that more accurately reflect the priorities and failings of our economic system, while dominant teacher-evaluation practices help to sustain hierarchical and authoritarian arrangements by which students and teachers are effectively silenced.

More concretely, there are a number of fundamental problems with dominant approaches to teacher evaluation that need to be exposed.

The separation of knowing from doing

In the most fundamental sense, the dominant paradigm of teacher evaluation is predicated on an indefensible dichotomy. There are a number of different ways of expressing this separation. Lundgren (1983), for example, speaks of a distinction between two educational contexts – those of 'formulation' and 'realization'. Put in slightly different terms, this means that distinction between 'knowing what' and 'knowing how', or a separation between theory and practice. In Braverman's (1975) language, this amounts to a separation of 'conception' from 'execution'; that is to say, a situation in which there is a temporal separation between those who actually do the work of teaching, as distinct from those who lay claim to planning and designing teaching. Whichever way it is described, what is at issue is a distinction with its origins in constructed and contested power relationships legitimated on the grounds of a technologization of reason (Kemmis, 1985). In this scheme, the distribution of educational tasks is based solely on the alleged sequencing of functions along bureaucratic or superordinate lines, which are 'scientifically' determined and allegedly based on information and techniques that are 'objectively' verifiable and quantatively validated.

Squeezed out of this objectified and stratified scheme is the notion that teachers could possibly have anything significant or worthwhile to say about teaching; their knowledge is treated as being incidental and largely relegated to the realm of folklore. This is not altogether surprising given what is known about the gendered nature of the teaching force. The struggle has to do with an enforced division of labour between those outside the classroom who lay claim to knowing good teaching on the basis of 'scientific research', and those inside the classroom who lay claim to knowing what constitutes good teaching by virtue of doing it. In many ways, these two exist in the tense atmosphere of a private cold war (Blumberg, 1980).

The interests embedded in the division of labour between teachers and evaluators need to be clearly understood. It is a separation that reinforces and maintains a constrained view of the teacher's role, in which teachers generally are prevented from developing their 'knowing' and are denied the opportunity of critically assessing the forms of teaching imposed upon them by others. While this separation can never be complete, and teachers always retain some control over the conceptualization of their work, it nevertheless reinforces an anti-educational approach to teaching. This promotes a self-fulfilling prophecy in which teachers continue to be denied access to assessing the ends towards which they work. This role further limits teachers' abilities to mediate and contest the hierarchical interests embedded in dominant approaches to the evaluation of teaching, and deflects them from uncovering the contradictions and unwarranted ranted effects these structures can have in their teaching. In this way, teachers have less and less control over their work, while at the same time being required to accept and shoulder more of the blame for the economic and social failure of society.

Part of the problem here is that dominant forms of teacher evaluation rely heavily on the assumption that 'science' can be harnessed to produce objective accounts of good teaching. Because these scientific generalizations are supposedly context-free, they ignore historical factors about the way teachers, schools and the practices of the teaching profession have been shaped and continue to be influenced. What has to be questioned is the assumption that science can produce objective accounts of good teaching by focusing only on teacher behaviour and ignoring the social, cultural and political conditions that surround it.

Using 'science' in support of evaluation

Those who endorse the dominant tradition of teacher evaluation assume that procedures originating in the physical sciences can be exported and applied to social contexts like teaching. Applying such procedures to social settings is to regard the inanimate as comparable with the animate. What this narrow view of science as applied to the evaluation of teaching does, of course, is hide the political interests that are served by portraying teaching in particular ways.

Knowledge acquired by using the methods of the physical sciences presupposes several things. Firstly, that the enquirer can and does take a disinterested view of the proceedings, so as to produce findings that are unbiased. Such an observer, so the claim goes, is able to remain uninvolved and thus able to measure the effects of different 'treatments' on groups and individuals, in much the same way that the effect of fertilizers can be measured on crop yields. The desirability and efficacy of this needs to be questioned. Second, such procedures are claimed consistently to predict a particular outcome; it is via this means that theories come to have the power of predictive generalization. While such principles may exist in the natural sciences, principles with such constancy and predictive validity are extremely rare in social situations like those prevailing in classrooms.

To make this point somewhat more directly, the practical consequences of not participating in a process of mutual understanding can be seen in the following scenario. If a teacher begins a lesson without giving clear directions to the students as to what they should be doing, then an evaluator watching might respond by pointing out that 'scientific' research suggests that students stay on-task, and therefore achieve better in tests, if the teacher starts the lesson with clear and unambiguous instructions. What is missing in this example is any kind of consensus about what teacher and evaluator respectively see as being important about teaching. We can impute that the evaluator holds a high regard for test results; but without any dialogue between the teacher and evaluator it is impossible to determine what the teacher holds to be important in this instance. Rather than being negligent, it is possible that the teacher may have been trying to make students more self-reliant by leaving them to their own devices.

Where the teacher's intentions are not considered and given an equal chance of legitimacy alongside those of the outsider, then teacher evaluation practices effectively silence the teacher. Using narrow forms of science to bolster and legitimate particular views of what constitutes 'good' teaching further reinforces oppressive hierarchies between teachers and evaluators, and avoids the crucial discussion of moral questions about what should rightfully be the aims of schooling. When this occurs, dominant forms of evaluation preserve the status quo by strengthening those school relations which structure classroom practices.

Evaluation as technique

Where the primary concern in teacher evaluation is allowed to remain at the level of a preoccupation with better ways of refining and perfecting teaching techniques, then broader questions to do with the moral and educational worth of teaching go unanswered. Those who support the dominant paradigm in teacher evaluation are thus able to claim that the techniques they use, such as rating scales and observational instruments (see for example, Suffolk Education Department, 1985; Borich, 1977; Harris, 1986) do not serve any particular interests; they simply produce raw data. Missing from the fragmented accounts of teaching constructed in this kind of technicist way, is the most important ingredient of all – whether such stories about schooling are recognizable by teachers and students. Almost without exception, such technicist approaches to teacher evaluation fail this ultimate test because teacher and students do not live their lives in the fragmented and dislocated ways suggested in the observation schedules.

The more general claim that evaluation methods are neutral and do not reflect political interests is problematic in several ways. While particular forms of science may be appropriate in controlling the physical world, they have severe limitations when it comes to the social world of teaching. Buchmann (1984) summed it up nicely:

> ... the public accepts scientific findings not because it shares the scientific conception of reality but because of the social authority of science. Scientific knowledge and judgement are opaque and indisputable for most people (p 431).

Teacher evaluation is portrayed as a neutral process of judging whether teachers 'measure-up' to common-sense standards. Broadfoot (1981) claims that this permits apparently objectivist notions of science to masquerade within a bureaucratic style of administration that twists and distorts the intent:

> In practice, this means that issues which are, in reality, questions of alternative values are perceived as technical problems to which a 'right answer – an optimum solution' exists, waiting only to be discovered (p 206).

Arguments about competing and contending values within teaching thus become hidden behind reputedly neutral technologies that claim to be measuring value-free aspects of teaching and learning according to behaviourally established normed references. What is not addressed in all of this is the 'conflict and political debate important to goal setting' (Popkewitz, 1984, p 167). Regarding evaluation as a political process that serves a set of interests, as opposed to a neutral technique, has significant consequences for the nature of evaluation. An evaluator can no longer rely on the 'authority' of science to determine what a teacher should and should not be doing. Teachers must be given the opportunity to take an active role in uncovering hidden interests, thereby replacing hierarchical and authoritarian relations with more dialogical and democratic ones.

The ahistorical nature of knowing

In its conventional or dominant form, teacher evaluation attempts to dissociate teaching from the various aspects of its context. As long as teachers are prevented from clearly seeing where educational ideas come from, they are cut off from the philosophy implicit in those ideas. Practices can thus be disguised in all sorts of ways to appear other than they really are. Rather than teaching being construed as a form of cultural politics (Simon, 1988) in which the give and take of ideas and the way they are negotiated continually act to shape and redefine what is meant by teaching, it is seen as a series of non-problematic and mechanical actions to be implemented in a designated way. Because teachers are unaccustomed to being exposed to the theory behind their practices, Boomer (1984) argues that they tend to 'remain spellbound by habit'. His claim is that having developed the habit of not looking closely at what they do (which is no indictment of them personally), teachers are inclined unwittingly to tell lies about what they do. In those circumstances where teachers work in ways that conform to the dominant view, they are caught-up in 'ensembles of power' (Foucault, 1980) that have been constructed and perpetrated as a consequence of unquestioned history, with even quite liberated teachers suffering from a certain amount of 'institutional contamination'.

Teachers are, therefore, trapped to varying degrees within their personal as well as their professional histories, with dominant practices of evaluation reinforcing rather than requiring them to question these pedagogical assumptions. Most teachers would be shocked and distressed, for example, to learn that the notion of 'individually prescribed instruction' which is still fashionable in some quarters, had its origins in attempts within industry in the early 1900s to standardize industrial production. The intent was to ensure a predictable output in which the 'worker's movements [were] made so elementary and routine that the product inevitably emerge[d] independent of will or conscious desire of the worker' (Kliebard, 1975, p 65). What might appear on the surface to be a humanistic process of catering for the individual needs of students is really a process designed to subjugate workers into submissiveness by removing any discretionary control they might have over the work process. As Kliebard (1975) has shown, the US rail industry was at the forefront of this process of standardization, using ideas that came originally from the military.

The point being made here is that when teachers are amputated, deliberately or otherwise, from the history of the ideas that infiltrate schools, then by adopting particular pedagogical practices they can unwittingly be taking on a philosophy quite opposed to educative intentions. The way in which dominant forms of teacher evaluation regard knowing in ahistorical terms minimizes the opportunity teachers have for questioning educational views, and where they come from. Treating teachers as objects not as subjects means that teachers' consciousness or 'range of vision' about what they do in classrooms is quite severely limited.

Rethinking teacher evaluation

The basic assumptions behind the dominant view of teacher evaluation, as sketched out above, must be confronted and roundly contested if evaluation is to do other than support narrowly conservative interests. Because teacher evaluation, in whatever form, expresses a particular view of social relationships in schools, a step in the direction of pursuing more educative (even, more 'empowering') interests, is to expose and acknowledge the nature of these relationships. Acknowledging whose interests are being served is crucial in moving away from alienating and oppressive hierarchical relations based on authority, towards educative and democratic ones based on reason. This amounts to putting the moral and educational ends back into the evaluation process. The relentless quest for certainty about what is appropriate teaching has led those who claim to be evaluators to rely heavily on procedures from science that disavow any disagreement about the goals or ends to which teaching is directed. The problem comes to be seen as one of diagnosing, inserting and policing the correct procedure.

The new thrust for more 'rigorous' forms of teacher evaluation is predicated on the alleged need for administrators to have access through increasingly hierarchical structures to more reliable information to assist in the remediation of poor teaching performance.[3] This claim is hard to sustain. As structures become more hierarchical, there is a displacement of judgement about teaching from the sites of educational practice, to quarters that are increasingly more distant, concerned with administrative and bureaucratic values and concerns. Devolving responsibility for teacher evaluation 'down' the hierarchy, is not a solution either – it creates an increasingly elaborated hierarchy and bureaucracy, resulting in the very opposite of what is required, namely 'informed' decision-making. Collegial decision-making in accordance with pedagogical and educative values become subservient to administrative expediency.

School and classroom-based forms of teacher evaluation have an extensive history of having worked successfully (see Elliott 1977; Hustler *et al* 1986; Goswami and Stillman, 1987; Comber and Hancock, 1987; Nixon, 1981; North Dakota Study group, 1986), whereby teachers themselves, with parents, administrators and members of the community, make collective decisions about what constitutes 'quality' teaching, are a more defensible alternative.

☐ They focus on the actual values and explicit practices that constitute the pedagogical work of the school, and of the teachers, students and parents within it.
☐ They amount to a regular and intensive process of review aimed at identifying shortcomings in existing practice, and identifying needs and opportunities for improvement.
☐ They embrace forms of collegial decision-making among peers jointly concerned about and/or jointly responsible for the quality of the work done.
☐ They amount to ways of placing emphasis in finding workable solutions within the resources of groups of teachers, or for requesting assistance to overcome structural problems teachers cannot address on their own.
☐ They view pedagogical work as the work of individuals and groups who have particular kinds of expertise, particular needs and circumstances, and particular requirements and opportunities for improvement.

Through promoting alternative forms of thinking and acting that endorse these kind of principles, Greene (1986) argues that we begin to counter the business-management model of teacher evaluation that goes something like this: '*If* we have the proper knowledge base, *if* we become more rigorous, *if* we pay more heed to content and less to method, *if* we underwrite merit and mastery, *if* we enlist more experts . . . we will solve what are largely technical problems and will be no longer at risk' (p 70). The starting point in opposing the increasingly enforced separation between those *who do the work of teaching* and those *who make the significant decisions about that work*, is to be found within the act of teaching itself. In part, it involves teachers coming to articulate theories about their own practice that enable them to see how the understandings they hold about teaching (which have been influenced by dominant forms of teacher evaluation) have become limited and distorted by non-educational forces, and supported in part by their own unwitting involvement in acquiescing to those forces. If teacher evaluation were considered against this kind of background then teacher-initiated theorizing would become a way of teachers beginning to figure out 'why things are the way they are, how they got that way, and what set of conditions are supporting the processes that maintain them' (Simon, 1984, p 380). As I expressed it in a previous publication:

☐ We need less measurement against standards of performance and more activity of an ethnographic, biographical and autobiographical kind that allows (even demands) that teachers connect with their students' personal lives (see Traver, 1987).

☐ We need better ways of helping teachers to see how their voices are being progressively silenced in the debates about school reform and how the media hype about accountability is being used as a device for legitimizing anti-educational forms of accountability.

☐ We need ways of enabling teachers to describe and analyse the pedagogical imperatives of their work, so as to expose and ultimately to transform the authoritarian structures that have come to captivate their professional lives and those of their students.

☐ We need ways of helping teachers to counteract 'negative pedagogy' and the kind of cultural illiteracy fostered by mindless measurement-oriented forms of teaching.

☐ We need ways of helping teachers to judge the 'political correctness' of what they do, case by case, not according to neatness-of-fit with some long-range goals or nebulous national priorities.

☐ We need better ways of helping teachers to celebrate what they do in their teaching as a means of developing robust self-images.

☐ We need ways of engaging teachers in the 'study of the academic culture of teaching' so as to shift from being 'passive, manipulated and silent' to providing an active, informed commentary on one another's teaching (Smyth, 1989, pp 168–9).

None of this is impossible; examples of teacher-to-teacher dialogue constituting the basis for a departure from the narrow accountability ethos can be found in the work of various teachers who have written about their work. To take the American scene by way of example (and I could equally well have taken any of a number of other countries), the illustrations below might serve to make the point about what is feasible and possible.

In his story of a group of high school teachers McDonald (1986) gives an account of the way the group (of which he was a part), met regularly (mostly outside school hours), to reflect upon and to make sense of their practical knowledge as teachers, and of the insights, uncertainties and paradoxes that emerged from these discussions. Given the power to determine their own agenda and to explore the role of academic theory in their teaching lives, these teachers found that they were able to stay in charge of the knowledge-creation process, rather than be subjugated by the ideas of others. From an initial concern about how to work as a group (or 'collegiality for collegiality's sake'), McDonald reported an increasing interest by these teachers in gaining policy power over their teaching, culminating in an increased confidence and realization that they could actually claim that power based upon knowledge generated about their own teaching.

Arguably the most insightful accounts of what teachers can achieve through discussions and support groups that have an evaluative agenda have come from the writings and activities of the Boston Women Teachers' Group. Their accounts (Freedman, Jackson & Boles, 1986) are perceptive analyses of the effect of teaching on the personal and professional lives of the teachers involved. More than this, their focus on the need to locate discussion and evaluation of teaching within wider considerations of institutional structures, amounts to a much needed radical shift in the nature of teacher-initiated discourse about schooling. Deflecting the spotlight from the alleged deficiencies in schooling that attach to presumed inadequacies of individual teachers actually enabled them to ask a different set of questions – ones that had more to do with the oppressive way schools are organized and administered. Moving away from the 'victim-blaming' rhetoric (Ryan, 1971), enabled them to open up the full range of the debate which has largely been stifled by educational reformers and policy-makers who profess to know about teaching. Emerging out of the kind of writings of the Boston Women Teachers' Group (Freedman, Jackson & Boles, 1983a; 1983b) are the beginnings of what Kanpol (1988) identifies as 'group solidarity' based upon collaborative and counter-hegemonic alliances that represent teachers' accounts of what it means to evaluate teaching.

The case for teacher-controlled forms of evaluation hinges on the fundamental nature of teaching. McDonald (1988) makes interrelated assertions, which are worth concluding this chapter with:

☐ Teaching is rooted in the teachers' own moral purpose and interests. Teachers teach what they do, and as they do, at least partly from a deep and often tacit sense of mission. . .

☐ Teaching is built on a pervasive and morally legitimate conflict between teachers and students. Such conflict arises from the fact that teachers must constrain students . . . in order to teach them . . .

☐ . . . There is great obliquity in the teacher's aim, and teaching is not, therefore, properly depicted as the deliberate application of means to technocratic ends. Teaching requires wilder images . . . [that encapsulate] three of our culture's villains: ambiguity, ambivalence and instability.

☐ The wildness helps explain why, despite so many exhortations to do otherwise, teachers tend to orient their work towards activities rather than goals, and to guide their planning by means of mental images of routines rather than by means of specific objectives, strategies and assessments (pp 482-3).

In short, we need to work harder at capitalizing on the re-discovery by at least *some* educational policy makers of the 'critical role teachers play in shaping the school experience of today's youth' (Flinders, 1988, p 17) and at incorporating this new-found spirit into treating teachers in ways that acknowledge this self-evident truth.

Notes

1. I use the terms teacher evaluation and teacher appraisal interchangeably in this chapter.
2. Some of the ideas contained in this section are reproduced from Gitlin, A, and Smyth, J, *Teacher Evaluation: Educative Alternatives*, Lewes: Falmer Press, 1989 with kind permission of the publisher. I am also grateful to Andrew Gitlin for helping me to sharpen these ideas through dialogue and debate.
3. Several of the ideas explored here are those of Stephen Kemmis, and I extend my appreciation to him for allowing me to use them. They are contained in Kemmis, S and Smyth, J, 'Management of the performance of academic staff', unpublished manuscript prepared for the Academic Board, Deakin University, 1989.

References

Apple, M (1983) 'Controlling the Work of Teachers', *Delta*, 32, pp 3–15

Apple, M (1988) 'What Reform Talk Does: Creating New Inequalities', *Educational Administration Quarterly*, 23(3), pp 272–81

Apple, M and Beyer, L (1983) 'Social Evaluation of Curriculum', *Educational Evaluation and Policy Analysis*, 5(4), pp 425–34

Beare, H (1987) 'Teacher Appraisal: The Australian Policy Context', paper to the Australian Council for Educational Research forum on 'Teacher Appraisal: An Emerging Issue in Australian Education', Melbourne, August

Beyer, L (1985) 'Educational reform: The political roots of national risk', *Curriculum Inquiry*, 15, Spring, pp 37–56

Blumberg, A (1980) *Supervisors and Teachers: A Private Cold War*, Berkeley, Ca: McCutchan, 2nd ed

Boomer, G (1984) 'Decyphering the teaching code', *Education News*, 19(1), pp 22–26

Borich, G (ed) (1977) *The Appraisal of Teaching: Concepts and Process*, Reading, Mass: Addison-Wesley

Braverman, H (1975) *Labour and Monopoly Capital*, New York: Monthly Review Press

Bridges, E (1986) *The Incompetent Teacher*, London: Falmer

Broadfoot, P (1981) 'Towards a sociology of assessment', in L Barton and S Walker (eds), *Schools, Teachers and Teaching*, London: Falmer

Buchmann, M (1984) 'The Use of Research Knowledge in Teacher Education and Teaching', *American Journal of Education*, 92(4), pp 421–39

Carnegie Corporation (1986) *A Nation Prepared: Teachers for the 21st Century*, New York: Carnegie Forum on Education and the Economy

Comber, B and Hancock, J (eds) (1987) *Developing Teachers: A Celebration of Teachers' Learning in Australia*, Sydney: Methuen

Dadds, M (1986) 'Those Being Tortured: Teachers Appraising Teacher Appraisal', *Cambridge Journal of Education*, 17(1)

Dadds, M (1987) 'Learning and Teacher Appraisal: The Heart of the Matter', *School Organization*, 8, pp 253–9

D'Alcan, F, Alexander, M, Machej, K and McCafferty, J (1986) 'Those Having Matches. . .; an Alternative Approach to Teacher Appraisal', *Cambridge Journal of Education*, 16(2), pp 154–6

Dale, R (1977) *The Structural Context of Teaching*, Milton Keynes, Open University Press

Darling-Hammond, L, Wise, A and Pease, S (1986), 'Teacher Evaluation in the Organizational Context: A Review of the Literature', in E House (ed), *New Directions in Educational Evaluation*, London: Falmer, 1986, pp 203–53

Diamond, P (1988) 'Benchmarks for Progress or Teacher Education on the Rails', *Australian Educational Researcher*, 15(4), pp 1–7

Dockrell, B, Nisbet, J, Nutall, D, Stones, E and Wilcox, B (1986) *Appraising Appraisal: A Critical Examination of Proposals for the Appraisal of Teachers in England and Wales*, Birmingham: British Educational Research Association

Elliott, J (1977) 'Developing Hypotheses about Classrooms from Teachers' Practical Constructs: An Account of the Work of the Ford Teaching Project', *Interchange*, 7(2), pp 2–22

Elliott, J (1989) 'The Emergence of Teacher Appraisal in the UK', paper to the annual meeting of the American Educational Research Association, San Francisco

Flinders, D (1988) 'Teacher Isolation and the New Reform', *Journal of Curriculum and Supervision*, 4(1), pp 17–29

Florida Coalition for the Development of a Performance Measurement System (1983) *Domains: Knowledge Base of the Florida Performance Measurement System*, Tallahassee, Florida: Office of Teacher Education and In-Service Staff Development

Foucault, M (1980) *Michel Foucault: Power/Knowledge, Selected Interviews and Other Writings*, C Gordon (ed), New York: Pantheon

Freedman, S, Jackson, J and Boles, K (1983a) (The Boston Women Teachers' Group) 'Teaching: An Imperilled "profession"', in L Shulman and G Sykes (eds), *Handbook of Teaching and Policy*, New York: Longmans, pp 261–99

Freedman, S, Jackson, J and Boles, K (1983b) (The Boston Women Teachers' Group) 'The Other End of the Corridor: The Effect of Teaching on Teachers', *The Radical Teacher*, 23(3), pp 2–23

Freedman, S, Jackson, J and Boles, K (1986) (The Boston Women Teachers' Group) *The Effect of Teaching on Teachers*, North Dakota Study Group on Evaluation, Center for Teaching & Learning: University of North Dakota, Grand Forks

Gitlin, A and Smyth, J (1989) *Teacher Evaluation: Educative Alternatives*, Lewes: Falmer Press

Goswami, D and Stillman, P (eds) (1987), *Reclaiming the Classroom: Teacher Research as an Agency for Change*, Boynton Cook, 1987

Greene, M (1986) 'Reflection and Passion in Teaching', *Journal of Curriculum and Supervision*, 2(1), pp 68–81

Hargreaves, A (1978) 'The Significance of Classroom Coping Strategies', in L Barton and R Meighan (eds), *Sociological Interpretations of Schooling and Classroom: A Reappraisal*, Driffield: Nafferton Books

Hargreaves, A (1988) 'Teacher Quality: A Sociological Analysis', *Journal of Curriculum Studies*, 20(3), pp 211–31

Harris, B (1986) *Developmental Teacher Evaluation*, New York: Allyn & Bacon

Hartley, L and Broadfoot, P (1986) 'Assessing Teacher Performance', *Journal of Educational Policy*, 3(1), pp 39–50

Hazi, H and Garman, N (1988) 'Legalizing Scientism Through Teacher Evaluation', unpublished manuscript, West Virginia University

Hextall, I and Sarup, M (1977) 'School Knowledge: Evaluation and Alienation', in G Whitty and M Young (eds), *Society, State and Schooling*, Lewes: Falmer Press

Hoetker, J and Ahlbrand, W (1969) 'The Persistence of Recitation', *American Educational Research Journal*, 6(2), pp 145–67

Hunter, C, Elliott, J, Marland, D and Wormald, E (1985) 'Teacher Education and Teaching Quality', *British Journal of Sociology of Education* 6(1), pp 97–107

Hustler, D *et al* (1986) *Action Research in Classrooms and Schools*, London: Allen & Unwin

Ingvarson, L 'Linking Teacher Appraisal and Professional Development: A Challenge for the Profession', unpublished manuscript, Monash University, nd

Jesson, D, Mayston, D and Smith, P (1987) 'Performance Assessment in the Education Sector: Educational and Economic Imperatives', *Oxford Review of Education*, 13(3), pp 249–66

Johnson, M (1988) 'Hell is the Place We don't Know We're in: The Control-dictions of Cultural Literacy, Story Reading and Poetry', *College English*, 50(3), pp 309–17

Jonathan, R (1983) 'The Manpower Service Model of Education', *Cambridge Journal of Education*, 13(2), pp 3–10

Kanpol, B (1988) 'Teacher Resistance and Accommodation to Structural Factors of Schooling: Possibilities and Limitations', paper presented to annual meeting of the American Education Research Association, New Orleans

Kemmis, S (1985) 'Action Research and the Politics of Reflection', in Boud, D, Keogh, R and Walker, D (eds), *Reflection: Turning Experience into Learning*

Kemmis, S and Smyth, J (April 1989) 'Management of the Performance of Academic Staff', unpublished manuscript

Kliebard, H (1975) 'Bureaucracy and Curriculum Theory', in W Pinar (ed), *Curriculum Theorizing: The Reconceptualists*, Berkeley, Ca: McCutchan

Larson, M (1980) 'Proletarianization and Educated Labor', *Theory and Society*, 9(2), pp 131–75

Lawn, M and Ozga, J (1986) 'Unequal Partners: Teachers under Indirect Rule', *British Journal of Sociology of Education*, 7(2), pp 225–38

Lundgren, U (1983) *Between Hope and Happening: Text and Context in Curriculum*, Geelong, Australia: Deakin University Press

McDonald, J (1986)'Raising the Teacher's Voice and the Ironic Role of Theory', *Harvard Education Review*, 56(4), pp 355–78

McDonald, J (1988) 'The Emergence of the Teachers' Voice: Implications for the New Reform', *Harvard Education Review*, 89(4), pp 471–86

McGreal, T (1983) *Successful Teacher Evaluation*, Alexandria, VA: Association for Supervision and Curriculum Development

McLaughlin, M (1984) 'Teacher Evaluation and School Improvement', *Teachers College Record*, 86(1)

Meisenhelder, T (1983) 'The Ideology of Professionalism in Higher Education', *Journal of Education*, 165(3), pp 295–307

Ministry of Education, New Zealand (1988) *Tomorrow's Schools: The Reform of Educational Administration in New Zealand*, Wellington: Government Printer

Mishler, E (1986) 'Meaning in Context and the Empowerment of Respondents', in E Mishler (ed), *Research Interviewing: Context and Narrative*, Cambridge, MA: Harvard University Press

Murphy, J (1987) 'Teacher Evaluation: A Comprehensive Framework for Supervisors', *Journal of Personnel Evaluation in Education*, 1, pp 157–80

National Commission on Excellence in Education (1983) *A Nation at Risk: The Imperative for Educational Reform*, Washington DC: US Government Printing Office

Nixon, J (ed) (1981) *A Teachers' Guide to Action Research: Evaluation, Enquiry and Development in the Classroom*, London: Grant McIntyre

North Dakota Study Group (1986) *Speaking Out: Teachers on Teaching*, Grand Forks, ND: University of North Dakota

Popkewitz, T (1984) *Paradigm and Ideology in Educational Research: The Social Functions of the Intellectual*, Lewes: Falmer Press

Preston, B (August 1987) 'Teacher Evaluation: Contextual Issues and Policy Development', paper to the Australian Council for Educational Research forum on 'Teacher appraisal: An emerging issue in Australian education', Melbourne

Ryan, W (1971) *Blaming the Victim*, New York: Pantheon

Sachs, J (1987) 'The Constitution of Teachers' Knowledge: A Literature Review', *Discourse*, 7(2), pp 86–98

Sachs, J and Smith, R (1988) 'Constructing Teacher Culture', *British Journal of Sociology of Education*, 9(4), pp 423–36

Schön, D (1984) 'Leadership as Reflection-in-action', in T Sergiovanni and J Corbally (eds), *Leadership and Organizational Culture: New Perspectives on Administrative Theory and Practice*, Urbana: University of Illinois Press, pp 36–63

Seddon, T (1988) 'Teachers as workers, the State as Employer: Restructuring the Work Relationship, 1929–32', *Curriculum Perspectives*, 8(1), pp 12–20

Simon, J (1979) 'Who and What is the APU?', *Forum*, 22(1), pp 7–11

Simon, R (1984) 'Signposts for a Critical Pedagogy: A Review of Henry Giroux's "Theory and Resistance in Education"', *Educational Theory*, 34(4), pp 379–88

Simon, R (1988) 'For a Pedagogy of Possibility', *Critical Pedagogy Networker*, 1(1), pp 1–4

Smyth, J (1989) 'An Alternative Vision and an "Educative" Agenda for Supervision as a Field of Study", *Journal of Curriculum and Supervision*, 4(2), pp 162–77

Smyth, J and Garman, N 'Supervision as School Reform: A "Critical" Perspective', *Journal of Education Policy*, (in press)

State Board of Education (December 1987) 'Monitoring the Achievements of Schools', working paper no 1, Ministry of Education, Victoria

Stenning, W and Stenning R (1984) 'The Assessment of Teacher's Performance: Some Practical Considerations', *School Organization and Management*, 3(2), pp 77–90

Stodolsky, S (1984) 'Teacher Evaluation: The Limits of Looking', *Educational Researcher*, 13(9), pp 11–18

Suffolk Education Department (1985) *Those Having Torches . . . Teacher Appraisal: A Study*, Suffolk: Department of Education and Science

Taskforce to Review Educational Administration (1988) (Picot report), *Administering for Excellence*, Wellington: Government Printer

Traver, R (1987) 'Autobiography, Feminism and the Study of Teaching', *Teachers College Record*, 88(3), pp 443–52

Tye, B (1985a) *Multiple Realities: A Study of Thirteen American High Schools*, Lanham: University Press of America

Tye, K (1985b) *The Junior High School: School in Search of a Mission*, Lanham: University Press of America

Walsh, K (1987) 'The Politics of Teacher Appraisal', in M Lawn and G Grace (eds), *Teachers: The Culture and Politics of Work*, London: Falmer

Westbury, I (1973) 'Conventional Classrooms, Open Classrooms and the Technology of Teaching', *Journal of Curriculum Studies*, 5(2), pp 99–121

White, R (1983) 'On Teachers and Proletarianisation', *Discourse*, pp 45–57

Whyte, J (1986) 'Teacher Assessment: A Review of the Performance Appraisal Literature with Special Reference to the Implications for Teacher Appraisal', *Research Papers in Education*, 1(2), pp 137–63

Wilby, P (1986) 'Teacher Appraisal', *Journal of Education Policy*, 1(1), pp 63–72

Wise, A (1977) 'Why Educational Policies Often Fail: The Hyper-Realization Hypothesis', *Journal of Curriculum Studies*, 9(1), pp 43–57

Wragg, E (1980) *Perspectives 2: The Core Curriculum*, Exeter: Exeter University, School of Education

22. Educational development in the mountain kingdom of Bhutan

John Bailey, G J Fishburne, Tsewang Choeden, Chitra Pradhan, Jerry Turner and Minchha Wangdi

Introduction

Very little has been written about the system of education being developed by the Royal Government of Bhutan in the Himalayas. Traditionally the education of the people has been on the farms where they learn from their famililes. For those who choose to become, (or whose families choose them to become) monks, education was in the monasteries. Subjects taught there were appropriate to religious and cultural life. For some students this form of education continues.

However, about 25 years ago an education system began to develop based on nineteenth-century British schools. It soon became apparent that in order to cope with the twenty-first century the education system would have to modernize.

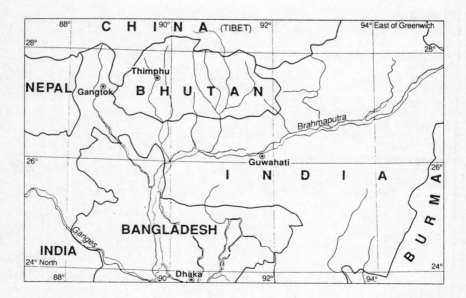

In Section 1 John Bailey briefly outlines the geographical and cultural context of the education system. This is followed by a concise description of the elements that make up the system including references to the various examination arrangements. Finally, mention is made of the Bhutan Board of Examinations.

In Section 2 Chitra Pradhan gives the background to curriculum activities in Bhutan. He describes the history of education and the establishment of the Curriculum Textbook and Development Division. Included is a summary of curriculum activities since 1985. The section closes with a summary of future intentions.

In Section 3 Tshewang Choeden describes how fundamental the changes are in introducing continuous assessment into the new primary-school curriculum.

In Section 4 Mincha Wangdi sets environmental studies first in an international setting and then describes the core rationale for including EVS (as it is always referred to locally) in the Bhutanese primary-school curriculum. In fact its aims and objectives have been adopted by the new national curriculum.

Lastly, in Section 5, Jerry Turner and Dr Fishburne describe the adoption of a common curriculum by the primary-teacher training institutes.

1 Bhutan: the education system
John Bailey

A Himalayan kingdom

It needs to be appreciated that in the independent monarchy of Bhutan teachers and schools are small in number compared with many other countries but that the geographical area is difficult and the isolation of some schools will influence the patterns and strategies of provision.

Bhutan is categorized by the United Nations as a least-developed nation with an estimated per capita income of $116 per annum. Small and landlocked, it is surrounded to the south, east and west by India and in the north by the Chinese Autonomous Region of Tibet. The country covers an area of 46,000 square kilometres.

The hills rise from the narrow strip of the plains with altitudes close to sea level (160m) through the foothills, to the fertile valleys of the Inner Himalaya, up to the peaks at 7,000m of the High Himalayas; in some places all three regions are spanned within a distance of 100km. The three regions are cut by generally north–south river valleys broadening in some places, in the Inner Himalaya, where a cultural heartland is found. The valleys are separated by ranges, with high passes often being the communication routes from west to east. An important north–south range is the Black Mountains which have traditionally separated eastern from western Bhutan culturally and ethnically as well as geographically.

The climate has perhaps the greatest diversity in any country its size in the world. The north features the perpetual ice and snow of the High Himalaya as well as the hot and humid semi-tropical conditions of the south. Due to various factors each valley has a unique climate, the result of the interplay between altitude, rainfall, exposure to sunlight and wind. Travel is particularly difficult during the monsoon period which lasts from mid-June to September. While

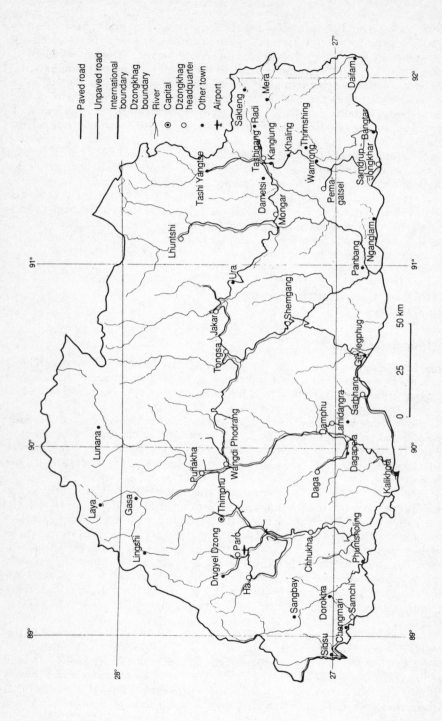

many of the secondary schools are accessible by motor road, the mountains, valleys and numerous rivers make communications difficult and the unit of travel is time – rather than distance – based. There is a lateral road across the country through the inner valleys and over the passes while feeder roads climb up from the Indian plains along four routes. The most important is that from Phuntsholing to Thimphu. These national roads are 95 per cent black-topped. Modern development in Bhutan began after 1959 when problems in Tibet resulted in Bhutan accepting more aid from India resulting in a close relationship that continues today.

While the precise ethnic composition of the 1.4 million Bhutanese is unknown, there are three main groups: the Sharchops from eastern Bhutan are thought to be the earliest settlers; the Ngalops are of Tibetan origin and their culture and the Buddhist religion has characterized northern Bhutan; in Southern Bhutan much of the population is of Nepali origin. Secondary co-educational boarding schools take students from all the regions as part of a national integration policy.

The official language is Dzongkha, derived from classical Tibetan. In southern Bhutan, Nepali is the major language and there are at least 11 other vernacular languages in the country. English plays an important role and is the language of instruction in schools and colleges as well as much official communication. Schools in southern Bhutan also teach Nepali while the monastery schools still teach Cheoke, the classical language of the monasteries.

King Jigme Singye Wangchuck has ruled the country since 1972 when he succeeded to the throne at the age of 16. He is head of state and head of government. The main legislative body, the National Assembly, meets twice a year. The Royal Advisory Council is always in session and advises the king on key issues and monitors the implementation of National Assembly policies. In addition a cabinet composed of ministers of government and councillors is responsible for advising on and carrying out policy. The Je Khenpo is the spiritual head of Bhutan. For a number of years the country had been administratively divided into *dzongkhags* (districts) and each *dzongkhag* was administered by a *dzongdha* (district officer) appointed by the king and reporting to the home minister. While this is still true, in 1989 an intermediate tier of Government was introduced. The *dzongkhags* have been grouped into four zones.

Except for religious and cultural education taught in monastic schools, little formal education existed in Bhutan until the early 1960s. In 1914 the first non-monastic school was started; this was followed by another the next year. The majority of the few Bhutanese who studied went to school in India. Opportunities for education were only expanded after 1955 when the government of India helped by sending 30 students a year to English medium schools. The state education system only began in 1962 and the first specially built primary school was opened in 1964, making Bhutan's one of the newest education systems in the world.

Over the past 25 years, considerable progress in supplying education has been made with the establishment of formal education including a teacher-training system. Indicators such as enrolment ratios of the age group for 1984 are low (primary 21 per cent, secondary 2.5 per cent) with adult literacy recorded as 10 per cent.

The education system

Education is administered and developed by the department of education within the ministry of social services. As has already been implied this system of education until recently had schools and a curriculum based largely on an earlier tradition of British education. These schools were based on similar schools in India and while this has served a useful role since the early 1960s, recently many changes have been planned which will modernize the system. Administratively there is a three-tier system of responsibility:

☐ Responsibility at the primary level is shared, administration being the responsibility of the *dzonghags* (districts) while the curriculum and examinations are national responsibilities. The *dzongkhag* also has the responsibility for teacher placement within the district.

☐ Until 1990 at the secondary level all the responsibilities were at the national level. However the national department of education is currently transferring authority and administrative responsibility to the zonal administrations. Again curriculum and examinations remain central responsibilities.

☐ Examinations and curriculum development are central responsibilities.

Education is not compulsory but is almost free (there is a token fee). English is the medium of instruction but a pass in Dzongkha (the national language) is compulsory at class VI, VIII, X and XII for further promotion. The school year is from March to December. All schools are co-educational.

THE STRUCTURE OF SCHOOLING

A 1+6+2+2+2+3 pattern of education is followed, consisting of seven years of primary education, four years of secondary education plus two years of higher secondary education, the latter in a single college, followed by a three-year period of higher education for a first degree.

PRIMARY EDUCATION

Primary education covers a seven-year period. Students enter a 5+ into a pre-primary year. Successful students complete primary education after six more years (class I to VI). There are 152 primary schools and 46,000 students. The syllabus covers various patterns depending on the stage:

☐ Stage 1   Pre-primary to class III
            English
            Dzongkha
            Mathematics
            Environmental science

☐ Stage 2   Class IV and V
            English
            Dzongkha
            Mathematics
            Social studies
            Science

☐ Stage 3   Class VI
            English

Dzongkha
Mathematics
History
Geography
Science

In the southern-belt schools, Nepali is also taught. A new primary education curriculum for classes PP–III has been piloted in about 20 per cent of the primary schools and an additional 50 schools will see the first phase of full implementation in 1990. This new curriculum is child-centred rather than subject orientated like the previous curriculum. This New Approach to Primary Education (NAPE) is described further in later sections of this chapter.

A selective examination is held by the Bhutan Board of Examinations at the end of class VI. About 50 per cent of the students pass and continue at secondary school. Until recently, training schemes existed for students who did not gain entry into class VII, but their entry requirements are consistently being raised.

SECONDARY EDUCATION

Secondary education has two stages. Class VII and VIII followed by classes IX and X. There are 22 junior high schools (11,900 students including primary sections). These are similar to primary schools but have a class VII and VIII. The 10 high schools (4,500 students) have classes VII and VIII and classes IX and X.

The class VII and VIII curriculum covers English, mathematics, Dzongkha, biology, chemistry, physics, geography and history. In southern-belt schools Nepali is also taught. There is a national selective examination at class VIII (The Bhutan Junior High School Certificate Examination) awarded by the Bhutan Board of Examinations. About 50 per cent of the students pass into class IX.

The curriculum for class IX and X is similar to class VII and class VIII except that there is an additional subject, economics. In one school, computer studies is taken as an alternative to economics. The school-leaving certificate is the Indian Certificate of Education. To continue to class XI English and Dzongkha must be passed. It is intended to replace the Indian Certificate of Secondary Education with the Bhutan Certificate of Education within the coming decade. It is hoped to do this initially by replacing the non-international subjects – Dzongkha, civics, history and geography – with local syllabuses. The international subjects – English, mathematics and science – will follow later.

HIGHER SECONDARY

A separate college has classes XI and XII and may be called higher secondary.

TECHNICAL/VOCATIONAL

There is one well-established institution, the Royal Technical Institute at Kharbandi. The Royal Technical Institute is basically a secondary/higher-secondary institution which requires a Bhutan Primary School Certificate for entry to the Technical Education Certificate Course. There is a foundation year followed by courses in motor mechanics, general mechanics, electrical and building construction. Girls were admitted from 1989.

FURTHER EDUCATION/ALTERNATIVE EDUCATION

The Royal Institute of Management has recently been inaugurated and has begun to run training courses. Various other government departments have training schools which include the Health School, the National Agricultural Training Institute, the Royal Veterinary Institute and the Forestry Institute. These award certificates and diplomas.

The Zangley Muenselling School for the Blind runs courses up to class VII. There is a Buddhist theological school at Tarpoling.

HIGHER EDUCATION

Higher education is offered at Sherubtse College (affiliated with Delhi University), Deothang Polytechnic and the National Institute of Education (NIE) has close links with the Institute of Education, University of London.

Sherubtse College at present offers a Bachelor of Science (General) degree course and Bachelor of Arts (Pass) degree courses in Arts and Commerce. The degrees are awarded by Delhi University.

The National Institute of Education offers Bachelor of Education degree courses at the pass level in arts and science.

Deothang Polytechnic offers three-year diploma courses in civil engineering and electrical engineering to candidates who have passed class X (ICSE). The polytechnic also runs two-year certificate courses, one in surveying and another in draughtmanship. Entry to these two courses is preferably at class X but class VIII is accepted.

TEACHER EDUCATION

Primary-school teachers take a two-year certificate course at the National Institute of Education at Samchi or at the Teachers Training College at Paro. This certificate-level course is assessed by course work (50 per cent) and examination (50 per cent). The certificate is awarded by the Bhutan Board of Examinations.

The National Institute of Education has a three-year Bachelor of Education Course. Entry is class XII certificate (normally Indian School Certificate) but for exceptional candidates a primary teachers' certificate plus five years' experience can meet entrance requirements. Currently the Bachelor of Education (Secondary) is either arts or science. There are plans to begin a Bachelor of Education (Primary) course in the near future. This programme is moderated by a London University team. A Postgraduate Certificate Course in Education has recently been added to the available choices.

Bhutan Board of Examinations

The public examination system was introduced in 1973. For four years, from 1973 to 1976, the two public examinations at the class V and class VIII levels were managed by the staff of the department of education. In 1977 an examination cell was created which has now been upgraded to the Bhutan Board of Examinations. Currently the Board of Examinations conducts examinations on completion of class VI and class VIII at the school level. It also conducts the Primary Teachers' Certificate examinations and helps to conduct the class X and XII examinations. Earlier it conducted Bachelor of Education and commercial course examinations. In the future it may be responsible for conducting all certificate and diploma examinations.

At present class X and class XII examinations are conducted by the Council for the Indian School Certificate Examinations. It is hoped in the first part of the current decade to establish a Bhutan Board of Examination exam for both class X and class XII. This will be a phased development. Initially a joint examination will be held in collaboration with the council followed by further development which will allow the Bhutan Board to issue its own certificates.

Summary

Over the past 25 years the education system has been set up and the basic structure is now clear and will allow future developments in all areas. Primary education, secondary education, technical and higher education adapt to the needs of the kingdom.

2 Curriculum past, present and future
Chitra K Pradhan

Background

Since the early 1960s the Royal Government of Bhutan has initiated a variety of development programmes throughout the country. Among all these, the education sector has always received the highest priority with a view to providing elementary education to the greatest possible number of the children of the kingdom. However the provision of a modern education geared to Bhutan's needs was constrained by three crucial elements:

☐ Content/Curriculum
☐ Teachers/Educators
☐ Evaluation/Examination system

In the initial stages, therefore, these three important elements of the education system were imported from outside the kingdom. Consequently, for example, our class III children learned about India, England and America but hardly knew anything of the geography of their own country. The system also relied heavily on rote learning and memorization of facts, and mostly suited students who had developed these skills. As a result the application of knowledge in the field was limited. Only a small proportion of children enrolled in the schools came out as successful academically orientated graduates.

The Royal Government, aware of these problems, constantly supported and encouraged the department of education in its efforts to bring about an education system more suited to the nation's needs. From the late sixties onwards efforts in teacher-education programmes were initiated which augmented and strengthened the national teacher population. Further, the Bhutan Board of Examinations was established to evaluate the academic standards at the end of both the primary and lower-secondary levels. The Bhutan Board of Examinations also coordinates the ICSE and ISC examinations with the ICSE Council.

Although the department of education has published textbooks for primary classes, most of these books have been developed and written without adequate overall syllabus/curriculum guidelines which met the national needs and aspirations. In fact, the textbooks were fundamentally the syllabuses. As a result degrees of difficulty, in the syllabuses and textbooks, for any particular class varies greatly from one class to another. However, it has to be mentioned here that the Dzongkha textbooks were totally developed and written by the department of education and therefore they are found more appropriate in terms of culture and values. Among the crucial elements mentioned earlier, curriculum, although it is the core of any education system, remained relatively neglected until the early 1980s. It was the recent National Education Policy in accordance with the king's concern and desire to develop a suitable education policy that would enable the provision of a sound education system, in line with our kingdom's needs and values, which envisaged the necessity of developing our own curriculum for educational institutions of our country.

To quote from the current National Education Policy, 'The major thrust of the objectives of the National Education Policy is on a qualitative improvement, re-orientation of curricular content to make education relevant, efficient and responsive to the merging national needs of the country; enhancing the capacity of the population to acquire knowledge, information, skills and healthy attitudes, improving the quality of teaching and administrative personnel; meeting the requirements for trained and technical personnel, and developing suitable and administrative structure for effective planning, management and monitoring of the education system.' Other statements in the policy also underlined strongly that a relevant and effective curriculum needed to be developed.

Establishment of a curriculum division

Considering the aims and objectives of the current National Education Policy, it was vital to establish a curriculum and textbook development division within the department of education to analyse both policy goals and needs of the country and then develop suitable curriculum, syllabuses, textbooks, and other relevant literature and teaching aids and to field test the materials produced. Consequently, the division was established in 1985–86 and given a major task which, according to the National Education Policy and Sixth Five-Year Plan, should be accomplished by 1992.

MAIN GOALS
 □ To make the content relevant to Bhutanese life, culture, tradition and the needs of the nation.
 □ To develop a curriculum which will augment our children's ability to apply their knowledge in their present as well as later life.
 □ To enhance the academic standards through more efficient processes of teaching and learning.

FUNCTIONAL OBJECTIVES
 □ Develop a relevant and comprehensive curriculum for lower-primary sections (first four years of schooling), and implement it through the New Approach to Primary Education (NAPE) project.

☐ Write appropriate and detailed syllabuses for upper-primary and secondary levels of the school system.
☐ Write the necessary textbooks for all levels of school education.
☐ Develop manuals and reference books for teachers.
☐ Design and develop teaching resources.
☐ Field test the materials developed in the division.
☐ Hold workshops for teachers to introduce new materials in collaboration with teacher-education colleges, inspectorate and other concerned divisions.
☐ At all times make constant effort to monitor and review the content of education, so as to keep it in line with the aims and objectives of the education policy and international standards.
☐ Initiate educational studies so that the findings can augment the curriculum work.

The curriculum and textbook development division (CTDD), after establishing the goals and functional objectives, took up various educational activities in the mid-1980s. It was crucial to formulate a national curriculum, and consequently the CTDD began the task immediately, working on NAPE the day it was established.

Major activities since 1985

In line with the current National Education Policy, work began on NAPE in May 1985. The initial task was to produce a new lower-primary syllabus covering languages, mathematics and the new subject of environmental studies (EVS). The new subject integrates history, geography, cultural education, health, agriculture, science and physical education into one so that learning takes place through and about the children's environment and is more effective and related to their needs. Under the auspices of various subject committees the syllabuses and attendant manuals were produced.

The last five years have seen considerable changes and progress in the NAPE project. It is important to understand that the NAPE project should not be considered in the narrow sense of a syllabus change. It takes into consideration various factors that contribute to children's educational needs. Relevant syllabuses and manuals, better-trained teachers, class and classroom size, better furniture, appropriate stationery supplies, improved monitoring and evaluation systems are some of the significant features that the project takes into account.

On the basis of the analysis of the curriculum and reports received from various teachers while experimenting with the new curriculum, the NAPE literature has been carefully rewritten. Many teachers have been trained to teach in the NAPE schools; NAPE conferences and project evaluations have been made.

The reviews, evaluations and reports have all suggested that we are on the right track. Initially NAPE started in 13 schools; by 1990 80 schools are under the NAPE project. It is hoped that by 1992 the NAPE programme will be implemented in all schools.

Besides the NAPE programme, CTDD has written comprehensive syllabuses for classes pre-primary (PP) to III for non-NAPE schools and IV to VIII standards for all the schools. Textbooks and course books in social studies, history and geography up to class VIII aim to be completed by 1990.

Biology textbooks and teacher manuals for classes VII and VIII have been written and are being used in the schools.

An ambitious project on English textbooks and readers was launched in August 1989. The project includes textbooks, workbooks, readers and teacher manuals from class PP to V and is expected to complete work in 1993.

Future plans

It has been envisaged that the CTDD will carry out various educational activities related to school curriculum in order to make school education relevant in terms of our cultural needs, international standards and usefulness in real life.

The nationalized syllabuses for secondary and higher secondary are planned to be completed and implemented before the turn of the century. Much work has been done developing the primary curriculum and 1995 should see a completely nationalized primary courses. In the secondary curriculum there is a great need to emphasize a drastic change both in humanities and science education.

The preservation of Bhutanese culture is based on the Buddhist philosophy of non-violence, tolerance, compassion, love and peace which have enabled our people to live in harmony, respecting human differences. In order to educate our children into this philosophy it is paramount that relevant history, geography and other related subjects are written. Books to teach Bhutan history and Bhutan geography for classes VI to VIII are being written and should be completed and implemented in 1990. As soon as these books are completed, further work on secondary humanities subjects will be started and it is expected that these will be produced by 1995.

It is the wish of the government that the nationalized humanities curriculum will educate our students into being good Bhutanese people. Studying the new curriculum, the children should learn to think not only for themselves but also for others, be self-disciplined and responsible, appreciate and practise age-old cultural and traditional values, develop into mature and humane persons by developing their innate talents, to use them for the good of the society in which they live, and be capable of applying their knowledge and skills in their everyday lives.

Science (including mathematics) education needs to be changed in terms of international standards and national needs. The present science and mathematics courses are at least 50 years behind the international level and applied science is almost non-existent in the present course. Bhutanese society envisages that science and technology will play a crucial role in uplifting the standard of living. In a developing country with a low population, it is important to have people with a higher level of thinking, problem-solving capabilities and able to use technological equipment and machinery.

The future science curriculum should aim at dealing with: understanding scientific ideas, developing scientific methods of investigation, relating science to other areas of knowledge, understanding the contribution science makes to society, recognizing the contribution science education makes to personal development and appreciating the nature of scientific knowledge.

Learning appropriate science and mathematics should make the educated population more comfortable with problem solving, using technological equipment and machines, improving living standards and health, and modern communication systems.

The primary course in science should be nationalized by the year 1995. It is planned to develop and complete a valid science course for the secondary schools so that it can be implemented by 1996 at the latest. A two-year biology course for classes VII and VIII has been written and was introduced in 1988. A systematic evaluation of the course will be undertaken in 1990 and on the basis of the evaluation the course will be updated.

Conclusion

There is a strong inclination in the CTDD, department of education, in line with the policy of the Royal Government of Bhutan to nationalize and modernize the school curriculum before the turn of the century. The aim of the curriculum should be to provide an education to our children that will enable them to solve real and practical problems as a farmer, a teacher or a doctor in any corner of our country; provide an education for our children that enables them to be resourceful and self-reliant; provide an education for our children that enables them to grow into mature persons capable of using their talents fully in the service of king, country and people. And finally, but most importantly we want our schools to inculcate in pupils the traditional, cultural and spiritual values that are such a crucial element of life in our country and will carry us into an auspicious future.

3 Fundamental changes in evaluation
Tshewang Choeden

Background

The New Approach to Primary Education (NAPE) will allow teachers to stop being slaves to syllabuses and to the textbooks with contents far from the lives and experiences of Bhutanese children. The system has been relying on rote learning and memorization of facts and figures for the purpose of examinations. When NAPE has been fully implemented in all the primary schools of Bhutan, the end of the nineteenth-century-style education will be seen.

To reorientate the education system developed over the past 25 years work began in 1985 on the New Approach to Primary Education. The new syllabus is divided into four main subjects: Dzongkha, English, mathematics and environmental studies. The emphasis is mainly on learning through participation and active involvement rather than by the mechanical memorization and repetition of facts spoonfed to the pupils by teachers.

This change of syllabus meant that it was essential to review and develop a compatible evaluation system.

The new evaluation system

The framework for evaluation techniques and instruments that teachers are encouraged to use is based on the following questions. The curriculum developers have tried to keep within this frame when giving advice to the teachers.

☐ Are there available evaluation materials which teachers may use?
☐ Are the goals, aims and objectives which may be inferred from these compatible with the goals, aims and objectives of the curriculum?
☐ Are there goals, aims and objectives for which no suggestions have been made for evaluation?
☐ Are material resources adequate to carry out the evaluation techniques suggested?
☐ Are the evaluation techniques suggested within the competency of the teachers?
☐ Are the teachers expected to produce some of the evaluation material on their own; do the teachers' guides contain adequate guidance?
☐ Have any suggestions been made to develop the skills of self-evaluation in pupils?
☐ Are there any words of caution or some indications that significant aims and objectives may not be adequately tested by certain of the techniques suggested?
☐ Do the suggested techniques leave any place for the subjective opinion of teachers based on extended observation of the students?

Reasons for evaluation

While in many education systems the following reasons may be self evident, in Bhutan the new approach had to lead the teachers away from the notion that the only form of evaluation was an examination and the only purpose of examinations was to pass to allow promotion to the next class. The main reasons for evaluation that the teachers were given are:

☐ To see if our teaching has been successful and whether the students have actually learned what we were trying to teach them.
☐ To judge the success or otherwise of our teaching methods.
☐ To get information on where we need to modify or re-teach parts of the syllabus and for further planning of lessons.
☐ To find out where the children are having special problems.
☐ To ensure that individual students have not been neglected.
☐ To encourage students to work better and learn better.
☐ To motivate students by giving them useful and constructive feedback on their work.
☐ To have information on hand so as to be able to give professional advice concerning a student's performance to the headteacher, parent or another teacher taking the class.
☐ To decide whether a student is ready for promotion to the next class.
☐ As teachers we are accountable to the department of education which demands that testing takes place periodically.

Evaluation techniques used under NAPE programme

The biggest change in the field of evaluation that the NAPE programme has brought about is continuous assessment, which forms the basis of examinations. Assessment is based on six projects per year per student, together with assessment of the children's planning procedures, powers of communication, social and physical development. Examples of question types are given in the general primary syllabuses and comprehensive guidance is given to the teachers in handbooks. Teachers are trained in evaluation techniques in the NAPE training workshops to help them become competent in correct evaluation. A number of sessions during the training workshop are devoted to an examination of the criteria of evaluation, and methods of analysis are suggested.

In NAPE the evaluation is used mainly as a criterion to identify instructional objectives achieved by students. The instructional objectives describe the students' behaviours which are observable and measurable. The teachers produce their own evaluation materials using information contained in the teachers' guides. In NAPE, self-evaluation for a section of a module is implemented. The resource teachers give the test. Resource teachers are experienced teachers whose task is to enhance the quality of education by developing educational resources within their school; developing appropriate teaching practices in school; and by working equally with all teachers of NAPE classes solving their day-to-day difficulties. For a block of modules the class teacher administers the test. It is noted that self-evaluation is quite effective as it encourages students to delve into the learning materials.

The teachers' guides include varied evaluation instruments and techniques within the competency level of the teachers. Written tests are reinforced by performance tests and other instruments such as questionnaires, checklists and interviews. Observation is regarded as a vital tool for the cross-checking of evaluation data. Most of the evaluation instruments recommended are prepared by teachers individually or by committees. All of these formal and informal evaluation techniques and tools are utilized in both formative and summative evaluations. Assessment procedures for granting school grades are clearly explained in the guide books and in in-service workshops.

A record system has been introduced in NAPE, which keeps track of each child's all-round development. This record includes information about a child's strengths and difficulties and social factors which influence personal views and views of their work at school. It provides necessary information when the child is transferred to another school, acts as a source of reports to parents and helps in preparing reports for the department of education. These records are kept in a file for each child and contain all the necessary documents like report copies, notes of unusual events or interviews with parents and also an accessible record of the termly assessments made by teachers. The class teacher files them and stores them, carefully in the cupboard in the class or in the headteacher's office for ready reference.

4 Environmental studies in the new curriculum
Minchha Wangdi

Introduction

There is an increasing awareness by educationalists in developing countries that the education being offered to children is not linked to their daily life. There is a recognition that education unrelated to the child's background inhibits free development of the child's intelligence and hence failure to find a bearing in the world.

Educationists through the ages have made the simple and obvious point that children are more likely to be interested in work that stems from things that are immediate and relevant to them. Learning best begins with the known and proceeds to the unknown and from the concrete to the abstract (Martin and Turner 1975). Piaget, Bruner and others have shown the role played by direct experience in the formation of basic concepts and the development of learning skills.

The role and aims of environment studies in Bhutan primary schools is described within an international perspective.

Concepts and meanings

The term 'environmental studies' is relatively new, coined some 20 years ago. However, the concept on which it is based has been evolving for some time. Environmental studies (Hammersley *et al* 1978) embraces a broad range of approaches and activities, many of which are not new. There are considerable differences in interpretation of the term. The variety of approaches within environmental studies is an important and valuable feature and no one approach can be looked upon as the right one. The actual term used to describe this approach seems relatively unimportant, provided that the environment of the child is used in providing integrated and meaningful studies. Environmental studies has been described in many different ways. These include: topic work, project work, integrated approach, social studies, humanities, environmental education, local studies, environmental science and agriculture, integrated day etc.

The terms are often confused, for each of these terms has been used in a variety of ways by teachers, writers and educationists. The terms have also been interpreted differently in different countries and by different local authorities and individual schools and teachers (Tan 1988). Each term has a different shade of meaning and concept for the individual school, authority and country. Despite such differences it seems fair to make the assumption that there are common methods of working. They may be summarized as follows: (Hoare 1971)

☐ They are all child centred, focusing on the interests and characteristics of the pupil.
☐ They generally break down the artificial barriers between the traditional subjects.
☐ They place greater responsibility for learning on the individual child.
☐ They involve children and provide the opportunity for developing skills, concepts and knowledge through practical activities.

There have been curriculum projects where an environmental-studies approach is adopted for the teaching of different subjects like history, geography, science, social studies, agriculture, health, music and creative activities. In this situation even mathematics and language are taught as components of environmental studies. However, it is acknowledged that mathematics and language as skill and tool subjects have their own syllabuses.

The main focus in the use of an environmental studies approach is that literacy, numeracy, skills and knowledge are developed, at least partially, through the experiences of children. This approach calls for a new look at how to teach different subject areas by sequencing and providing experiences from the immediate environment.

Why teach environmental studies?

As the concepts and meanings of the term environmental education varies amongst people, societies and countries, the aims also differ. Martin (1975), while reviewing the aims states that 'the aims for environmental education vary according to the values and interests held by those advocates.' For instance, an educator's principal aim would be to use the environment as a vehicle for teaching the concepts and skills of various subject disciplines. The conservationist on the other hand would aim firmly at the protection of the environment and the wise use of natural resources. It is also the case that environmental-education aims for primary education may differ from middle and secondary aims. From this it is apparent that the aims of environmental studies cannot be defined without taking into account each society's actual economic, social and ecological circumstances and the objectives established by that society for its development (UNESCO 1977).

Nevertheless, it seems possible, and indeed necessary, to reach an agreement on certain common aims for a well-rounded environmental-education programme. The following list of aims is a summary chosen from 'Education for relevance in developing countries' (Knamiller 1985).

To help children to:

- ☐ Become critically aware of issues and problems in their own community.
- ☐ Become effective environmental investigators.
- ☐ Develop an ability to make decisions consciously.
- ☐ Explore alternatives for social action.

As one can see, these aims are almost all related to education *for* the environment. However, for primary education it seems both education *about* and *from* the environment are equally important, as children learn from the concrete to the abstract and need to develop the skills of observation, data collection and communication. It is also suggested that learning *from* the environment and studies *about* the environment lead on to a responsibility *for* the environment. This again shows that the three approaches are interrelated. The younger the children are, however, the more 'about' and 'from' the programme should be.

Environmental studies in the primary-school curriculum

Environmental studies in primary education should be seen as an integral part of the total curriculum. It is important to ensure that environmental studies is not seen so much as a subject but as an educative method or medium (Martin *et al* 1975). This is because children view their world as a single unit. They do not see it in a compartmentalized form. Children in their natural learning do not divide knowledge into subjects. For them any dividing line that exists simply separates what they know from what they do not know (Martin *et al* 1975).

The real beauty of environmental studies is its integrated approach to learning. Integrated learning emphasizes teaching and learning through topics/themes where all the disciplines and skills are found interwoven. For the child, subject materials cannot readily be broken down into compartments. Good topics are clearly interdisciplinary. The work involves various subjects which are difficult to separate because they are found in one string of beads.

The role of environmental studies in NAPE

As already implied in an earlier section, Bhutan may perhaps be the last Shangri-La, practically unmarred by modern highways, railways, and industrial plants. The country's geography has influenced its history, culture and the life of the people. Its inaccessible mountainous terrain, wild rivers and thick forests have for centuries endowed it with an isolation from the outside world. At the same time lack of contact with the outside world allowed Bhutan to evolve through the centuries a distinct pattern of civilization, social and economic life and religious and political institutions.

It has a diverse climate and altitudinal variations. The climate ranges from hot and humid to very cold. This contributes to its biological diversity of flora and fauna. Bhutan has the greatest biological diversity for its size. It has some of the best remaining representatives of the unique Himalayan ecosystems which include species threatened with extinction. Bhutan still has around 60 per cent of forest undisturbed. The National Forest Policy of 1974 and 1985 further supports conservation of nature and natural resources.

THE PLACE OF EVS
The imported education system which survived long enough in Bhutan has been relying on rote learning and memorization of facts and figures for the purpose of examination. The contents of the textbooks are far removed from the Bhutanese children's lives and experience. The underlying assumption has been that a fixed body of information, once acquired, constituted being educated. The system believed that an active year of learning could be validly measured by an examination of a few hours at the end of the year. The system as a whole has been against child-centred education and the needs of the country.

In NAPE EVS is one of the new subjects. Unlike in other countries EVS is not considered an integral part of the total curriculum. It is regarded only as one-quarter of the NAPE curriculum. It was felt that key subjects like English, mathematics and Dzongkha would need special attention as EVS topics may not be able to cover some of the important areas, whereas certain other areas sit very well with EVS topics. History, geography, culture and traditions, science, health education, physical education, agriculture and creative activities are indeed merged in the wider subject of environmental studies. It is considered that any local study which is based on topics cuts across the formal subject boundaries.

The topics are the means of enabling the children to observe and work with the environment around them and acquire knowledge and skills through personal experience and discovery.

AIMS OF ENVIRONMENTAL STUDIES
Children will be able to:

☐ Observe, gather and record information through field and class work.
☐ Look at and interpret real surroundings in pictorial, verbal, written and graphic form.
☐ Proceed from direct observation and manipulation of information gained at first hand to the indirect use of reference and resource materials: library, textbooks, documents etc.
☐ Choose and recognize the most important point from a larger body of knowledge.
☐ Organize and present their discoveries in a clear and interesting way.
☐ Study the materials purposefully and draw conclusions from their work.
☐ Develop a sense of team spirit by the encouragement to participate in activities.
☐ Express their own opinions while understanding the importance of listening, compromise and reaching agreement in discussion and activity.

Summary

The practical EVS activities are also used as a vehicle for the purposeful development of literacy, numeracy and learning skills. This means the education *from* and *about* the environment which would lead on to a responsibility for the environment. To summarize the role of environmental studies in Bhutanese primary education, it is a vehicle for teaching children the skills of how to learn and communicate. It is used as a medium for enquiry and discovery-learning activities. It is also used as a source of material for real-life activities in different disciplines (Scottham 1981).

5 Primary-teacher education institutes of Bhutan adopt a core curriculum: a case study
J K Turner and G J Fishburne

Education in Bhutan before the 1960s was mainly for the benefit of the male population. Some boys would have had the opportunity to attend a Buddhist monastery while a few children, whose parents could afford the expense, were sent to India for formal schooling. During the past 20 years, Bhutan has grown tremendously in all areas of development with education being no exception. The government of Bhutan has initiated a series of five-year plans for the growth of the country and the fifth five-year plan (1981–86) was aimed at creating a more solid educational foundation.

Bhutan's primary education system is made up of one year of kindergarten followed by six years of formal schooling. However, this categorization was only implemented in March 1987; before that date children undertook two years of kindergarten before proceeding.

Today primary schools in the country number 149 – still a far cry from the number needed to house all school-aged children. It is reported that only 25 per cent of the primary-aged population were enrolled in schools in 1987; this reflects the low literacy rate of 23 per cent for this country. The literacy level and the number of children attending primary school form the lowest levels in the south Asia region and are among the lowest in the world (Department of

Education, Royal Government of Bhutan, 1988).

To combat these problems, the Royal Government of Bhutan (RGOB) is placing a greater emphasis on the training of Bhutanese primary teachers at both the National Institute of Education (NIE) in Samchi and the Teachers' Training Centre and Demonstration School (TTC/DS) situated in Paro. For example, it is expected that during the sixth five-year plan (1987–92) the enrolment capacity of the primary teachers' training centres (including a newly constructed centre in Eastern Bhutan) will increase from 170 to about 400 trainees. Furthermore, in order to educate prospective primary teachers in a more standardized and effective manner, NIE and TTC/DS jointly planned and implemented the same primary-teacher education curriculum in July of 1986. Detailed reasons for this amalgamation, and the effects of adopting the same core curriculum, will be discussed after presentation of a brief historical sketch of NIE and TTC/DS.

A brief historical account of the National Institute of Education (NIE) and the Teachers' Training Centre and Demonstration School (TTC/DS)

During the RGOB's second five-year plan (1966–67) the National Institute of Education (NIE) was opened with financial and human resource assistance from the United Nations Development Programme (UNDP). Initially, NIE focused on the training of primary-school teachers, and in 1981, again with the support of UNDP, a major project was begun in order to:

- ☐ educate secondary teachers;
- ☐ provide in-service training; and
- ☐ create programmes leading to a Bachelor's degree in education.

In 1987, 34 students were enrolled in the Bachelor's degree programme while another 62 were part of a two-year primary-teacher education programme.

The Teachers' Training Centre and Demonstration School (TTC/DS) was opened in 1974 with assistance from the United Nations Children's Fund (UNICEF). Initially, TTC/DS was to focus on the education of pre-school teachers and children, but the need for trained primary teachers created a change in focus. From November 1977 to July 1986, TTC/DS offered a two-year teacher-training programme focusing on the first four years of schooling which included two years of kindergarten: namely, lower kindergarten (LKG) and upper kindergarten (UKG).

Ideally, children should be five years of age on or before the first day of the month that school begins. In reality, children may be much younger as a systematic procedure for the recording and issuing of birth certificates is not in effect. This situation is compounded by the fact that many children are born at home with no official record of their birth. Moreover, it is not unusual for a child of ten or eleven years of age to be admitted to the first year of schooling.

Obviously, a primary teacher in Bhutan is commonly faced with a wide age range of children in the classroom; this is one reason why TTC/DS began educating prospective school teachers for all primary-class levels from July of 1986. It was at this time that NIE and TTC/DS chose to adopt the same core curriculum. The major reasons for this decision and its effects after a two-year period will now be discussed.

A core curriculum and its effects (1986–1988)

As stated above, in July 1986, NIE and TTC/DS implemented the same curriculum as outlined in the document *Primary Teacher Certificate Course: NIE, Samchi and TTC, Paro, July 1985*. The Royal Government of Bhutan, through its department of education and two teacher-training institutes, believed that a joint programme would have the following advantages:

☐ standardization in the education and evaluation of prospective primary teachers would occur;

☐ an equitable status for the institutions would emerge within the country;

☐ there would be an increase in the number of teachers capable of teaching all levels within the primary school; and

☐ there would be an improvement in communication between and among the two institutes and the department of education.

However, it was not until April 1987 that some form of correspondence did take place between the two institutes (Turner, 1987).

This situation highlights a general problem within Bhutan and creates obstacles for any form of centralization in that regular communication can be difficult to maintain. The telephone system in Bhutan is improving but is still technologically unreliable; travel through the Himalayan mountains is naturally difficult and time-consuming; as a result, a personal conference between NIE and TTC/DS may take up to one week to complete. Finally, though the mail system is reliable it tends to be used less frequently than the telegraph system which is immediate but only adequate for brief messages. The hardship of communication and travel within Bhutan may be illustrated by the fact that some graduates of NIE and TTC/DS have to trek for six days through the Himalayan mountains before reaching their posting (Tshering Lhaden, personal communication, August 24, 1988).

The major issue that necessitated communication between NIE and TTC/DS in April 1987, was how the trainees at NIE and TTC/DS would be assessed. It is important to note that in past years there would not have been a need for these institutes to correspond as they were essentially independent of each other. Now, however, their curriculum document, the *Primary Teacher Certificate Course: NIE, Samchi and TTC, Paro, July 1985* states that:

A common annual/final examination will be conducted by the two institutes. The Board of Examinations will moderate the marking done by the institutes in order to maintain standards. (1985, p 4)

The Bhutan Board of Examinations (BBE) is the body which typically administers formal examinations within the public school system of Bhutan. Their role as cited above was to 'moderate the marking'; however, at a meeting held in Thimphu, the capital in April 1987, attended by two senior education officials along with a representative from the BBE and a representative from one of the teacher-education institutes, it was decided that the Bhutan Board of Examinations would conduct the year-end examinations. Following this, the two institutes were immediately asked to submit model question papers to the BBE who would in turn administer the assessment procedure.

It should be noted that when NIE and TTC/DS adopted their curriculum it was to be for a two-year pilot period, and at the end of that time a review and subsequent revision was to take place. However, a formal policy-decision body had not been officially created by the department of education with a mandate for considering and sanctioning policy changes to this new teacher-education curriculum. Therefore, the meeting of April 1987 made a significant change in the curriculum of these two institutes, a meeting at which one of the institutes was not represented.

A number of difficulties did result during the initial year-end examination and assessment period. Firstly, NIE and TTC/DS had hastily to submit model question papers to the BBE. Subsequently, the BBE followed a procedure in which they sent the model question papers and a copy of the syllabus for the specific subject to an examination setter. It was subsequently the responsibility of the examination setter to create a comon final examination based on the materials received from the BBE. Furthermore, the examination setter may or may not have been the person who was to mark the examinations.

The problem with this system of assessment was a lack of personnel in the education sector with adequate experience in the field of primary education. Since the majority of primary teacher educators are on staff at one of the two teacher training centres, examination setters and markers would often be secondary-school specialists. This situation resulted in both institutes lodging appeals relating to the reliability and validity of the examinations set by the BBE in June 1987.

Although the problems incurred with formal assessment of the trainees resulted in a certain amount of turbulence, a significant educational benefit did result as this experience was the impetus for the creation of the Teacher Education Committee.

In September 1987 a group of fifteen senior education officials met in order to resolve the initial problems encountered with the adoption of a common core curriculum. The officials included: Director of Education; Deputy Director of Education; Dzongkha Language Adviser; Dzongkha Language Development Officer; Secretary, BBE; Chief Inspector of Schools; Assistant Planning Officer; Controller, BBE; Director, NIE; Coordinator of Primary Education, NIE; Principal of TTC, along with one lecturer; personnel officer; Deputy Coordinator of the Curriculum Development Division (CDD); and finally, Head of the Teacher Education Division. These senior education officials agreed on the need for a Teacher Education Committee. As stated in the minutes of the above meeting, 'the establishment of such a body was an absolute necessity for making decisions on all matters pertaining to teacher education in the country' (Dukpa, 1987, p 5). Hence, the Teacher Education Committee would be composed of: Director of Education; Head of the Teacher Education Division as Secretary; and the following members, Secretary, BBE; Dzongkha Language Adviser; Dzongkha Language Development Officer; Chief Inspector of Schools; Coordinator of CDD; Planning Officer; Heads of the Teacher Education Institutes along with one other representative from each institute.

The major functions of the Teacher Education Committee were to be:

☐ to lay down policy guidelines for both pre-service and in-service teacher-training programmes, including Dzongkha Language Training;
☐ appointment of Committees for review and revision of teacher education syllabuses and examinations for the core teacher-education curriculum;

☐ do final review of existing programmes and make recommendations for further changes that may need to take place from time to time. (Dukpa, 1987, p 5)

In accordance with the original plan, it was also decided at the September meeting that the present curriculum for NIE and TTC/DS needed to be reviewed and amended prior to the beginning of the next academic year in July 1988. Consequently, three meetings were scheduled in which the two teacher-education institutes would meet twice and amend the present syllabuses and lastly present their revised draft to the Teacher Education Committee for recommendations and final approval. These conferences went as planned and a revised primary-teacher education curriculum was implemented in the July of 1988.

Turning now to the initial reasons why these institutes adopted a centralized curriculum, it has been stated that an initial lack of communication spawned the necessity for regular correspondence and will be required if the standardization and evaluation of primary-teacher trainees is to be realized. Secondly, as reported by the teacher trainees at TTC/DS from 1986 to 1988, the qualification to teach at all levels of the primary school would create a sense of equality between the two institutes and the graduates. Since before adoption of a common core curriculum feelings of inequity existed between the two teacher training institutes (Turner, 1987). An attitude does exist within the country that teachers of upper-primary classes (IV–VI) are somehow superior to teachers of lower-primary classes. This attitude is based on the perception that upper-primary teachers possess more content knowledge in their specific subject area and are thus considered to be intellectually superior (Turner, 1987). Lastly, having graduates from both institutes qualified to teach at all class levels will help accommodate an educational situation where primary classes often consist of children of varying ages.

It is essential to note that the importance the Royal Government of Bhutan is placing on primary-teacher education is not just to improve its literacy level and to increase the number of children attending school; the RGOB would also like to alter a situation in which 36 per cent of the primary teachers within the country are expatriates.

The government of Bhutan headed by King Jigme Singe Wangchuk, envisions that Bhutan will remain a country rich in Buddhist heritage and culture. Thus, if this rich culture and strong sense of identity are to be preserved, the RGOB believes that the country's children should be taught and educated by Bhutanese teachers. As a matter of fact, the king and his government regard the pedagogical skills of classroom teachers to be of secondary importance to the ability to inculcate the highest standard of Bhutanese customs, values and traditions in their students. Evidence of this came in February 1988, when the king met with a group of 15 leaders of educational institutions along with 24 prospective heads of various schools. *Kuensel:* Bhutan's national newspaper (March 5, 1988), in a special report entitled 'Teachers to Play a Growing Role' reported that:

His Majesty told the group that their abilities as classroom teachers were of secondary importance. What was required most from them were the following qualities: (a) initiative, dedication and the ability to effectively implement the new government policies and programmes; (b) effective and sound administration of their respective institutions, and (c) the ability to instill the highest standard of Bhutanese values in the students so that they will develop into loyal and dedicated citizens of the country.

Concluding remarks

In conclusion, the adoption of a centralized curriculum by the two teacher-education institutes of Bhutan has created a unique bridge between them which was not present in the past. Although centralization resulted in a variety of developmental problems this change has generated an awareness, by both institutes, of each other's educational environment and culture, and how both can work together in meeting the human-resource needs of the country. This awareness is essential as Bhutan enters its sixth five-year plan (1987–92) having already decided to place 42 per cent of its sectoral development expenditure – an increase of 26 per cent from the previous plan – on primary education (Department of Education, Royal Government of Bhutan, 1988).

References

Bhutan – United Nations Development Programme (UNDP) (1985) A Profile of Technical Co-operation Royal Government of Bhutan, Thimphu, Bhutan

Department of Education, Royal Government of Bhutan (1988) Terms of Reference for Technical Assistance to Paro Teachers' Training Centre: Primary Education Project Thimphu, Bhutan

Dukpa, M (1987) Minutes of the Meeting on Teacher Education held on 17 and 18 of September, 1987 at the Bhutan Board of Examinations Thimphu, Bhutan

Hammersley, A, Jones, E and Perry, G (1987) Approaches to Environmental Studies, Blandford

Hoare, R (1971) Topic Work with Book, Geoffrey Chapman

Knamiller, G (1985) Environmental Studies for Relevance in Developing Countries, The Environmentalist

Kuensel (March 5, 1988) Teachers to play a growing role.

Martin, G and Turner, E (1975) Environment Studies, Blond Educational Press

Primary Teacher Certificate Course (1985) National Institute of Education, Samchi (NIE), and Teachers' Training Centre (TTC), Paro, Bhutan

School Council (1974) Project Environment: Learning from Trails, School Council Publication, Longman

Scottham, S (1981) Using the School Surrounding, Topman Press

Statistical Yearbook of Bhutan (1987) Central Statistical Office Planning Commission – Royal Government of Bhutan, Thimphu, Bhutan

Tan, C (1988) Developing Topic Work, Taylor and Francis

Turner, J K (1987) Field notes and observations: Bhutan, Unpublished raw data

UNESCO (1977) Education and the Challenge of Environmental Problems, Tbilisi, USSR

UNESCO (1985, December) Expanding Physical Facilities for Primary Education in Bhutan (Educational Buildings Occasional Paper No 4) Bangkok

Bibliography

Abramson, T (1979) *Handbook of Vocational Education Evaluation* Sage Publications

Ahmad, Y J & Sammy, G K (1985) *Guidelines to Environmental Impact Assessment in Developing Countries* Hodder Educational

Akahori, K (1988) Evaluation of educational computer software in Japan (I): methods and results *Programmed Learning & Educational Technology* 25, 1, 46–57

Akahori, K (1988) Evaluation of educational computer software in Japan (II): practical problems *Programmed Learning & Educational Technology* 25, 1, 57–66

Albas D & Albas, C (1988) The staging of examinations: a student response to the institutional perspective *Canadian Journal of Higher Education* 18, 3, 69–81

Alexander, D J (1989) Issues in evaluating non-formal education in Thailand *International Journal of Lifelong Education* 8, 1, 57–82

Arubayi, E A (1986) Students' evaluation of instruction in higher education – a review *Assessment and Evaluation in Higher Education* 11, 1, 1–10

Ashworth, A B (1982) *Testing for Continuous Assessment: Handbook for Teachers in Schools and Colleges* Evans Brothers

Baker, E A & Quellmalz, E S (Ed) (1980) *Educational Testing and Evaluation: Design, Analysis and Policy* Sage Publications

Baker, A M (1986) Validity of Palestinian university students' responses in evaluating their instructors *Assessment and Evaluation in Higher Education* 11, 1, 70–75

Barker, B O & Platten, M R (1988) Student perceptions of the effectiveness of college credit courses taught via satellite *American Journal of Distance Education* 2, 2, 44–50

Barnett, R (1988) Does higher education have aims? *Journal of Philosophy of Education* 22, 2, 239–250

Beal, L F (1987–1988) On-line computer testing: implementation and endorsement *Journal of Educational Technology Systems* 16, 3, 239–252

Beeby, C E (1979) *Assessment of Indonesian Education: A Guide in Planning* Oxford University Press

Bejar, I I (1988) *A Sentence-Based Approach to the Assessment of Writing: a Feasibility Study* Machine Mediated Learning 2, 4, 321–332

Bertrand, A & Cebula, J P (1980) *Tests, Measurement and Evaluation: A Developmental Approach* Addison-Wesley

Black, T R (1987) A discrimination index for criterion-referenced test items *British Journal of Educational Psychology* 57, 3, 380–388

Black, H D & Dockrell, W B (ed) (1988) *New Developments in Educational Assessment* Scottish Academic Press

Bloom, B S & Madaus, G (1981) *Evaluation of Student Learning* McGraw

Blume, S S & Spaapen, J B (1988) External assessment and 'conditional financing' of research in Dutch universities *Minerva* 26, 1, 1–30

Bramley, P & Hullah, H (1987) Auditing training *Journal of European Industrial Training* 11, 6, 5–10

Brewer, M & Nevison, M (1989) Models for assessing the learning potential of placements *Journal of Further and Higher Education* 13, 1, 34–45

Brown, S A & Munn, P (Ed) (1986) *Changing Face of Education 14 to 16: Curriculum and Assessment* NFER-Nelson

Brohn, D M (1986) The use of computers in assessment in higher education *Assessment and Evaluation in Higher Education* 11, 3, 231–239

Bryce, T G K (1983) *Teaching for the Assessment of Practical Skills in Foundation Science* Heinemann Educational

Buckle, C F & Riding, R J (1988) Current problems in assessment: some reflections *Educational Psychology* 8, 4, 299–306

Campbell, C P & Armonstrong, R B (1988) A methodology for testing job task performance *Journal of European Industrial Training* 12, 1, 17–25

Carter, C (1984) The value and purpose of monitoring, evaluation and review in further and higher education *Journal of Further and Higher Education in Scotland* 9, 1, 36–44

Chater, P (1984) *Marking and Assessment in English* Methuen

Comfort, L K (1982) *Education Policy and Evaluation: A Context for Change* Pergamon Press

Cook, J (1988) An investigation of the validity of the British Ability Scales with respect to the Wechsler Intelligence Scale for a group of Canadian children *British Journal of Educational Psychology* 58, 2, 212–216

Cowan, J & George, J (1989) Opinion: Formative evaluation of study skills workshops: an unsolved problem *Educational & Training Technology International* 26, 1, 56–59

Cox, S & Hobson, B (1988) User appreciation of open learning at Jaguar Cars Ltd *Open Learning* 3, 1, 50–52

Creemers, B & Verloop, N (1984) *Educational Evaluation in the Netherlands* Pergamon Press

Cresswell, M J (1988) Combining grades from different assessments: how reliable is the result? *Educational Review* 40, 3, 361–382

Cruse, D B (1987) Student evaluations and the university professor-caveat professor *Higher Education* 16, 6, 723–737

Day, C (1989) Issues in the management of appraisal for professional development *Westminster Studies in Education* 12, 3–15

de Winter Hebron, C (1984) An aid for evaluating teaching in higher education *Assessment and Evaluation in Higher Education* 9, 2, 145–163

DeJoy, J K & Mills, H H (1989) Criteria for evaluating interactive instructional materials for adult self-directed learners *Educational Technology* 29, 2, 39–41

DES (1986) *Education in the Federal Republic of Germany: Aspects of Curriculum Assessment* HMSO

DES (1985) *Quality in Schools: Evaluation and Appraisal* HMSO

Dodson, C J (Ed) (1985) *Bilingual Education: Evaluation, Assessment and Methodology* University of Wales Press

Donald, J G (1982) A critical appraisal of the state of evaluation in higher education in Canada *Assessment and Evaluation in Higher Education* 7, 2, 108–126

Drenth, P (1986) Quality in higher education: evaluation and promotion *CRE-Information* 74, 2nd Quarter 1986, 57–69

Drope, P (198) The epistemology of assessment *Educational Psychology* 8, 4, 281–289

Duby, A (1988) Early formative evaluation of educational television *Journal of Educational Television* 14, 1, 43–51

Dudley-Marling, C, Owston, R G, & Searle, D (1988) A field-testing approach to software evaluation *Computers in Schools* 5, 1–2, 241–249

Edwards, R M (1989) An experiment in student self-assessment *British Journal of Educational Technology* 20, 1, 5–10

Elsayed, S S (1988) Surveys: a different picture *Development Communication Report* 60, 13–14

Elton, L (1988) Appraisal and accountability in higher education: some current issues *Higher Education Quarterly* 42, 3, 207–229

Elton, L (1984) Evaluating teaching and assessing teachers in universities *Assessment and Evaluation in Higher Education* 9, 2, 97–115

Englert, D C, Bedient, D & Garoan, G S (1986) Evaluation techniques for individualized instruction: revision and summative evaluation *Journal of Educational Technology Systems* 15, 2, 191–200

Estrin, H A (1988) Graduate engineers evaluate their in-house oral presentation course *Journal of Technical Writing and Communications* 18, 2, 135–142

Farnsworth, B H & Wilkinson, J C (1987) A fully integrated management system for tracking student mastery *THE Journal* 15, 4, 96–100

Forehand, G A & Rice, M W (1988) Diagnostic assessment in instruction *Machine-Mediated Learning* 2, 4, 287–296
Fraser, B J, Treagust, D F & Dennis, N C (1986) Development of an instrument for assessing classroom psychosocial environment at universities and colleges *Studies in Higher Education* 11, 1, 43–54
Fuchs, L S (1988) Effects of computer-managed instruction on teachers' implementation of systematic monitoring programs and student achievement *Journal of Educational Research* 81, 5, 294–304

Gillett, R (1989) Research performance indicators based on peer review: a critical analysis *Higher Education Quarterly* 43, 1, 20–38
Glasser, J, Gach, S & Levine, P (1988) Approaches to program validation *Video Systems* 14, 1, 56–61
Good, F (1989) Setting common examination papers that differentiate *Educational Studies* 15, 1, 67–82
Goodge, P (1988) Task-based assessment *Journal of European Industrial Training* 12, 6, 22–27
Gorrell, J & Cramond, B (1988) Students' attitudes toward and use of written justifications for multiple-choice answers *Educational and Psychological Measurement* 48, 4, 935–943
Gronlund, N E (1985) *Measurement and Evaluation in Teaching* Collier
Guri, S (1987) Quality control in distance learning *Open Learning* 2, 2, 16–21
Guskey, T R & Pigott, T D (1988) Research on group-based mastery learning programs: a meta-analysis *Journal of Educational Research* 81, 4, 197–216

Hargrove, L J & Proteet, J A (1984) *Assessment in Special Education: The Education Evaluation* Prentice-Hall
Harris, D & Bell, CD (1986) *Evaluating and Assessment for Learning* Kogan Page
Hazelwood, R D (1989) Extremism in response to quesionnaires and its relationship to ability *Educational Research* 31, 1, 46–51
Hegarty, S & Evans, P (1985) *Research and Evaluation Methods in Special Education* NFER-Nelson
Hewton, E (1983) Getting it right: assessing undergraduates at a university *International Journal of Educational Development* 3, 2, 139–147
Heywood, J (1989) *Assessment in Higher Education* John Wiley
Ho, J K (1987) Academic testing and grading with spreadsheet software *Collegiate Microcomputer* 5, 3, 274–278
Hoelscher, K (1988) Evaluating interactive video at Harvard Law School *Video-disc Monitor* 6, 8–9
Hoko, J A (1987) Evaluating instructional effects *Educational Technology* 26, 10, 44–47
Hopkins, K D & Stanley, J C (1981) *Education and Psychological Measurement and Evaluation* Prentice-Hall
Hort, L K (1988) Staff assessment: the development of procedures for Australian universities *Assessment and Evaluation in Higher Education* 13, 1, 73–78
Hubbard, J I & Seddon, G M (1989) Changes in the marking standard and reliability of successive assessments of practical skills in science *British Educational Research Journal* 15, 1, 53–60

Irwin, C C (1988) The assessment of values: Some methodological considerations *Scientia Paedagogica Experimentalis* 25, 2, 289–298

Jackson, E A (1988) Marking reliability in BSc Engineering examinations *European Journal of Engineering Education* 13, 4, 487–494
Jackson, T (1988) Evaluation in training: the value of current performance *Training and Development* 6, 9, 35–36
Jackson, T (1988) Evaluation in training: measurement and assessment *Training and Development* 7, 2, 32–33
Johnstone, J N (1983) An analysis of the perceptions teaching staff hold towards factors useful for evaluating an institution of higher education *Higher Education* 12, 2, 215–229
Johnstone, V M (1987) Evaluating interactive video *Interactive Update* November 8–10
Johnstone, V M (1987) The evaluation of microcomputer programs; an area of debate *Journal of Computer Assisted Learning* 3, 1, 40–50
Jones, R L & Bray, E (1985) *Assessment: From Principles in Action* Macmillan Education
Jones, J (1988) Student grades and rating of teaching quality *Higher Education Research and Development* 7, 2, 131–140
Juell, P & Wassor, J (1988) A comparison of input and output for a knowledge-based system for educational diagnosis *Educational Technology* 28, 3, 19–23

Kasten, K L & Young, I P (1983) Bias and the intended use of student evaluations of university faculty *Instructional Science* 12, 2, 161–169

Kempa, R (1986) *Assessment in Science* Cambridge University Press

Kikumba, N & Cryer, P (1987) Evaluating at a distance using cassette tape *Open Learning* 2, 1, 59–61

Kulik, J A (1987) Mastery testing and student learning: a meta analysis *Journal of Educational Technology Systems* 15, 3, 325–436

Ledwith, F (1986) Can evaluation be cost effective or even effective? *Health Education Research* 1, 4, 295–298

Lewis, C & Sheenan, K (1988) Computerized mastery testing *Machine-Mediated Learning* 2, 4, 283–286

Lindsay, A W (1981) Assessing institutional performance in higher education: a managerial perspective *Higher Education* 10, 6, 687–706

Llabre, M M *et al* (1987) The effect of computer-administered testing on test anxiety and performance *Educational Computing Research* 3, 4, 429–433

Lombard, M J & Bunting, B P (1989) Teacher's views on methods of appraisal *Educational Research* 31, 2, 150–162

Lomax, P M & McLeman, P (1984) The uses and abuses of nominal group technique in polytechnic course evaluation *Studies in Higher Education* 9, 2, 183–190

Maassen, P A M (1987) Quality control in Dutch higher education: internal versus external evaluation *European Journal of Education* 22, 2, 161–170

MacDougall, M & Roussie, G (1984) *Handbook of Testing and Evaluation in Business Education* Clark Publishing Company

Marshall, S (1987) EVAL: an expert system for evaluating written reports *International Journal of Electrical Engineering Education* 24, 1, 23–31

Marsh, H W (1982) SEEQ: a reliable, valid and useful instrument for collecting students' evaluations of university teaching *British Journal of Educational Psychology* 52, 1, 77–95

Marsh, H W (1987) Students' evaluations of university teaching: research findings, methodological issues and directions for future research *International Journal of Educational Research* 11, 3, 253–388

Markowitz, H (1987) Financial decision making; calculating the costs of distance education *Distance Education* 8, 2, 147–161

McCormick, R & James, M (1987) *Curriculum Evaluation in Schools* Croom Helm

McGaw, B (1985) Combining school-based and external assessments of performance to determine university admissions *Studies in Educational Evaluation* 11, 3, 303–314

McLeod, P J & Tenehouse, A (1988) Peer review of class handouts *Medical Teacher* 10, 1, 69–73

Mehrens, W A & Lehmann, I J (1983) *Measurement and Evaluation in Education and Psychology* Holt, Rinehart and Winston

Miller, A H (1979) Influencing assessment policy in a university *Assessment in Higher Education* 5, 1, 3–15

Miller, A H (1988) Student assessment of teaching in higher education *Higher Education* 17, 1, 3–15

Miller, C A (1988) Questionnaires by computer *Assessment and Evaluation in Higher Education* 13, 1, 50–60

Millman, J (Ed) (1981) *Handbook of Teacher Evaluation* Sage Publications

Miller, R P & Miller, S D (1988) The need for systematic evaluation of educational instructional materials *Technology Trends* 3, 3, 24–26

Miron, M (1988) Students' evaluation and instructors' self-evaluation of university instruction *Higher Education* 17, 2, 175–181

Moe, K C & Johnstone, M F (1988) Participant's reaction to computerized testing *Journal of Educational Computing Research* 4, 1, 79–86

Mohammad, Y H J & Almahmeed, M A H (1988) An evaluation of traditional admission standards in predicting Kuwait University students' academic performance *Higher Education* 17, 2, 203–217

Moses, I (1980) Assessment in Australian higher education 1974–1979 *Assessment in Higher Education* 5, 3, 294–312

Moses, I (1986) Student evaluation of teaching in an Australian university: staff perceptions and reactions *Assessment and Evaluation in Higher Education* 11, 2, 117–129

Murphy, R & Torrance, H (1988) *Changing Face of Educational Assessment* Open University Press

Murray, H G (1984) The impact of formative and summative evaluation of teaching in North American universities *Assessment and Evaluation in Higher Education* 9, 2, 117–132

Natarajan, V (1988) A critical evaluative study on distance learning programmes in Indian universities *Studies in Educational Evaluation* 14, 2, 147–150

Newman, P W (1985) *Assessment and Remediation of Articulatory and Phonological Disorders* Merrill

Nixon, J (1989) Curriculum evaluation: towards the vanishing point *Westminster Studies in Education* 12, 91–98

Norcini, J J, Shea, J A, Hancock, E W, Webster, G D & Baranowski, R A (1988) A criterion-referenced examination in cardiovascular disease *Medical Education* 22, 1, 32–39

Noss, R, Goldstein, H & Hoyles, C (1989) Graded assessment and learning hierarchies in Mathematics *BERJ* 15, 2, 109–120

O'Grady, M (1989) Change in assessment procedures and practices *NASD Journal* 21, 4–8

O'Sulivan, D (1987) Individualized qualitative evaluation *Adult Education* 60, 3, 250–256

Ogunniyi, M B (1984) *Educational Measurement and Evaluation* Longman

Open University (1981) *Contemporary Issues in Education Block 4, Unit 18–19: Educational Standards – Examinations and Assessment* Open University Press

Open University (1981) *Curriculum Evaluation and Assessment in Educational Institutions. Unit 3: Observing Classroom Processes* Open University Press

Open University (1981) *Curriculum Evaluation and Assessment in Educational Institutions. Unit 4: Measuring Learning Outcomes* Open University Press

Open University (1981) *Curriculum Evaluation and Assessment in Educational Institutions. Unit 5: Analysing Curriculum Materials* Open University Press

Open University (1982) *Curriculum Evaluation and Assessment in Educational Institutions. Unit 1: Accountability and Evaluation* Open University Press

Open University (1982) *Curriculum Evaluation and Assessment in Educational Institutions. Unit 6: Organization and Use of Evaluation* Open University Press

Open University (1982) *Curriculum Evaluation and Assessment in Educational Institutions. Case Study 3: The CNAA* Open University Press

Open University (1982) *Curriculum Evaluation and Assessment in Educational Institutions. Unit 2, Pt 4: Approaches to Evaluation – Audited Self-evaluation* Open University Press

Os Willem van, Drenth, P J D & Bernaert, G F (1987) AMOS: an evaluation model for institutions of higher education *Higher Education* 16, 3, 143–256

Patterson, A C & Bloch, B (1987) Formative evaluation: a process required in computer-assisted instruction *Educational Technology* 27, 11, 26–30

Pedro, F (1988) Higher education in Spain: setting the conditions for an evaluative state *European Journal of Education* 23, 1–2, 125–139

Pollitt, C (1987) The politics of performance assessment: lessons for higher education? *Studies in Higher Education* 12, 1, 87–98

Popham, W J (1988) *Educational Evaluation* Prentice-Hall

Potton, A (1983) *Guides to Assessment in Education: Screening* Macmillan Educational

Raggatt, P C M & Weiner, G (1985) *Curriculum and Assessment* Pergamon

Raizen, S A & Rossi, P H (Ed) (1981) *Programme Evaluation in Education: When? How? To What Ends?* National Academy Press

Reeves, T C (1988) Evaluation review: guidelines, introduction and overview *Videodisc Monitor* 6, 4, 24–25

Reiser, R A, Driscoll, M P & Vergara, A (1987) The effects of ascending, descending and fixed criteria on student performance and attitude in a mastery-orientated course *Educational Communication & Technology Journal* 35, 4, 195–202

Rice, L C (1988) Student evaluation of teaching: problems and prospects *Teaching Philosophy* 11, 4, 329–344

Ridgway, B (1988) Analysis of training costs *Videodisc Monitor* 6, 1, 27

Robinson, C G (1988) Assessment and the curriculum *Educational Psychology* 8, 4, 221–227

Roe, E & McDonald, R (1985) *Informed Professional Judgement: Guide to Evaluation in Postsecondary Education* University of Queensland Press

Roopchand, G & Moss, D (1988) A systematic approach to the design of secondary school lessons in Guyana *British Journal of Educational Technology* 19, 1, 42–52

Ross, M (1986) *Assessment in Arts Education* Pergamon

Rule, S, DeWulf, M J & Stowitschek, J J (1988) An economic analysis of inservice teacher training *American Journal of Distance Education* 2, 2, 12–22

Russell, J D & Blake, BL (1988) Formative and summative evaluation products and learners *Educational Technology* 28, 9, 22–28

Rutherford, D & Parkin, I (1988) Staff appraisal systems in universities: profiles from student questionnaires *Programmed Learning & Educational Technology* 25, 2, 159–164

Sadler, D R (1987) Specifying and promulgating achievement standards *Oxford Preview of Education* 13, 2, 191–210

Sadiku, M N O & Galade, C I (1987) Using objective tests in engineering *International Journal of Applied Engineering Education* 3, 6, 583–589

Safi, A Q & Miller, R I (1986) Student evaluations of courses and instructors at Kuwait University *Higher Education Review* 18, 3, 17–25

Scottish Education Department (1980) *What Do They Know?: A Review of Criterion-referenced Assessment* HMSO

Seddon, G M (1987) A method of item-analysis and item-selection for the construction of criterion-referenced tests *British Journal of Educational Psychology* 57, 3, 371–379

Seddon, G M (1988) The validity of reliability measures *British Educational Research Journal* 14, 1, 89–97

Shertzer, B & Linden, J D (1979) *Fundamentals of Individual Appraisal: Assessment Techniques for Counsellors* Houghton Mifflin

Stone, H R (1988) Capabilities of traditional quantitative admissions criteria in predicting performance of off-campus engineering graduate students enrolled in videotaped courses *Distance Education* 9, 2, 250–272

Straughan, R & Wrigley, J (Ed) (1980) *Values and Evaluation in Education* Harper & Row

Swanson, R A & Sleezer, C M (1987) Training effectiveness evaluation *Journal of European Industrial Training* 11, 4, 7–16

Taylor, R L (1984) *Assessment of Exceptional Students: Educational and Psychological Procedures* Prentice-Hall

Taylor, T (1985) A value-added student assessment model: Northeast Missouri State University *Assessment and Evalution in Higher Education* 10, 3, 190–202

Taylor, J & Johnes, J (1989) An evaluation of performance indicators based upon the first destination of university graduates *Studies in Higher Education* 14, 2, 201–217

Thyer, B A (1988) Teaching without testing: a preliminary report of an innovative technique for social work evaluation *Innovative Higher Education* 13, 1, 47–53

Tofts, S W (1988) The evaluation of RAF training *Royal Air Force Education Bulletin* 25, 73–80

Tyler, R W (1985) *Changing Concepts of Educational Evaluation* Pergamon Press

Van Der Vleuten, C P M, Van Luyk, S J & Beckers, J M (1989) A written test as an alternative to performance testing *Medical Education* 23, 1, 97–107

Walberg, H J & Postlethwaite, T N (1984) *Evaluation in Education* Pergamon Press

Watson, K & Oxenham, J (1985) *Research, Cooperation and Evaluation of Educational Programmes in the Third World* Pergamon Press

Whitehead, J (1982) Assessing and evaluating an individual's higher education *Assessment and Evaluation in Higher Education* 7, 1, 74–84

Wiig, E H & Mintz, E S (1984) *Learning Assessment and Intervention for the Learning Disabled* Merrill

Wilcox, B (1989) Inspection and its contribution to practical evaluation *Educational Research* 31, 3, 163–175

Willis, J A (1988) Learning outcome testing: a statewide approach to accountability *THE Journal* 16, 1, 69–73

Woodhall, H L (1987) Performance appraised reviews in academic settings *ACA Bulletin* 61, 50–64

Worthen, B R & Saunders, J (1987) *Educational Evaluation: Alternative Approaches and Practical Guidelines* Longman

Wright, D & Wiese, M J (1988) Teacher judgment in student evaluation: a comparison of grading methods *Journal of Educational Research* 82, 1, 10–14

Yoloye, E (1984) *Continuous Assessment: A Simple Guide for Teachers* Cassell

Contributor details

Dr Nurit Adler
Hadassah Vocational Guidance
Institute
POB 1406
Jerusalem
Israel 91031

Dr John Bailey
Department of Education
Royal Government of Bhutan
Thimphu
Bhutan

Dr Antonio Calvani
Department of Educational Sciences
Florence
Italy

Ms Lynne Cameron
College of Ripon & York St John
English Language and Linguistics
Ripon
HG4 1NA
UK

Mr Tshewang Choeden
Royal Government of Bhutan
Department of Education
Thimphu
Bhutan

Mr David Clemson
Liverpool Polytechnic
School of Education
Liverpool L17 6BD
UK

Dr Betty Collis
University of Twente
PO Box 217
7500 AE Enchede
Netherlands

Dr A di Carlo
Liceo Scientifico 'E Majorana'
Torino
Italy

Prof Avram Eskenasi
Bulgarian Academy of Sciences
Institute of Mathematics
ul.Acad.Georgi Bontchev Str
1113 Sofia
Bulgaria

Dr Maria Ferraris
Instituto Tecnologie Didattiche
Via all'Opera
Pia 11
16145 Genova
Italy

Dr Maria Ferretti
Scuola Don Milani
Genova
Italy

Dr G J Fishburne
University of Alberta
Faculty of Education
Edmonton
Canada T6G 2G5

Kim Foss Hansen
Research Institute for Pedagogy and
Education
Copenhagen
Denmark

Dr Claude Kennedy
Ngee Ann Polytechnic
Mathematics and Science Centre
535 Clementi Road
Singapore 2159

Dr Bob Kowalski
Wolverhampton Polytechnic
Agricultural Education Training Unit
Faculty of Education
Dudley
West Midlands
UK

Dr Lorento Laviosa
Scuola Don Milani
Genova
Italy

Ms Michela Mayer
European Centre of Education
Villa Falconieri
Frascati
Italy

Prof Elchanan Meir
Hadassah Vocational Guidance
Institute
POB 1406
Jerusalem
Israel 91031

Mr Nigel Nixon
CNAA
344–354 Grays Inn Road
London
WC1X 8BP
UK

Dr Donatella Persico
Istituto Tecnologie Didattiche
Via all'Opera
Pia 11
16145 Genova
Italy

Mr Chitra Pradhan
Royal Government of Bhutan
Department of Education
Thimphu
Bhutan

Dr Jaap Scheerens
University of Twente
PO Box 217
7500 AE Enchede
Netherlands

Mr Tom Schuller
University of Warwick
Continuing Education
Coventry
CV4 7AL
UK

Prof Blagovest Sendov
Bulgarian Acadamy of Sciences
1000 Sofia
Bulgaria

Mr Roger Singer
DRS Data and Research Services
Linford Wood
Milton Keynes
MK14 6LR
UK

Mr David Smith
Research and Consultancy in
Education
29 Milner Lane
Burnham
Slough
SL1 7PA
UK

Prof John Smyth
Deakin University
Geelong
Victoria 3217
Australia

Dr G Trentin
Instituto Tecnologie Didattiche
Via all'Opera
Pia 11
16145 Genova
Italy

Mr Jerome Turner
St Francis Xavier University
Faculty of Education
Nova Scotia
Canada B2G 1C0

Mr Minchha Wangdi
Royal Government of Bhutan
Department of Education
Thimphu
Bhutan

Dr David Warren Piper
University of Queensland
Tertiary Education Institute
St Lucia
QLD
Australia 4067

Index